結界師

KEKKAISHI

20

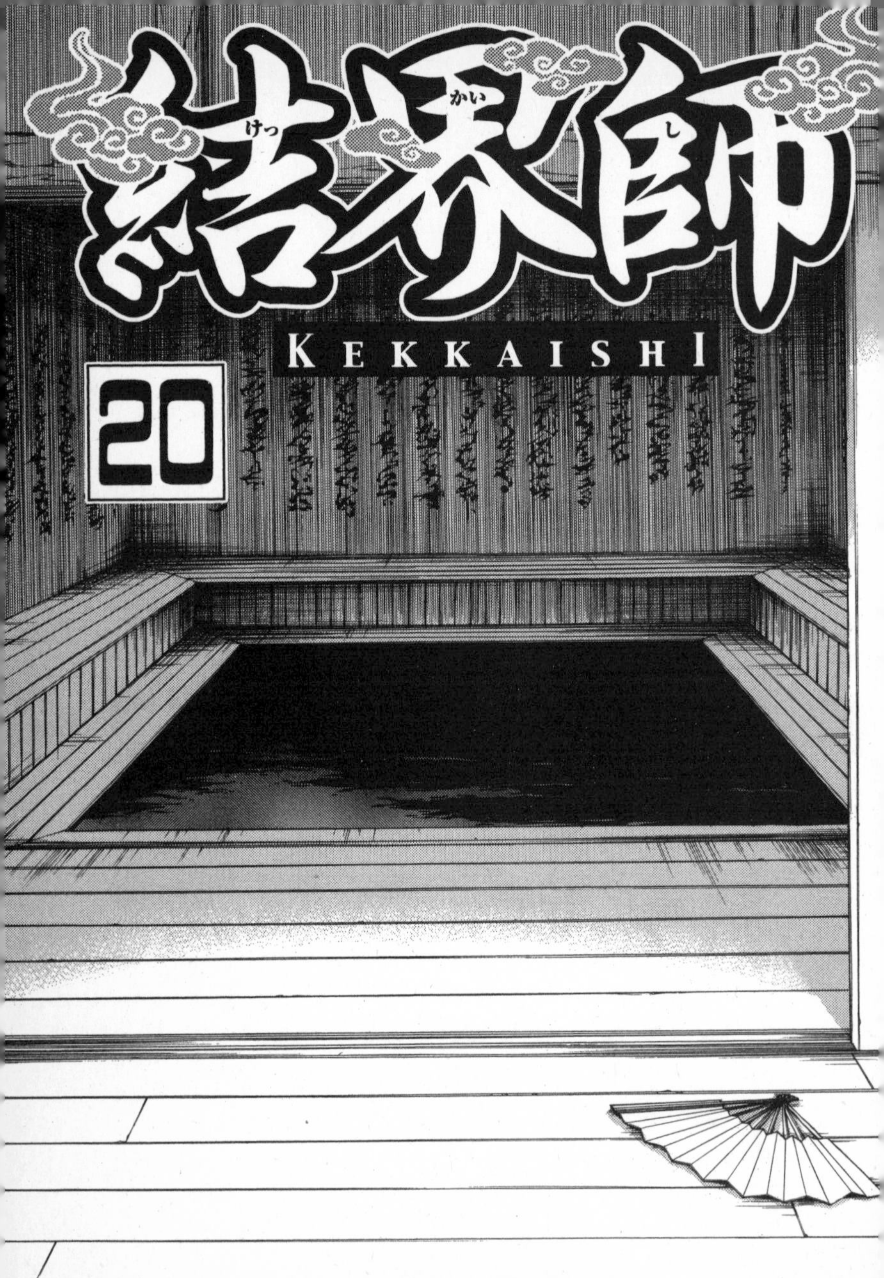

田辺イエロウ

YELLOW TANABE PRESENTS

THE STORY THUS FAR

Yoshimori Sumimura and Tokine Yukimura have an ancestral duty to protect the Karasumori Forest from supernatural beings called ayakashi. People with their gift for terminating ayakashi are called kekkaishi, or "barrier masters."

One day, ayakashi butterflies bring a prophecy of impending doom to Karasumori. Then a major mystical site, Lake Mashiro, is attacked.

In the aftermath of these disturbing developments, an investigator visits Yoshimori's family. It appears the Shadow Organization suspects Yoshimori's mother is behind the attacks on the mystical sites!

Angered by the accusation against his mother, Yoshimori threatens the investigator's companion, Rokuro Ogi, a "wind master."

Meanwhile, Ichiro Ogi, Masamori's archrival, lures Masamori to one of the mystical sites...

KEKKAISHI VOL. 20
TABLE OF CONTENTS

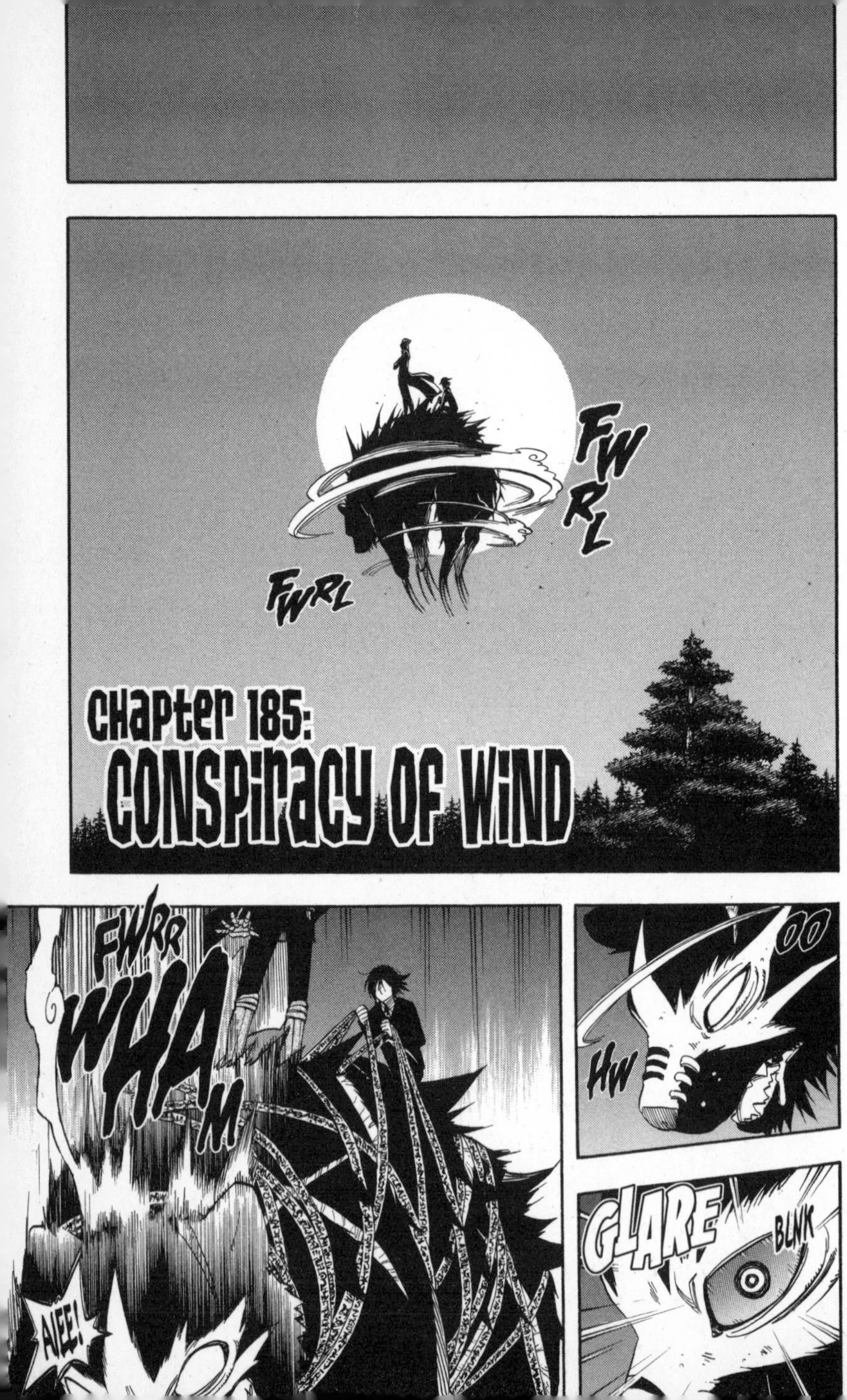
FWRL
FWRL
Chapter 185:
CONSPIRACY OF WIND
OO
HW
GLARE
BLNK
FWRR
WHAM
AIEE!

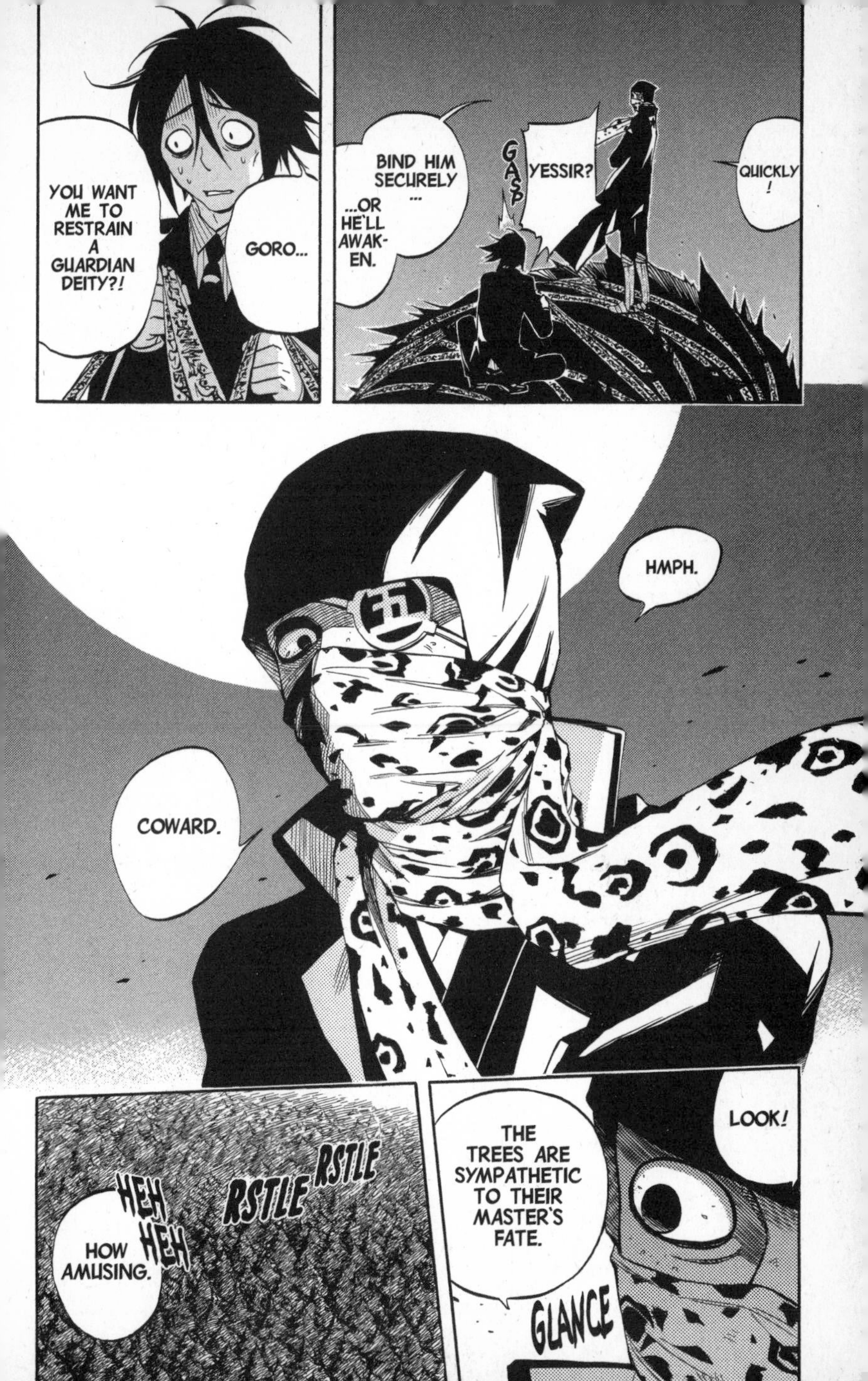
BIND HIM SECURELY...
...OR HE'LL AWAKEN.
GASP
YESSIR?
QUICKLY!
GORO...
YOU WANT ME TO RESTRAIN A GUARDIAN DEITY?!
HMPH.
COWARD.
LOOK!
THE TREES ARE SYMPATHETIC TO THEIR MASTER'S FATE.
GLANCE
RSTLE RSTLE
HEH HEH
HOW AMUSING.

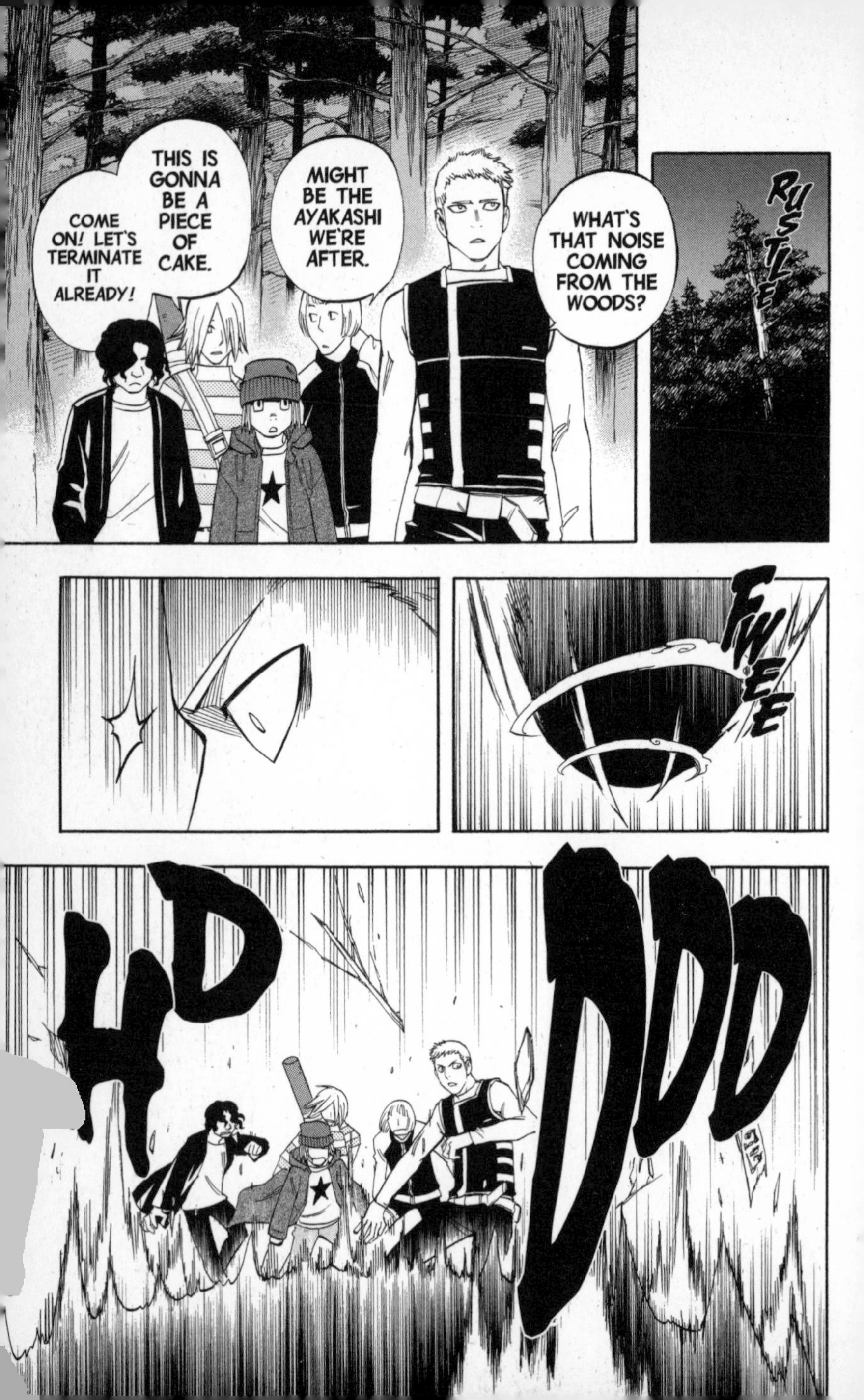
RUSTLE
WHAT'S THAT NOISE COMING FROM THE WOODS?
MIGHT BE THE AYAKASHI WE'RE AFTER.
THIS IS GONNA BE A PIECE OF CAKE.
COME ON! LET'S TERMINATE IT ALREADY!
FWEE

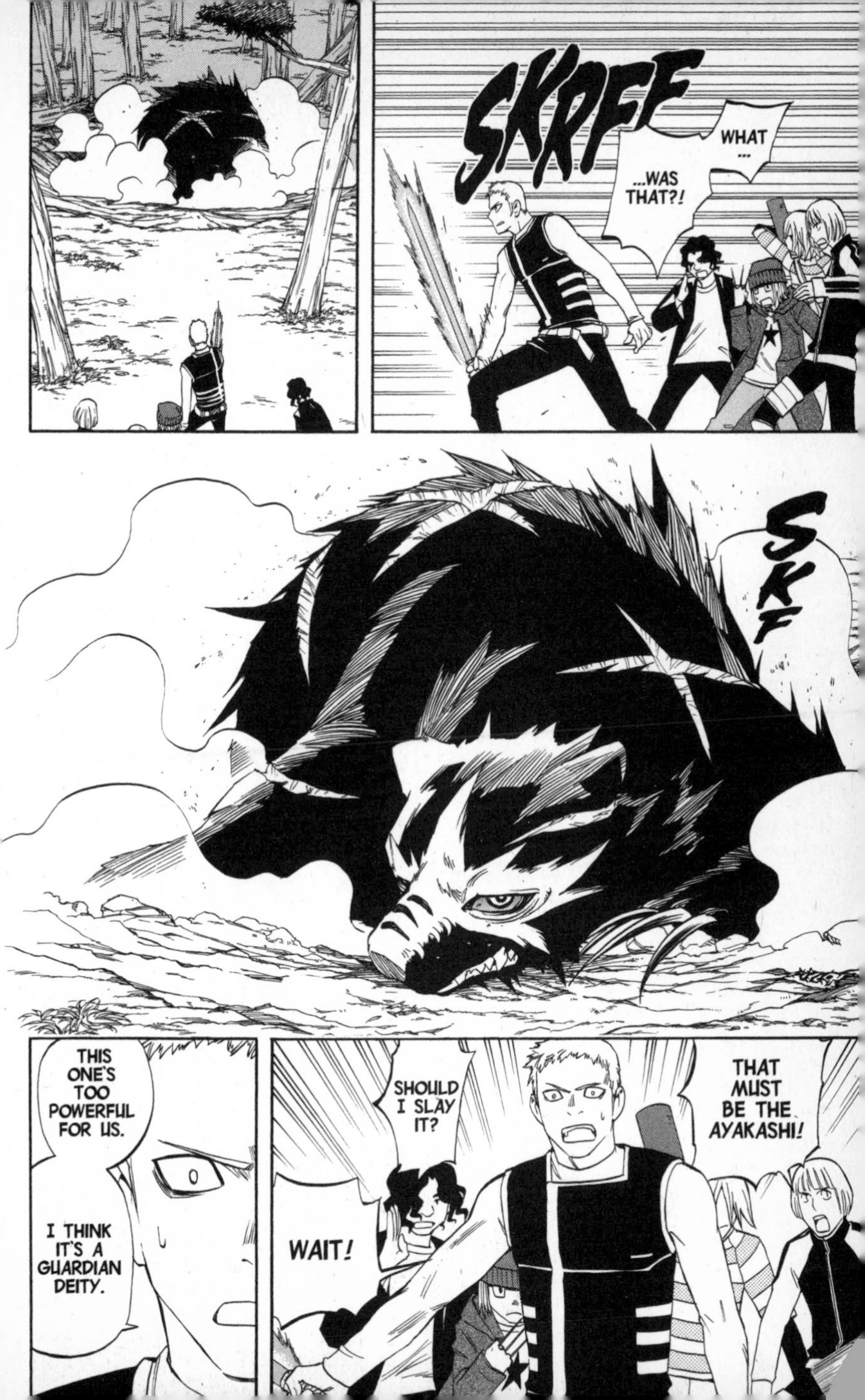
SKRFF
WHAT ...
...WAS THAT?!
SKF
THAT MUST BE THE AYAKASHI!
SHOULD I SLAY IT?
WAIT!
THIS ONE'S TOO POWERFUL FOR US.
I THINK IT'S A GUARDIAN DEITY.

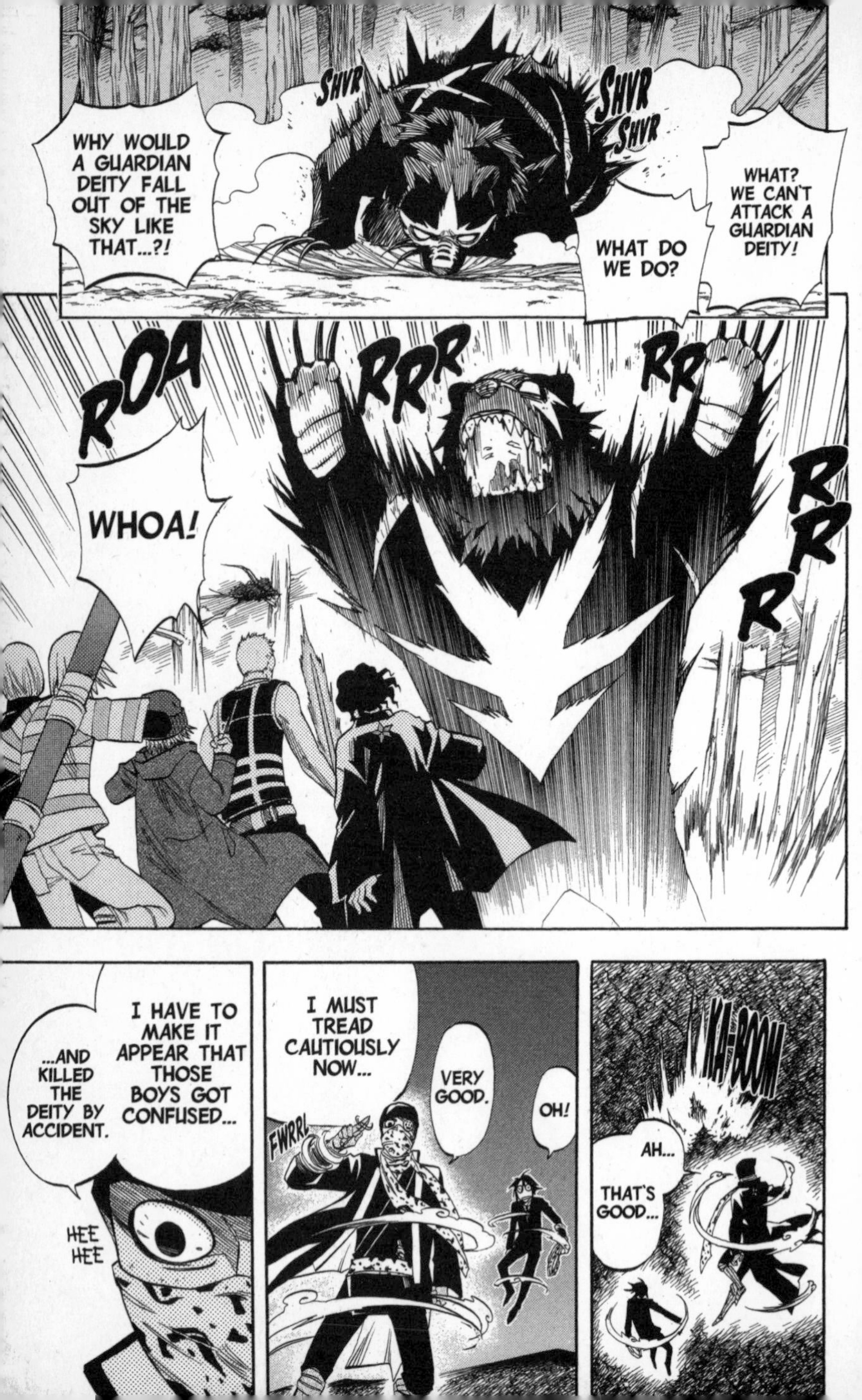
WHAT? WE CAN'T ATTACK A GUARDIAN DEITY!
WHAT DO WE DO?
SHVR SHVR
SHVR
WHY WOULD A GUARDIAN DEITY FALL OUT OF THE SKY LIKE THAT...?!
RRRR
ROA RRR RR
WHOA!
KA-BOOM
AH...
THAT'S GOOD...
OH!
VERY GOOD.
I MUST TREAD CAUTIOUSLY NOW...
FWRRL
I HAVE TO MAKE IT APPEAR THAT THOSE BOYS GOT CONFUSED...
...AND KILLED THE DEITY BY ACCIDENT.
HEE HEE

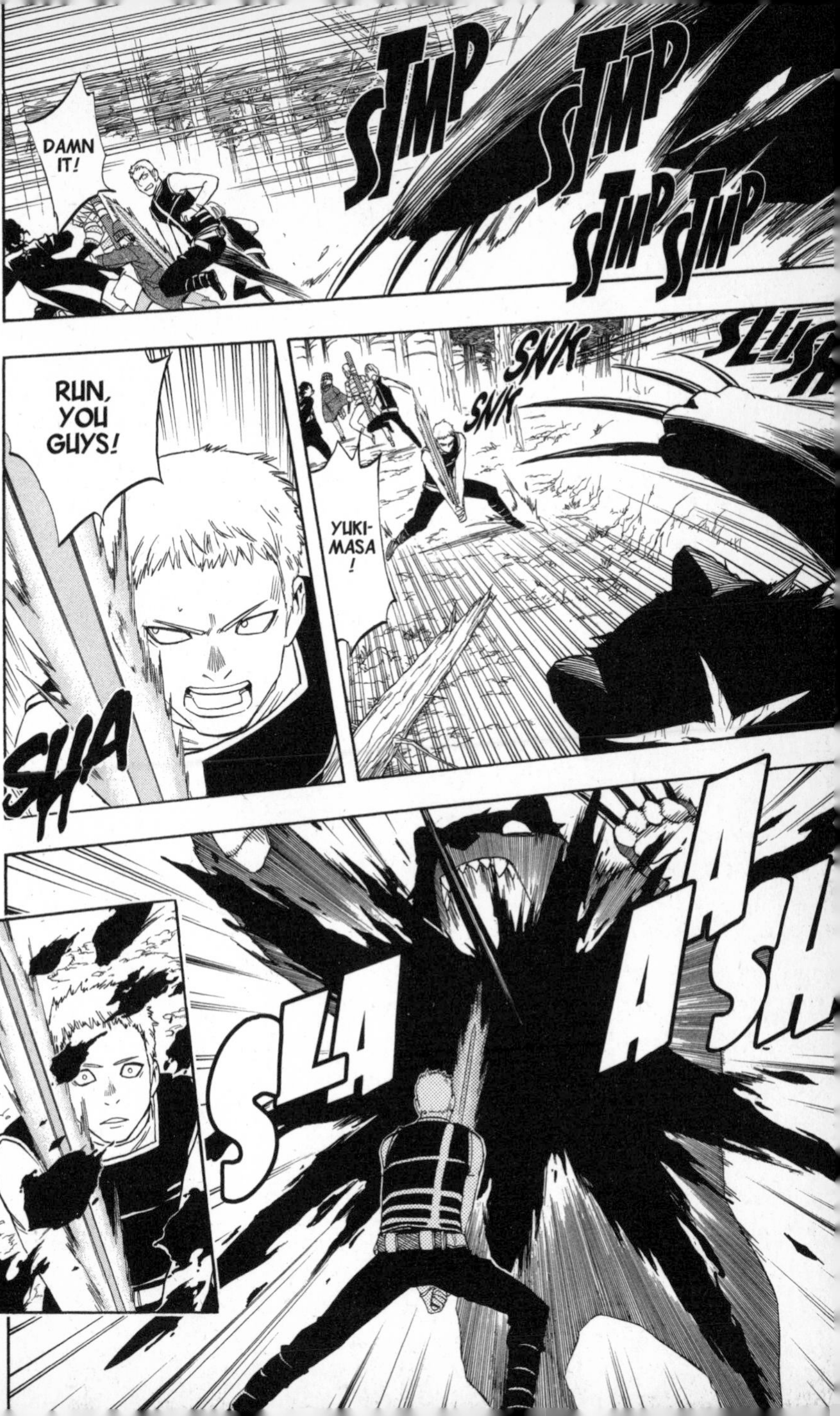

STMP STMP
STMP STMP
DAMN IT!
SLISH
SNK SNK
YUKI-MASA!
RUN, YOU GUYS!
SHA
SLAASH

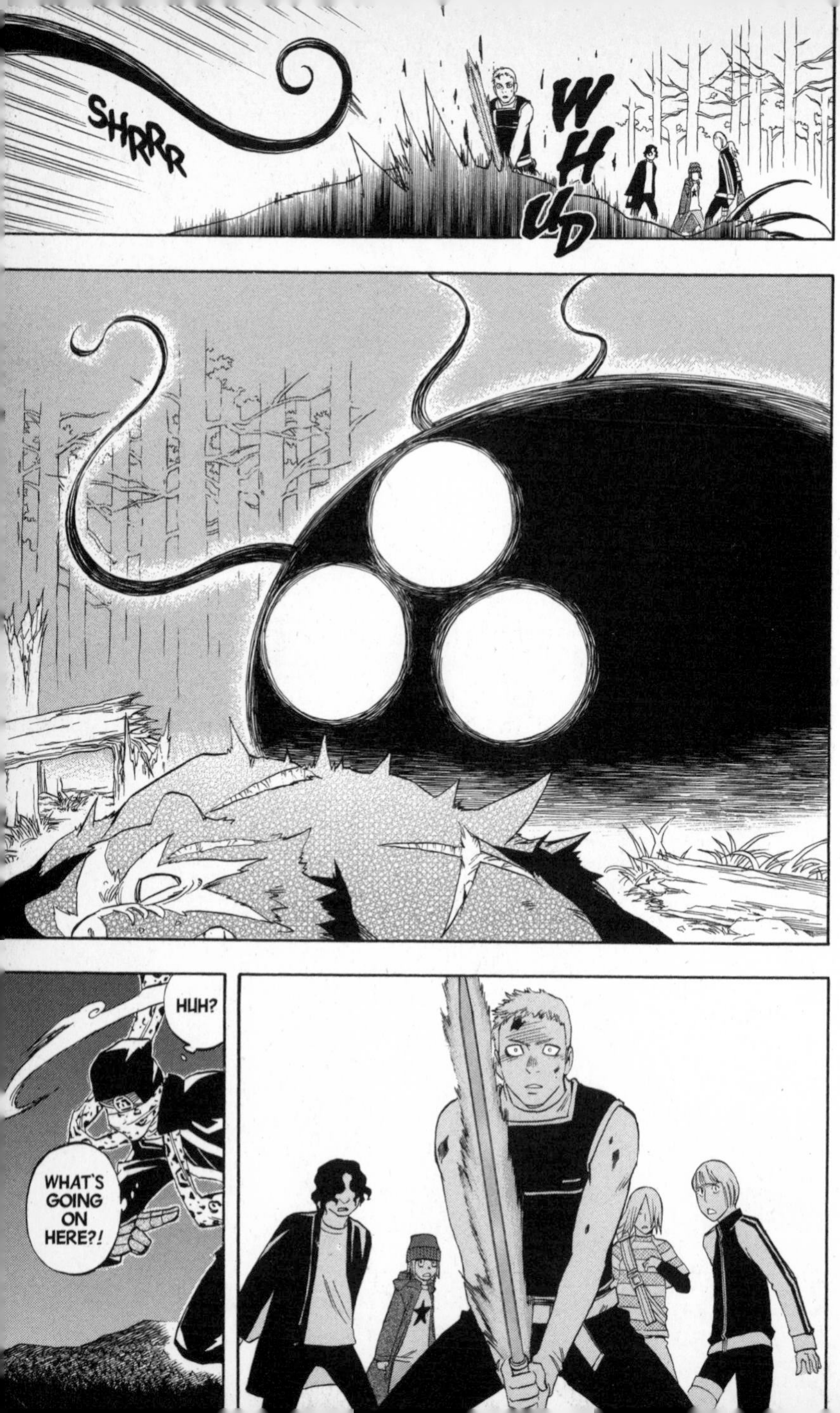
WHUD
SHRRR
HUH?
WHAT'S GOING ON HERE?!

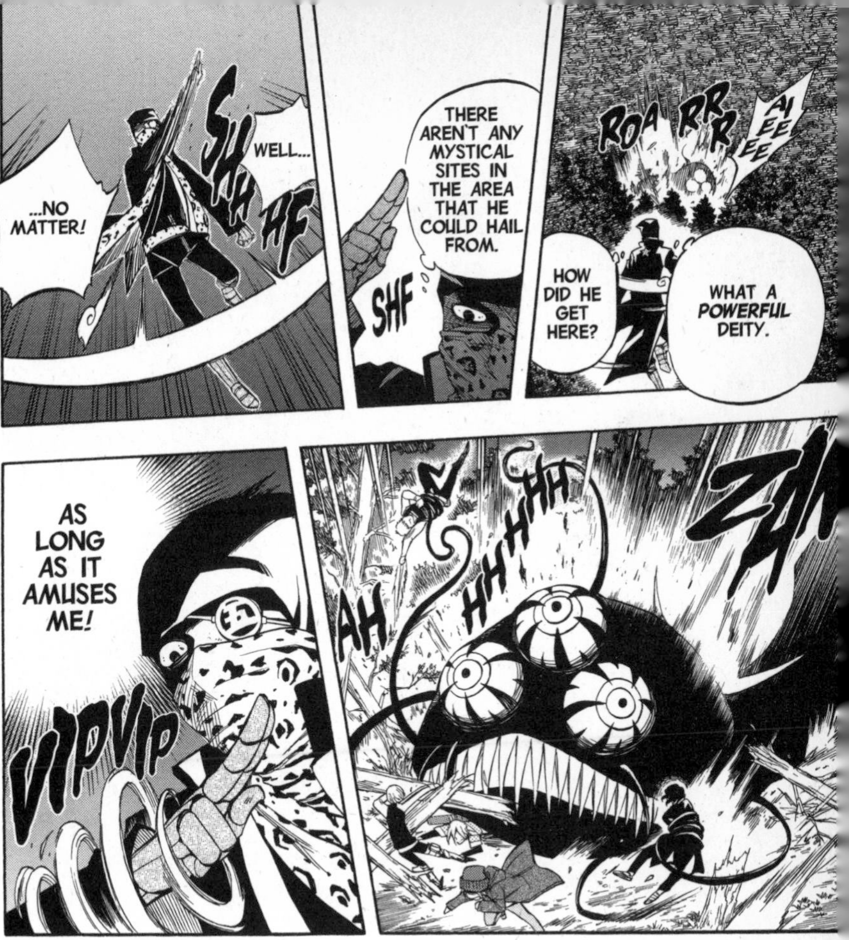
ROAARRRR
AIEEE
WHAT A POWERFUL DEITY.
HOW DID HE GET HERE?
THERE AREN'T ANY MYSTICAL SITES IN THE AREA THAT HE COULD HAIL FROM.
SHF
WELL...
SHHHF
...NO MATTER!
AHHHHHHHHH
AS LONG AS IT AMUSES ME!
VIPVIP

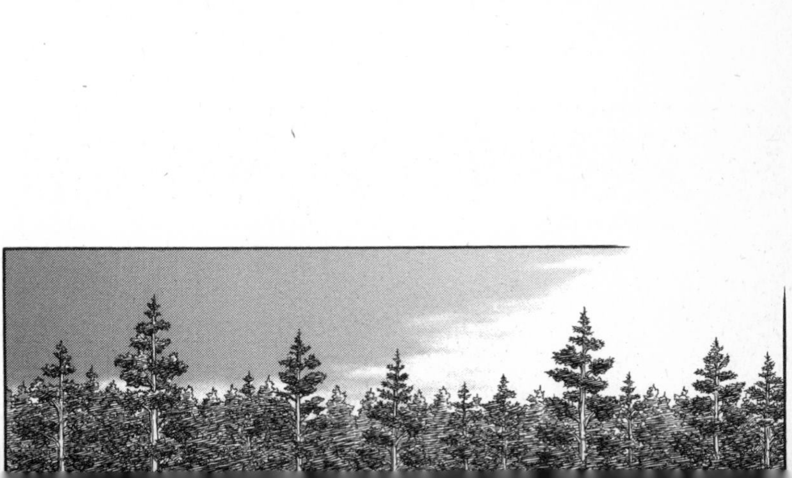

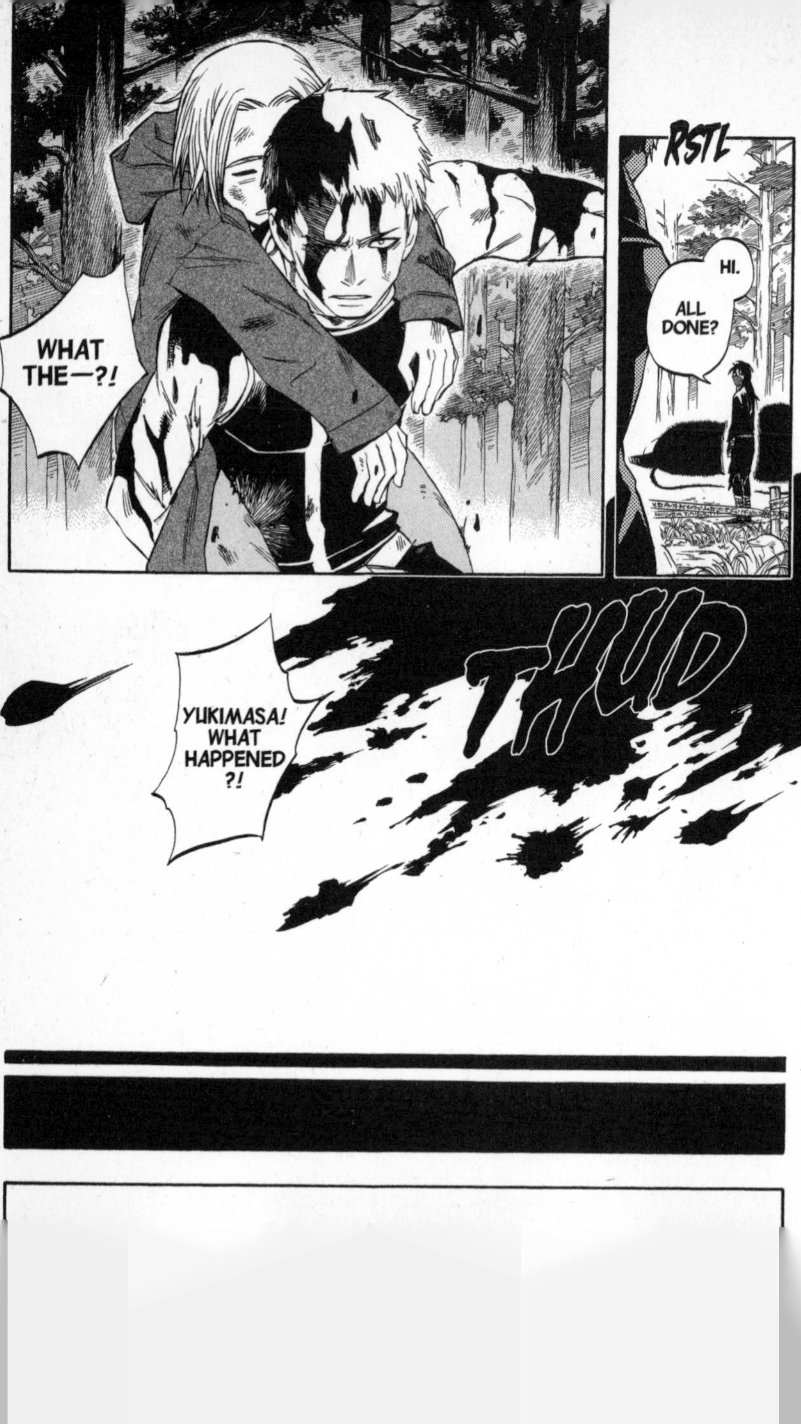
RSTL
HI.
ALL DONE?
WHAT THE—?!
THUD
YUKIMASA! WHAT HAPPENED?!

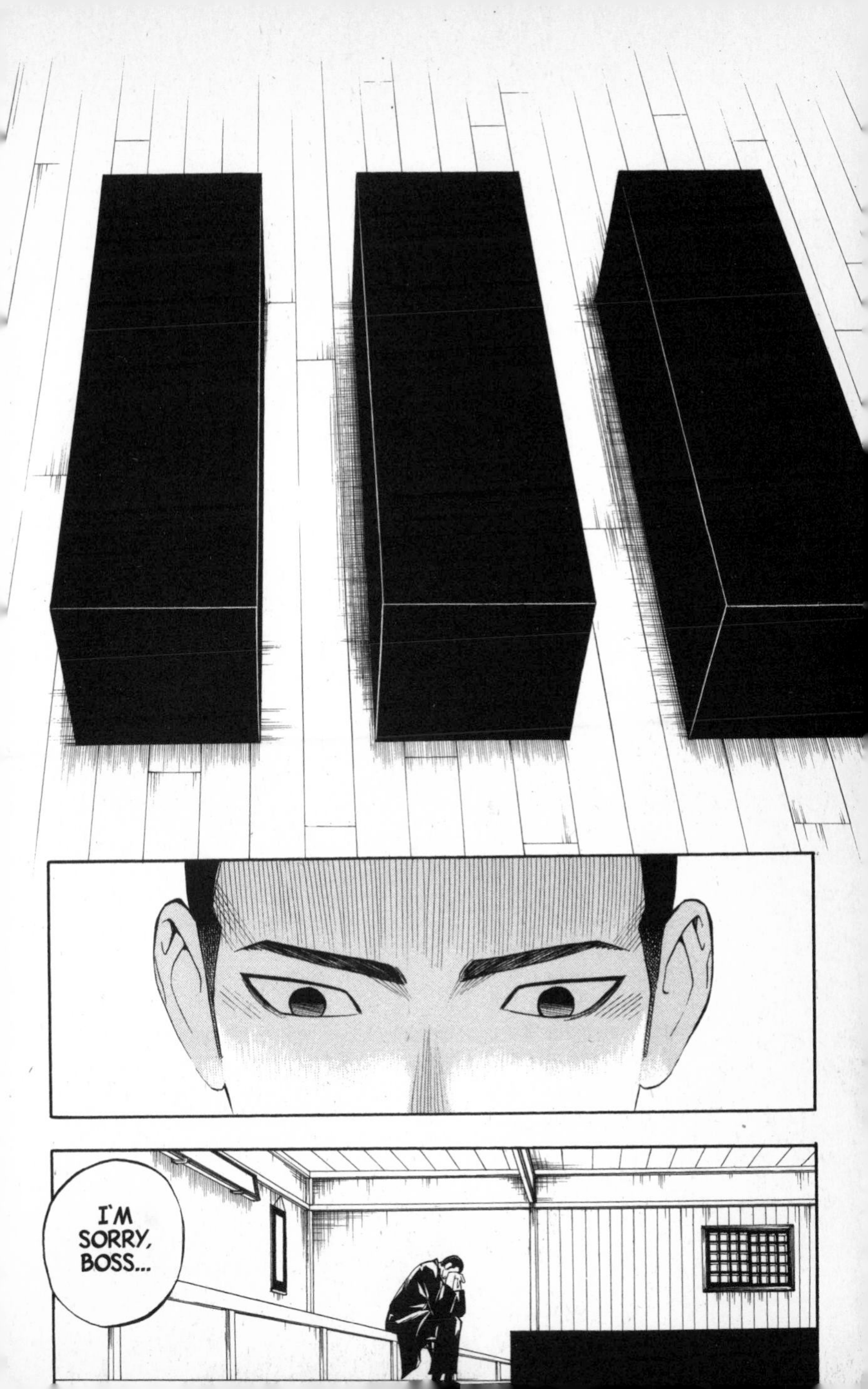
I'M SORRY, BOSS...

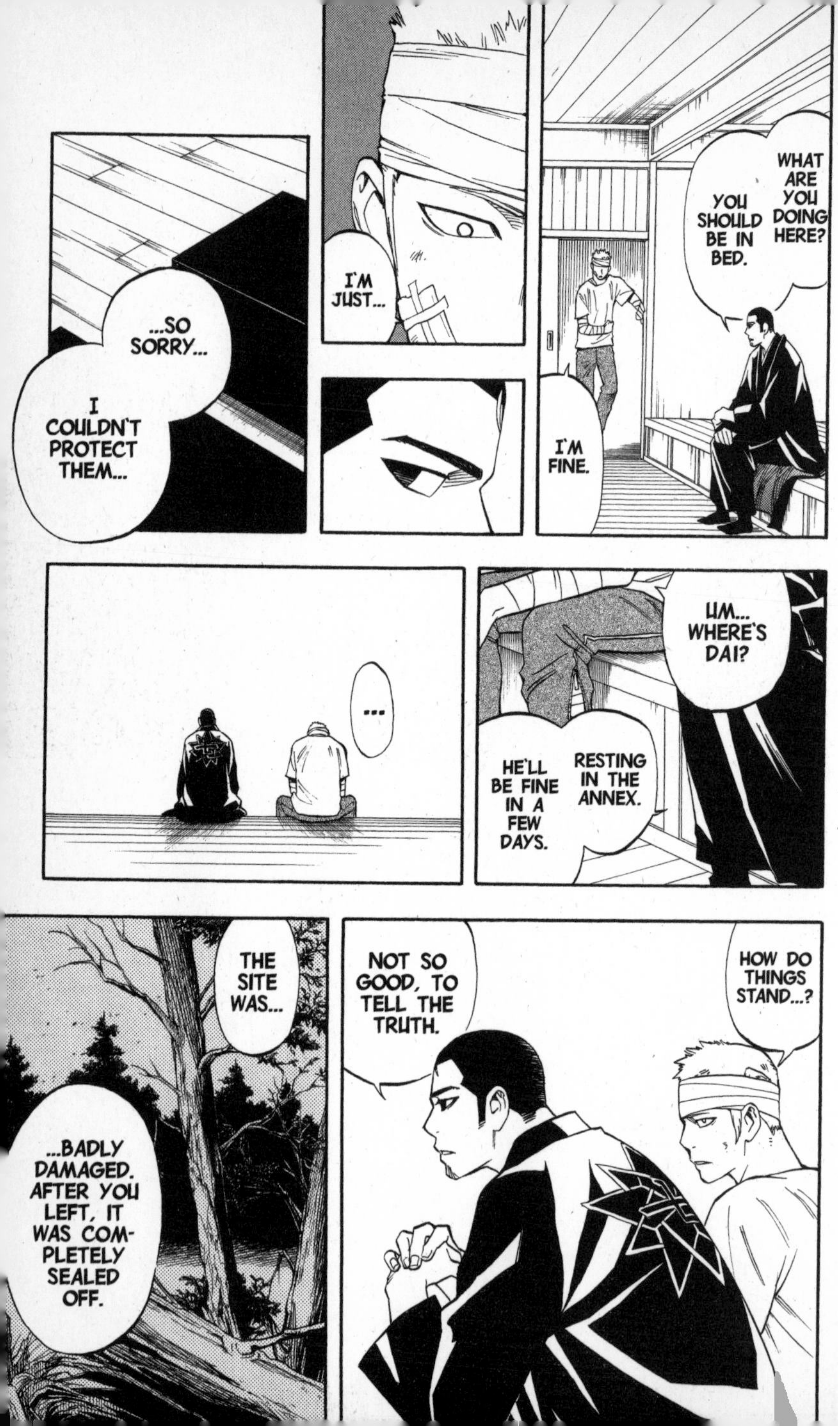
WHAT ARE YOU DOING HERE?
YOU SHOULD BE IN BED.
I'M FINE.
I'M JUST...
...SO SORRY...
I COULDN'T PROTECT THEM...
UM... WHERE'S DAI?
RESTING IN THE ANNEX.
HE'LL BE FINE IN A FEW DAYS.
...
HOW DO THINGS STAND...?
NOT SO GOOD, TO TELL THE TRUTH.
THE SITE WAS...
...BADLY DAMAGED. AFTER YOU LEFT, IT WAS COMPLETELY SEALED OFF.

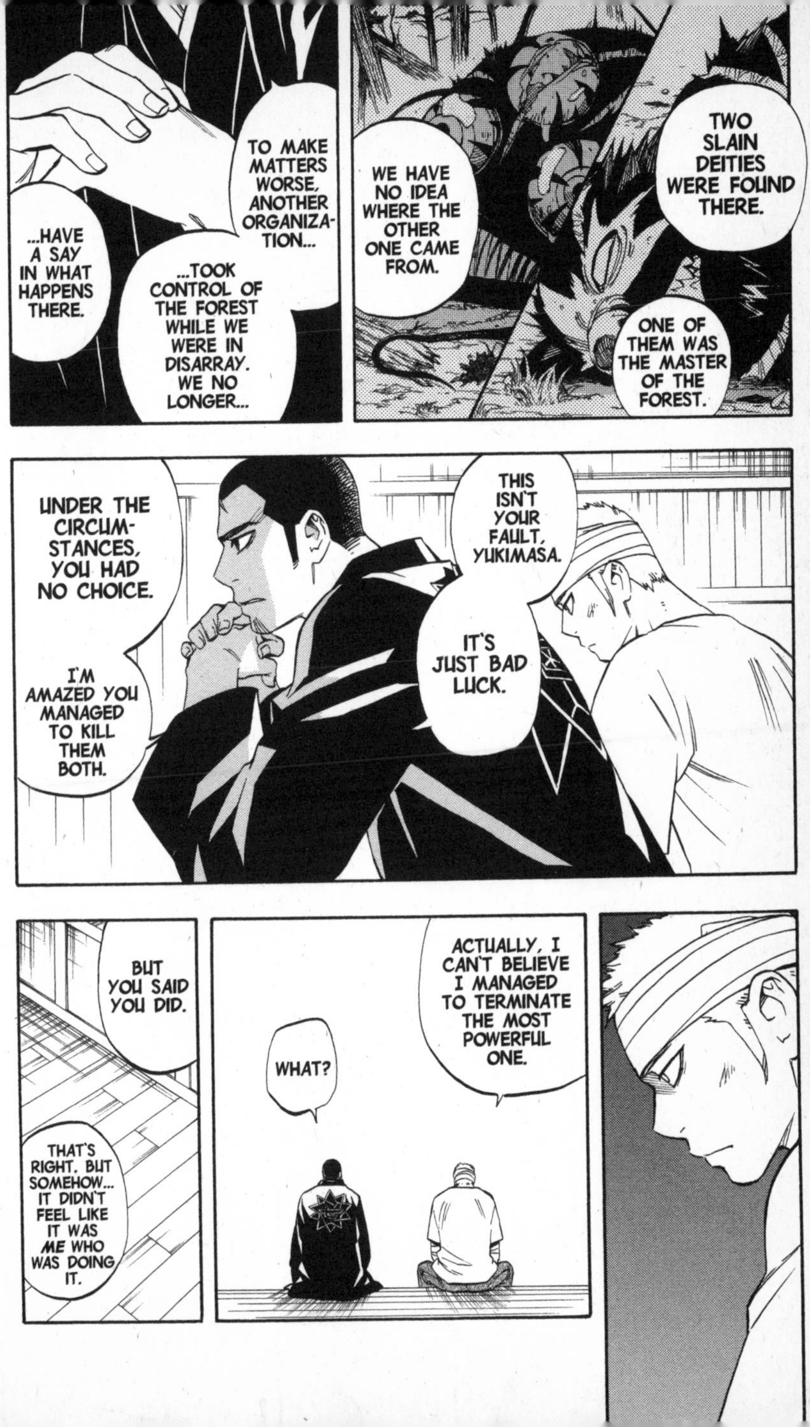
TWO SLAIN DEITIES WERE FOUND THERE.
ONE OF THEM WAS THE MASTER OF THE FOREST.
WE HAVE NO IDEA WHERE THE OTHER ONE CAME FROM.
TO MAKE MATTERS WORSE, ANOTHER ORGANIZATION...
...TOOK CONTROL OF THE FOREST WHILE WE WERE IN DISARRAY. WE NO LONGER...
...HAVE A SAY IN WHAT HAPPENS THERE.
THIS ISN'T YOUR FAULT, YUKIMASA.
IT'S JUST BAD LUCK.
UNDER THE CIRCUMSTANCES, YOU HAD NO CHOICE.
I'M AMAZED YOU MANAGED TO KILL THEM BOTH.
ACTUALLY, I CAN'T BELIEVE I MANAGED TO TERMINATE THE MOST POWERFUL ONE.
WHAT?
BUT YOU SAID YOU DID.
THAT'S RIGHT, BUT SOMEHOW... IT DIDN'T FEEL LIKE IT WAS *ME* WHO WAS DOING IT.

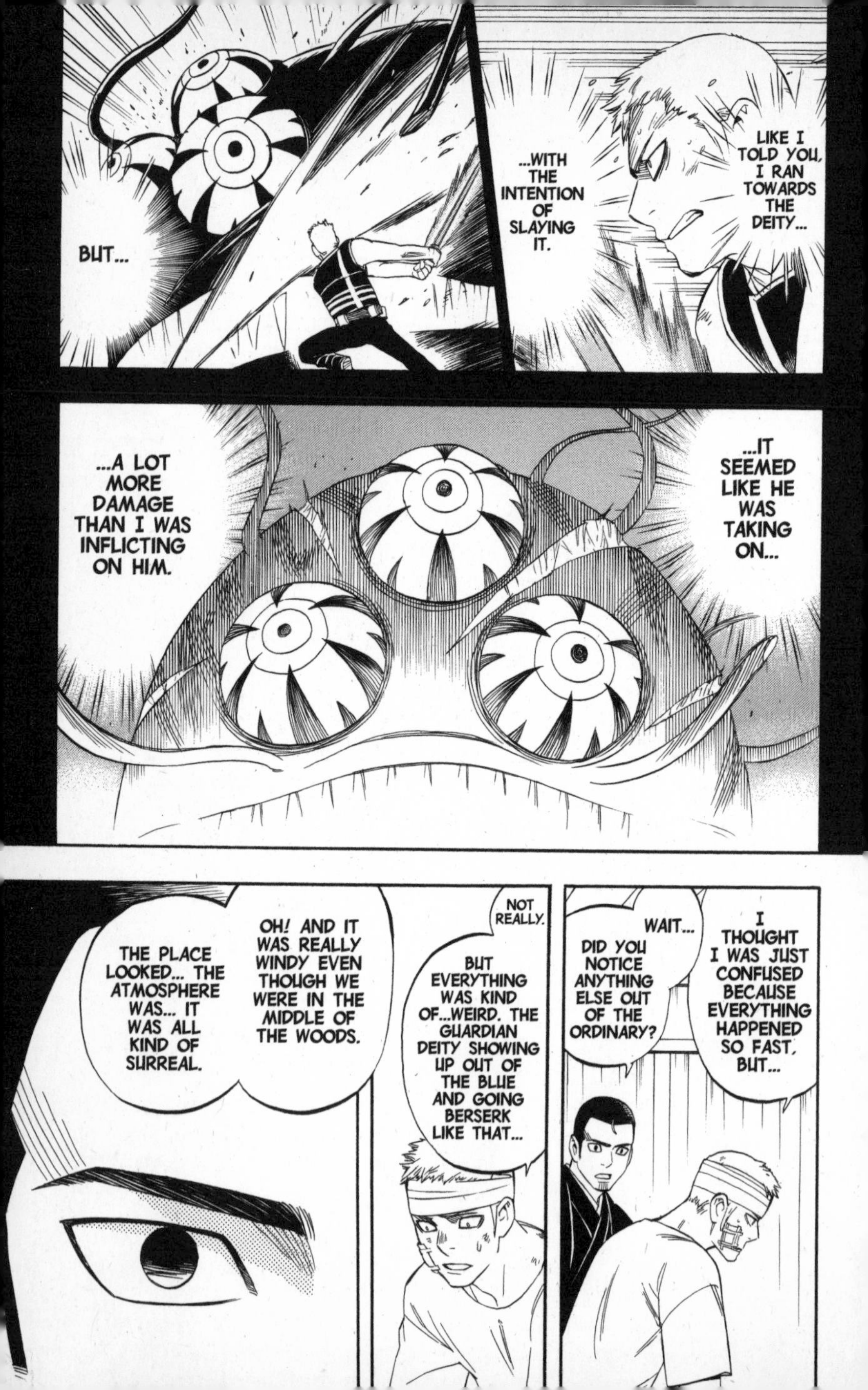
LIKE I TOLD YOU, I RAN TOWARDS THE DEITY...
...WITH THE INTENTION OF SLAYING IT.
BUT...
...IT SEEMED LIKE HE WAS TAKING ON...
...A LOT MORE DAMAGE THAN I WAS INFLICTING ON HIM.
I THOUGHT I WAS JUST CONFUSED BECAUSE EVERYTHING HAPPENED SO FAST, BUT...
WAIT...
DID YOU NOTICE ANYTHING ELSE OUT OF THE ORDINARY?
NOT REALLY.
BUT EVERYTHING WAS KIND OF...WEIRD. THE GUARDIAN DEITY SHOWING UP OUT OF THE BLUE AND GOING BERSERK LIKE THAT...
OH! AND IT WAS REALLY WINDY EVEN THOUGH WE WERE IN THE MIDDLE OF THE WOODS.
THE PLACE LOOKED... THE ATMOSPHERE WAS... IT WAS ALL KIND OF SURREAL.

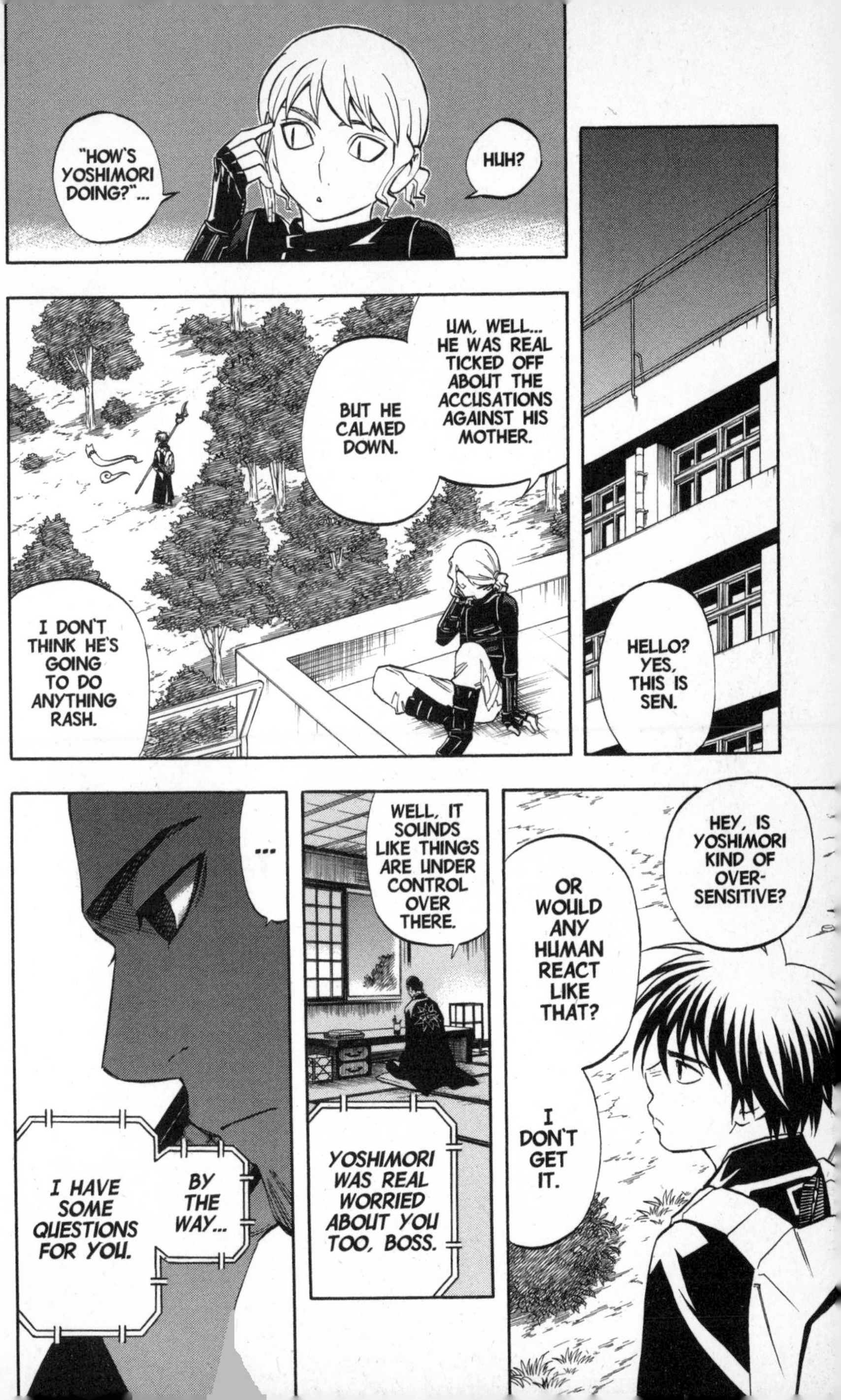
HELLO? YES, THIS IS SEN.
HUH?
"HOW'S YOSHIMORI DOING?"...
UM, WELL... HE WAS REAL TICKED OFF ABOUT THE ACCUSATIONS AGAINST HIS MOTHER.
BUT HE CALMED DOWN.
I DON'T THINK HE'S GOING TO DO ANYTHING RASH.
HEY, IS YOSHIMORI KIND OF OVER-SENSITIVE?
OR WOULD ANY HUMAN REACT LIKE THAT?
I DON'T GET IT.
WELL, IT SOUNDS LIKE THINGS ARE UNDER CONTROL OVER THERE.
YOSHIMORI WAS REAL WORRIED ABOUT YOU TOO, BOSS.
...
BY THE WAY...
I HAVE SOME QUESTIONS FOR YOU.

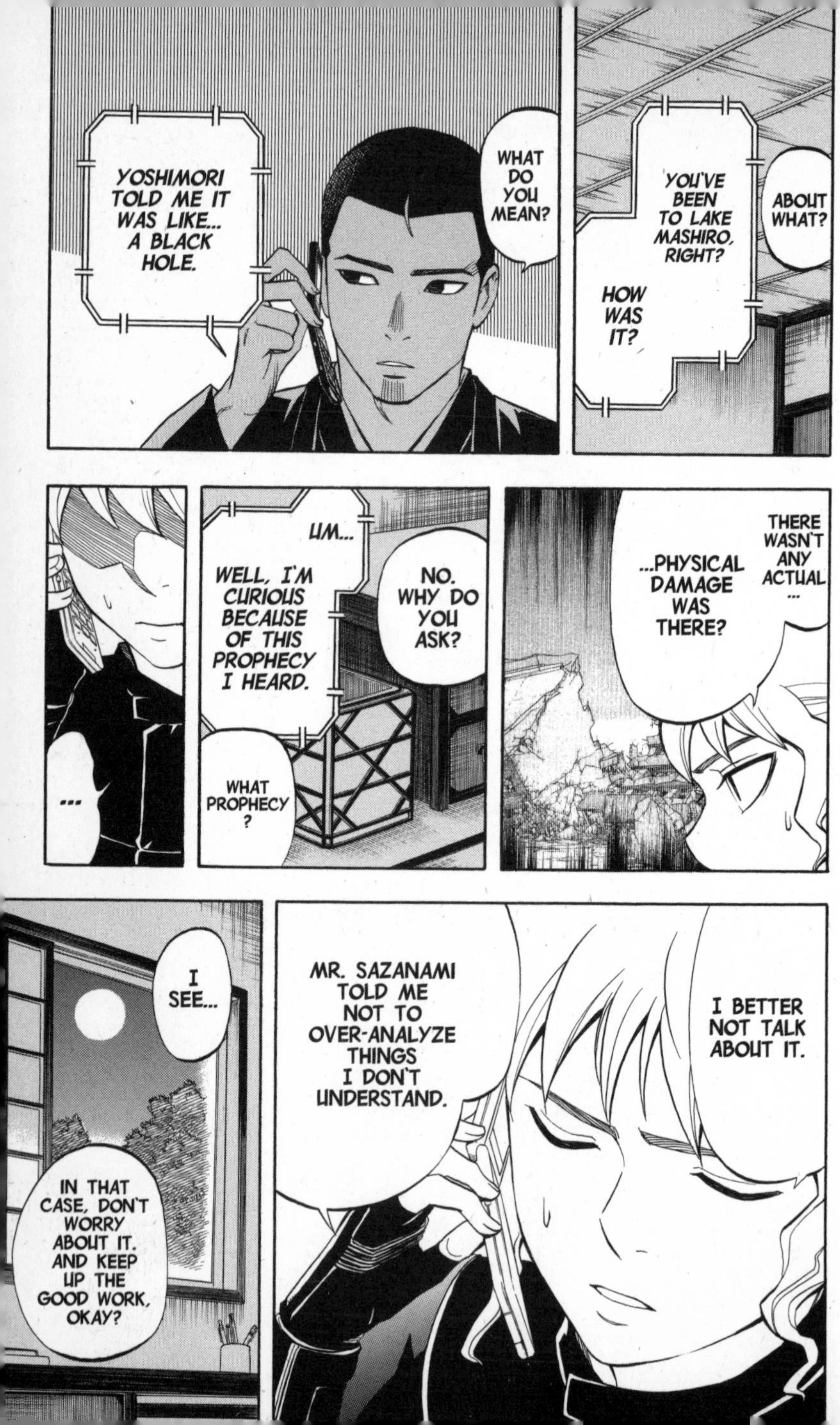
YOU'VE BEEN TO LAKE MASHIRO, RIGHT?
HOW WAS IT?
ABOUT WHAT?
YOSHIMORI TOLD ME IT WAS LIKE... A BLACK HOLE.
WHAT DO YOU MEAN?
THERE WASN'T ANY ACTUAL...
...PHYSICAL DAMAGE WAS THERE?
NO. WHY DO YOU ASK?
UM...
WELL, I'M CURIOUS BECAUSE OF THIS PROPHECY I HEARD.
WHAT PROPHECY?
...
I BETTER NOT TALK ABOUT IT.
MR. SAZANAMI TOLD ME NOT TO OVER-ANALYZE THINGS I DON'T UNDERSTAND.
I SEE...
IN THAT CASE, DON'T WORRY ABOUT IT. AND KEEP UP THE GOOD WORK, OKAY?

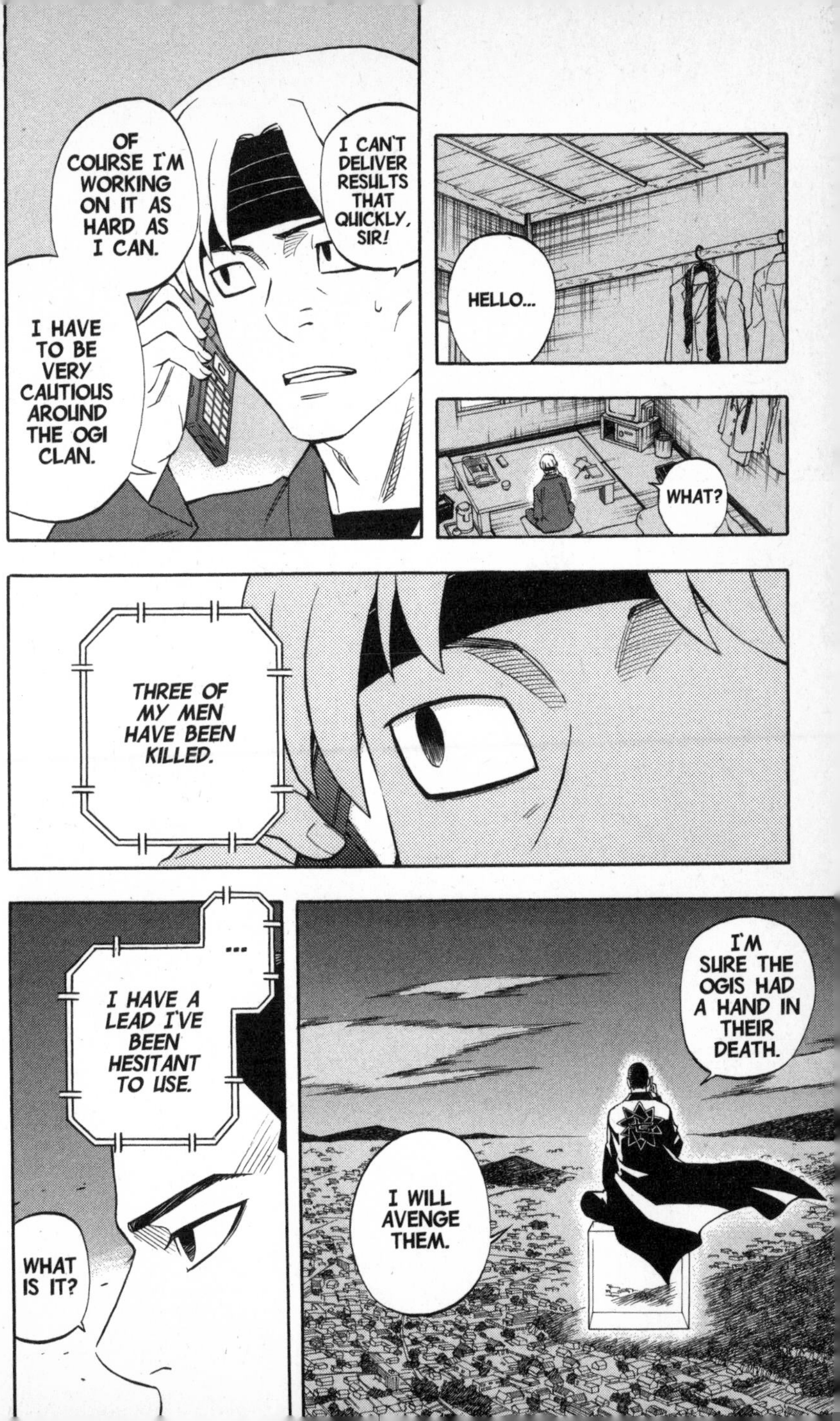
HELLO...
WHAT?
I CAN'T DELIVER RESULTS THAT QUICKLY, SIR!
OF COURSE I'M WORKING ON IT AS HARD AS I CAN.
I HAVE TO BE VERY CAUTIOUS AROUND THE OGI CLAN.
THREE OF MY MEN HAVE BEEN KILLED.
I'M SURE THE OGIS HAD A HAND IN THEIR DEATH.
I WILL AVENGE THEM.
...
I HAVE A LEAD I'VE BEEN HESITANT TO USE.
WHAT IS IT?

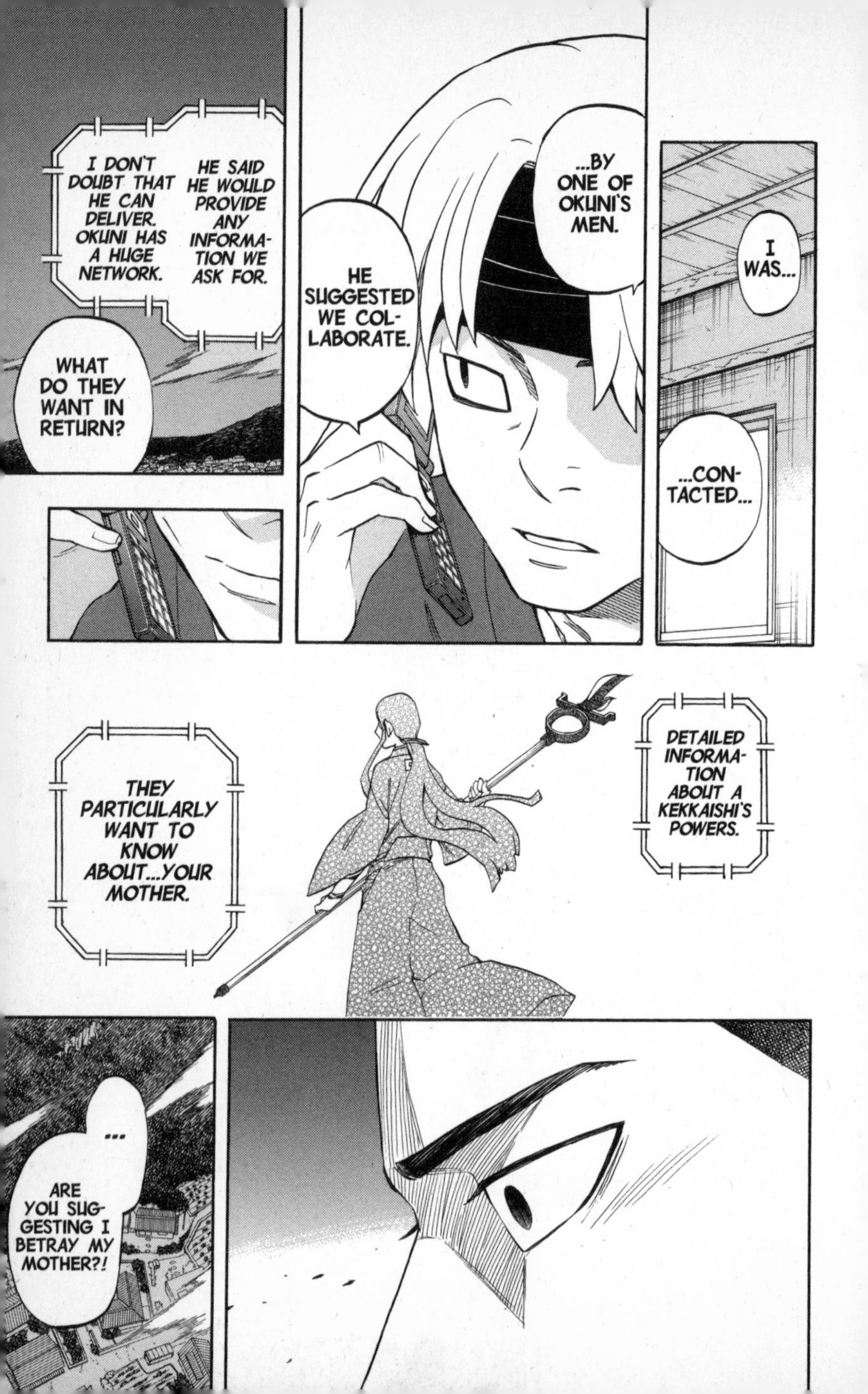
I WAS...
...CONTACTED...
...BY ONE OF OKUNI'S MEN.
HE SUGGESTED WE COLLABORATE.
HE SAID HE WOULD PROVIDE ANY INFORMATION WE ASK FOR.
I DON'T DOUBT THAT HE CAN DELIVER. OKUNI HAS A HUGE NETWORK.
WHAT DO THEY WANT IN RETURN?
DETAILED INFORMATION ABOUT A KEKKAISHI'S POWERS.
THEY PARTICULARLY WANT TO KNOW ABOUT...YOUR MOTHER.
...
ARE YOU SUGGESTING I BETRAY MY MOTHER?!

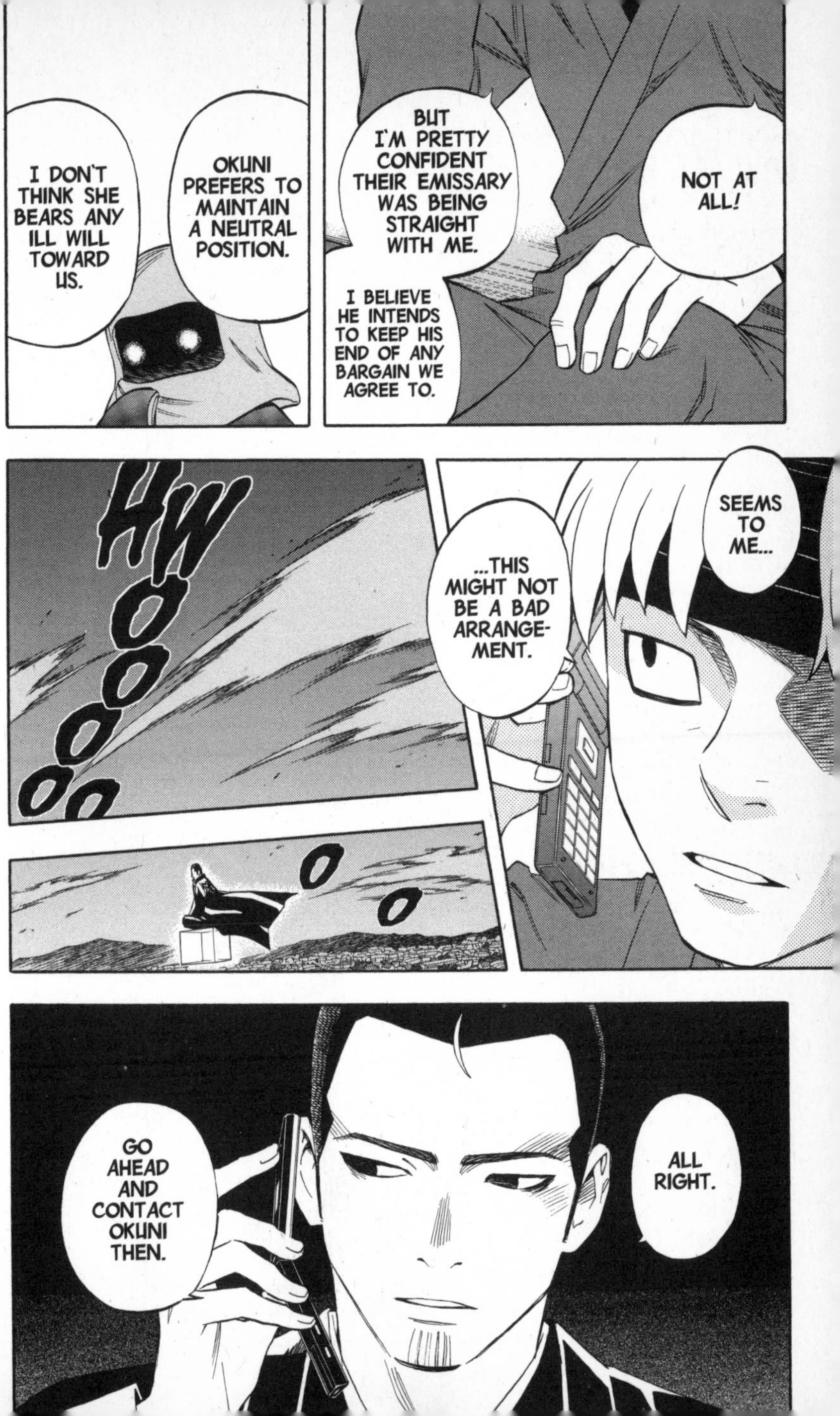
NOT AT ALL!
BUT I'M PRETTY CONFIDENT THEIR EMISSARY WAS BEING STRAIGHT WITH ME.
I BELIEVE HE INTENDS TO KEEP HIS END OF ANY BARGAIN WE AGREE TO.
OKUNI PREFERS TO MAINTAIN A NEUTRAL POSITION.
I DON'T THINK SHE BEARS ANY ILL WILL TOWARD US.
SEEMS TO ME...
...THIS MIGHT NOT BE A BAD ARRANGE-MENT.
HWOOOOOOO
OO
ALL RIGHT.
GO AHEAD AND CONTACT OKUNI THEN.

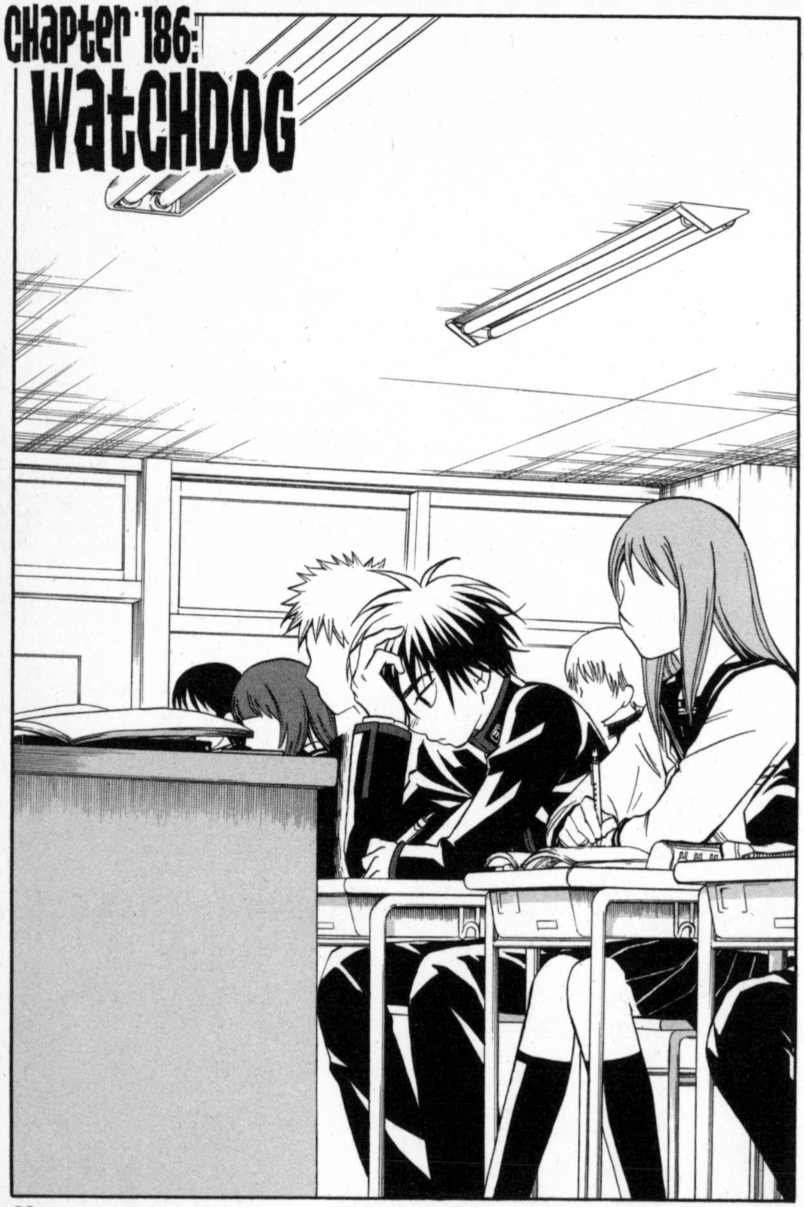
Chapter 186:
Watchdog

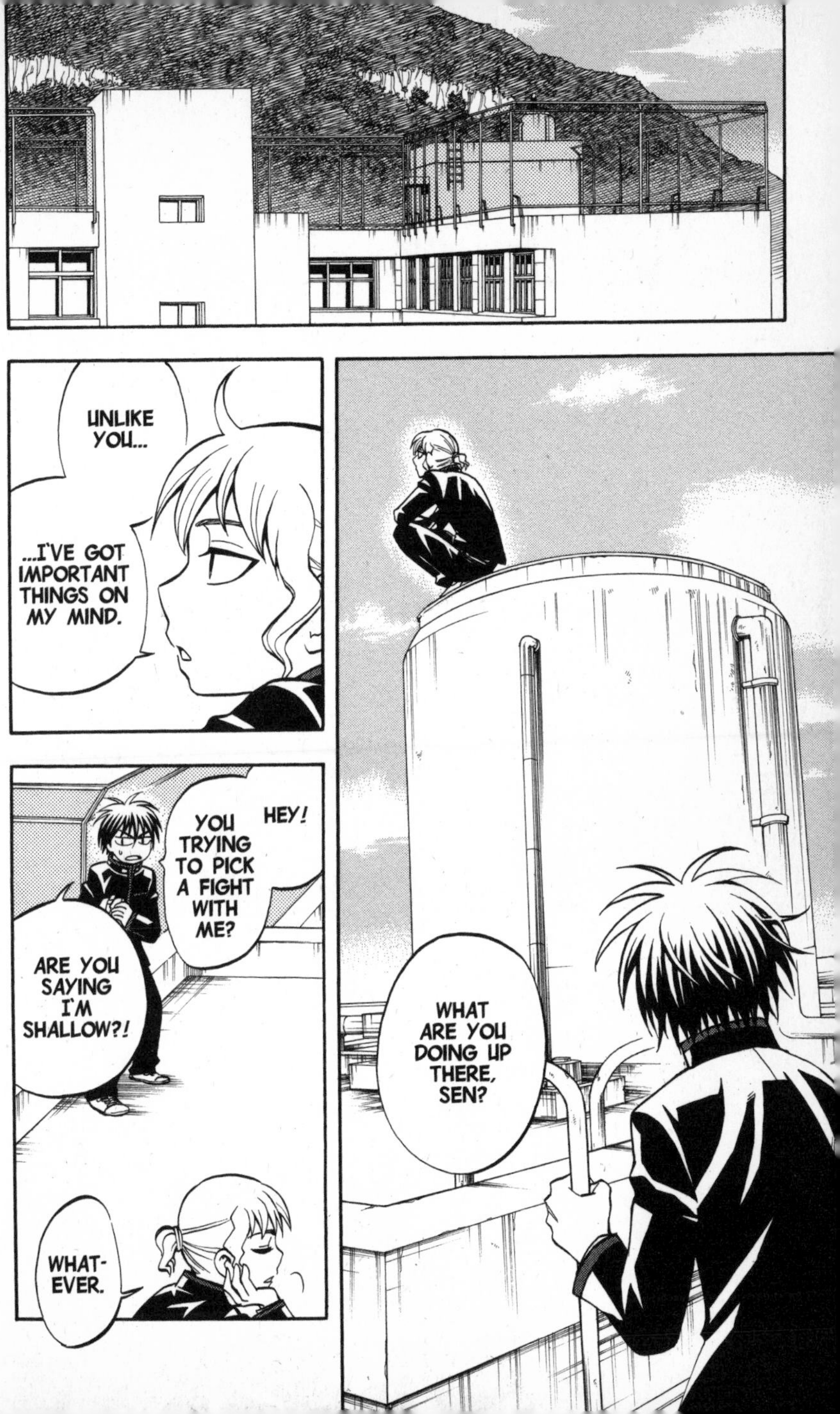
WHAT ARE YOU DOING UP THERE, SEN?
UNLIKE YOU...
...I'VE GOT IMPORTANT THINGS ON MY MIND.
HEY!
YOU TRYING TO PICK A FIGHT WITH ME?
ARE YOU SAYING I'M SHALLOW?!
WHAT-EVER.

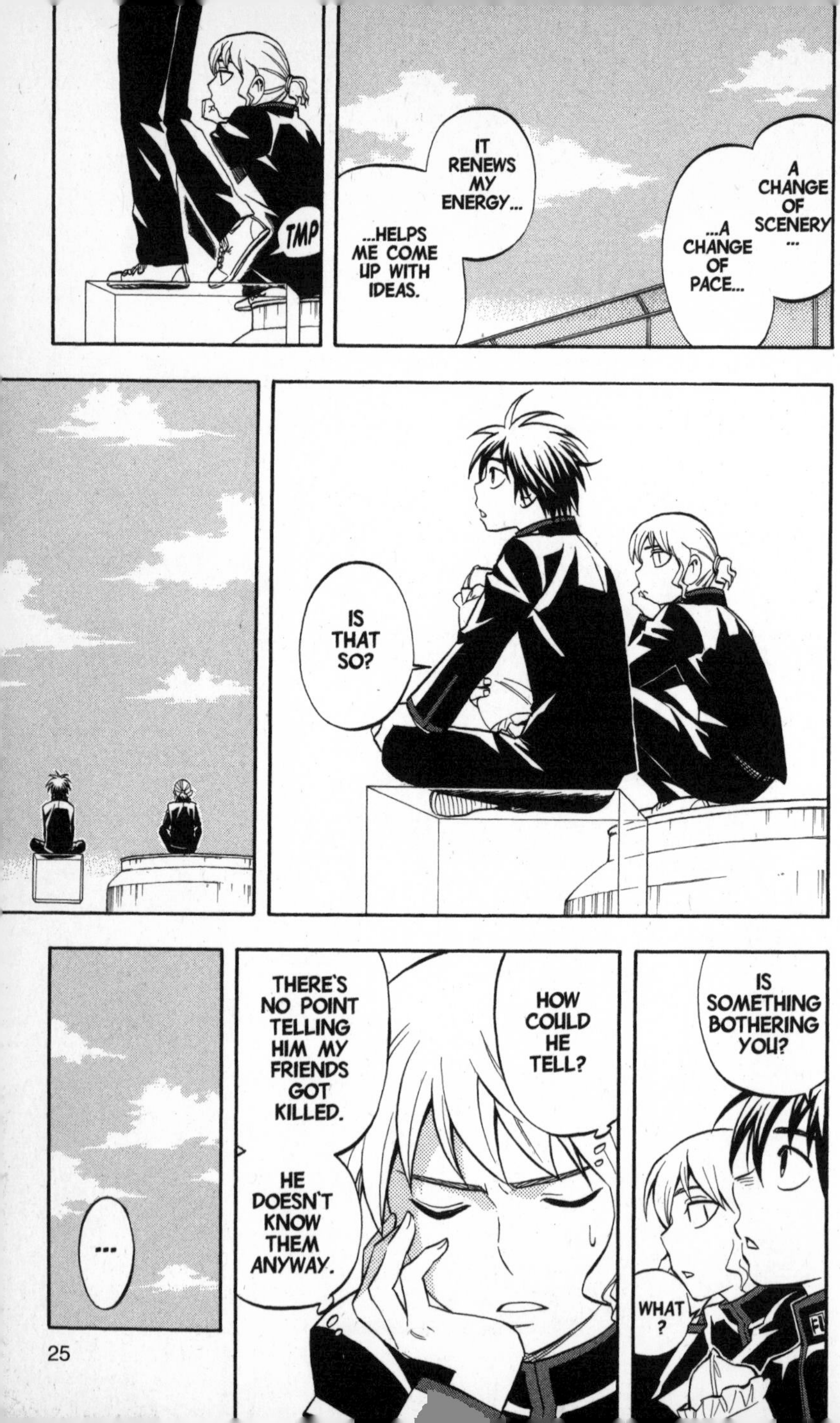
A CHANGE OF SCENERY...
...A CHANGE OF PACE...
IT RENEWS MY ENERGY...
...HELPS ME COME UP WITH IDEAS.
TMP
IS THAT SO?
IS SOMETHING BOTHERING YOU?
WHAT?
HOW COULD HE TELL?
THERE'S NO POINT TELLING HIM MY FRIENDS GOT KILLED.
HE DOESN'T KNOW THEM ANYWAY.
...

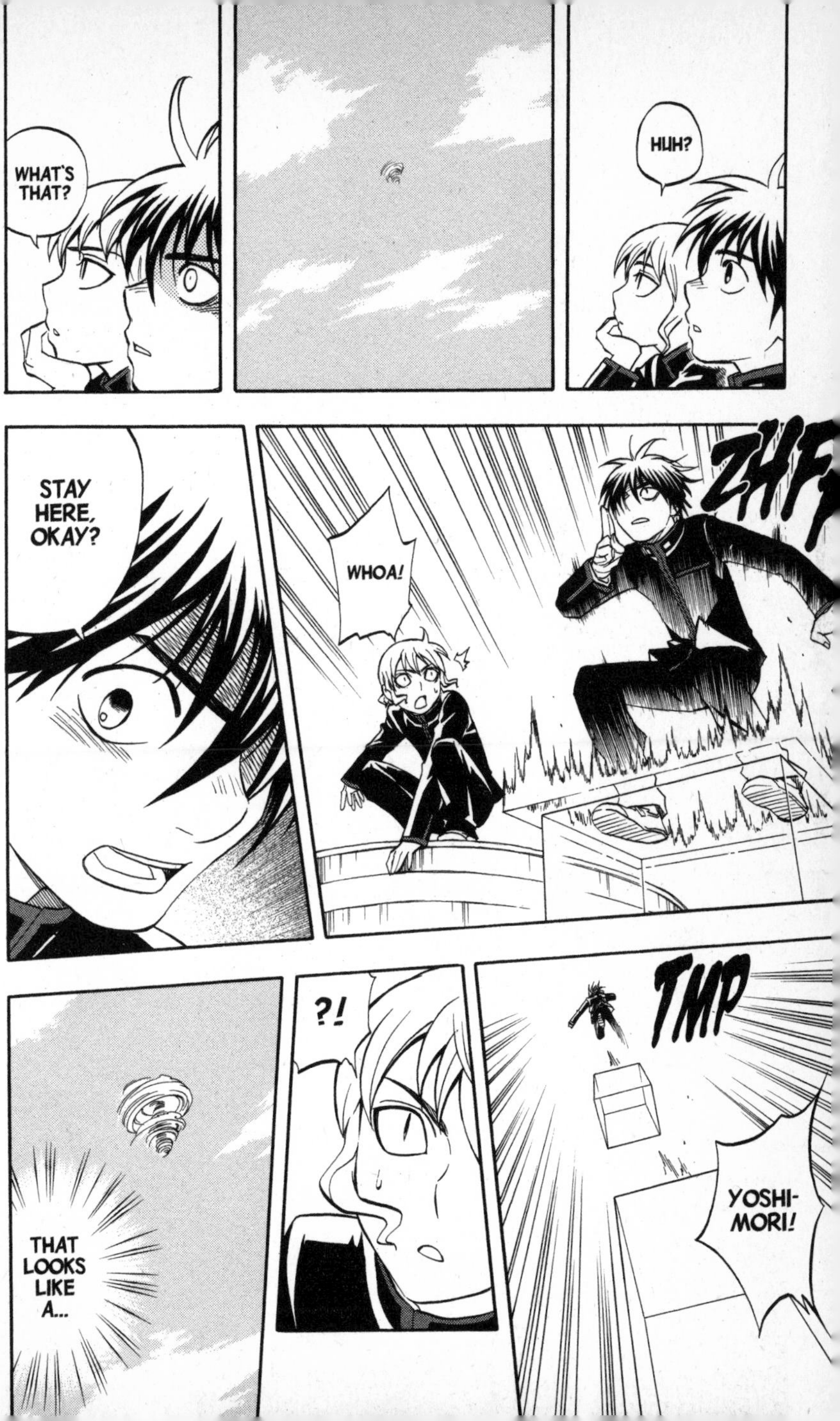
HUH?
WHAT'S THAT?
ZHF
WHOA!
STAY HERE, OKAY?
TMP
YOSHIMORI!
?!
THAT LOOKS LIKE A...

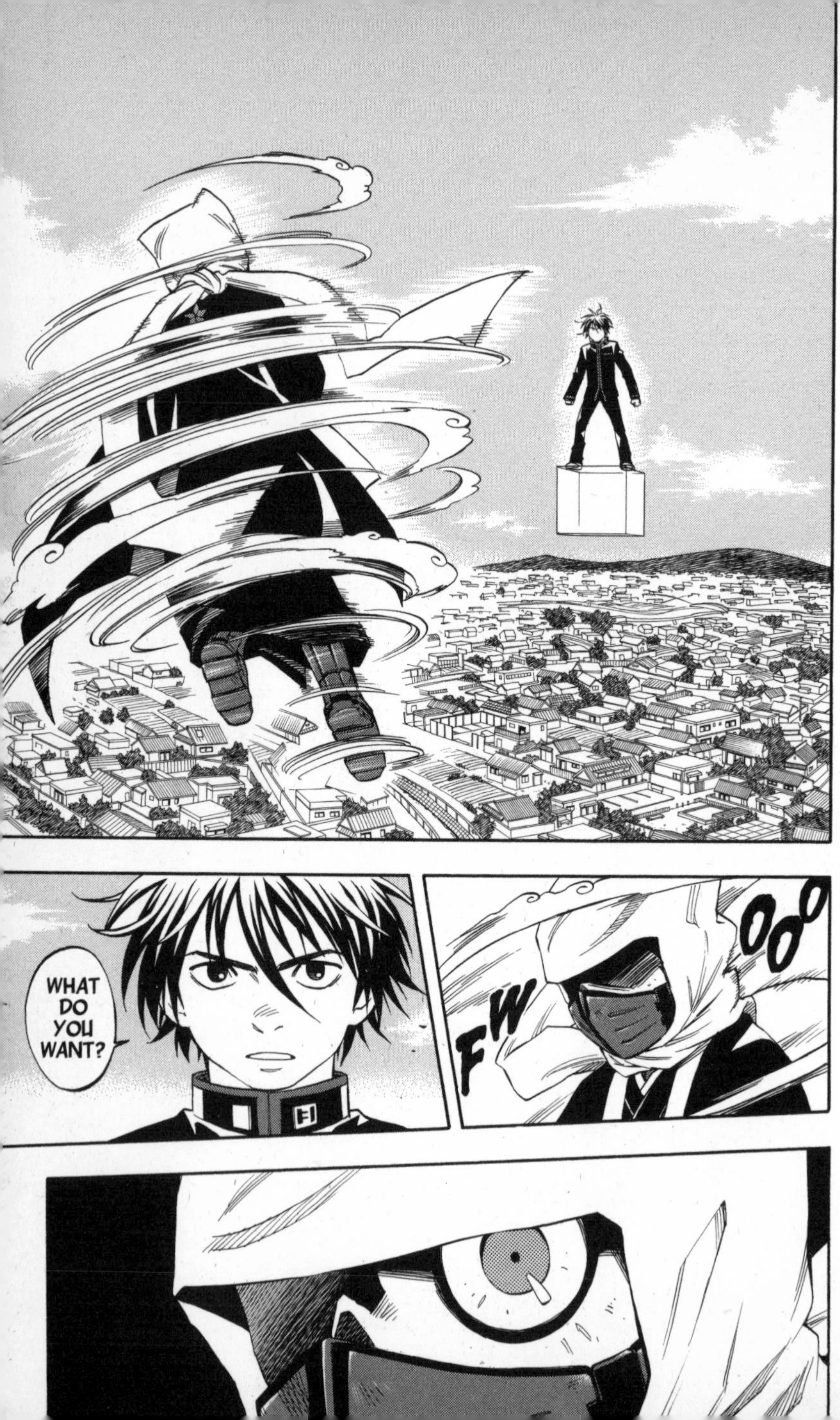
FWOOO
WHAT DO YOU WANT?

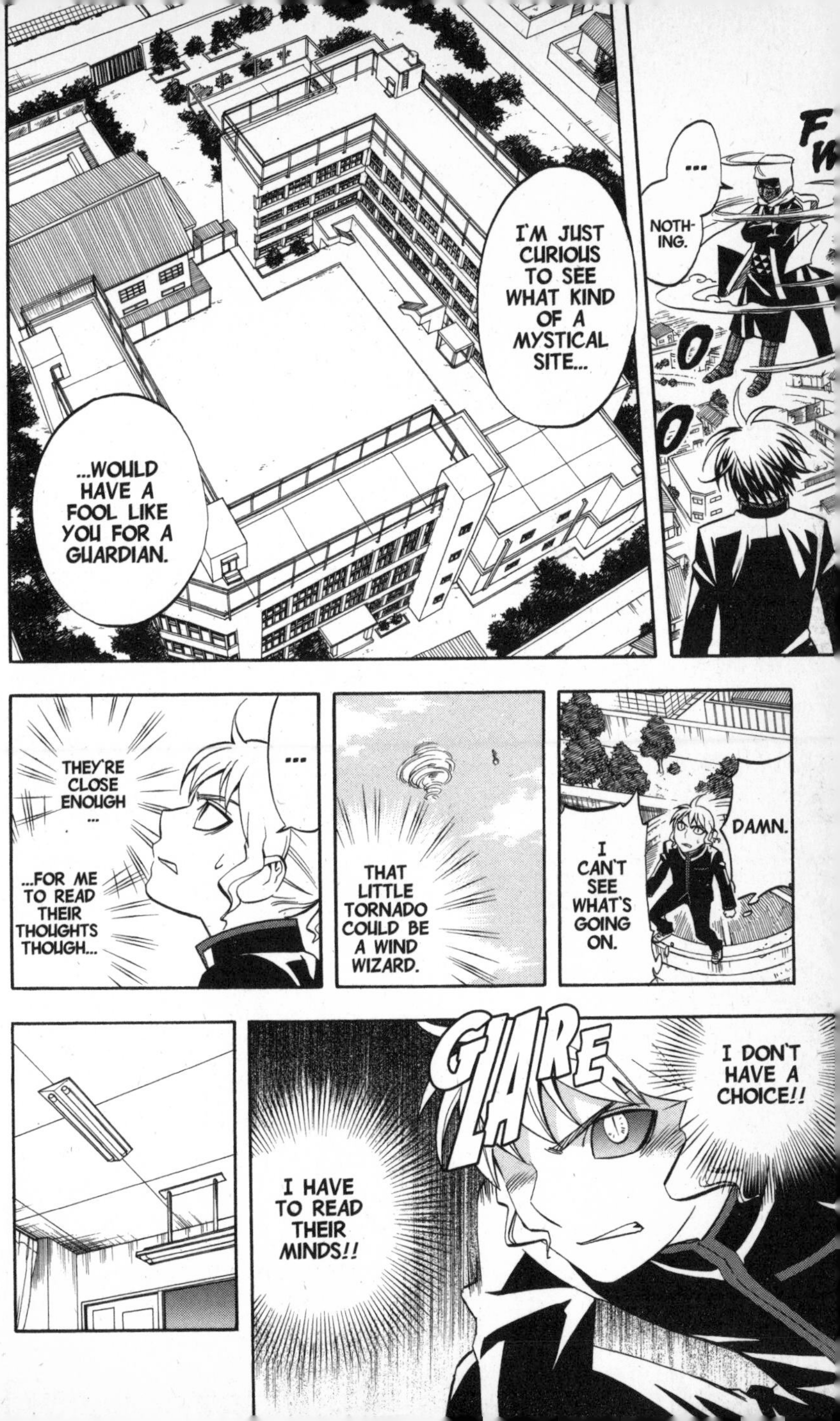
FW
...
NOTHING.
I'M JUST CURIOUS TO SEE WHAT KIND OF A MYSTICAL SITE...
...WOULD HAVE A FOOL LIKE YOU FOR A GUARDIAN.
DAMN.
I CAN'T SEE WHAT'S GOING ON.
THAT LITTLE TORNADO COULD BE A WIND WIZARD.
...
THEY'RE CLOSE ENOUGH...
...FOR ME TO READ THEIR THOUGHTS THOUGH...
GLARE
I DON'T HAVE A CHOICE!!
I HAVE TO READ THEIR MINDS!!

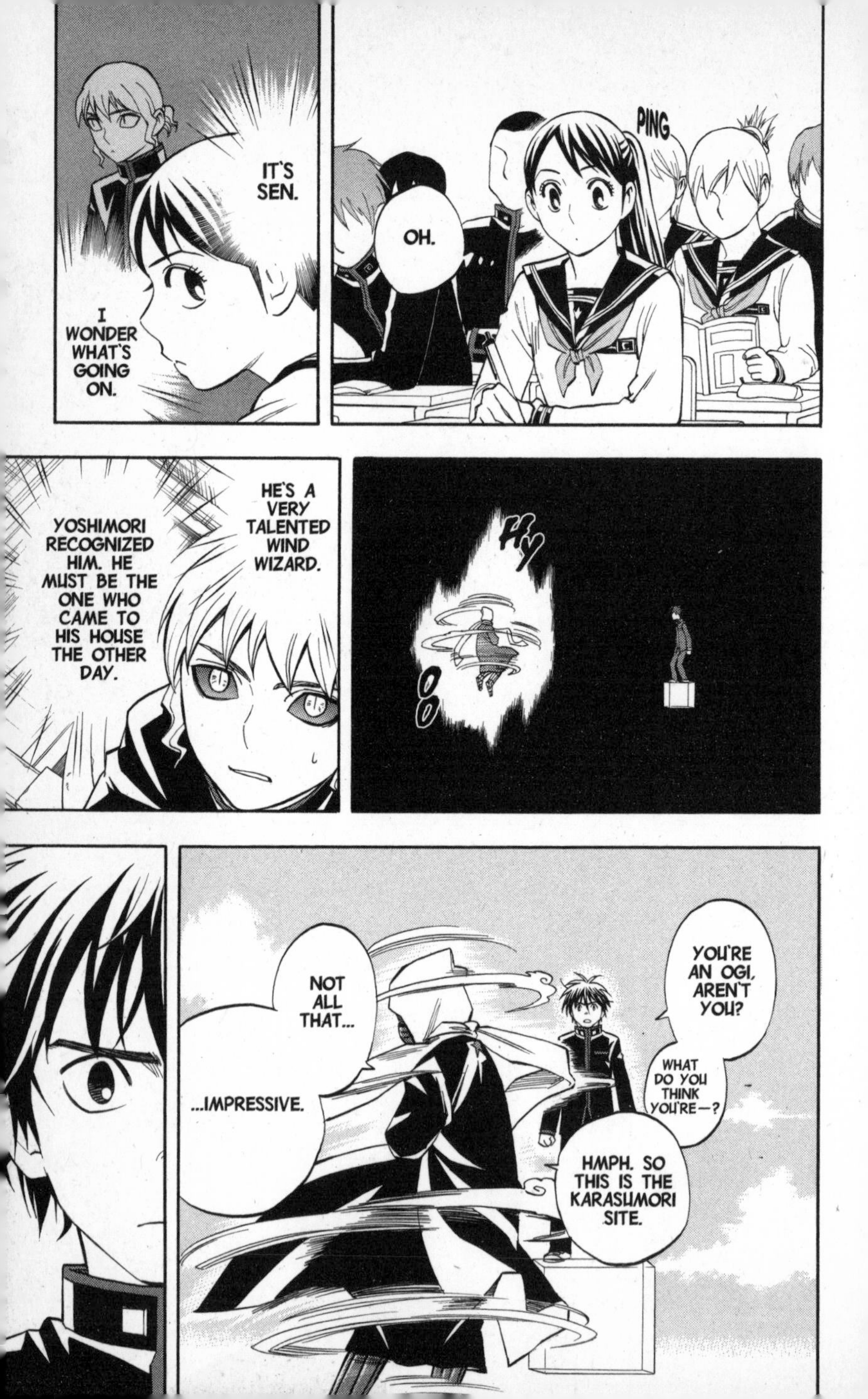
PING
OH.
IT'S SEN.
I WONDER WHAT'S GOING ON.
HE'S A VERY TALENTED WIND WIZARD.
YOSHIMORI RECOGNIZED HIM. HE MUST BE THE ONE WHO CAME TO HIS HOUSE THE OTHER DAY.
YOU'RE AN OGI, AREN'T YOU?
WHAT DO YOU THINK YOU'RE—?
HMPH. SO THIS IS THE KARASUMORI SITE.
NOT ALL THAT...
...IMPRESSIVE.

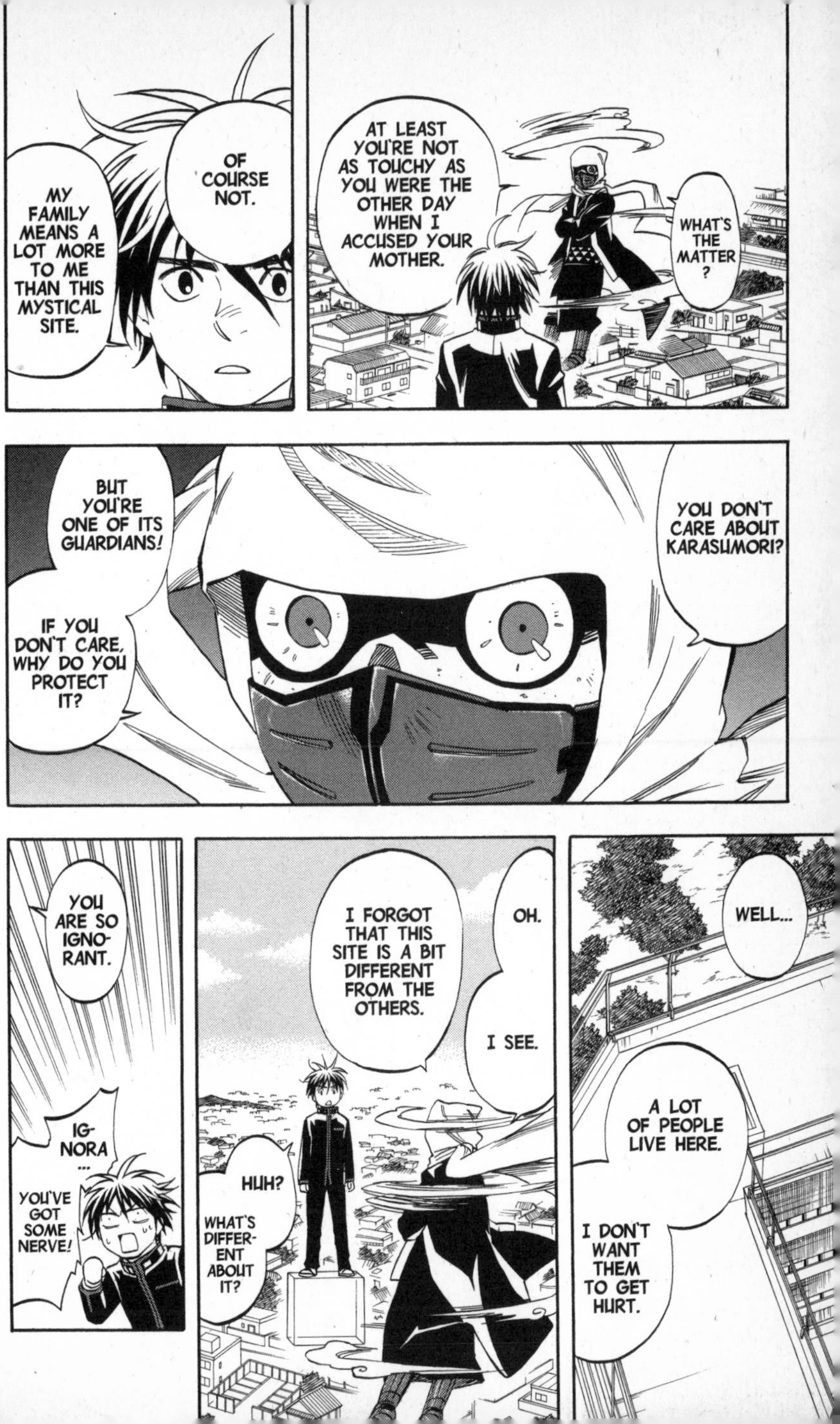
WHAT'S THE MATTER?
AT LEAST YOU'RE NOT AS TOUCHY AS YOU WERE THE OTHER DAY WHEN I ACCUSED YOUR MOTHER.
OF COURSE NOT.
MY FAMILY MEANS A LOT MORE TO ME THAN THIS MYSTICAL SITE.
YOU DON'T CARE ABOUT KARASUMORI?
BUT YOU'RE ONE OF ITS GUARDIANS!
IF YOU DON'T CARE, WHY DO YOU PROTECT IT?
WELL...
A LOT OF PEOPLE LIVE HERE.
I DON'T WANT THEM TO GET HURT.
OH.
I SEE.
I FORGOT THAT THIS SITE IS A BIT DIFFERENT FROM THE OTHERS.
HUH?
WHAT'S DIFFER-ENT ABOUT IT?
YOU ARE SO IGNO-RANT.
IG-NORA...
YOU'VE GOT SOME NERVE!

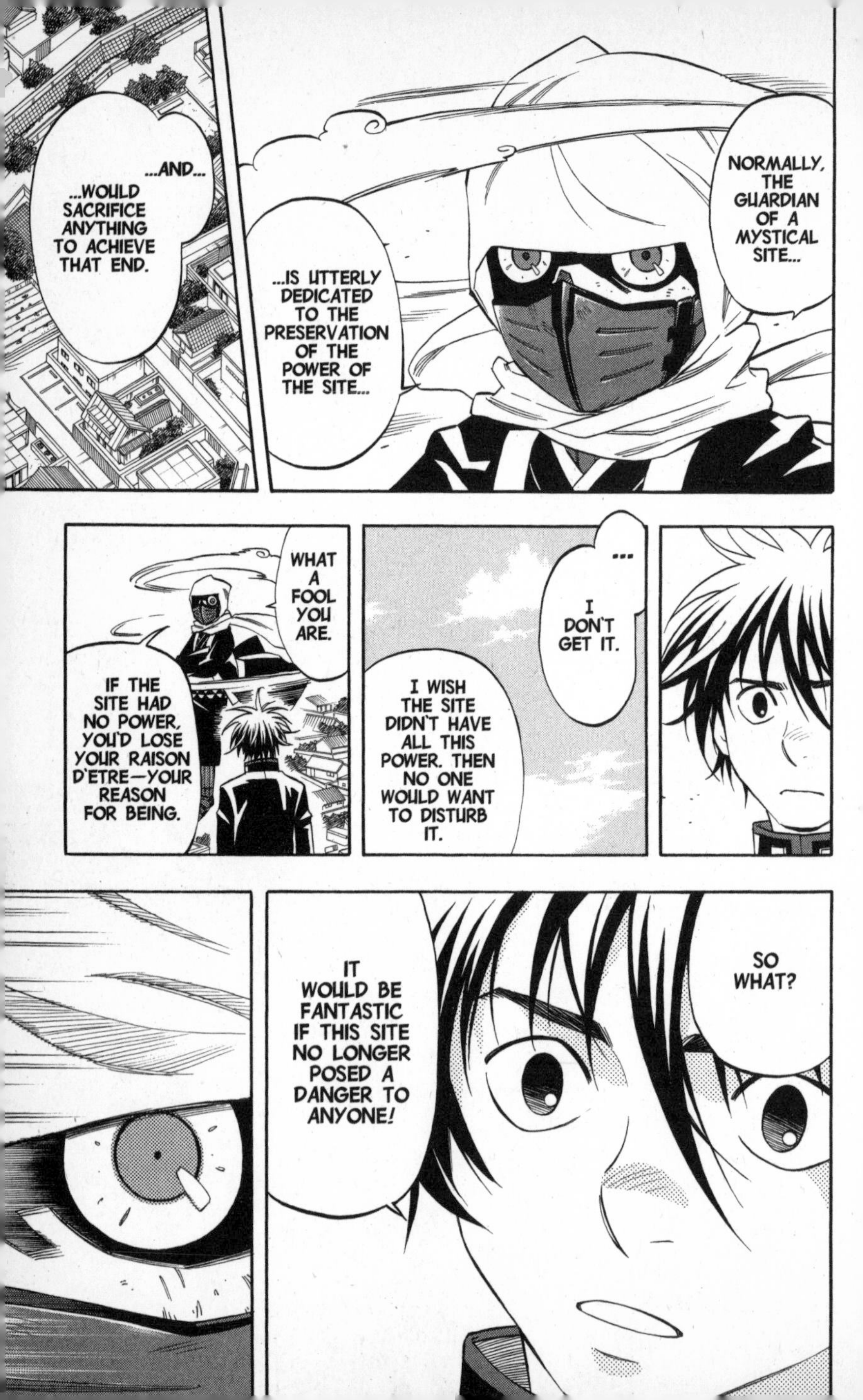
NORMALLY, THE GUARDIAN OF A MYSTICAL SITE...
...IS UTTERLY DEDICATED TO THE PRESERVATION OF THE POWER OF THE SITE...
...AND...
...WOULD SACRIFICE ANYTHING TO ACHIEVE THAT END.
...
I DON'T GET IT.
I WISH THE SITE DIDN'T HAVE ALL THIS POWER. THEN NO ONE WOULD WANT TO DISTURB IT.
WHAT A FOOL YOU ARE.
IF THE SITE HAD NO POWER, YOU'D LOSE YOUR RAISON D'ETRE—YOUR REASON FOR BEING.
SO WHAT?
IT WOULD BE FANTASTIC IF THIS SITE NO LONGER POSED A DANGER TO ANYONE!

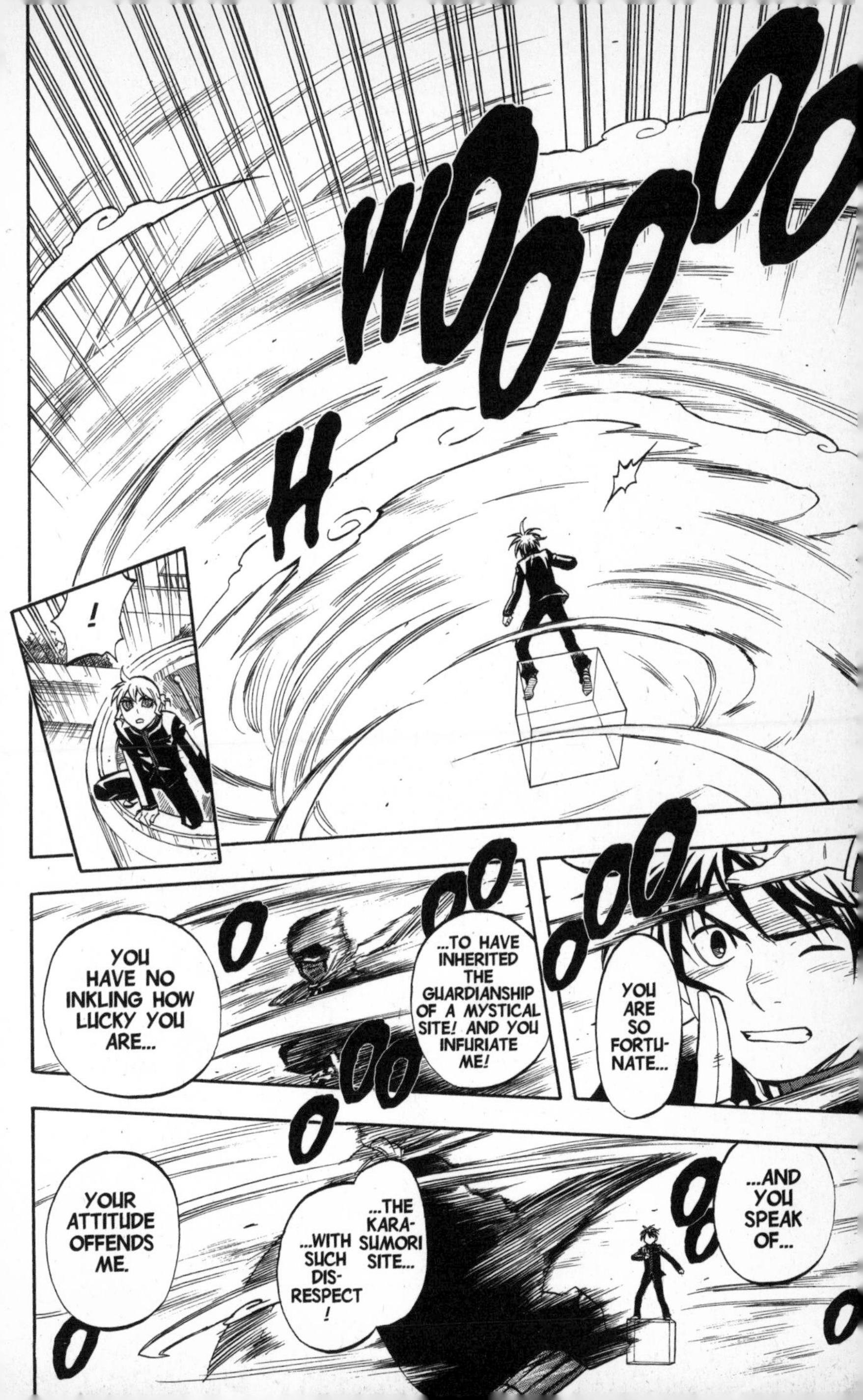
WOOOOOOOOOH
!
YOU ARE SO FORTUNATE...
YOU HAVE NO INKLING HOW LUCKY YOU ARE...
...TO HAVE INHERITED THE GUARDIANSHIP OF A MYSTICAL SITE! AND YOU INFURIATE ME!
...AND YOU SPEAK OF...
...THE KARASUMORI SITE...
...WITH SUCH DISRESPECT!
YOUR ATTITUDE OFFENDS ME.

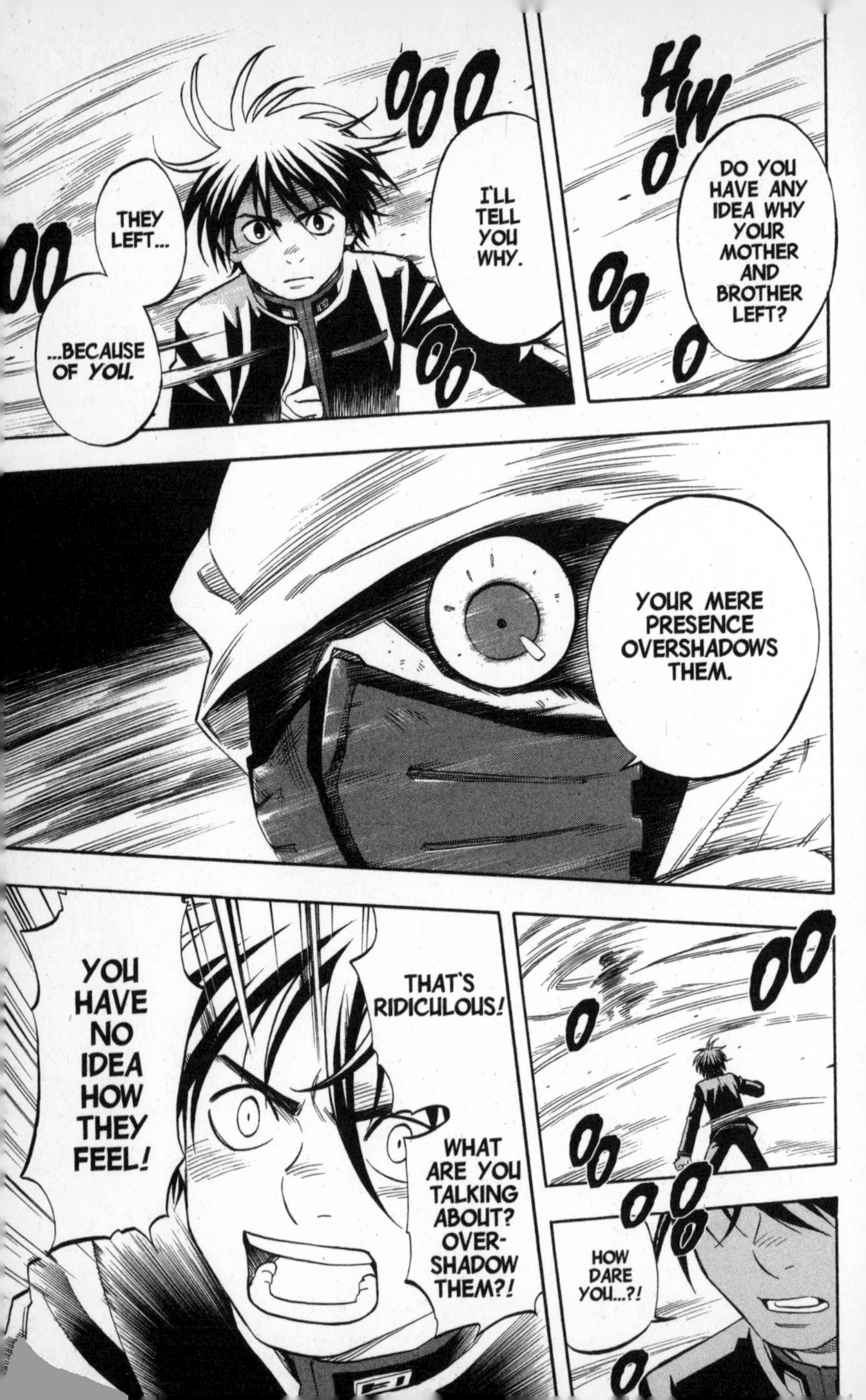
HWOOO
DO YOU HAVE ANY IDEA WHY YOUR MOTHER AND BROTHER LEFT?
I'LL TELL YOU WHY.
THEY LEFT...
...BECAUSE OF *YOU.*
YOUR MERE PRESENCE OVERSHADOWS THEM.
HOW DARE YOU...?!
THAT'S RIDICULOUS!
WHAT ARE YOU TALKING ABOUT? OVER-SHADOW THEM?!
YOU HAVE NO IDEA HOW THEY FEEL!

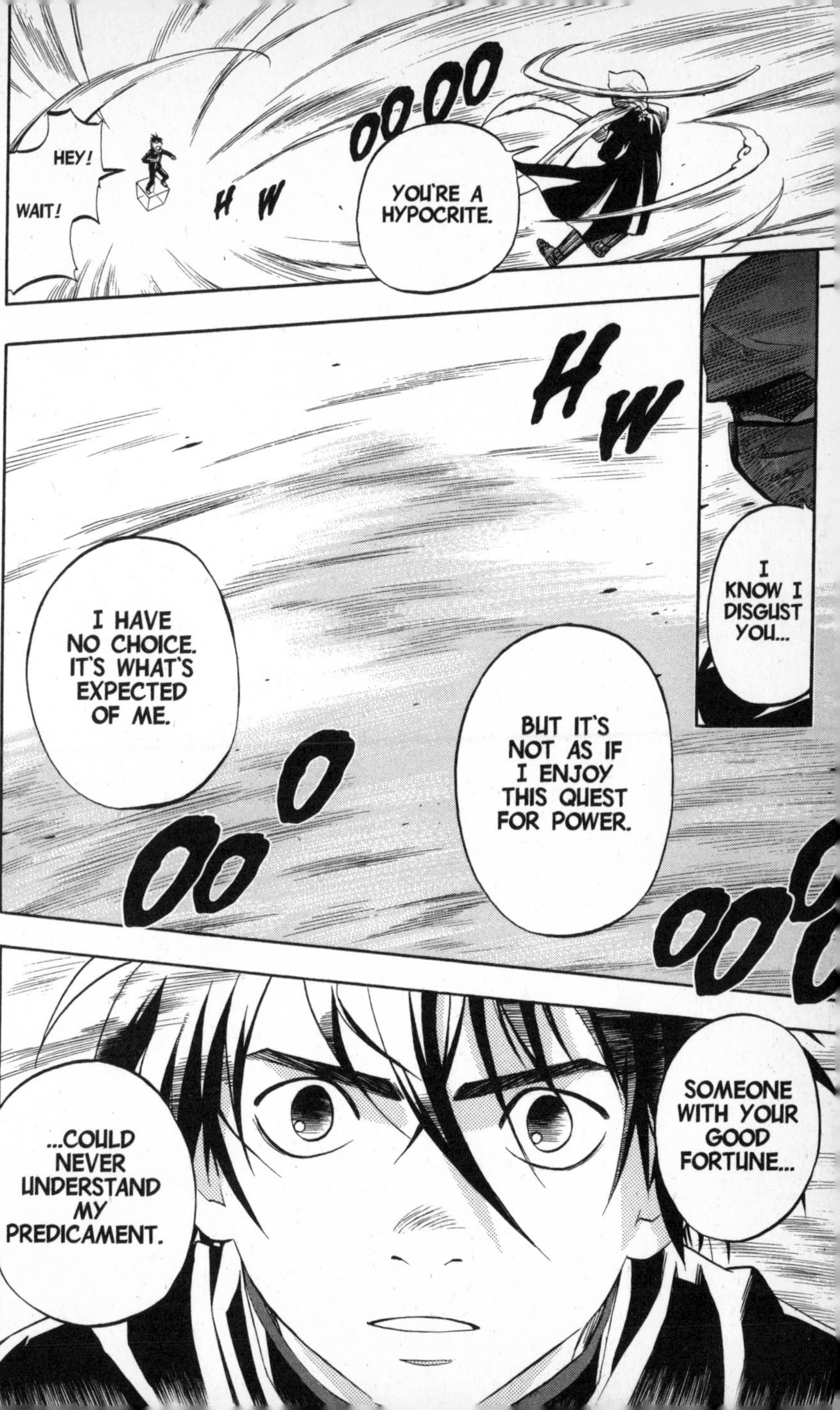
HWOOOO
YOU'RE A HYPOCRITE.
HEY! WAIT!
I KNOW I DISGUST YOU...
HWOOOOO
BUT IT'S NOT AS IF I ENJOY THIS QUEST FOR POWER.
I HAVE NO CHOICE. IT'S WHAT'S EXPECTED OF ME.
SOMEONE WITH YOUR GOOD FORTUNE...
...COULD NEVER UNDERSTAND MY PREDICAMENT.

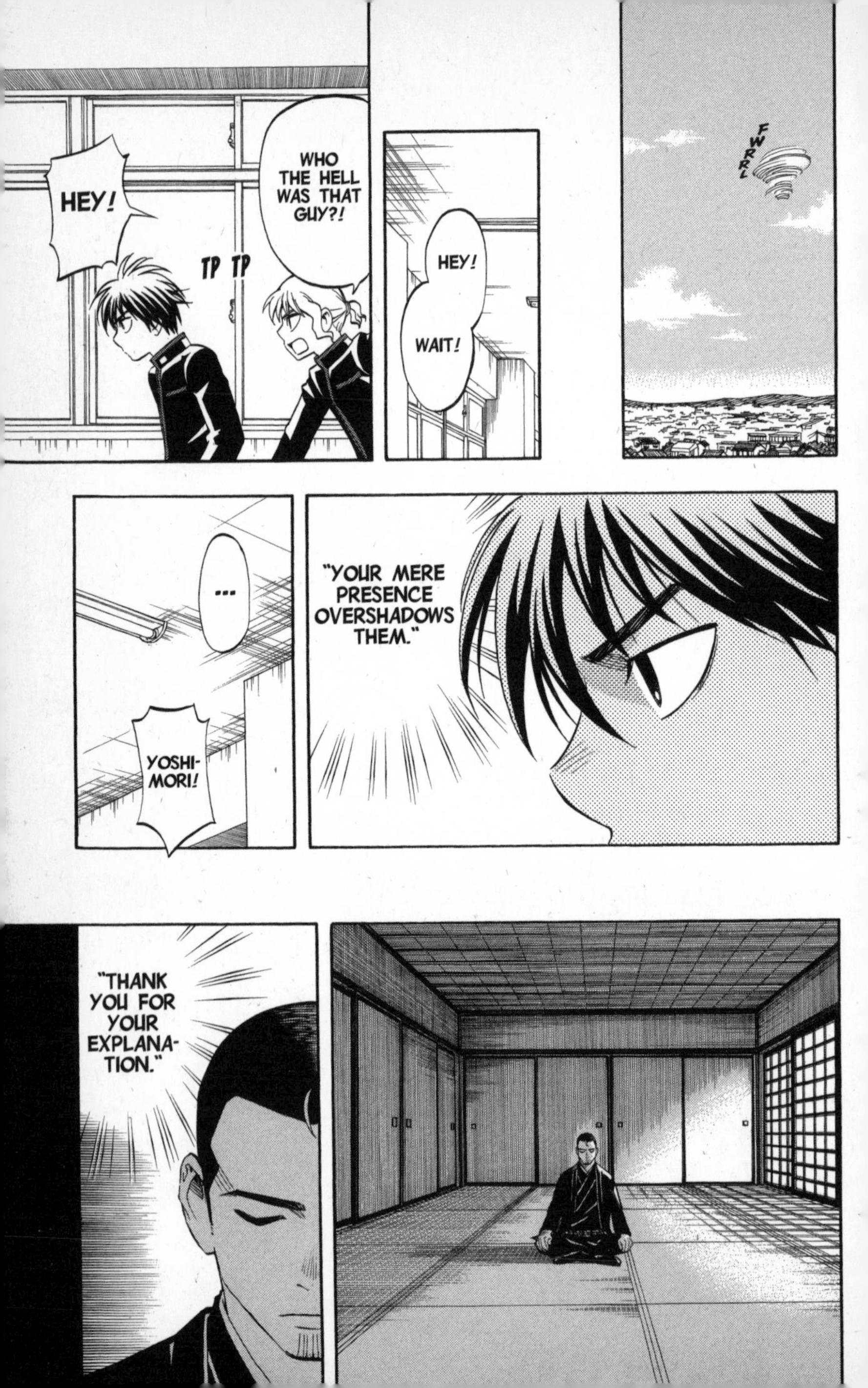
FWRRL
HEY!
WAIT!
WHO THE HELL WAS THAT GUY?!
HEY!
TP TP
"YOUR MERE PRESENCE OVERSHADOWS THEM."
...
YOSHIMORI!
"THANK YOU FOR YOUR EXPLANATION."

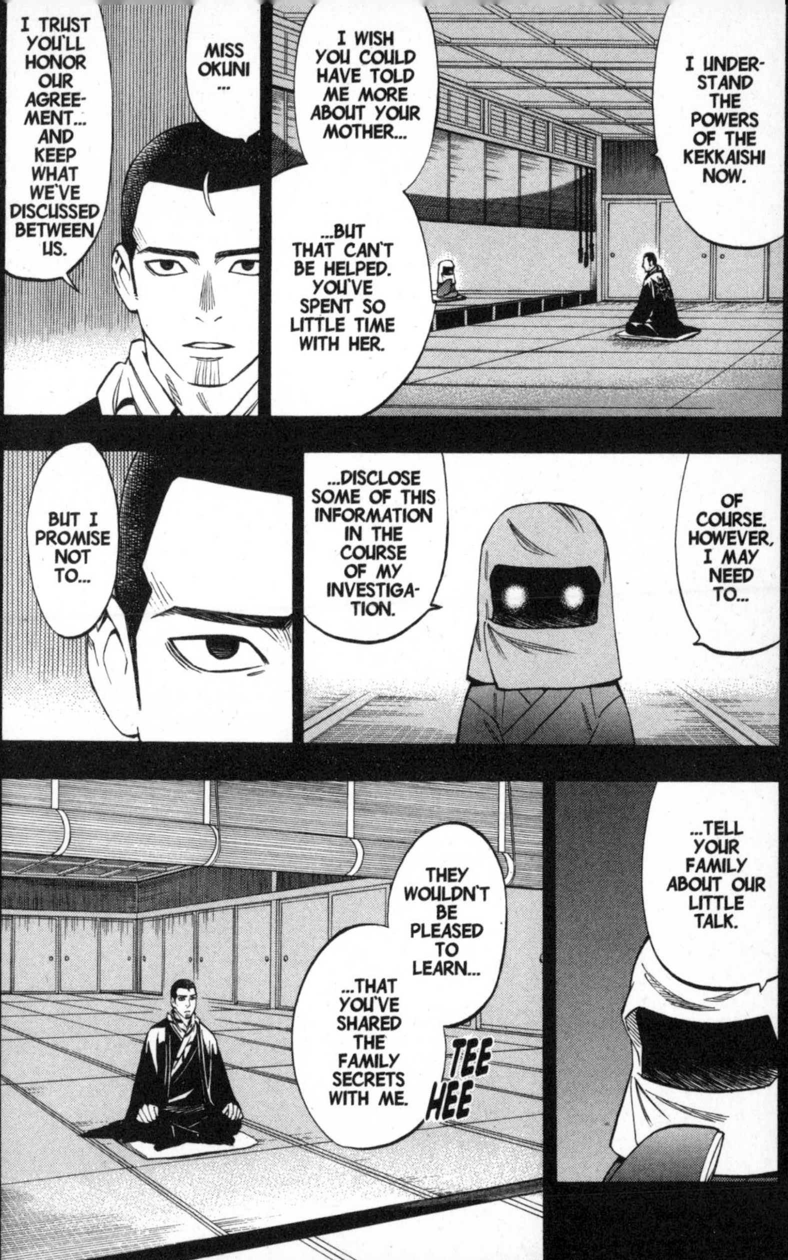
I UNDER-STAND THE POWERS OF THE KEKKAISHI NOW.
I WISH YOU COULD HAVE TOLD ME MORE ABOUT YOUR MOTHER...
...BUT THAT CAN'T BE HELPED. YOU'VE SPENT SO LITTLE TIME WITH HER.
MISS OKUNI...
I TRUST YOU'LL HONOR OUR AGREEMENT... AND KEEP WHAT WE'VE DISCUSSED BETWEEN US.
OF COURSE. HOWEVER, I MAY NEED TO...
...DISCLOSE SOME OF THIS INFORMATION IN THE COURSE OF MY INVESTIGA-TION.
BUT I PROMISE NOT TO...
...TELL YOUR FAMILY ABOUT OUR LITTLE TALK.
THEY WOULDN'T BE PLEASED TO LEARN...
...THAT YOU'VE SHARED THE FAMILY SECRETS WITH ME.
TEE HEE

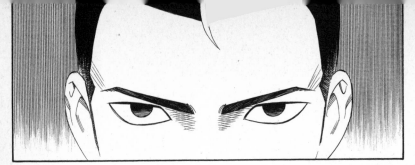

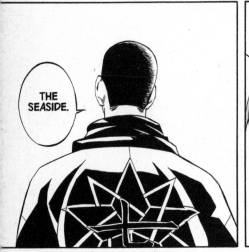

THE SEASIDE.

WHERE TO...?

GOING OUT, CHIEF?

ZHF

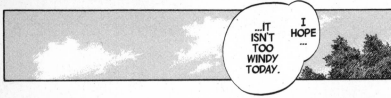

I HOPE...

...IT ISN'T TOO WINDY TODAY.

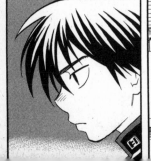

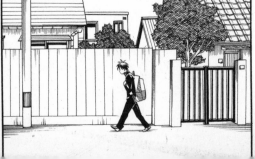

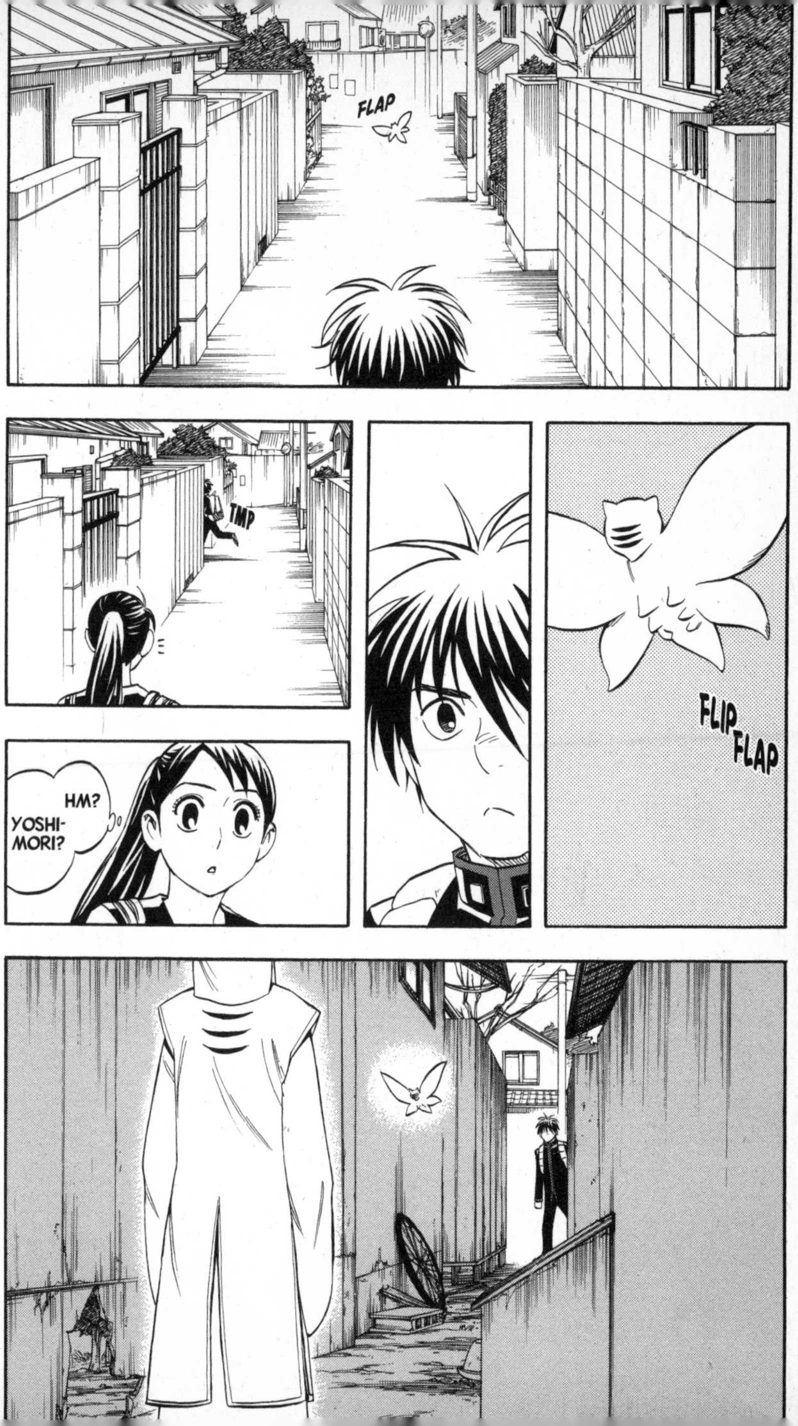
FLAP
FLIP FLAP
TMP
HM? YOSHIMORI?

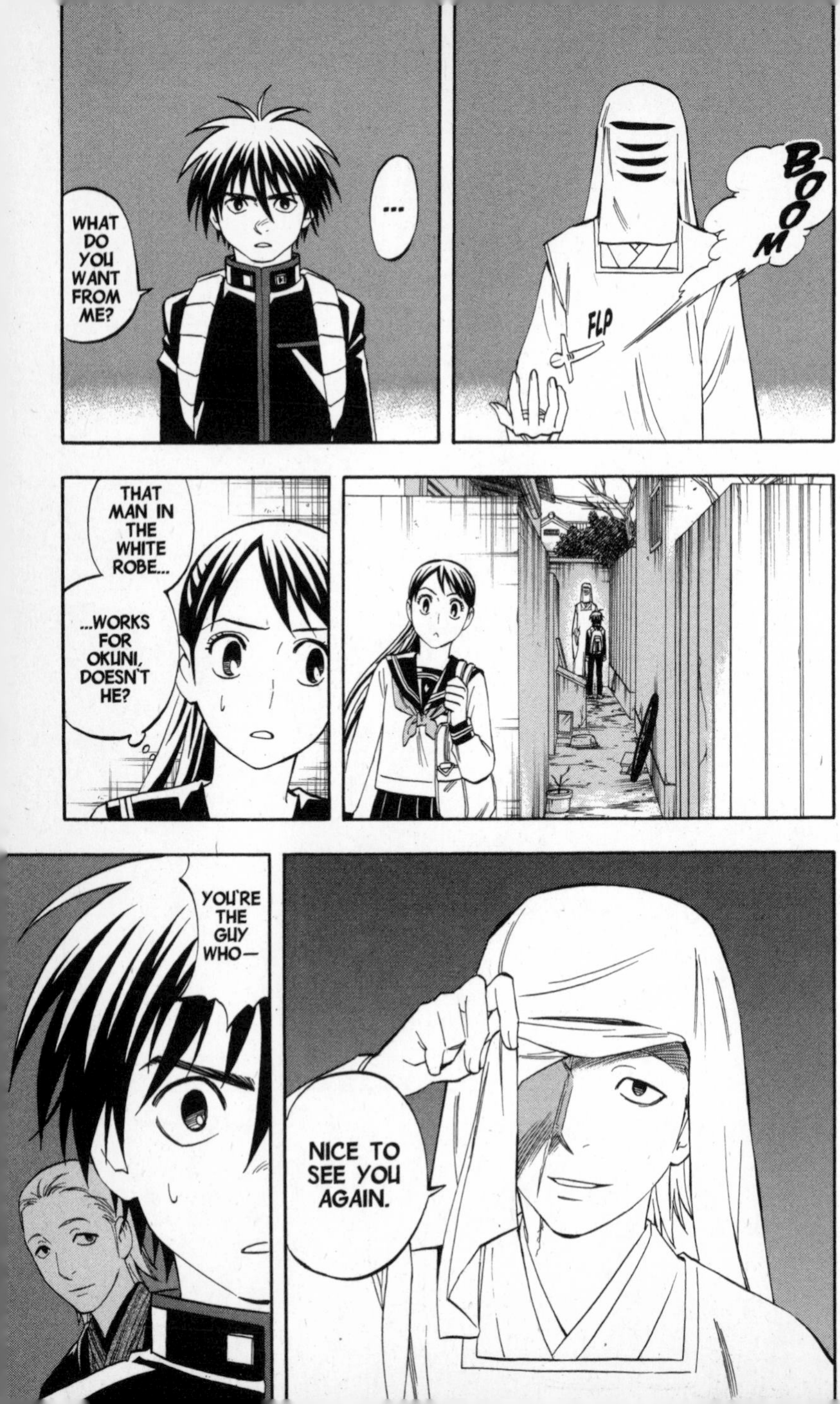
BOOOM
FLP
...
WHAT DO YOU WANT FROM ME?
THAT MAN IN THE WHITE ROBE...
...WORKS FOR OKUNI, DOESN'T HE?
NICE TO SEE YOU AGAIN.
YOU'RE THE GUY WHO—

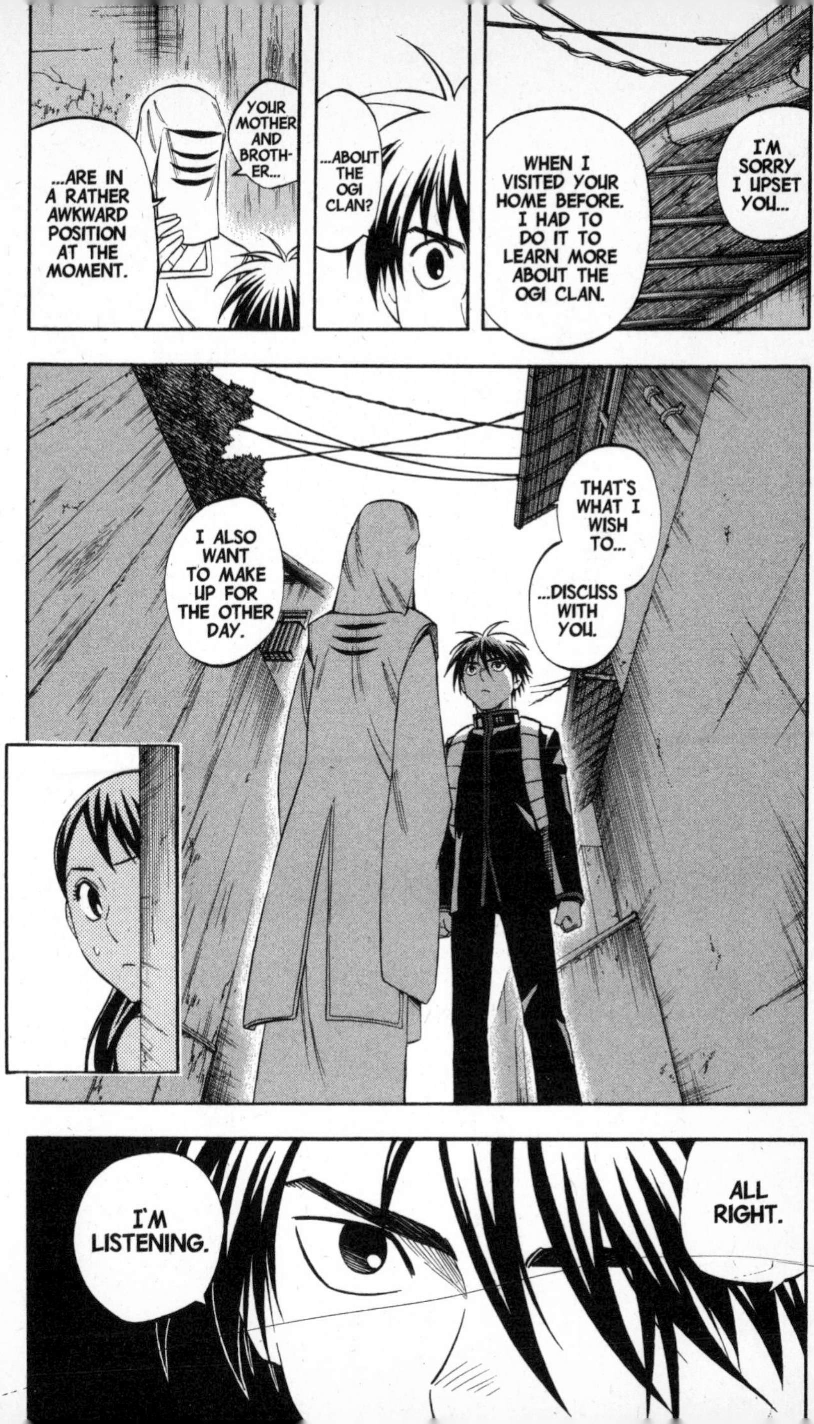
I'M SORRY I UPSET YOU...
WHEN I VISITED YOUR HOME BEFORE. I HAD TO DO IT TO LEARN MORE ABOUT THE OGI CLAN.
...ABOUT THE OGI CLAN?
YOUR MOTHER AND BROTH-ER...
...ARE IN A RATHER AWKWARD POSITION AT THE MOMENT.
THAT'S WHAT I WISH TO...
...DISCUSS WITH YOU.
I ALSO WANT TO MAKE UP FOR THE OTHER DAY.
ALL RIGHT.
I'M LISTENING.

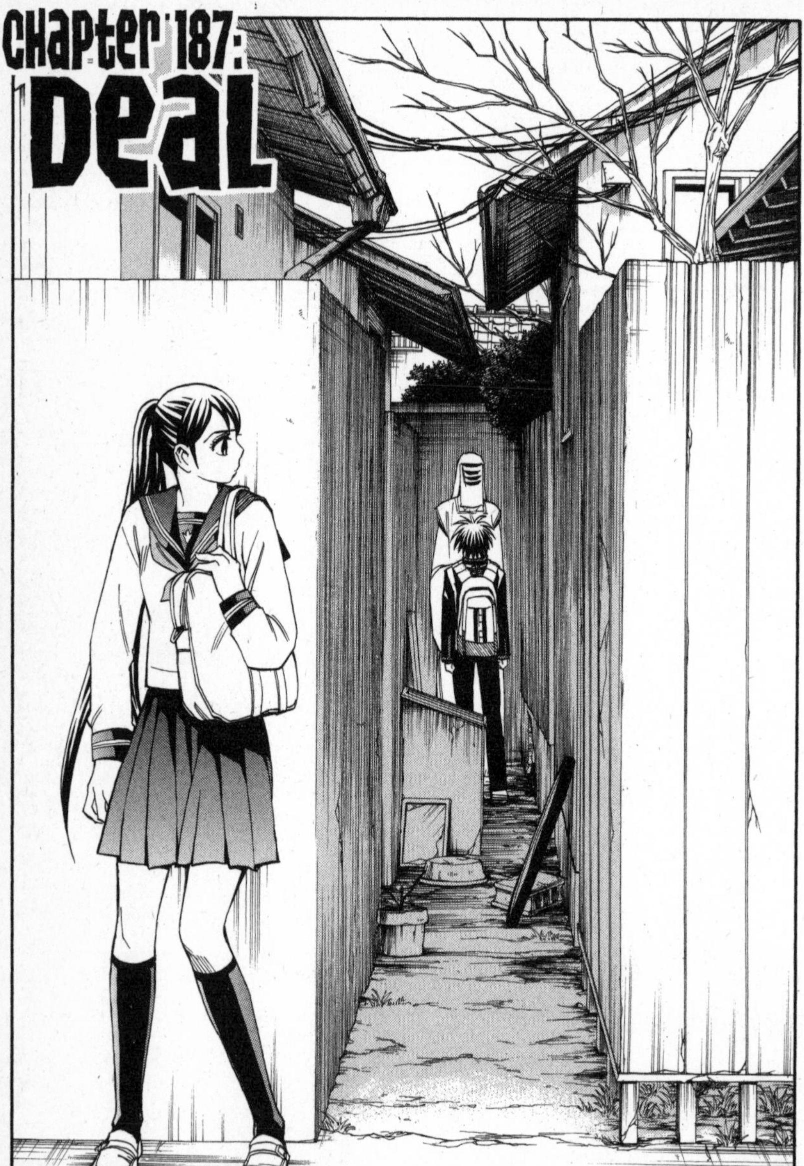
Chapter 187:
Deal
1

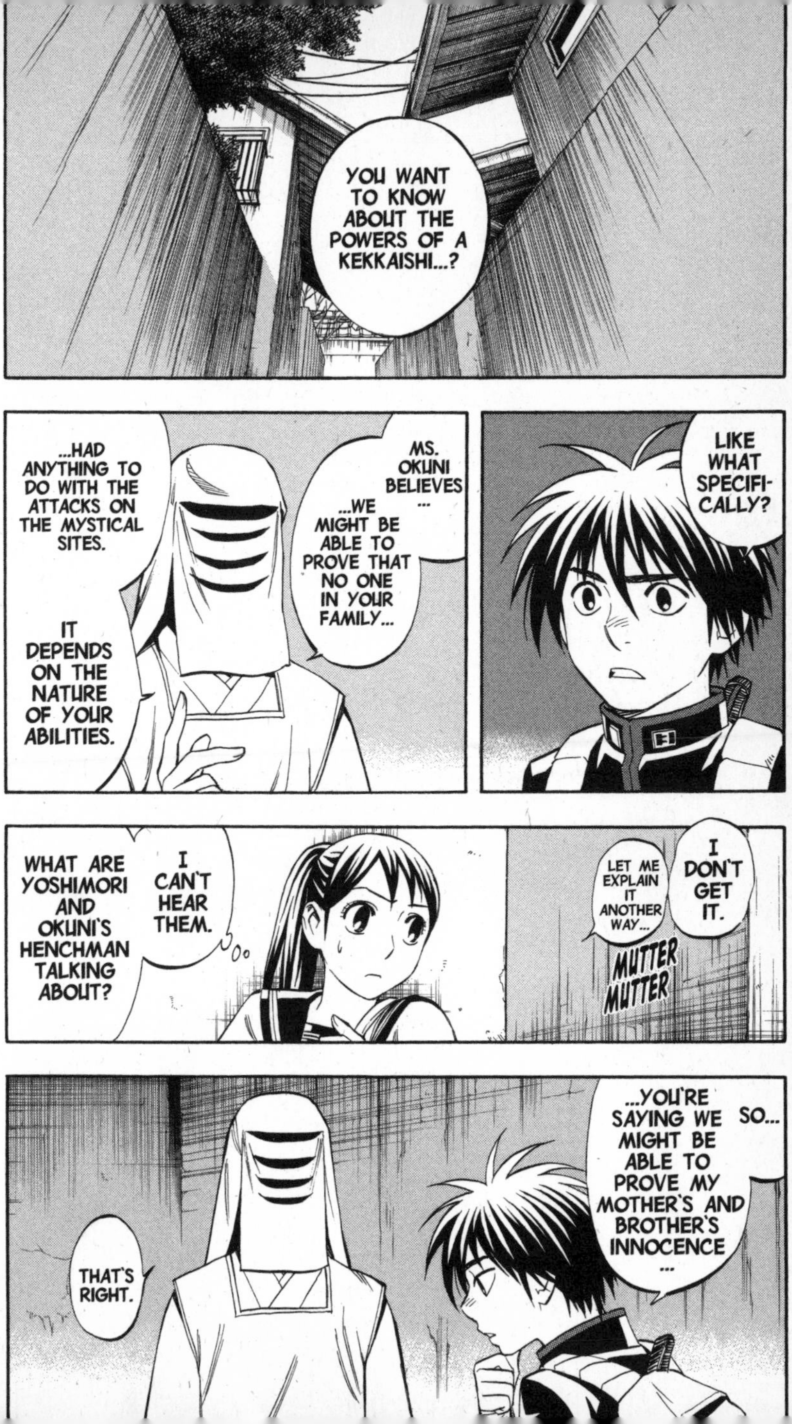
YOU WANT TO KNOW ABOUT THE POWERS OF A KEKKAISHI...?
LIKE WHAT SPECIFICALLY?
MS. OKUNI BELIEVES...
...WE MIGHT BE ABLE TO PROVE THAT NO ONE IN YOUR FAMILY...
...HAD ANYTHING TO DO WITH THE ATTACKS ON THE MYSTICAL SITES.
IT DEPENDS ON THE NATURE OF YOUR ABILITIES.
I DON'T GET IT.
LET ME EXPLAIN IT ANOTHER WAY...
MUTTER MUTTER
I CAN'T HEAR THEM.
WHAT ARE YOSHIMORI AND OKUNI'S HENCHMAN TALKING ABOUT?
SO...
...YOU'RE SAYING WE MIGHT BE ABLE TO PROVE MY MOTHER'S AND BROTHER'S INNOCENCE...
THAT'S RIGHT.

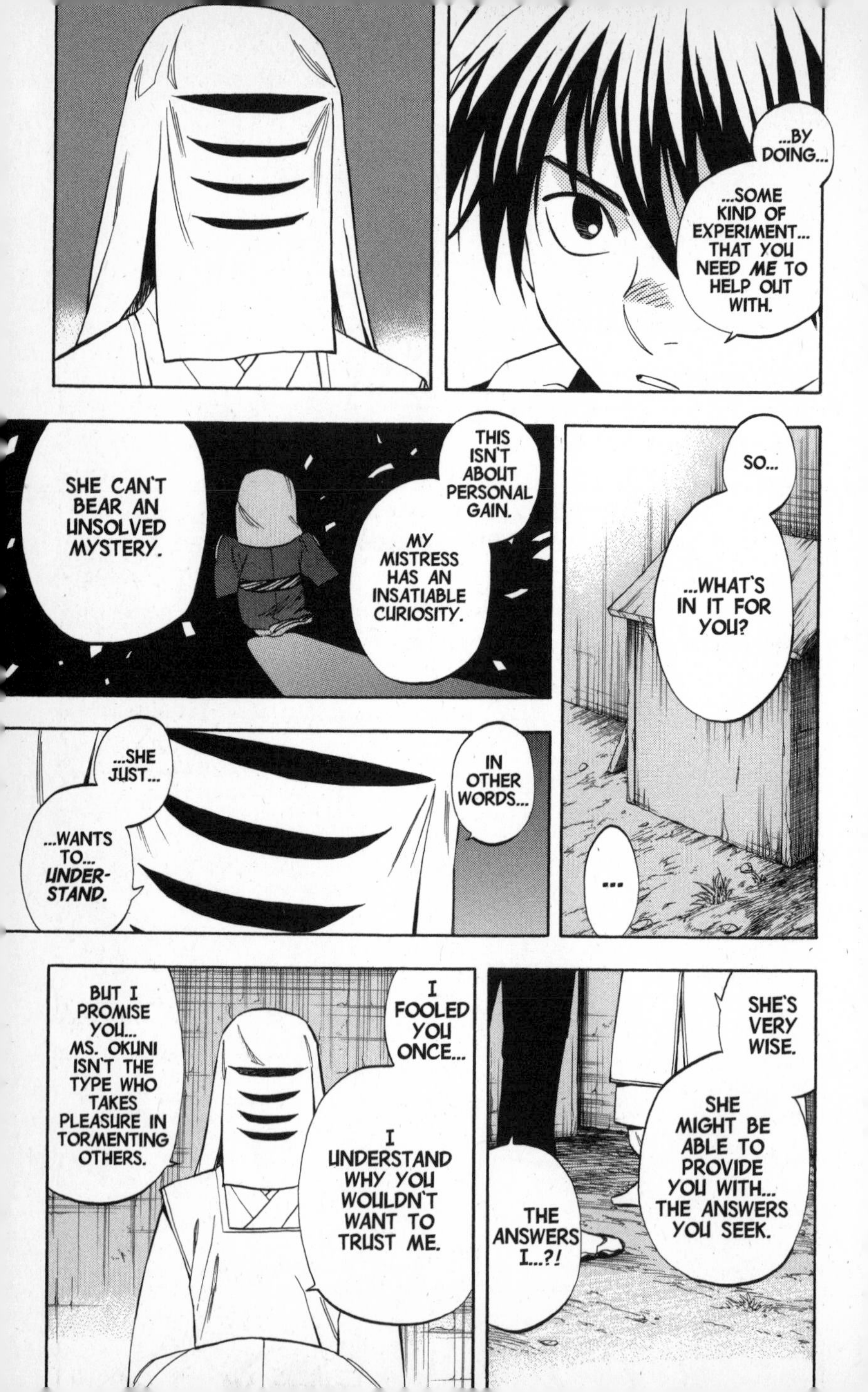
...BY DOING...
...SOME KIND OF EXPERIMENT... THAT YOU NEED *ME* TO HELP OUT WITH.
SO...
...WHAT'S IN IT FOR YOU?
...
THIS ISN'T ABOUT PERSONAL GAIN.
MY MISTRESS HAS AN INSATIABLE CURIOSITY.
SHE CAN'T BEAR AN UNSOLVED MYSTERY.
IN OTHER WORDS...
...SHE JUST...
...WANTS TO... *UNDER-STAND.*
SHE'S VERY WISE.
SHE MIGHT BE ABLE TO PROVIDE YOU WITH... THE ANSWERS YOU SEEK.
THE ANSWERS I...?!
I FOOLED YOU ONCE...
I UNDERSTAND WHY YOU WOULDN'T WANT TO TRUST ME.
BUT I PROMISE YOU... MS. OKUNI ISN'T THE TYPE WHO TAKES PLEASURE IN TORMENTING OTHERS.

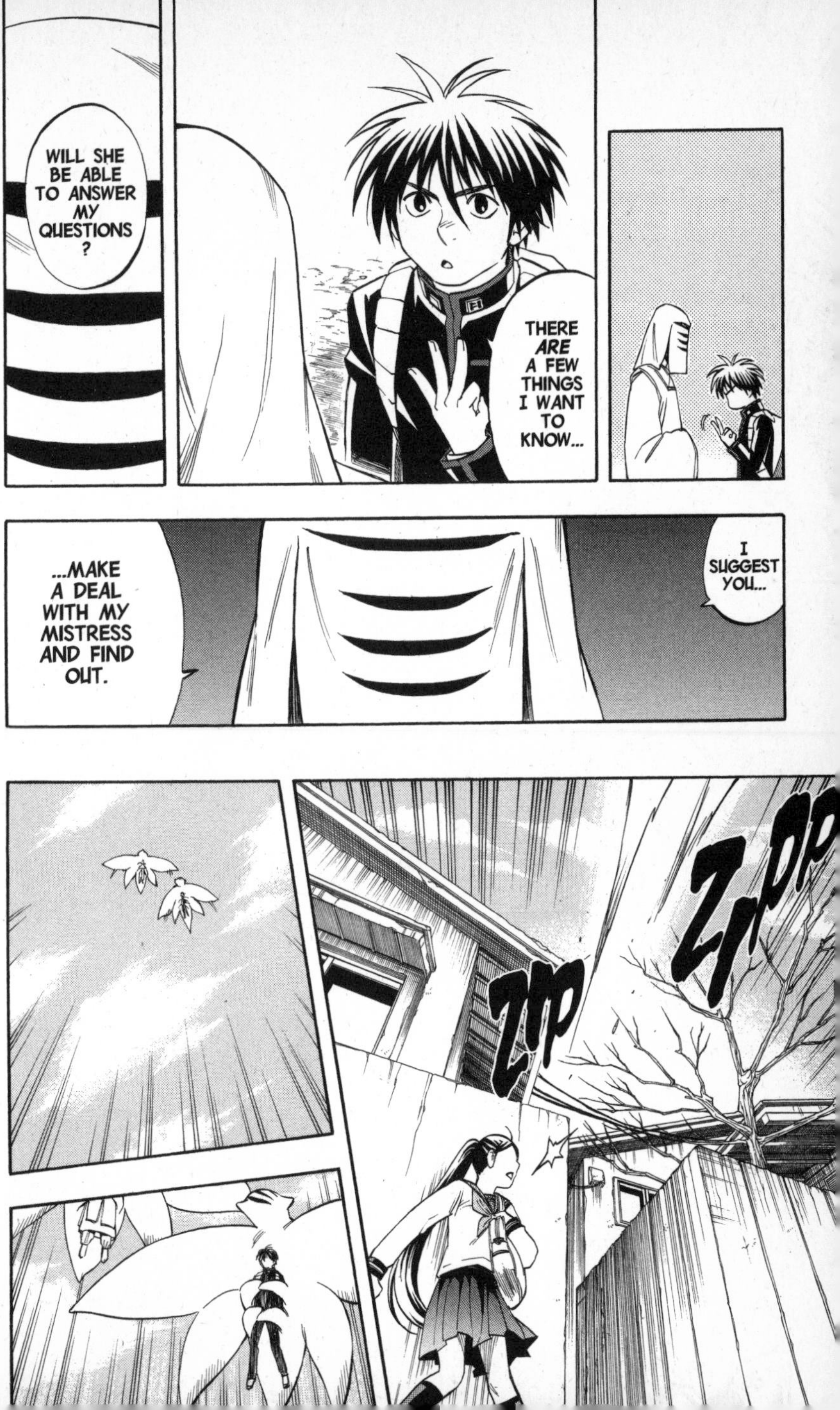
THERE *ARE* A FEW THINGS I WANT TO KNOW...
WILL SHE BE ABLE TO ANSWER MY QUESTIONS?
I SUGGEST YOU...
...MAKE A DEAL WITH MY MISTRESS AND FIND OUT.
ZIPP
ZIP

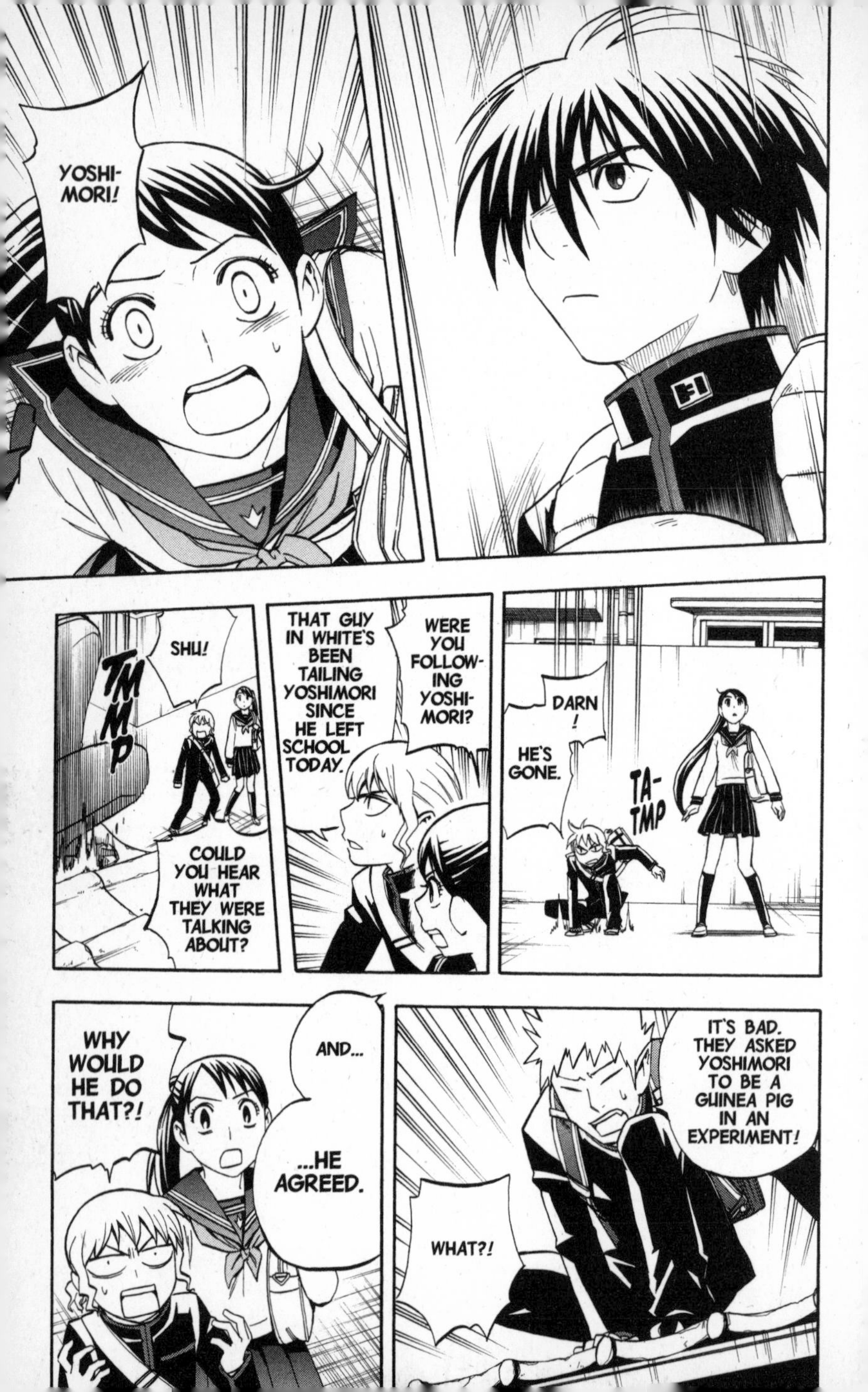
YOSHI-MORI!
DARN!
HE'S GONE.
TA-TMP
WERE YOU FOLLOWING YOSHIMORI?
THAT GUY IN WHITE'S BEEN TAILING YOSHIMORI SINCE HE LEFT SCHOOL TODAY.
SHU!
TMMP
COULD YOU HEAR WHAT THEY WERE TALKING ABOUT?
IT'S BAD. THEY ASKED YOSHIMORI TO BE A GUINEA PIG IN AN EXPERIMENT!
WHAT?!
AND...
...HE AGREED.
WHY WOULD HE DO THAT?!

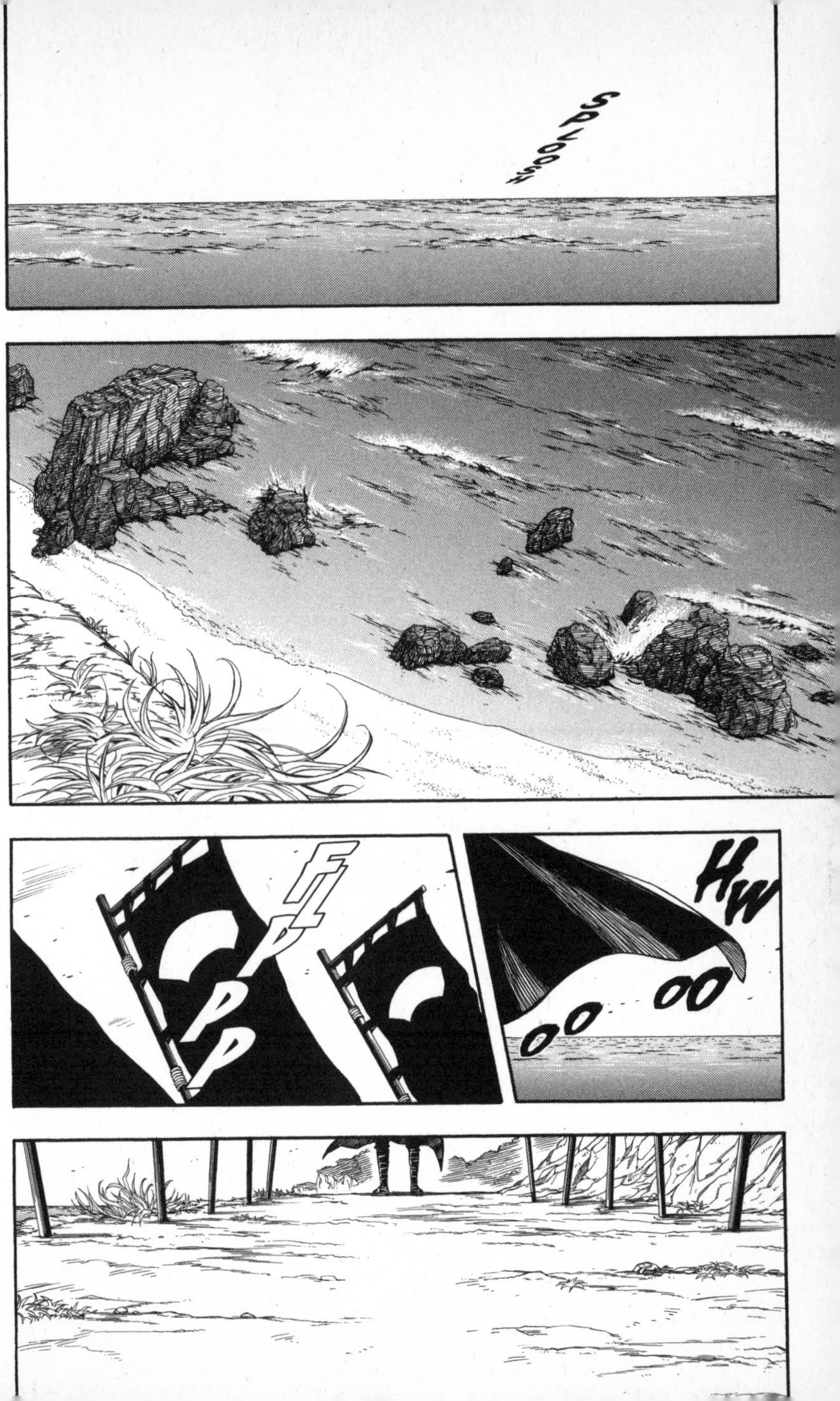
SPLOOSH
HWOOOO
FLPPP

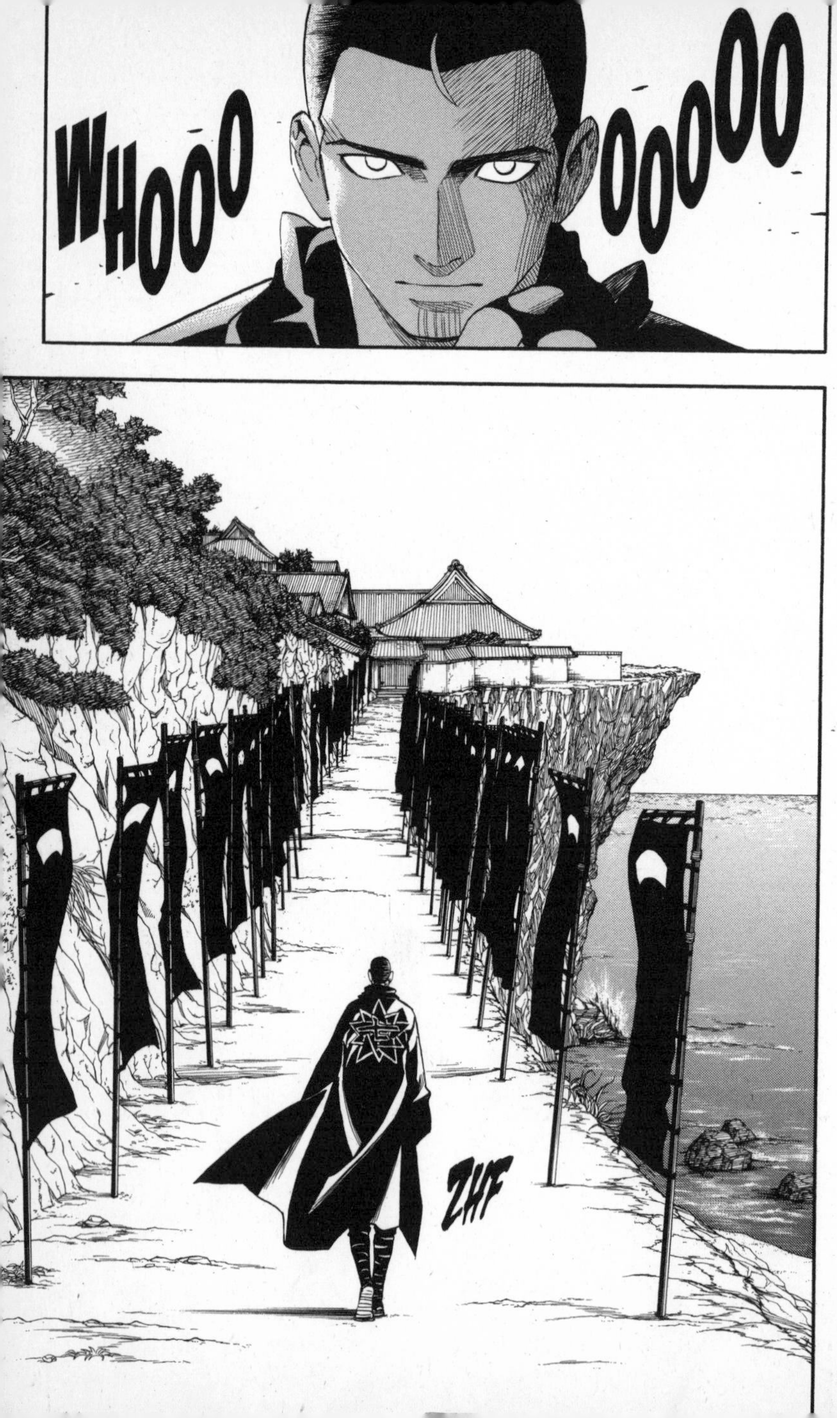
WHOOO
OOOOOO
ZHF

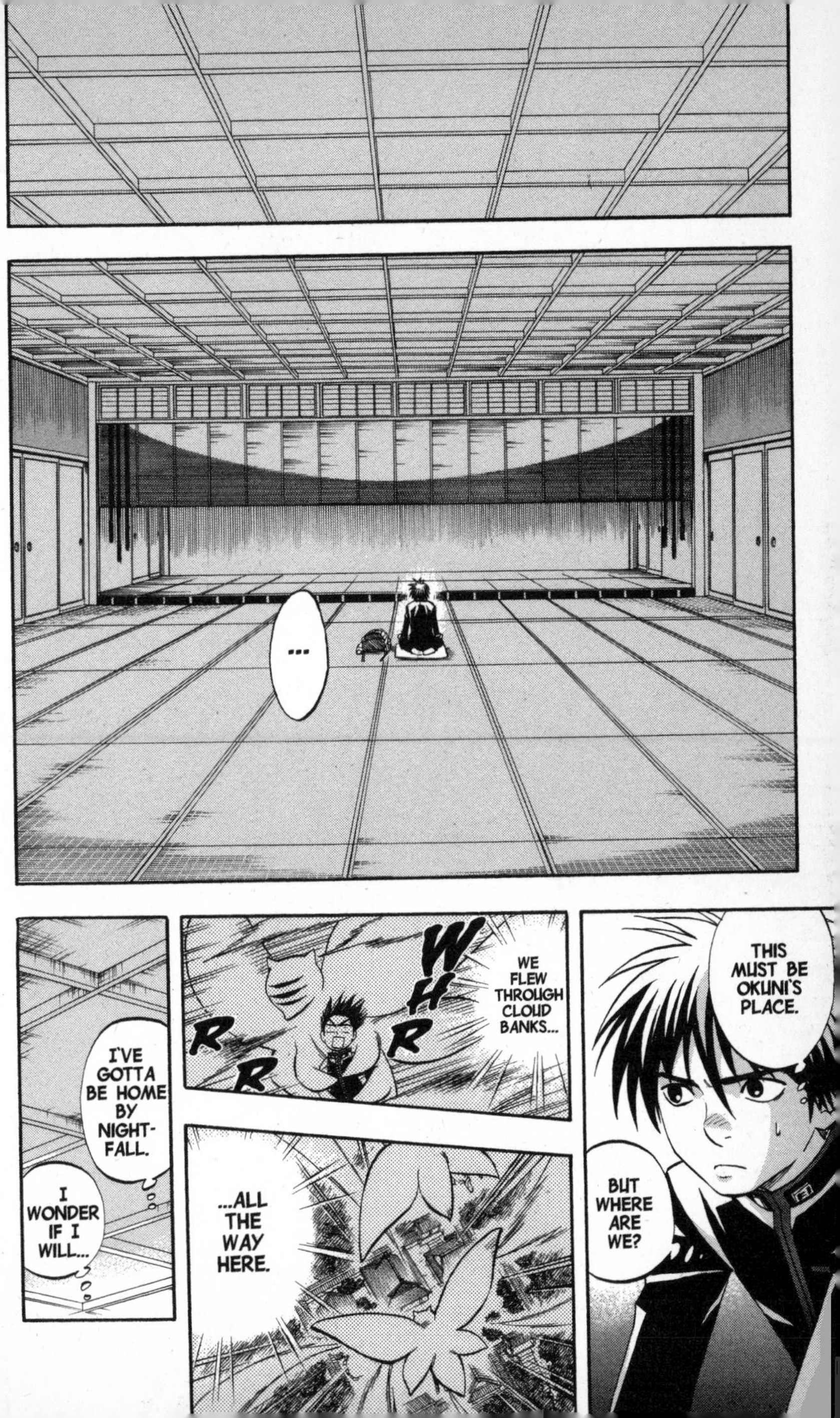
...
THIS MUST BE OKUNI'S PLACE.
BUT WHERE ARE WE?
WHRRR
WE FLEW THROUGH CLOUD BANKS...
...ALL THE WAY HERE.
I'VE GOTTA BE HOME BY NIGHT-FALL.
I WONDER IF I WILL...

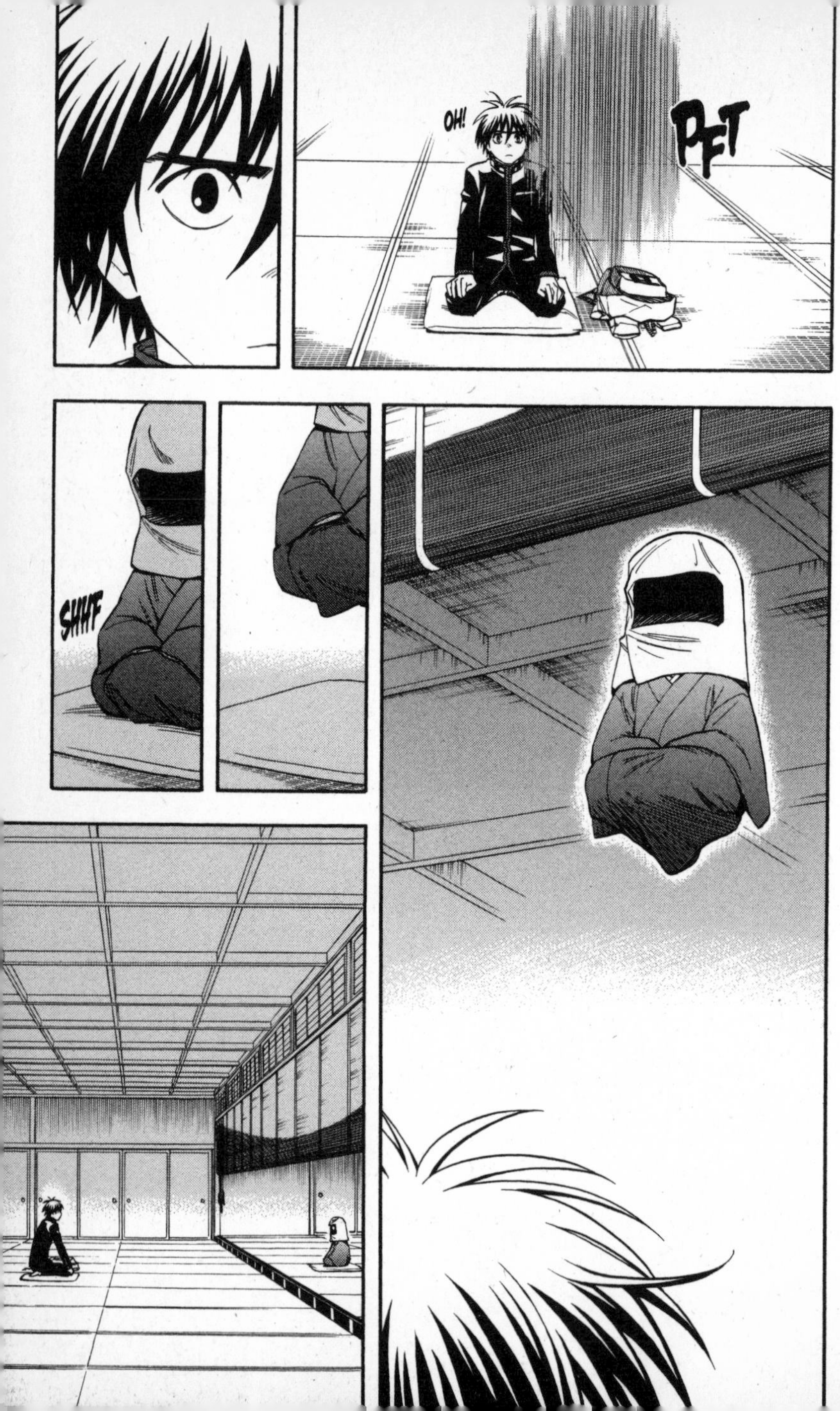
PFT
OH!
SHHF

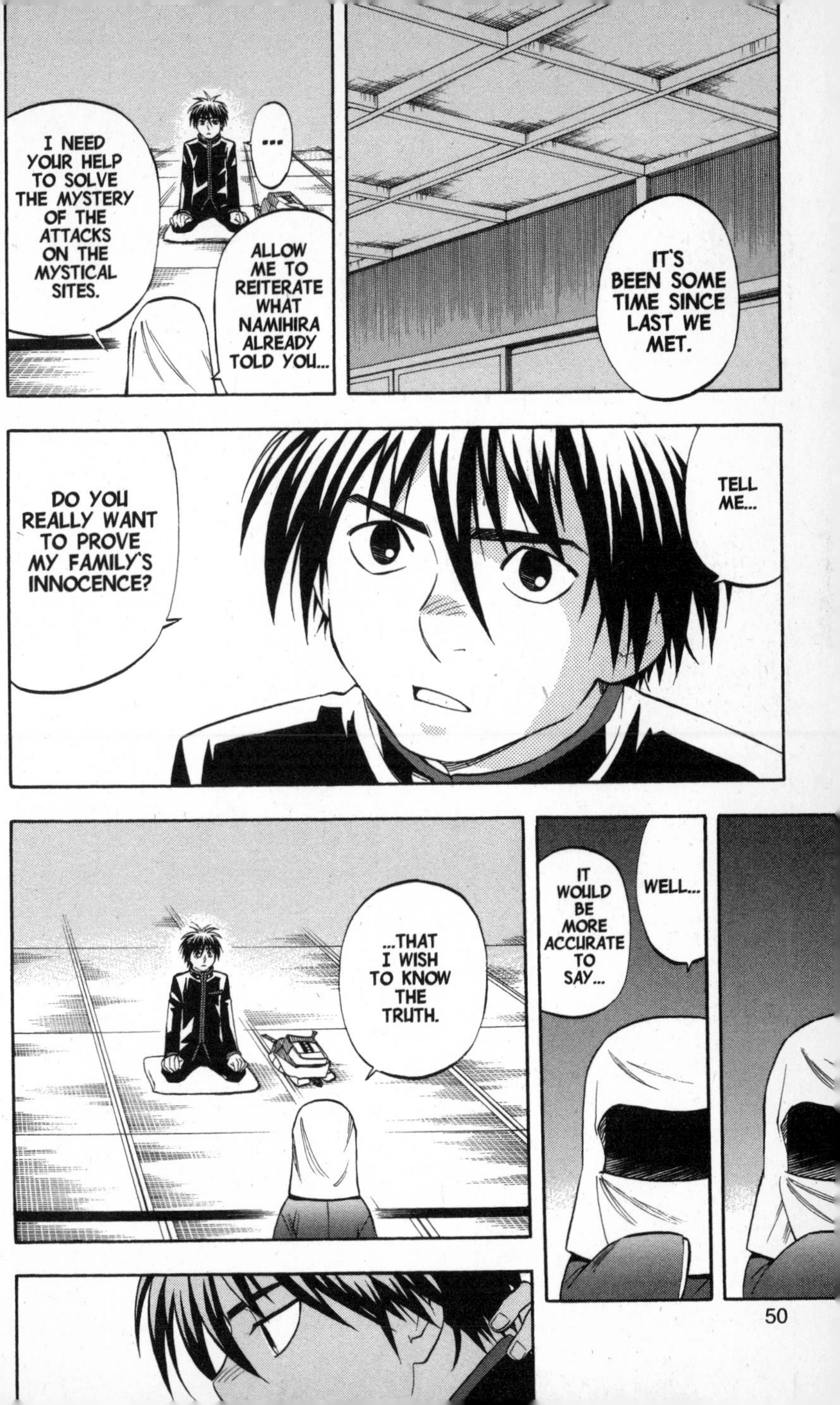
IT'S BEEN SOME TIME SINCE LAST WE MET.
...
ALLOW ME TO REITERATE WHAT NAMIHIRA ALREADY TOLD YOU...
I NEED YOUR HELP TO SOLVE THE MYSTERY OF THE ATTACKS ON THE MYSTICAL SITES.
TELL ME...
DO YOU REALLY WANT TO PROVE MY FAMILY'S INNOCENCE?
WELL...
IT WOULD BE MORE ACCURATE TO SAY...
...THAT I WISH TO KNOW THE TRUTH.

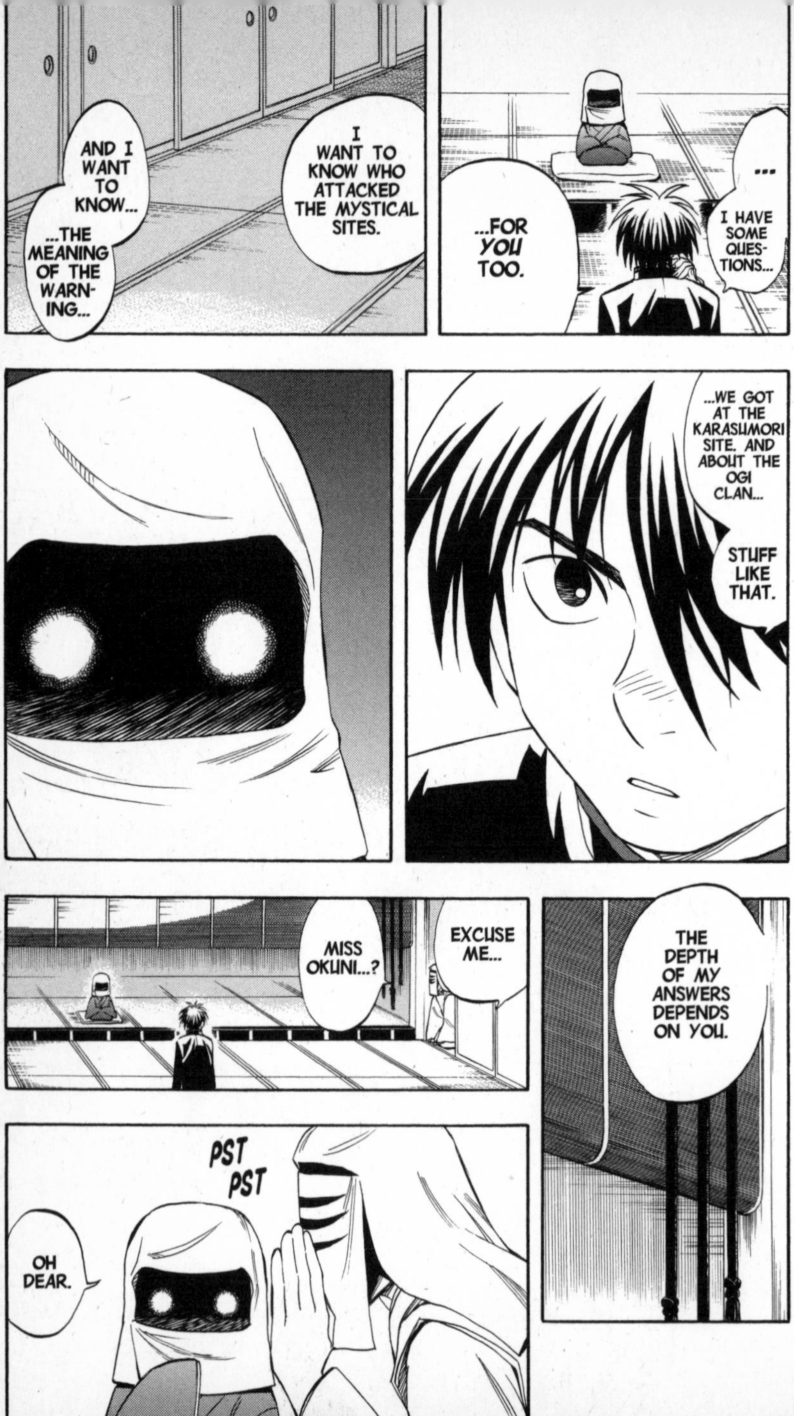
...
I HAVE SOME QUES-TIONS...
...FOR YOU TOO.
I WANT TO KNOW WHO ATTACKED THE MYSTICAL SITES.
AND I WANT TO KNOW...
...THE MEANING OF THE WARN-ING...
...WE GOT AT THE KARASUMORI SITE. AND ABOUT THE OGI CLAN...
STUFF LIKE THAT.
THE DEPTH OF MY ANSWERS DEPENDS ON YOU.
EXCUSE ME...
MISS OKUNI...?
PST PST
OH DEAR.

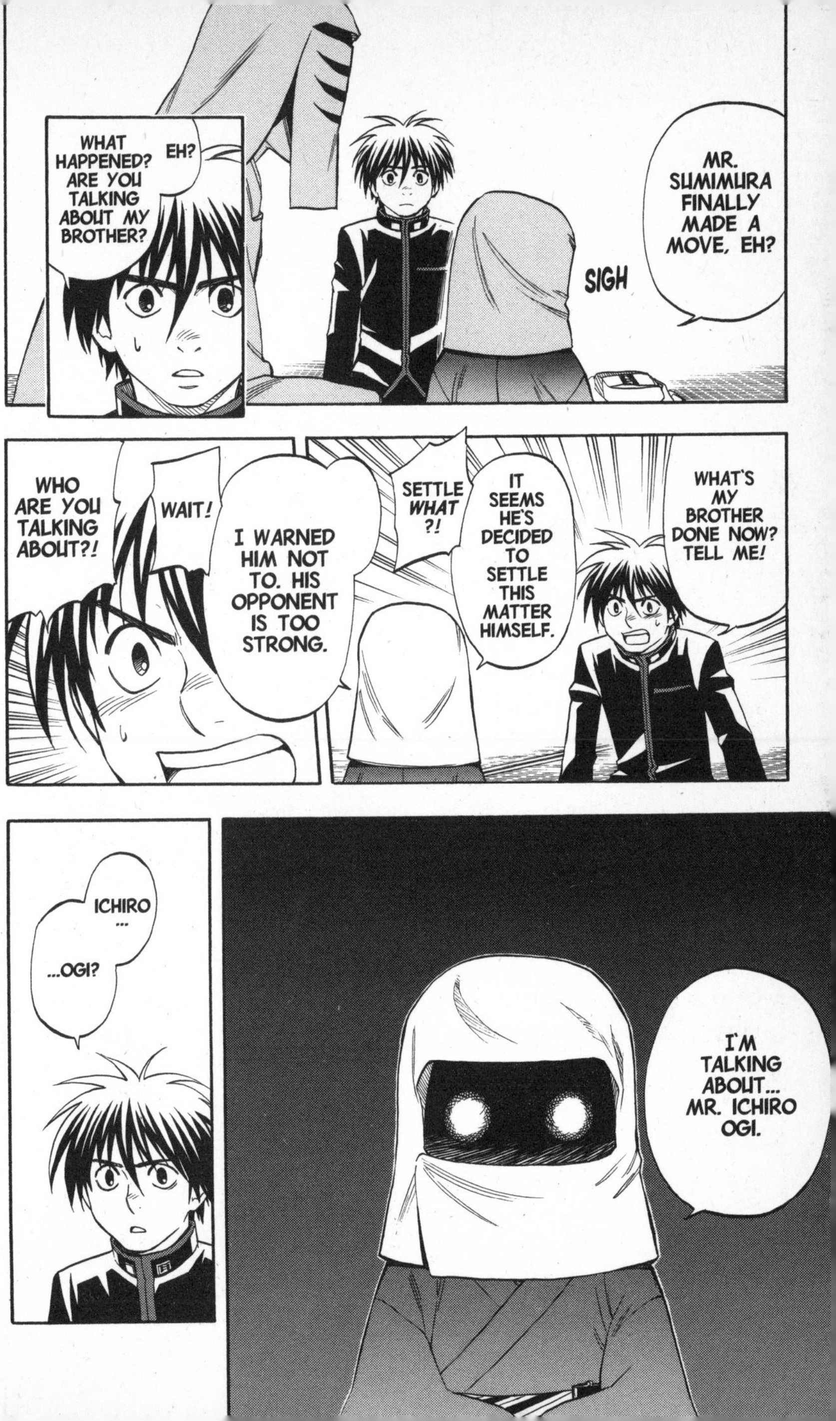
MR. SUMIMURA FINALLY MADE A MOVE, EH?
SIGH
EH?
WHAT HAPPENED? ARE YOU TALKING ABOUT MY BROTHER?
WHAT'S MY BROTHER DONE NOW? TELL ME!
IT SEEMS HE'S DECIDED TO SETTLE THIS MATTER HIMSELF.
SETTLE *WHAT*?!
I WARNED HIM NOT TO. HIS OPPONENT IS TOO STRONG.
WAIT!
WHO ARE YOU TALKING ABOUT?!
I'M TALKING ABOUT... MR. ICHIRO OGI.
ICHIRO ...
...OGI?

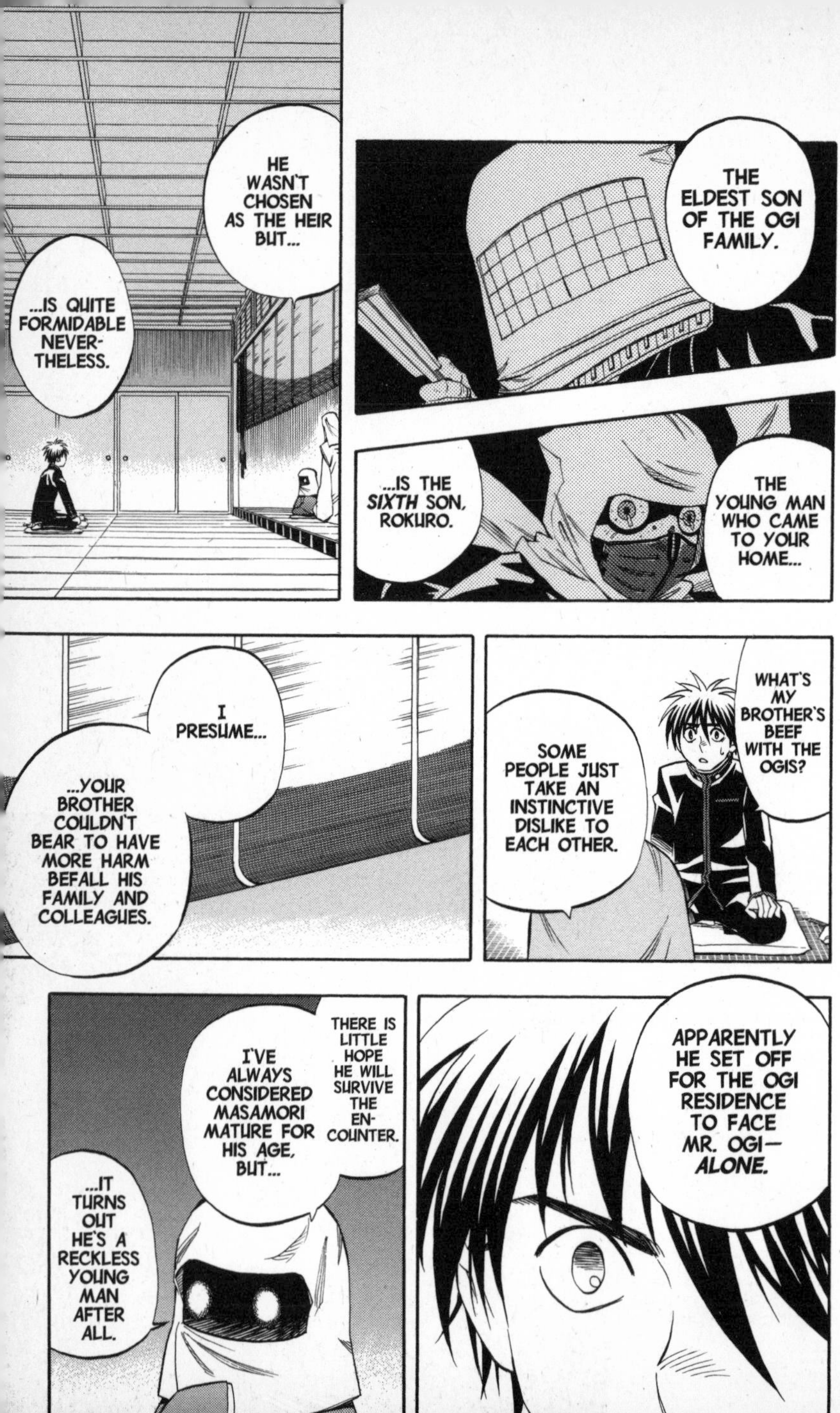
THE ELDEST SON OF THE OGI FAMILY.
THE YOUNG MAN WHO CAME TO YOUR HOME...
...IS THE *SIXTH* SON, ROKURO.
HE WASN'T CHOSEN AS THE HEIR BUT...
...IS QUITE FORMIDABLE NEVERTHELESS.
WHAT'S MY BROTHER'S BEEF WITH THE OGIS?
SOME PEOPLE JUST TAKE AN INSTINCTIVE DISLIKE TO EACH OTHER.
I PRESUME...
...YOUR BROTHER COULDN'T BEAR TO HAVE MORE HARM BEFALL HIS FAMILY AND COLLEAGUES.
APPARENTLY HE SET OFF FOR THE OGI RESIDENCE TO FACE MR. OGI—*ALONE.*
THERE IS LITTLE HOPE HE WILL SURVIVE THE ENCOUNTER.
I'VE ALWAYS CONSIDERED MASAMORI MATURE FOR HIS AGE, BUT...
...IT TURNS OUT HE'S A RECKLESS YOUNG MAN AFTER ALL.

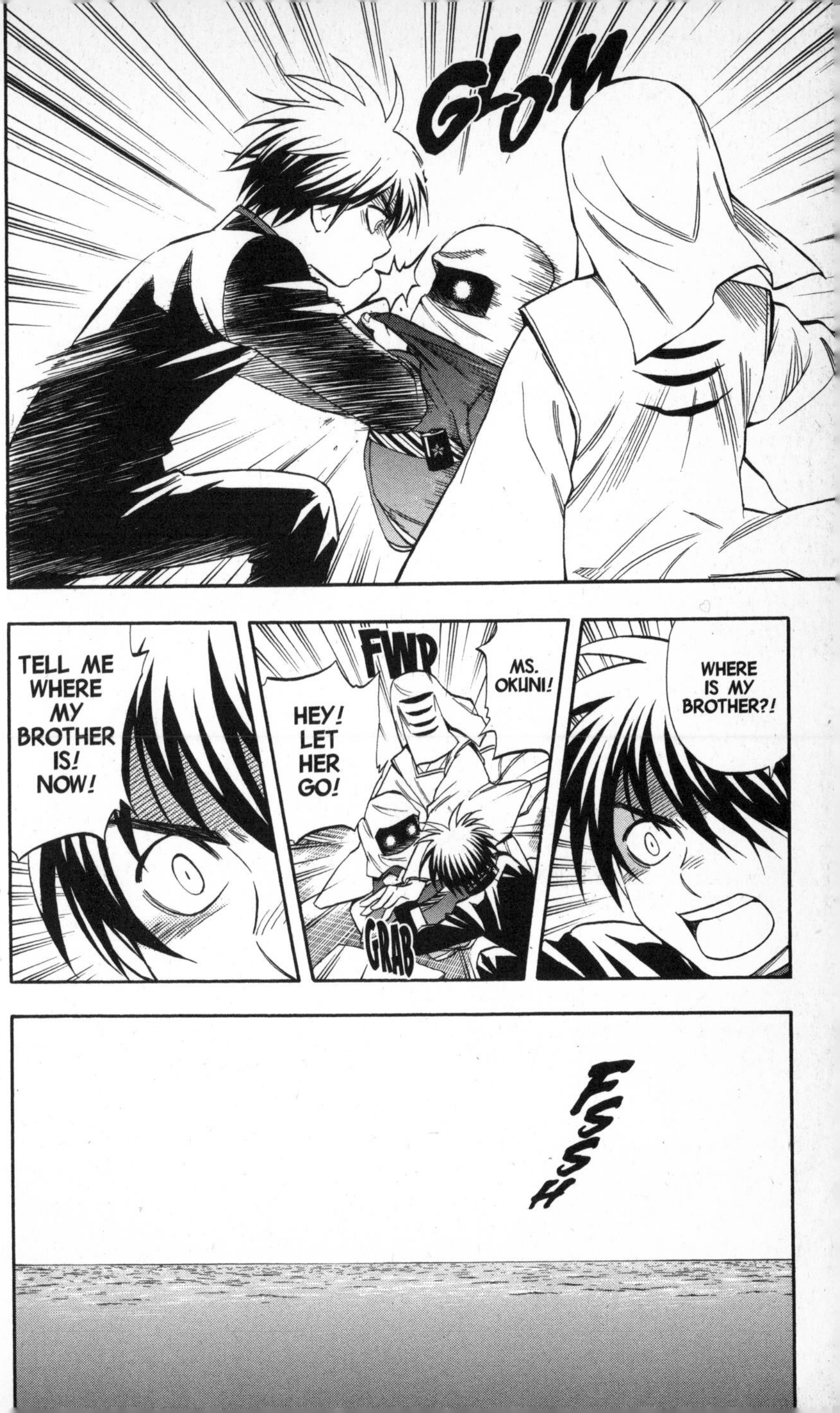
GLOM
WHERE IS MY BROTHER?!
MS. OKUNI!
FWP
HEY! LET HER GO!
GRAB
TELL ME WHERE MY BROTHER IS! NOW!
FSSH

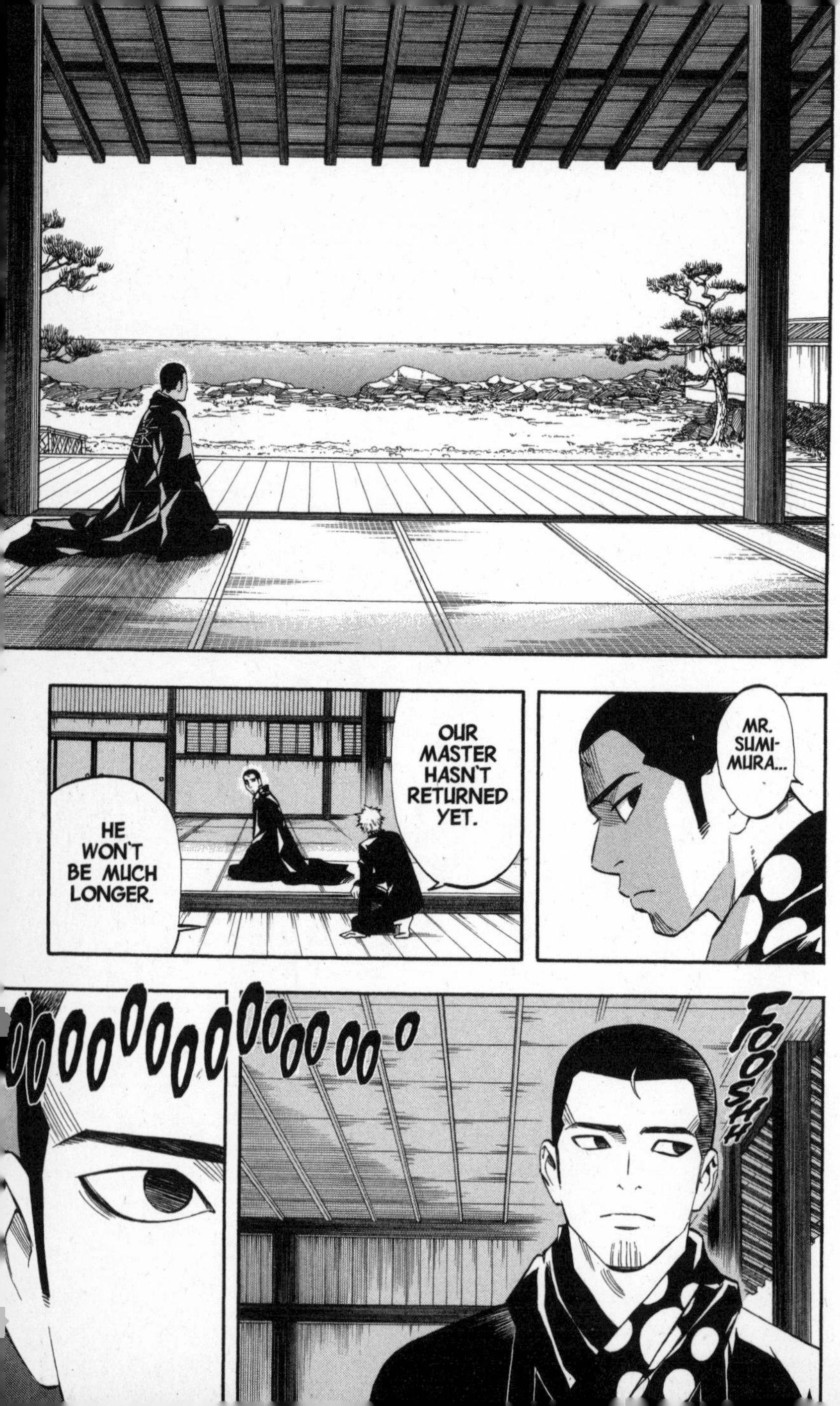
MR. SUMIMURA...
OUR MASTER HASN'T RETURNED YET.
HE WON'T BE MUCH LONGER.
FOOSHH
OOOOOOOOOOOO OO O

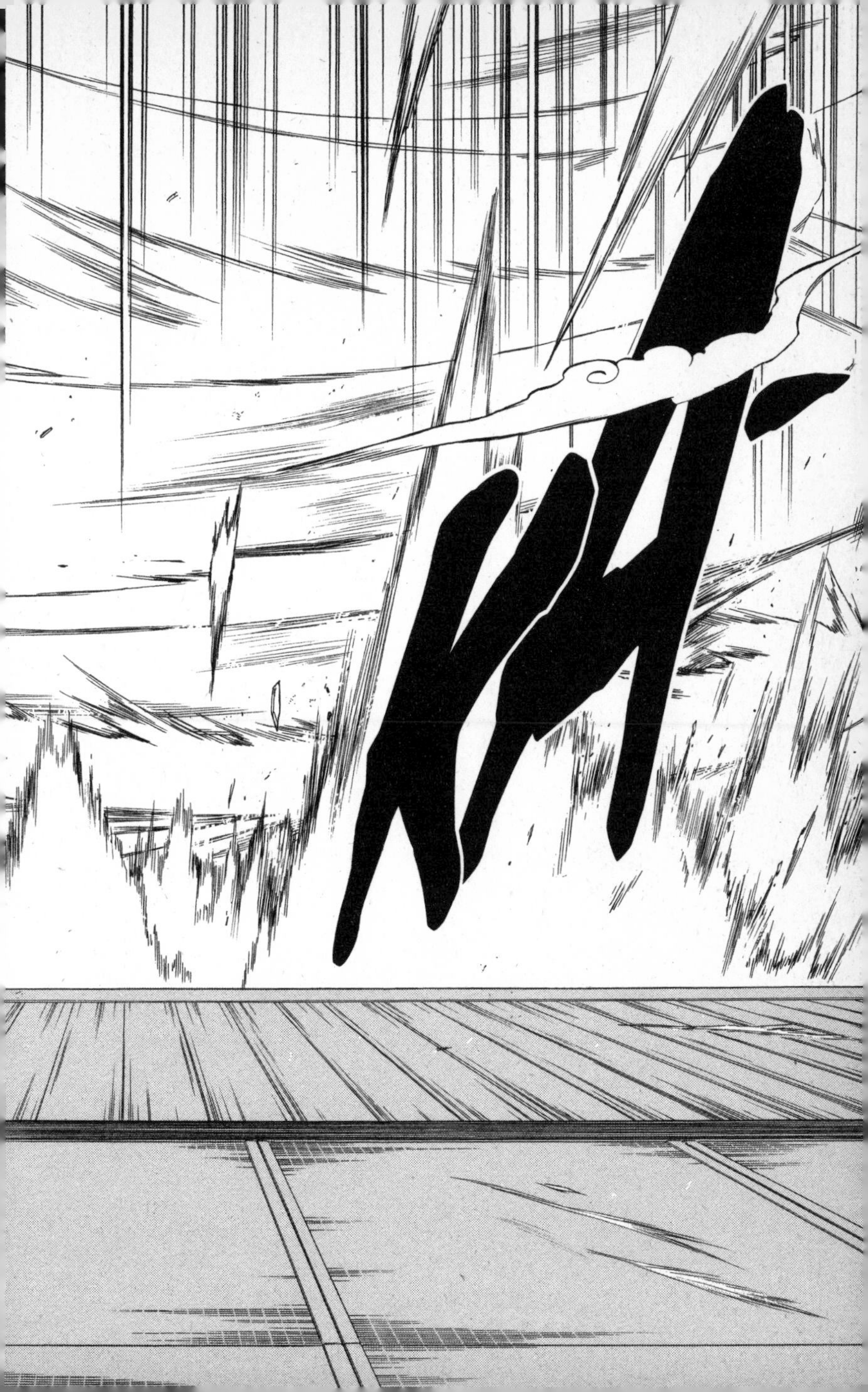
KSH

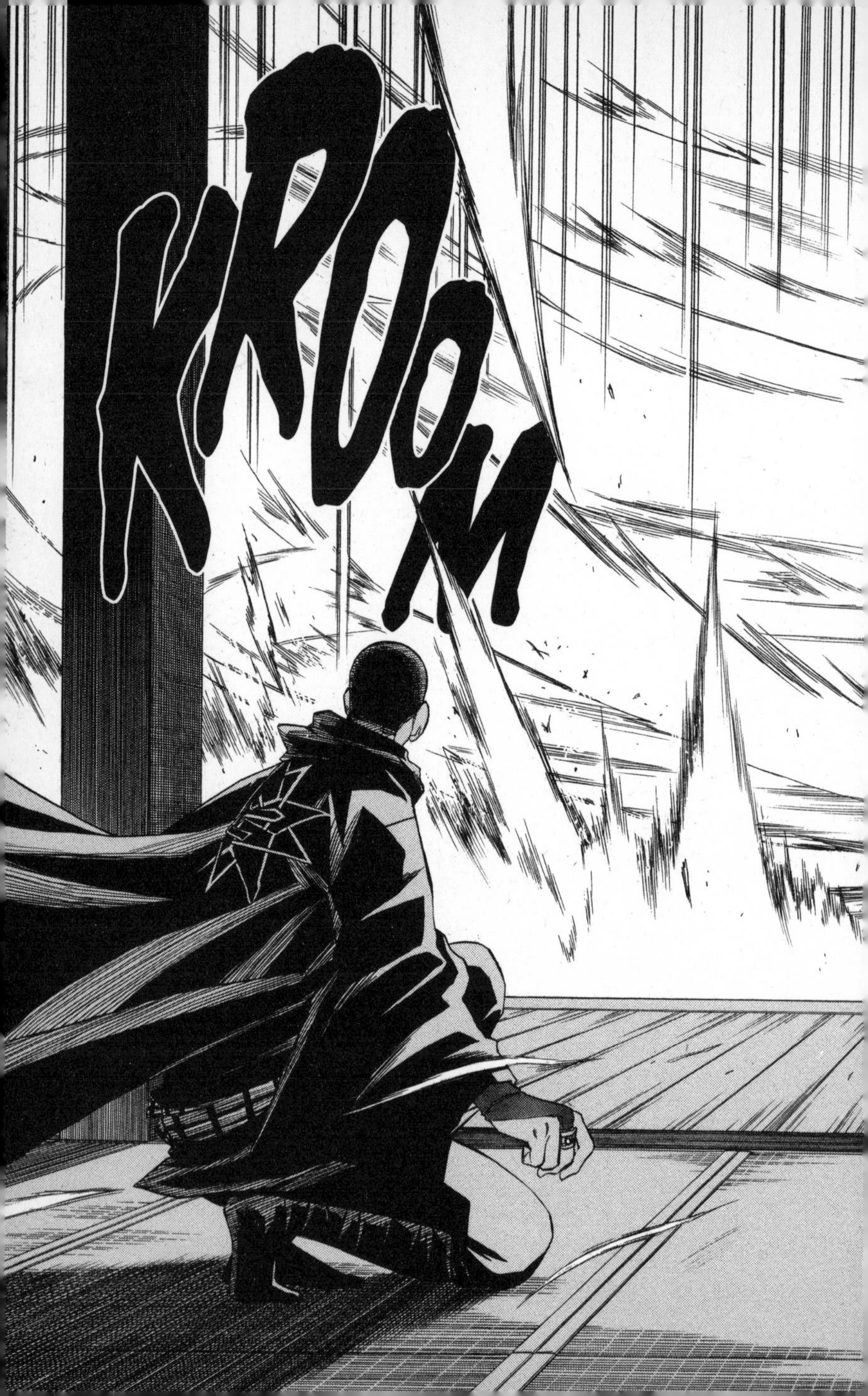
KRoom

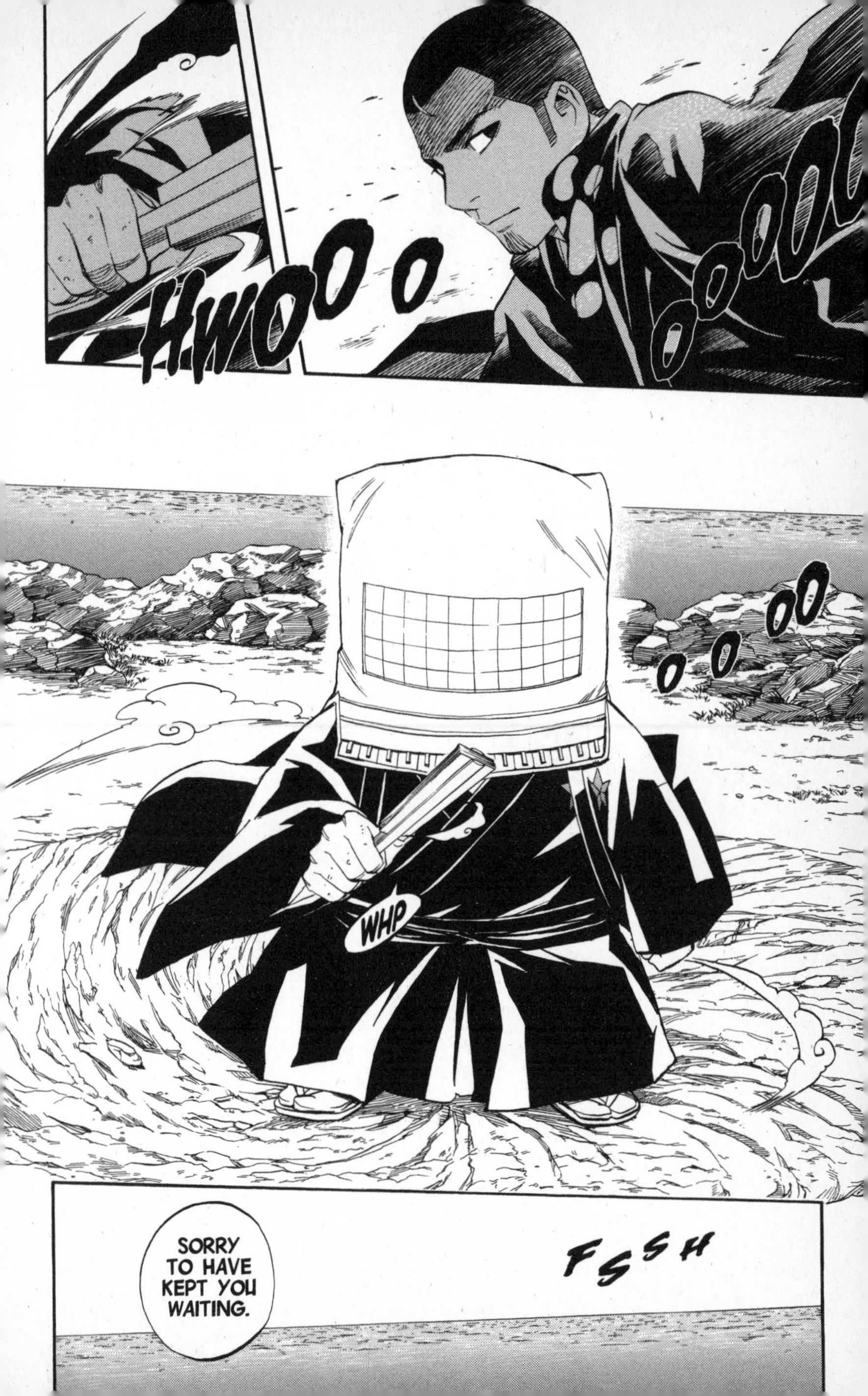

HWOOO
OOO
WHP
SORRY TO HAVE KEPT YOU WAITING.
FSSH

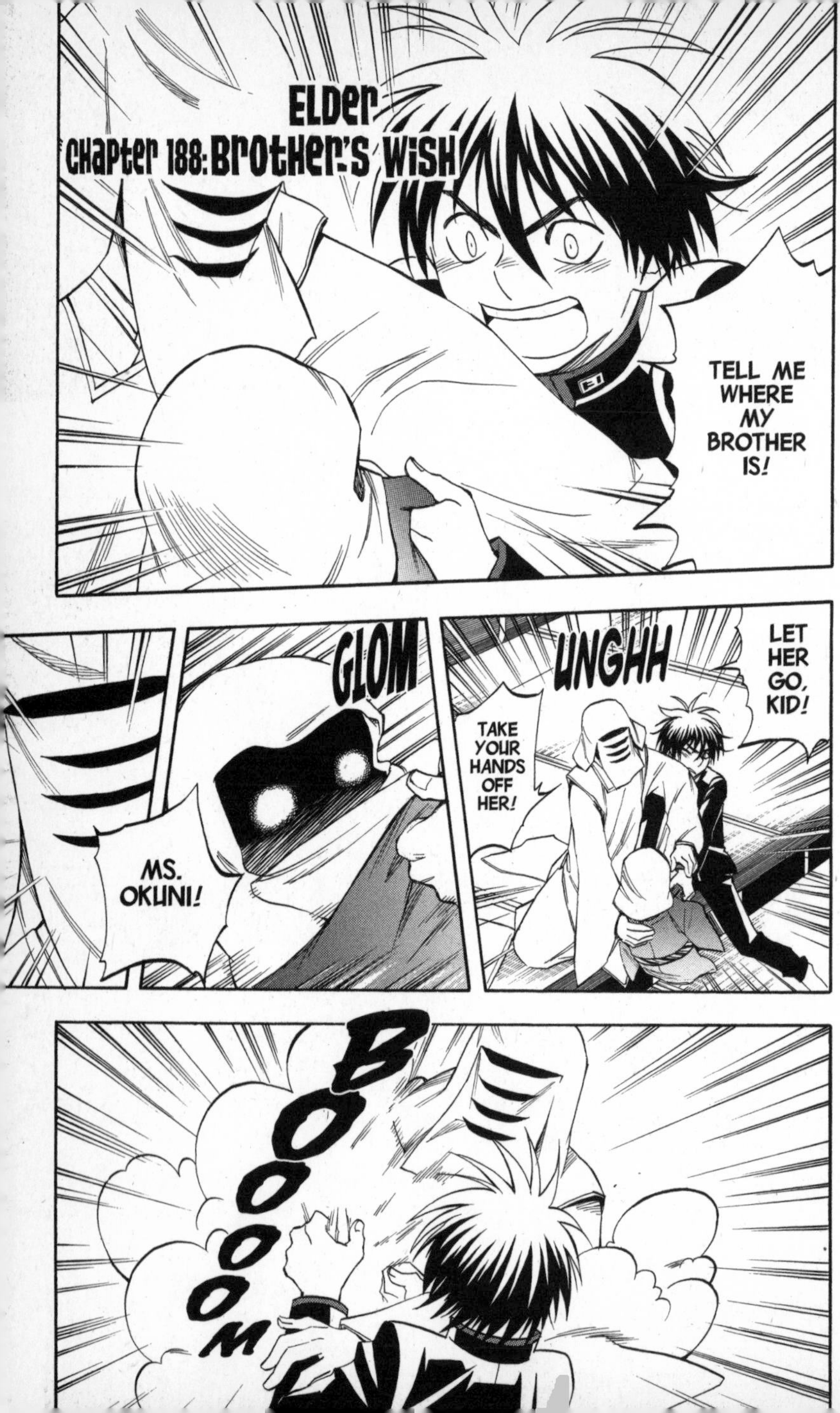
Chapter 188: Elder Brother's Wish
TELL ME WHERE MY BROTHER IS!
UNGHH
LET HER GO, KID!
TAKE YOUR HANDS OFF HER!
GLOM
MS. OKUNI!
BOOOOOOM

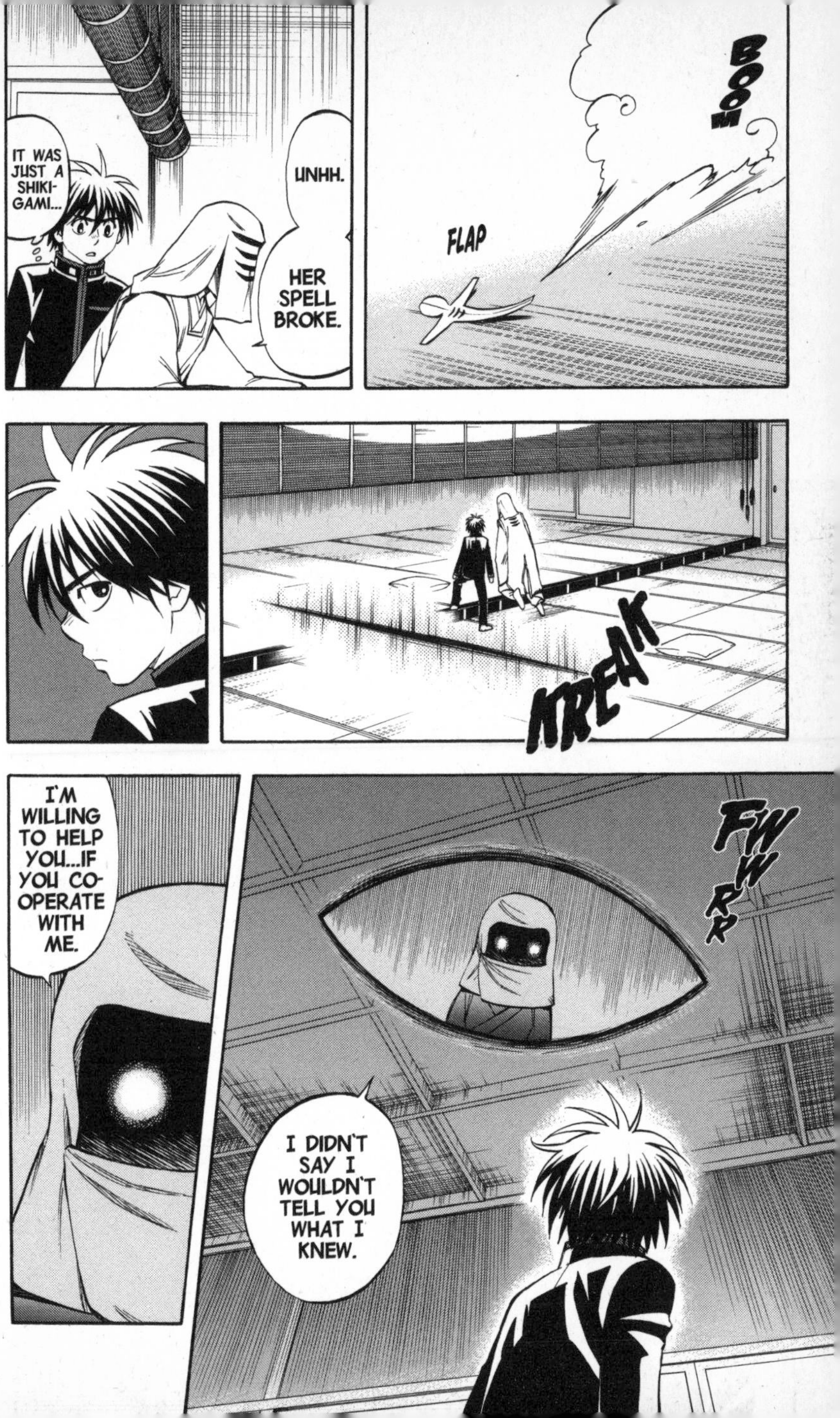
BOOM
FLAP
UNHH.
HER SPELL BROKE.
IT WAS JUST A SHIKI-GAMI...
KREAK
FWWRR
I DIDN'T SAY I WOULDN'T TELL YOU WHAT I KNEW.
I'M WILLING TO HELP YOU...IF YOU CO-OPERATE WITH ME.

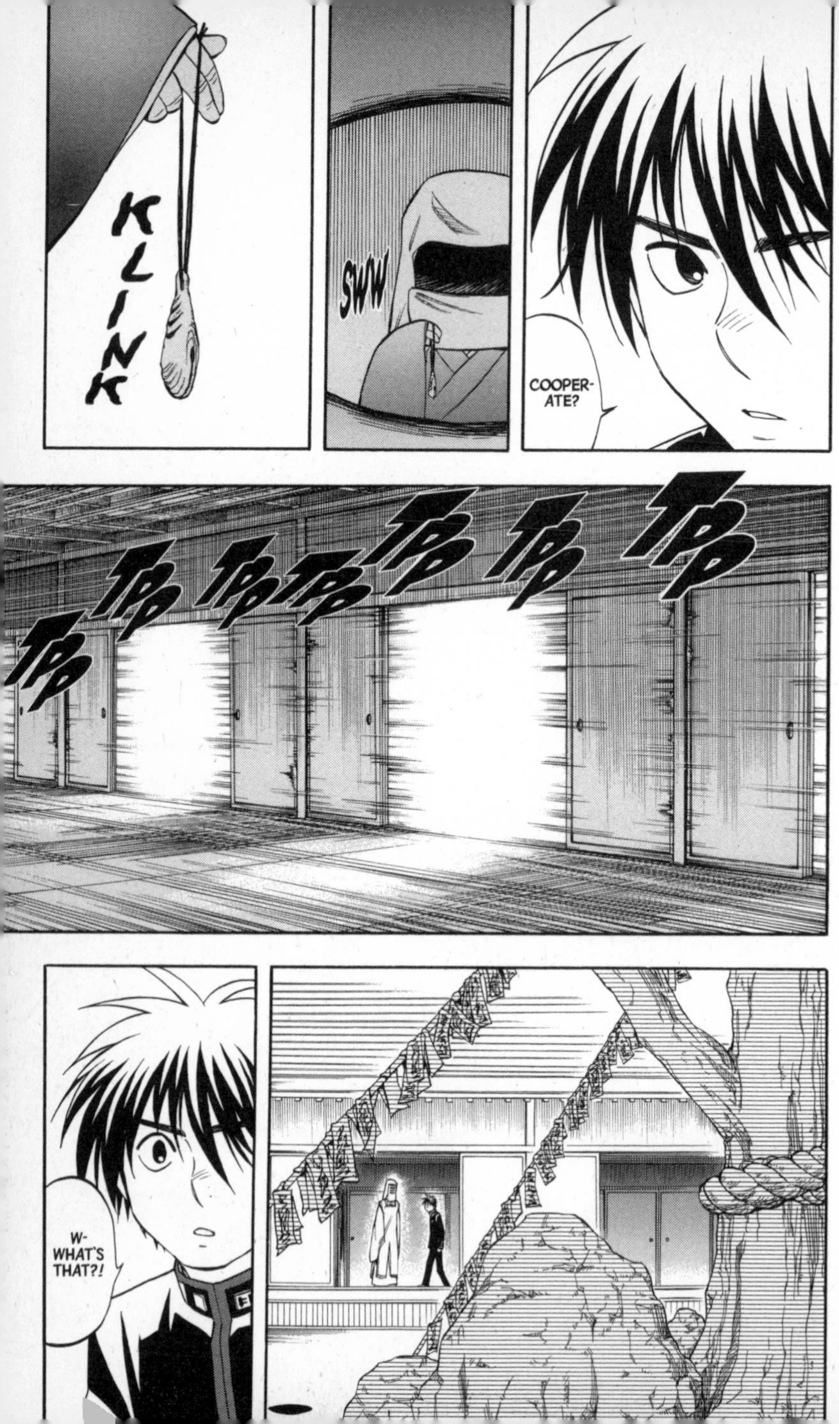
COOPER-ATE?
SWW
KLINK
TPP TPP TPP TPP TPP TPP TPP TPP
W- WHAT'S THAT?!

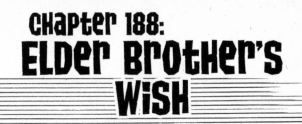

CHAPTER 188: ELDER BROTHER'S WISH

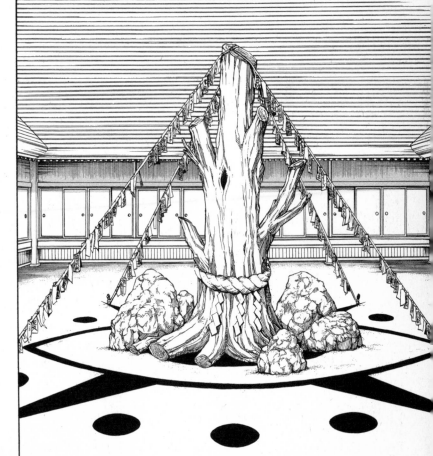

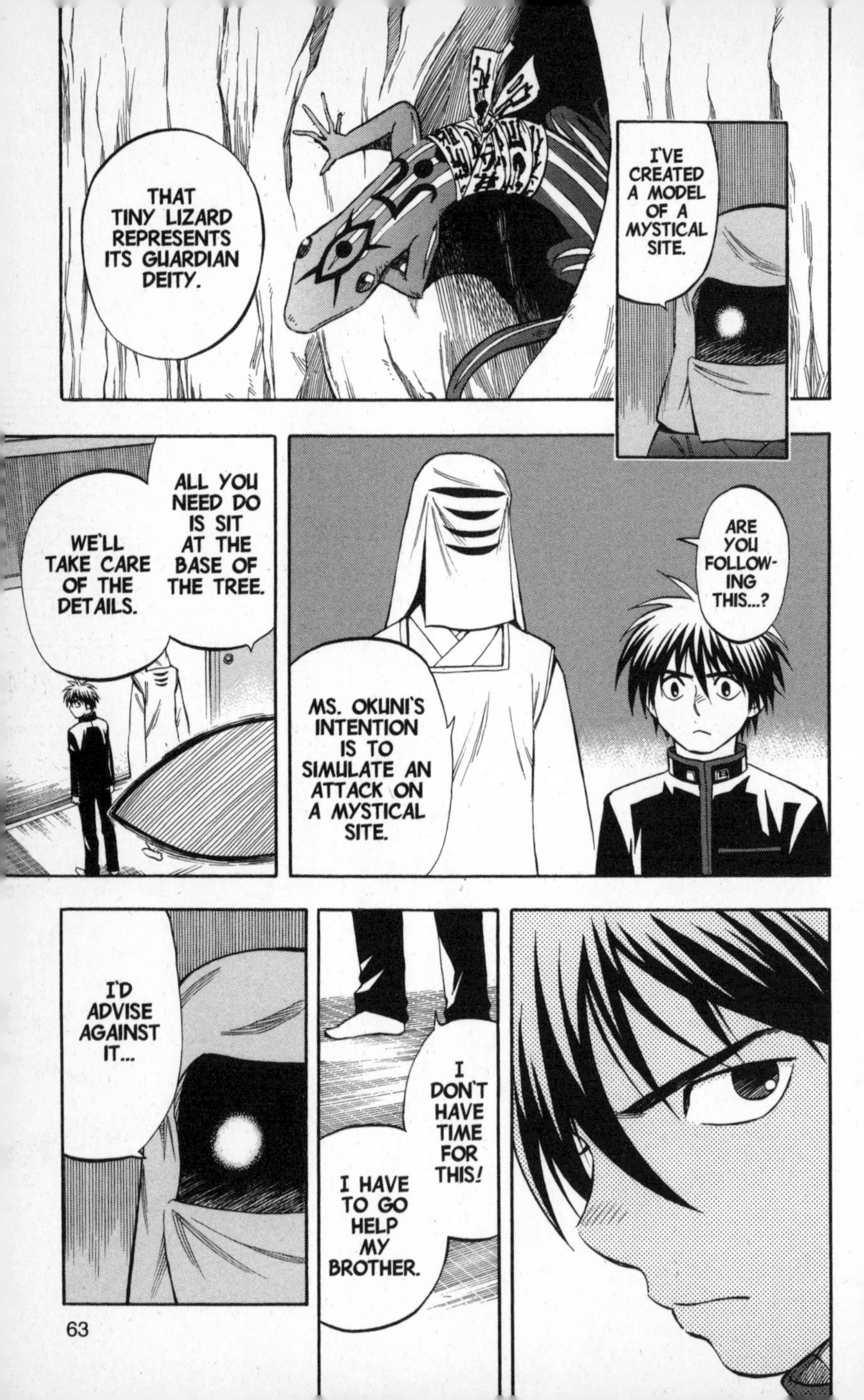
I'VE CREATED A MODEL OF A MYSTICAL SITE.
THAT TINY LIZARD REPRESENTS ITS GUARDIAN DEITY.
ARE YOU FOLLOWING THIS...?
MS. OKUNI'S INTENTION IS TO SIMULATE AN ATTACK ON A MYSTICAL SITE.
ALL YOU NEED DO IS SIT AT THE BASE OF THE TREE.
WE'LL TAKE CARE OF THE DETAILS.
I DON'T HAVE TIME FOR THIS!
I HAVE TO GO HELP MY BROTHER.
I'D ADVISE AGAINST IT...

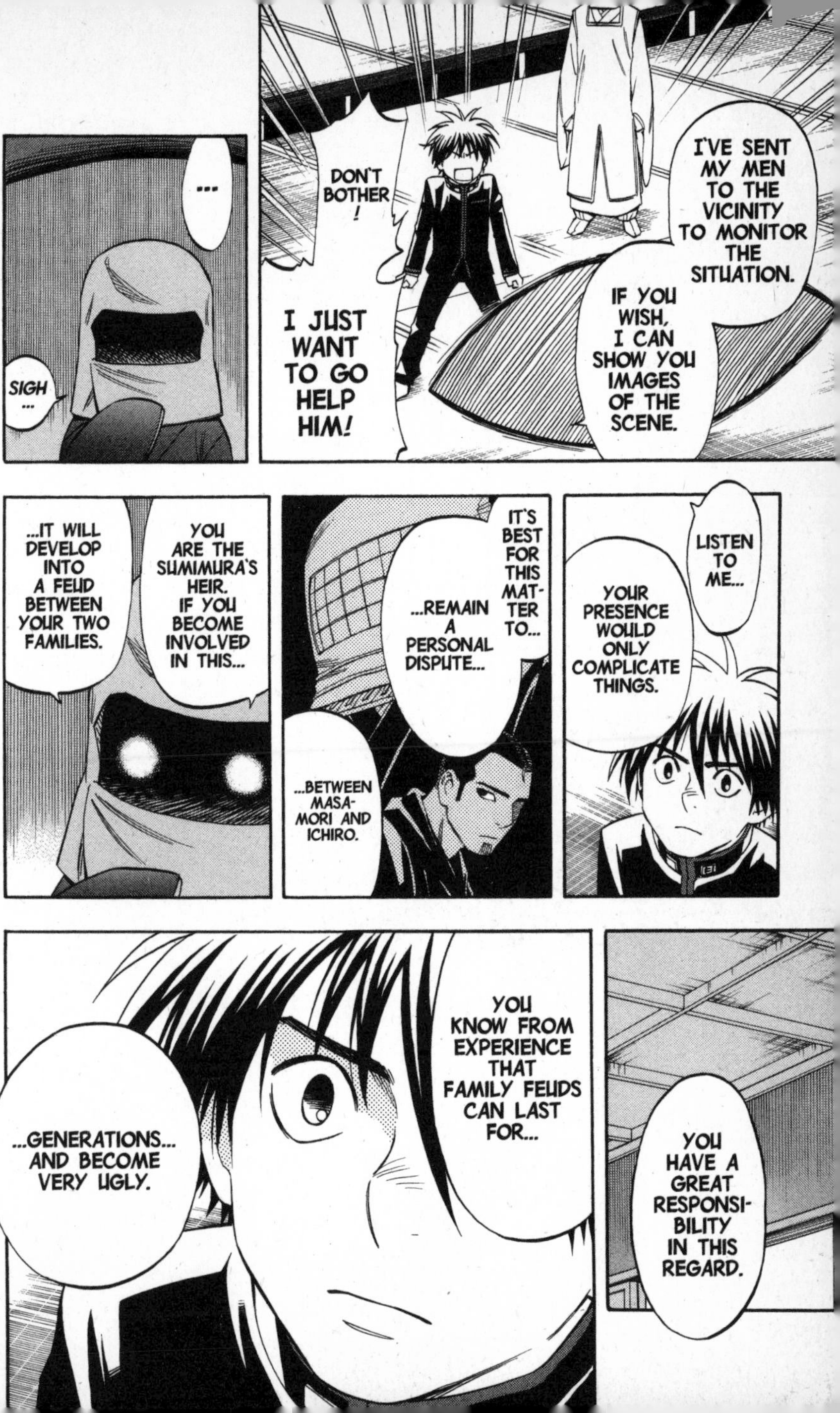
I'VE SENT MY MEN TO THE VICINITY TO MONITOR THE SITUATION.
IF YOU WISH, I CAN SHOW YOU IMAGES OF THE SCENE.
DON'T BOTHER!
I JUST WANT TO GO HELP HIM!
...
SIGH...
LISTEN TO ME...
YOUR PRESENCE WOULD ONLY COMPLICATE THINGS.
IT'S BEST FOR THIS MATTER TO...
...REMAIN A PERSONAL DISPUTE...
...BETWEEN MASAMORI AND ICHIRO.
YOU ARE THE SUMIMURA'S HEIR. IF YOU BECOME INVOLVED IN THIS...
...IT WILL DEVELOP INTO A FEUD BETWEEN YOUR TWO FAMILIES.
YOU HAVE A GREAT RESPONSIBILITY IN THIS REGARD.
YOU KNOW FROM EXPERIENCE THAT FAMILY FEUDS CAN LAST FOR...
...GENERATIONS... AND BECOME VERY UGLY.

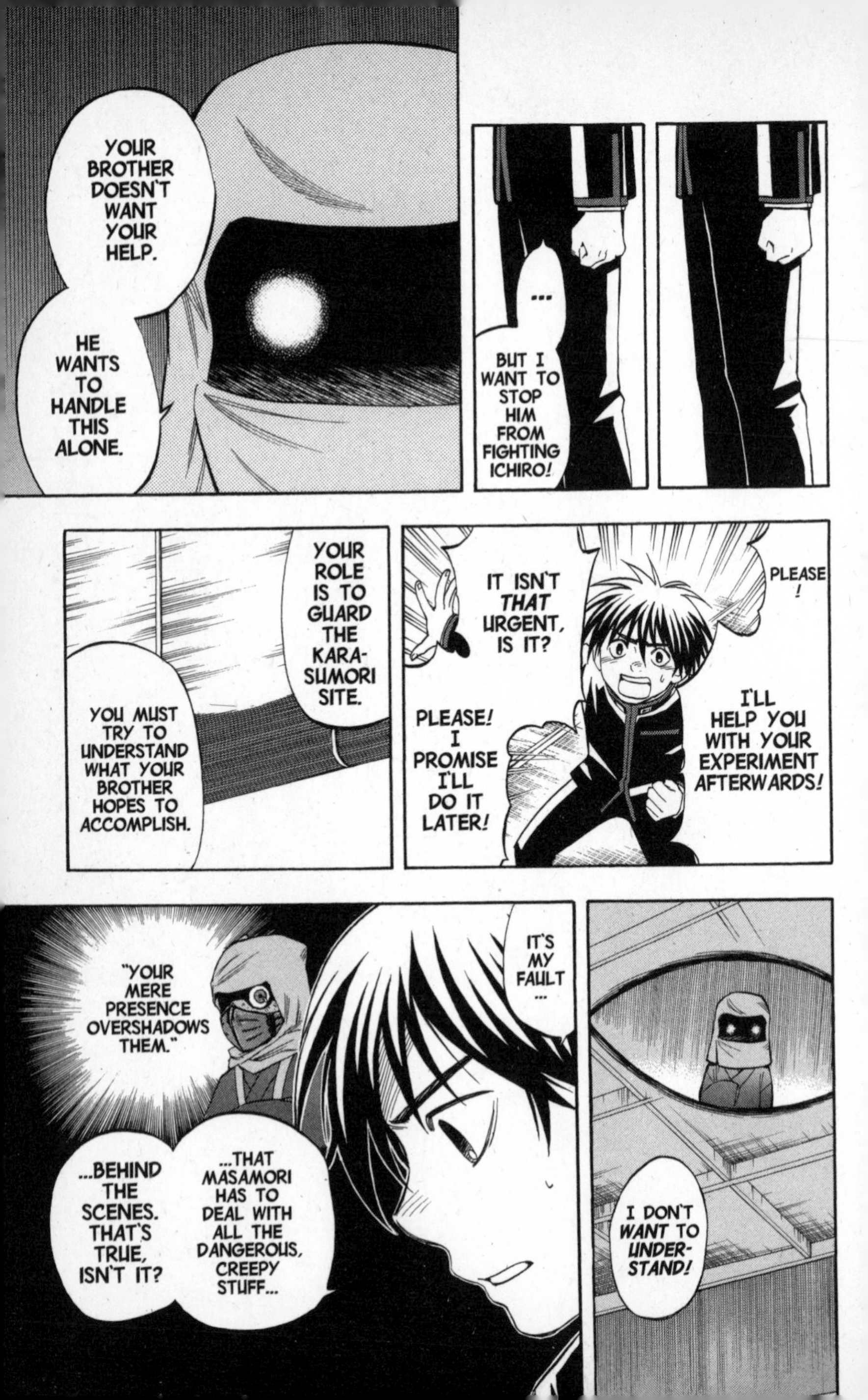
...
BUT I WANT TO STOP HIM FROM FIGHTING ICHIRO!
YOUR BROTHER DOESN'T WANT YOUR HELP.
HE WANTS TO HANDLE THIS ALONE.
PLEASE!
IT ISN'T *THAT* URGENT, IS IT?
I'LL HELP YOU WITH YOUR EXPERIMENT AFTERWARDS!
PLEASE! I PROMISE I'LL DO IT LATER!
YOUR ROLE IS TO GUARD THE KARA-SUMORI SITE.
YOU MUST TRY TO UNDERSTAND WHAT YOUR BROTHER HOPES TO ACCOMPLISH.
I DON'T *WANT* TO *UNDER-STAND!*
IT'S MY FAULT...
...THAT MASAMORI HAS TO DEAL WITH ALL THE DANGEROUS, CREEPY STUFF...
...BEHIND THE SCENES. THAT'S TRUE, ISN'T IT?
"YOUR MERE PRESENCE OVERSHADOWS THEM."

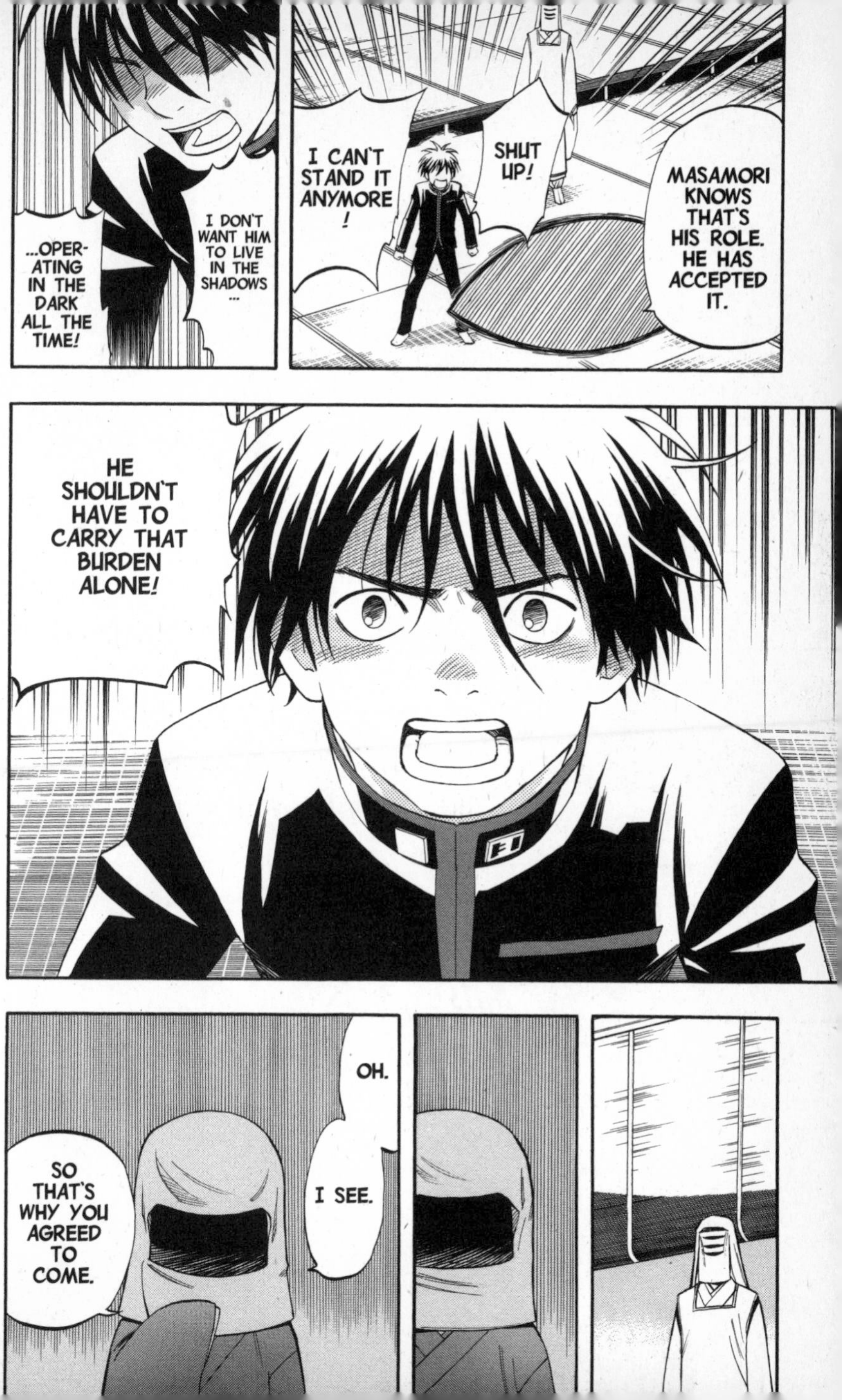
MASAMORI KNOWS THAT'S HIS ROLE. HE HAS ACCEPTED IT.
SHUT UP!
I CAN'T STAND IT ANYMORE!
I DON'T WANT HIM TO LIVE IN THE SHADOWS...
...OPERATING IN THE DARK ALL THE TIME!
HE SHOULDN'T HAVE TO CARRY THAT BURDEN ALONE!
OH.
I SEE.
SO THAT'S WHY YOU AGREED TO COME.

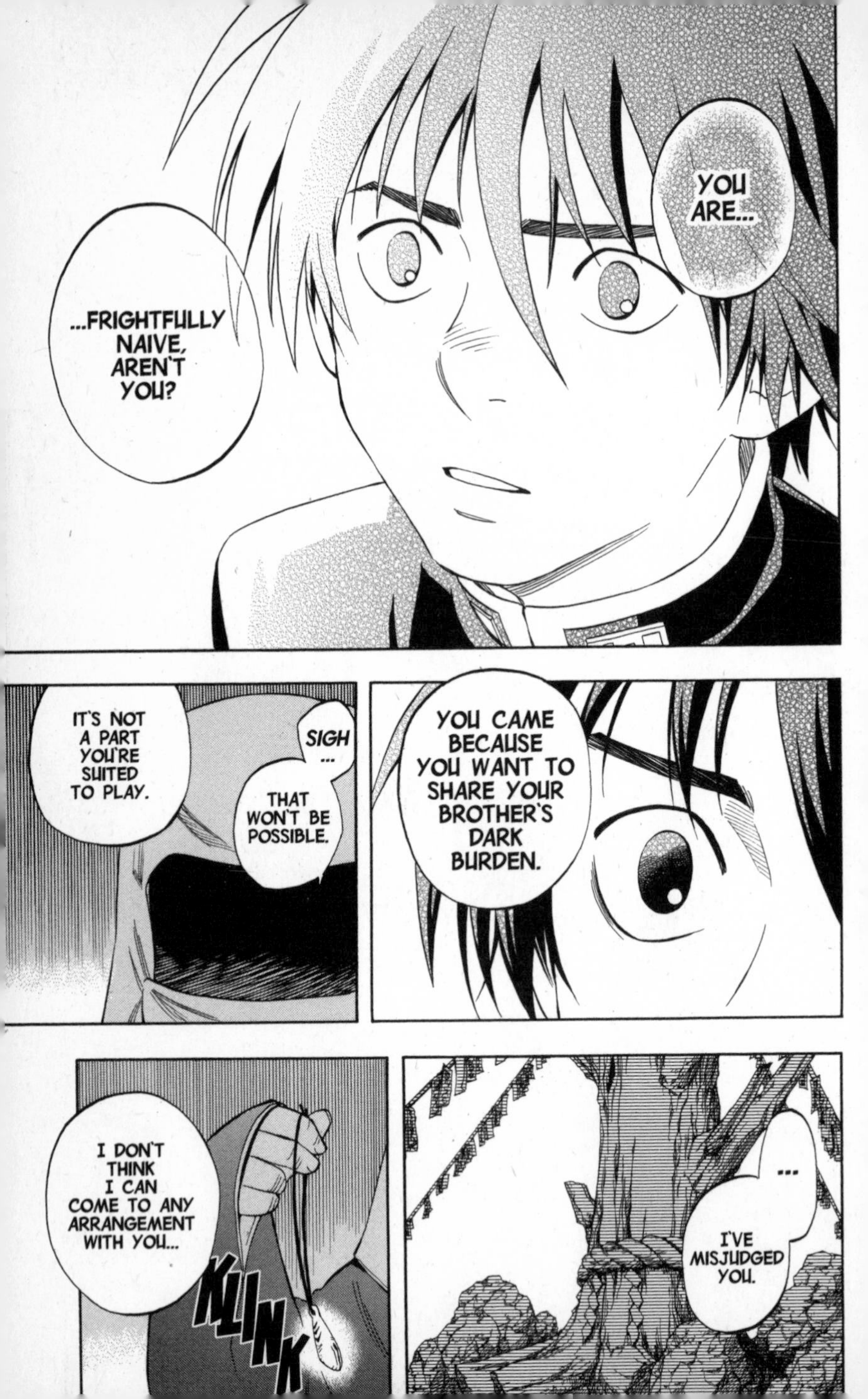
YOU ARE...
...FRIGHTFULLY NAIVE, AREN'T YOU?
YOU CAME BECAUSE YOU WANT TO SHARE YOUR BROTHER'S DARK BURDEN.
SIGH...
THAT WON'T BE POSSIBLE.
IT'S NOT A PART YOU'RE SUITED TO PLAY.
...
I'VE MISJUDGED YOU.
I DON'T THINK I CAN COME TO ANY ARRANGEMENT WITH YOU...
KLINK

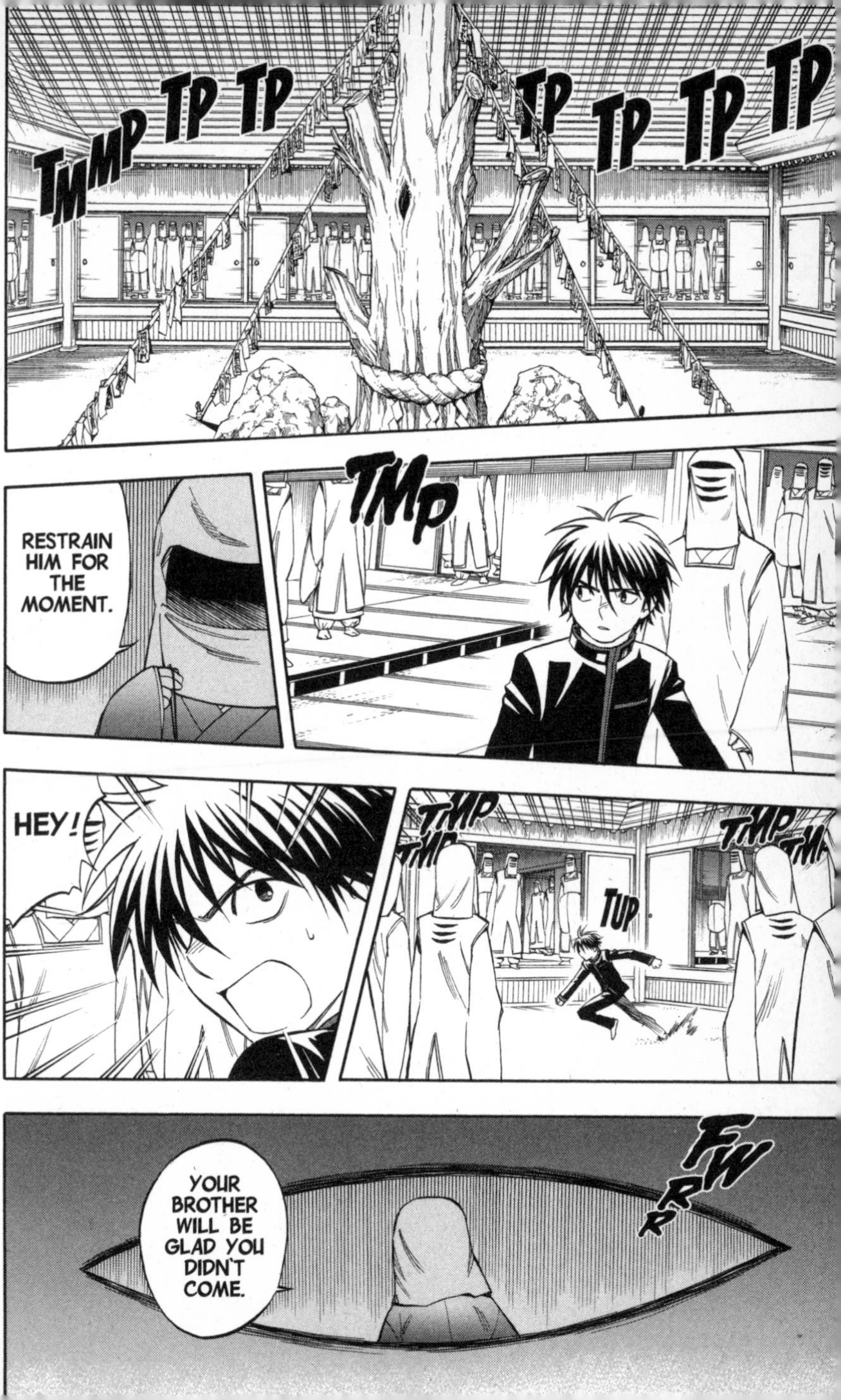
TP TP TP TP
TMMP TP TP
TMP
RESTRAIN HIM FOR THE MOMENT.
TMP TMP
TMP TMP
TUP
HEY!
FWRR
YOUR BROTHER WILL BE GLAD YOU DIDN'T COME.

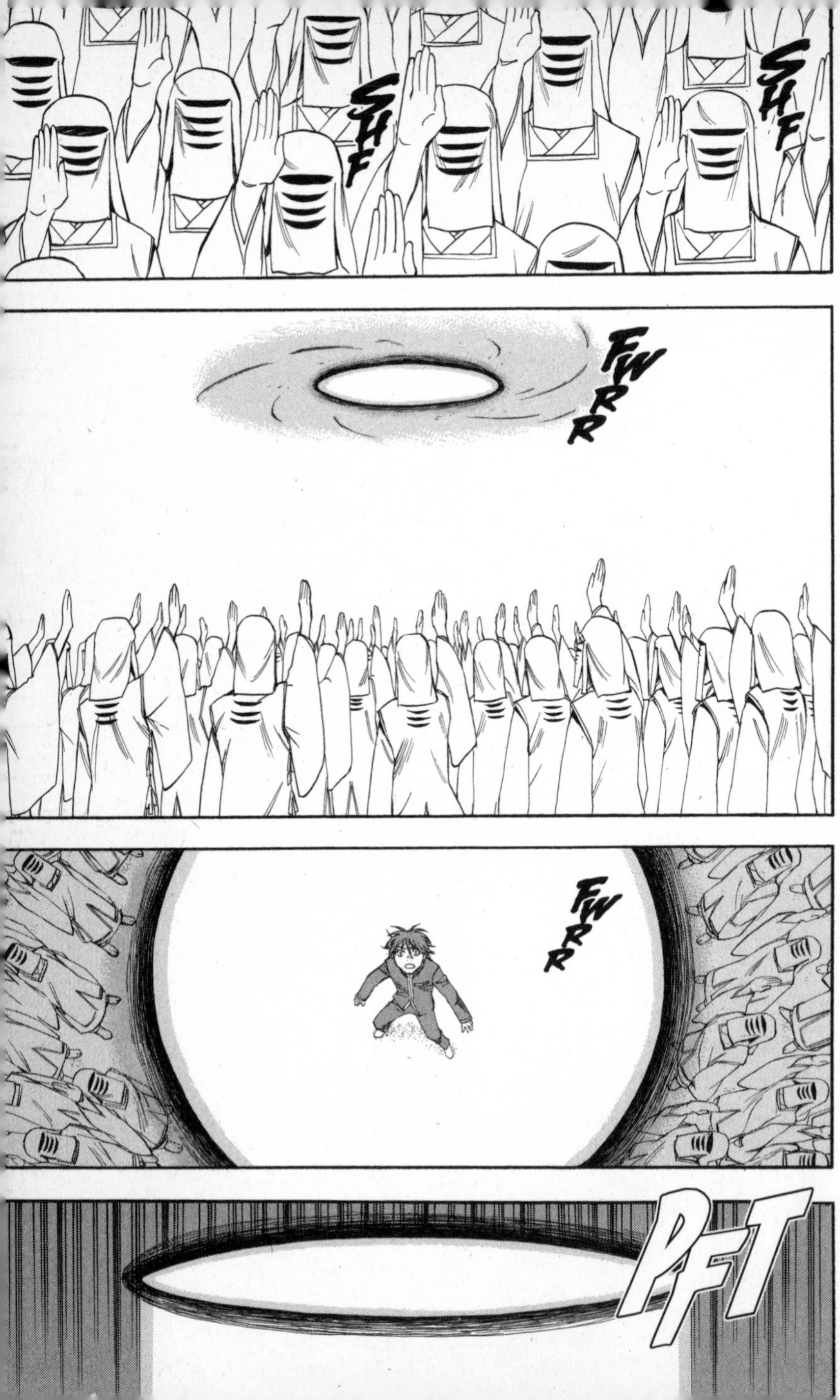
SHF
SHF
FWRR
FWRR
PFT

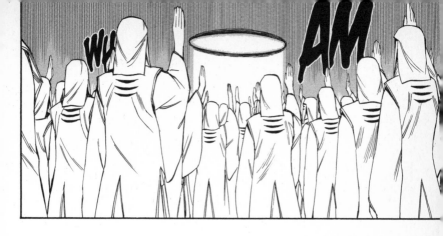

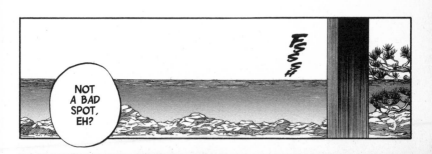

NOT A BAD SPOT, EH?

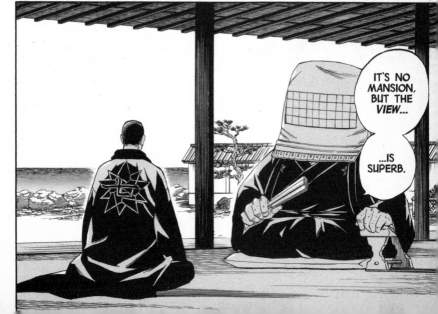

IT'S NO MANSION, BUT THE VIEW...

...IS SUPERB.

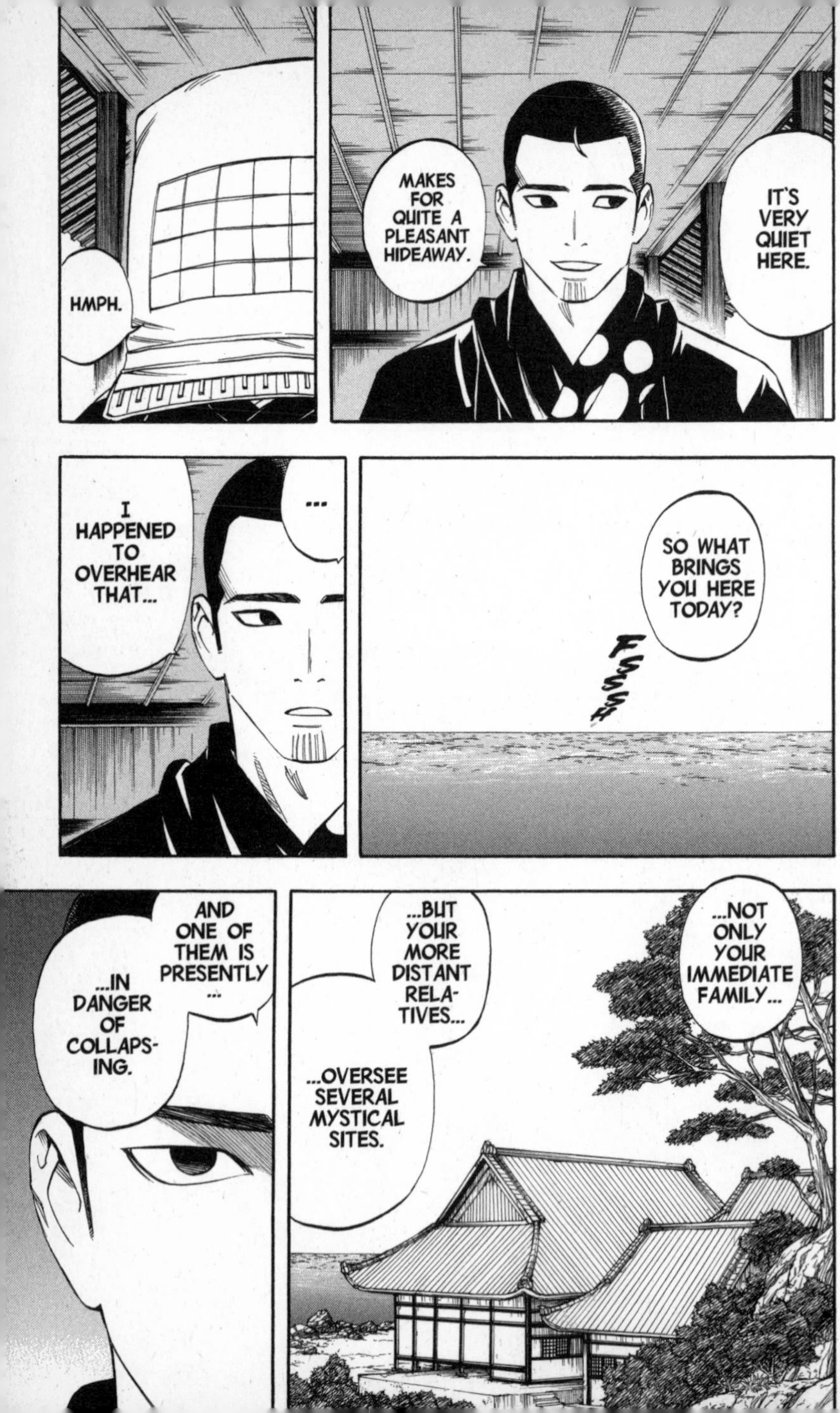
IT'S VERY QUIET HERE.
MAKES FOR QUITE A PLEASANT HIDEAWAY.
HMPH.
SO WHAT BRINGS YOU HERE TODAY?
...
I HAPPENED TO OVERHEAR THAT...
...NOT ONLY YOUR IMMEDIATE FAMILY...
...BUT YOUR MORE DISTANT RELA-TIVES...
...OVERSEE SEVERAL MYSTICAL SITES.
AND ONE OF THEM IS PRESENTLY...
...IN DANGER OF COLLAPS-ING.

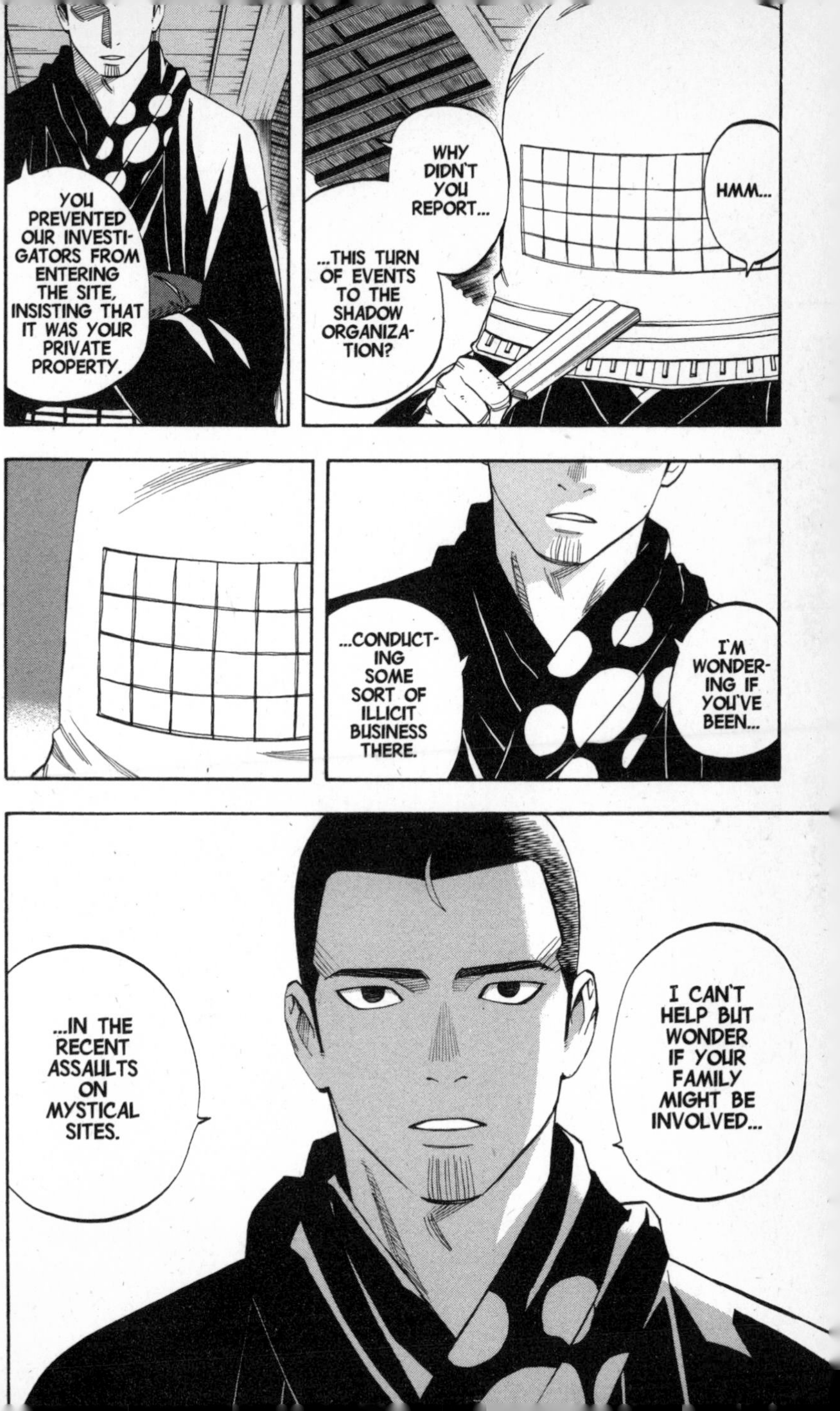

HMM...
WHY DIDN'T YOU REPORT...
...THIS TURN OF EVENTS TO THE SHADOW ORGANIZATION?
YOU PREVENTED OUR INVESTIGATORS FROM ENTERING THE SITE, INSISTING THAT IT WAS YOUR PRIVATE PROPERTY.
I'M WONDERING IF YOU'VE BEEN...
...CONDUCTING SOME SORT OF ILLICIT BUSINESS THERE.
I CAN'T HELP BUT WONDER IF YOUR FAMILY MIGHT BE INVOLVED...
...IN THE RECENT ASSAULTS ON MYSTICAL SITES.

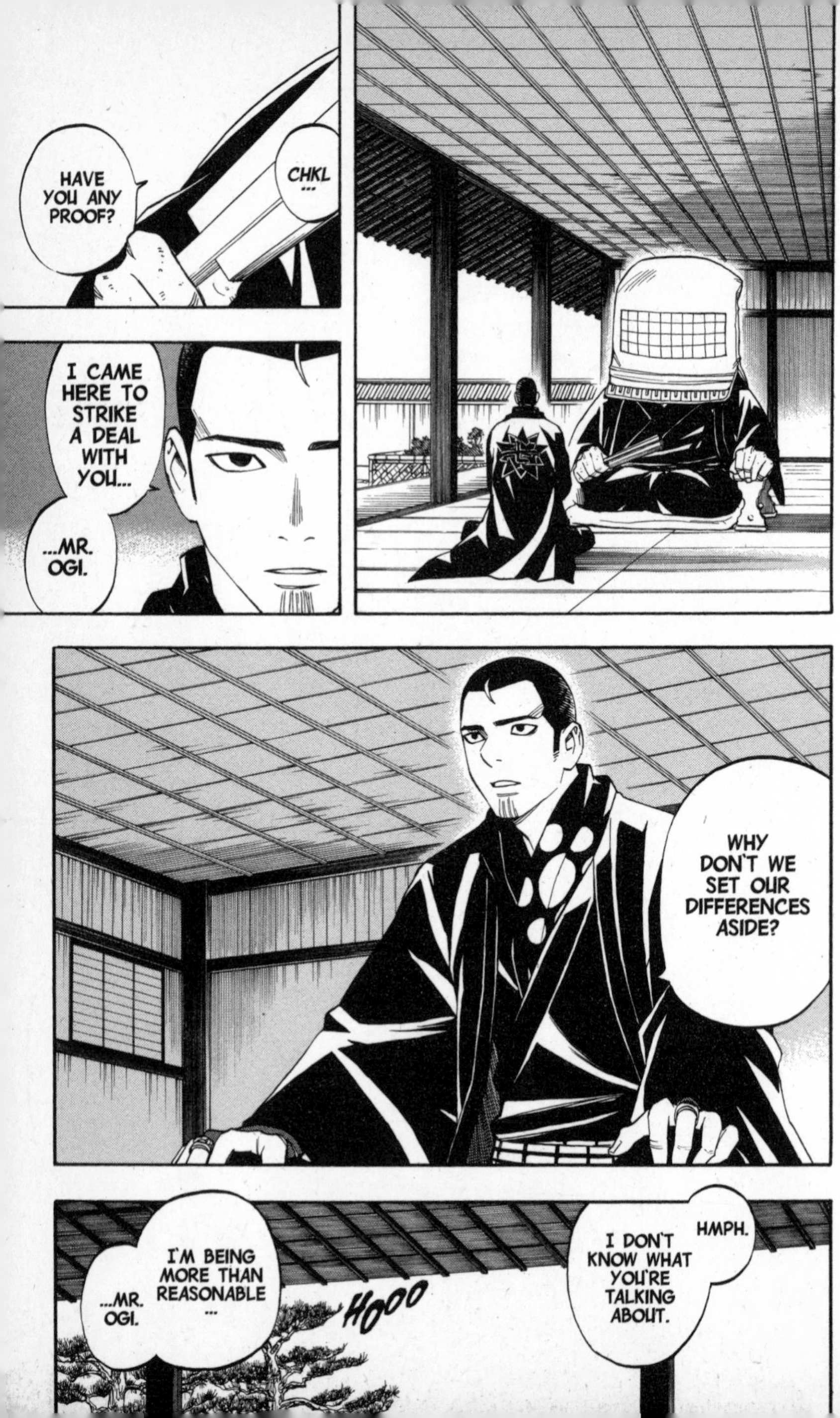

CHKL...
HAVE YOU ANY PROOF?
I CAME HERE TO STRIKE A DEAL WITH YOU...
...MR. OGI.
WHY DON'T WE SET OUR DIFFERENCES ASIDE?
HMPH.
I DON'T KNOW WHAT YOU'RE TALKING ABOUT.
HOOO
I'M BEING MORE THAN REASONABLE...
...MR. OGI.

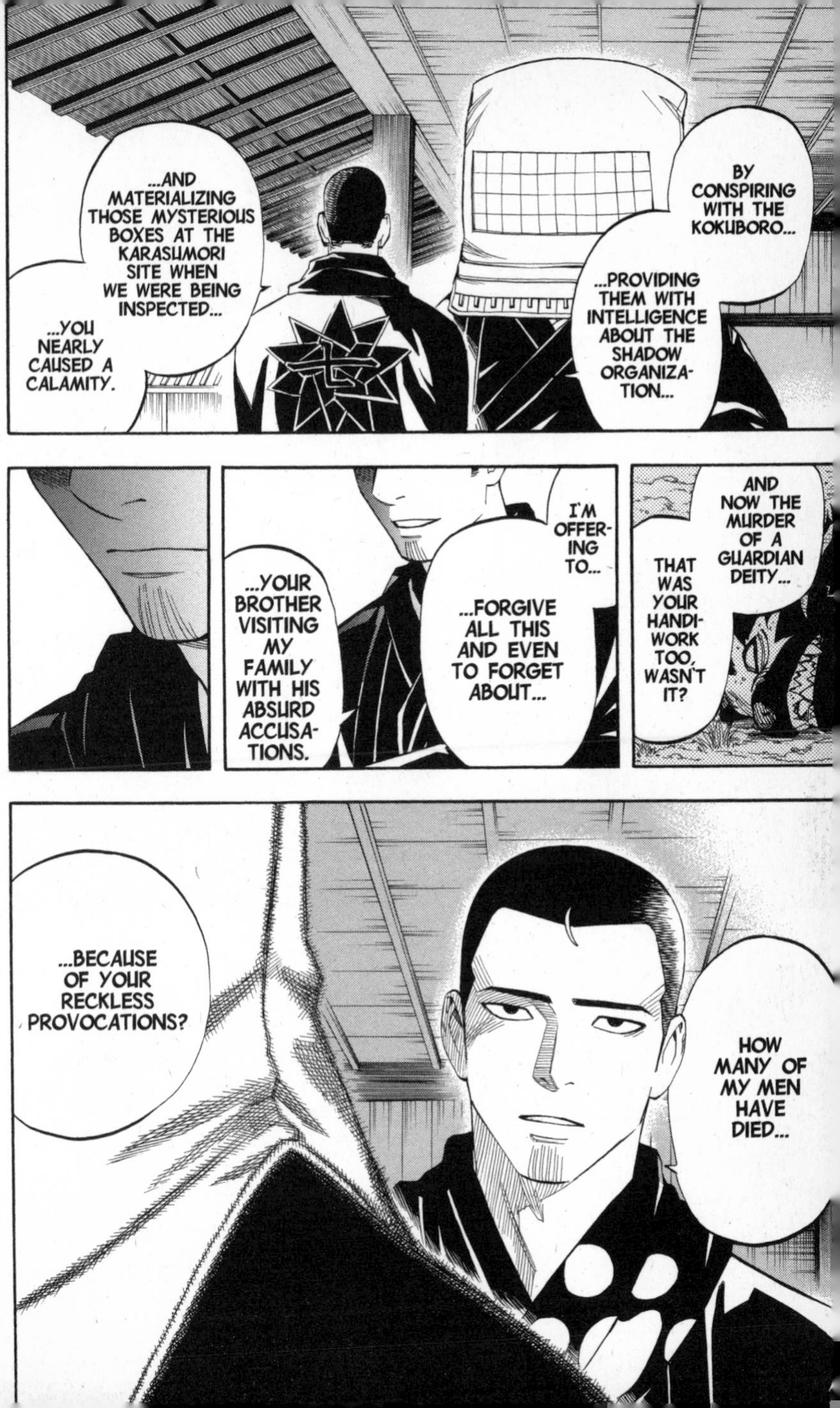
BY CONSPIRING WITH THE KOKUBORO...
...PROVIDING THEM WITH INTELLIGENCE ABOUT THE SHADOW ORGANIZATION...
...AND MATERIALIZING THOSE MYSTERIOUS BOXES AT THE KARASUMORI SITE WHEN WE WERE BEING INSPECTED...
...YOU NEARLY CAUSED A CALAMITY.
AND NOW THE MURDER OF A GUARDIAN DEITY...
THAT WAS YOUR HANDIWORK TOO, WASN'T IT?
I'M OFFERING TO...
...FORGIVE ALL THIS AND EVEN TO FORGET ABOUT...
...YOUR BROTHER VISITING MY FAMILY WITH HIS ABSURD ACCUSATIONS.
HOW MANY OF MY MEN HAVE DIED...
...BECAUSE OF YOUR RECKLESS PROVOCATIONS?

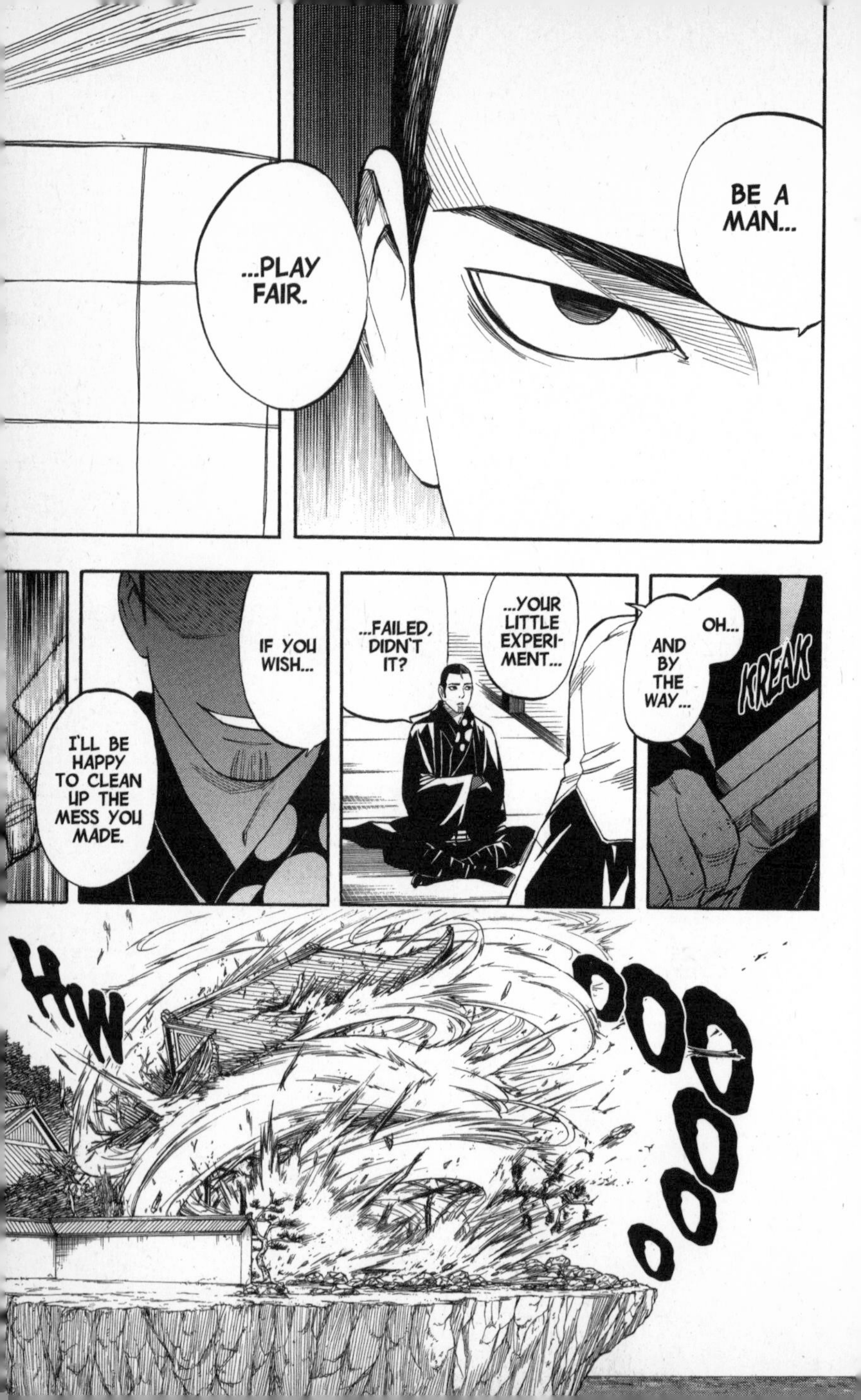
BE A MAN...
...PLAY FAIR.
OH... AND BY THE WAY...
KREAK
...YOUR LITTLE EXPERIMENT...
...FAILED, DIDN'T IT?
IF YOU WISH...
I'LL BE HAPPY TO CLEAN UP THE MESS YOU MADE.
HWOOOOOOOOO

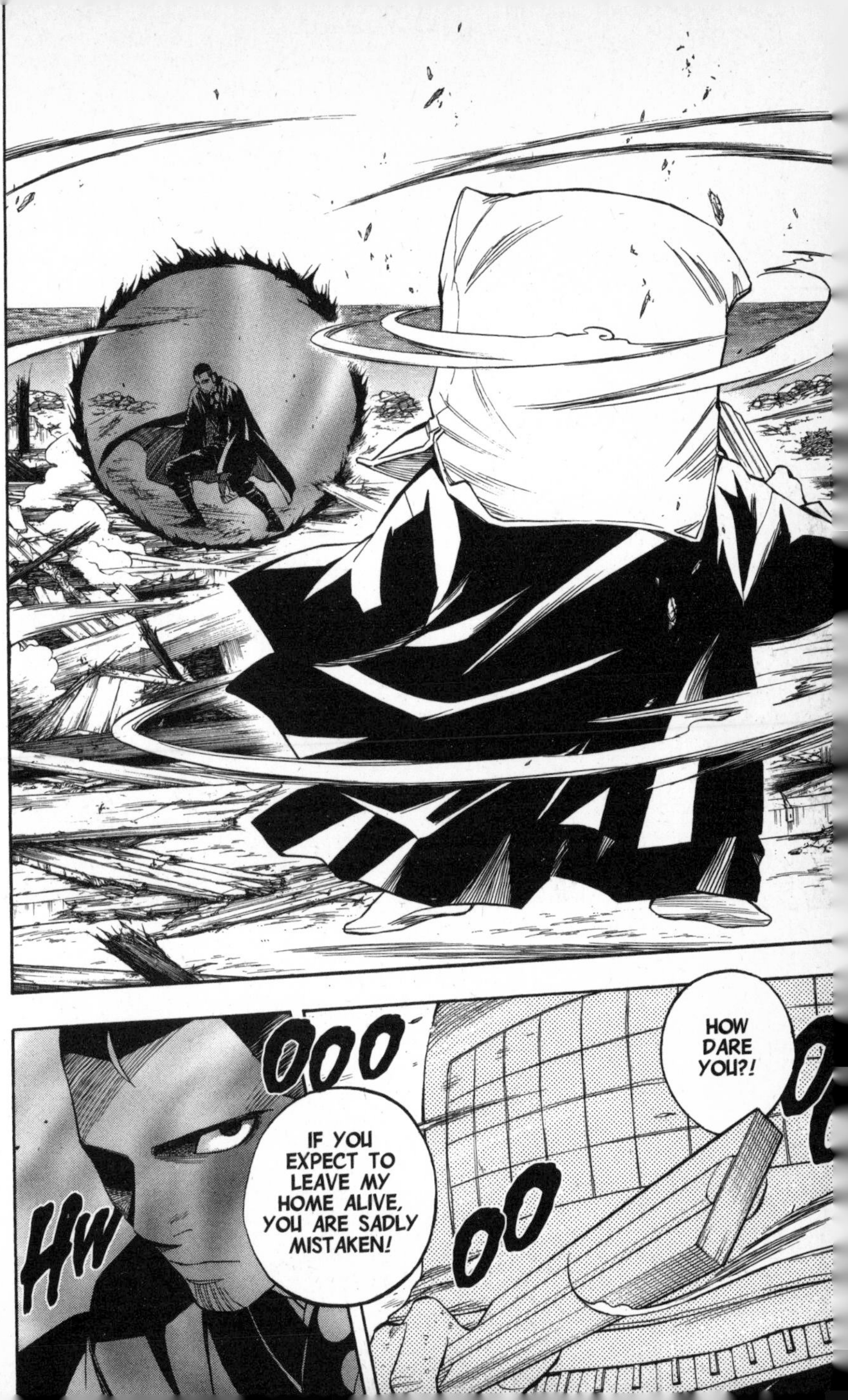
HOW DARE YOU?!
IF YOU EXPECT TO LEAVE MY HOME ALIVE, YOU ARE SADLY MISTAKEN!
OOO
OO
HW

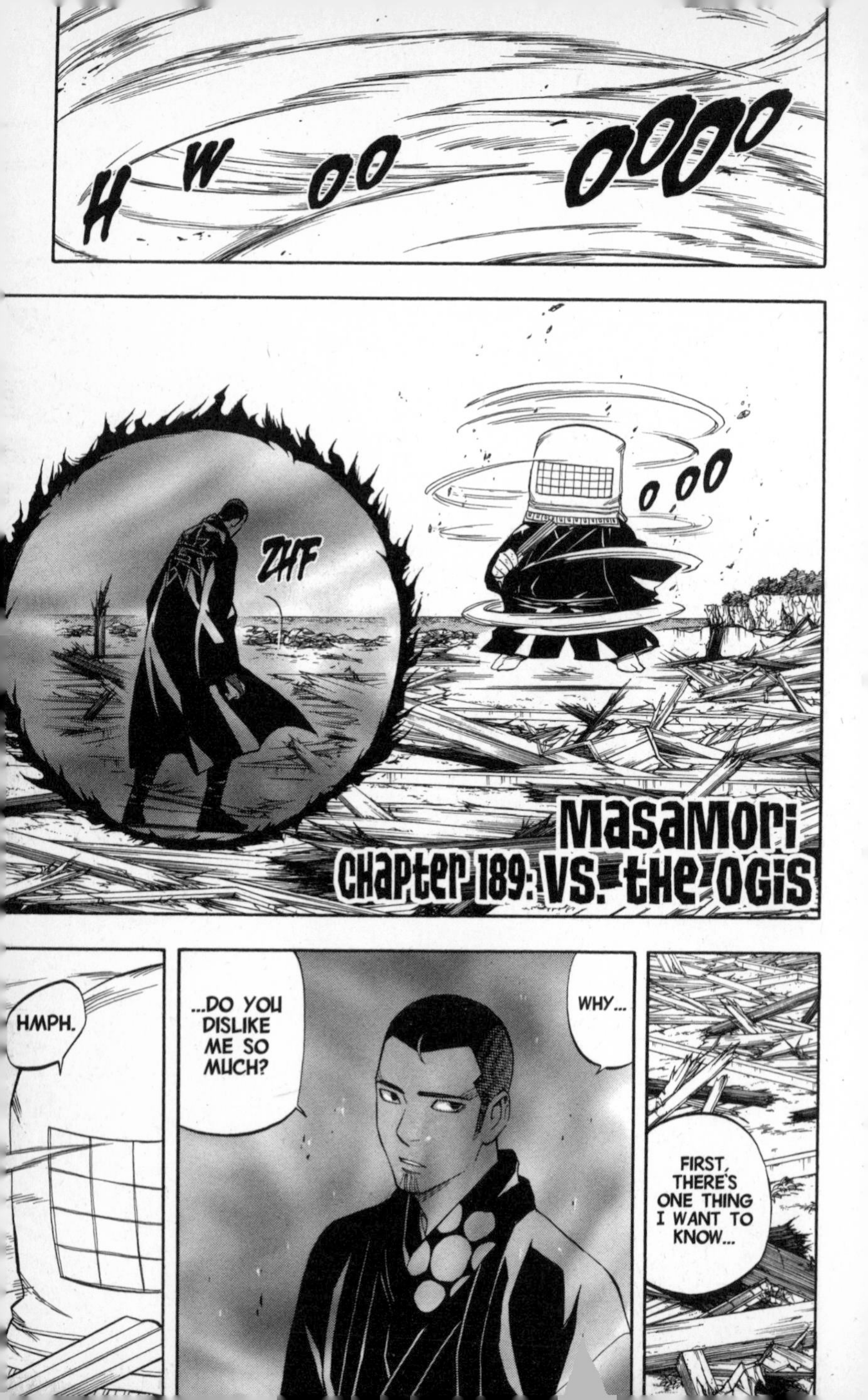
HWOOOOOOO
ZHF
O OO
Masamori
Chapter 189: VS. the Ogis
FIRST, THERE'S ONE THING I WANT TO KNOW...
WHY...
...DO YOU DISLIKE ME SO MUCH?
HMPH.

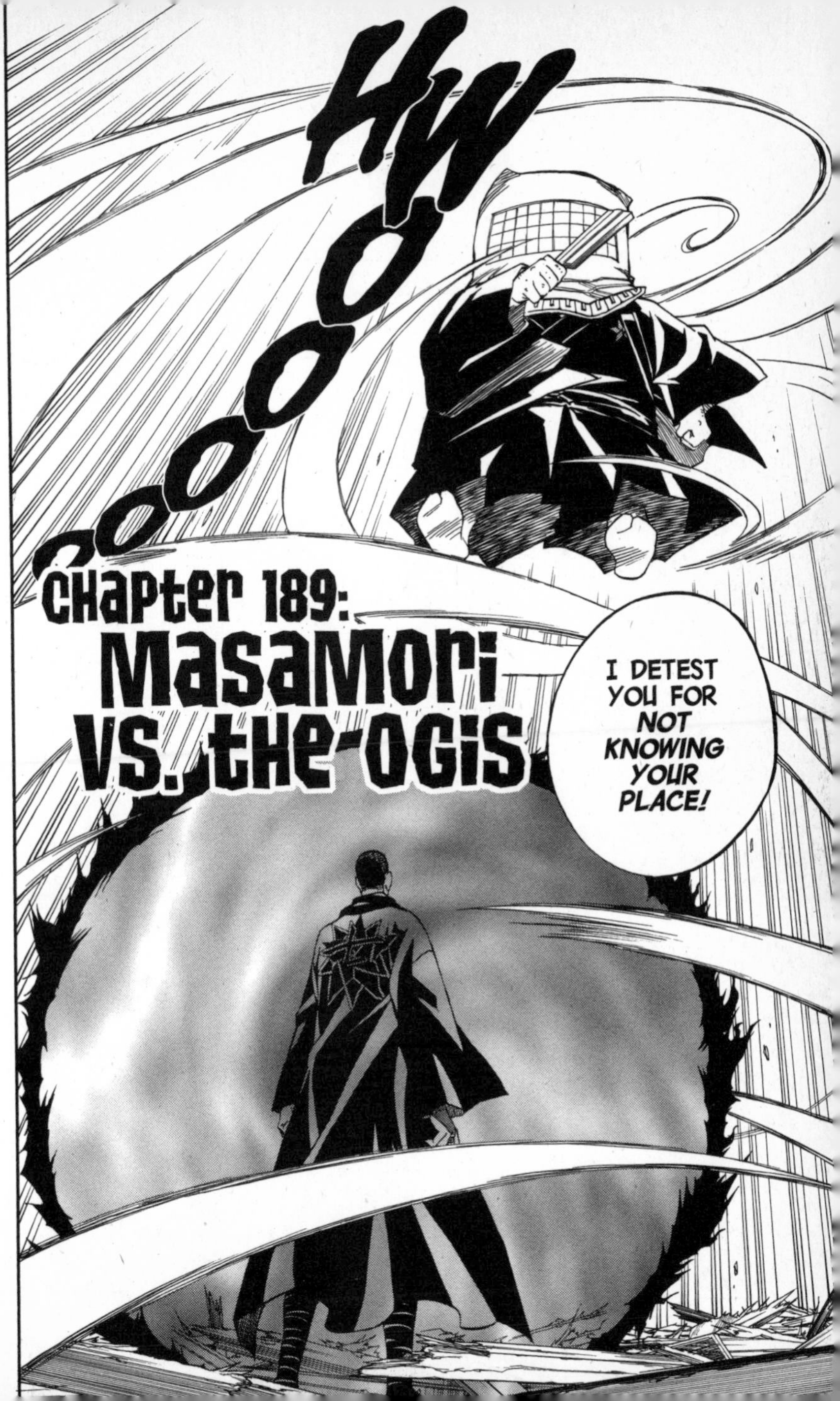

HWOOOOOOO
Chapter 189: Masamori vs. the Ogis
I DETEST YOU FOR NOT KNOWING YOUR PLACE!

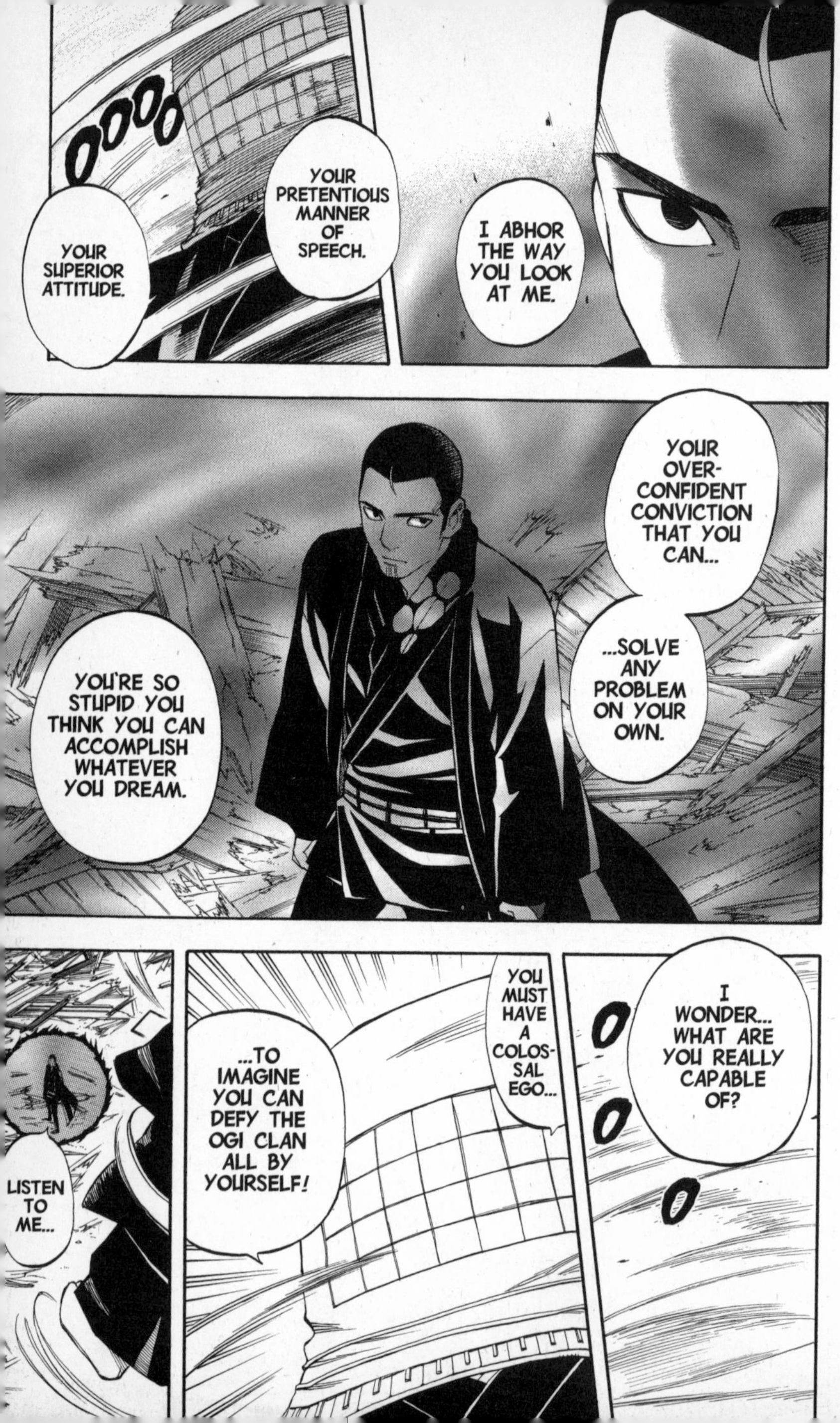
I ABHOR THE WAY YOU LOOK AT ME.
YOUR PRETENTIOUS MANNER OF SPEECH.
YOUR SUPERIOR ATTITUDE.
OOOO
YOUR OVER-CONFIDENT CONVICTION THAT YOU CAN...
...SOLVE ANY PROBLEM ON YOUR OWN.
YOU'RE SO STUPID YOU THINK YOU CAN ACCOMPLISH WHATEVER YOU DREAM.
I WONDER... WHAT ARE YOU REALLY CAPABLE OF?
OOO
YOU MUST HAVE A COLOS-SAL EGO...
...TO IMAGINE YOU CAN DEFY THE OGI CLAN ALL BY YOURSELF!
LISTEN TO ME...

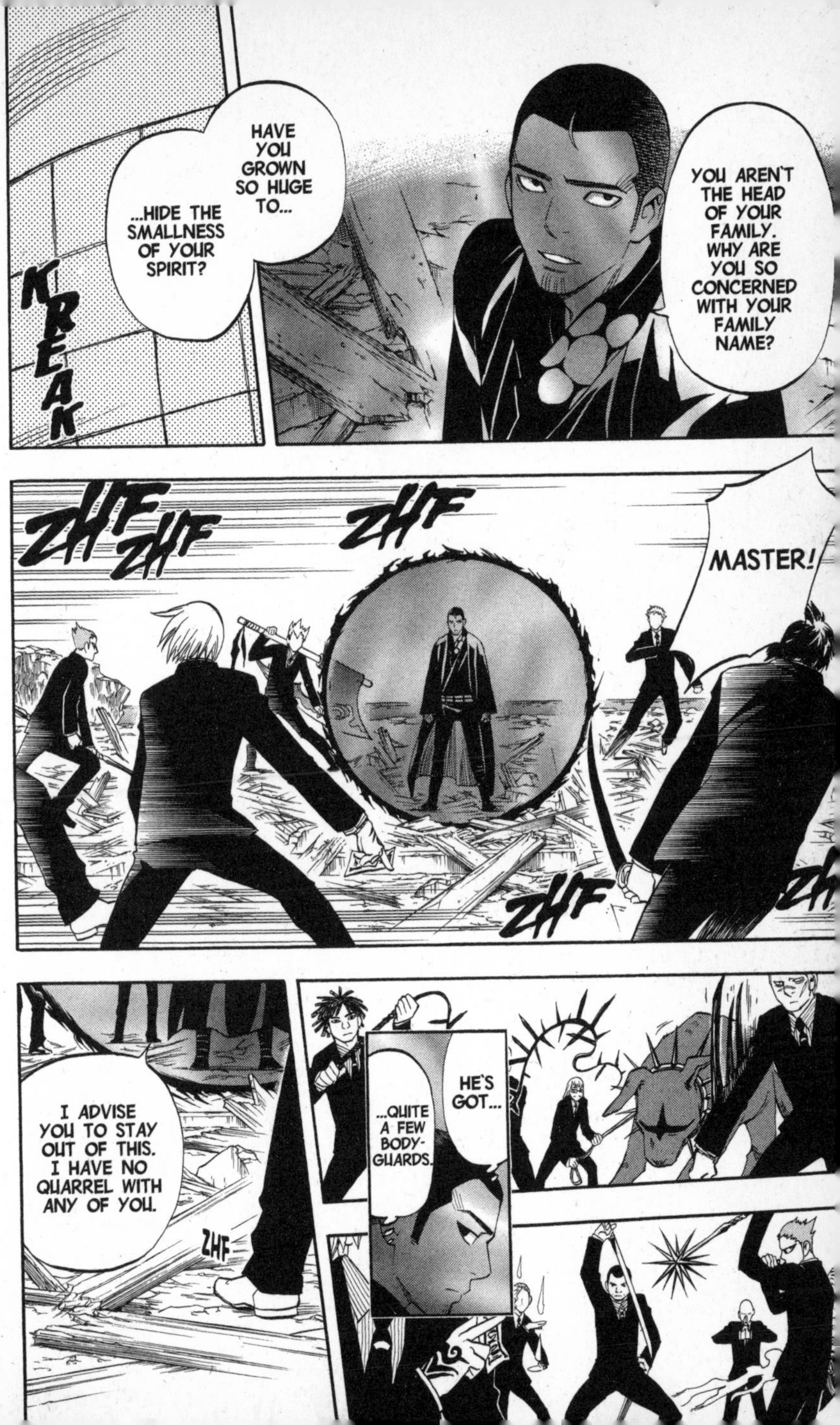

YOU AREN'T THE HEAD OF YOUR FAMILY. WHY ARE YOU SO CONCERNED WITH YOUR FAMILY NAME?
HAVE YOU GROWN SO HUGE TO...
...HIDE THE SMALLNESS OF YOUR SPIRIT?
KREAK
MASTER!
ZHF
ZHF
ZHF
ZHF
HE'S GOT...
...QUITE A FEW BODY-GUARDS.
I ADVISE YOU TO STAY OUT OF THIS. I HAVE NO QUARREL WITH ANY OF YOU.
ZHF

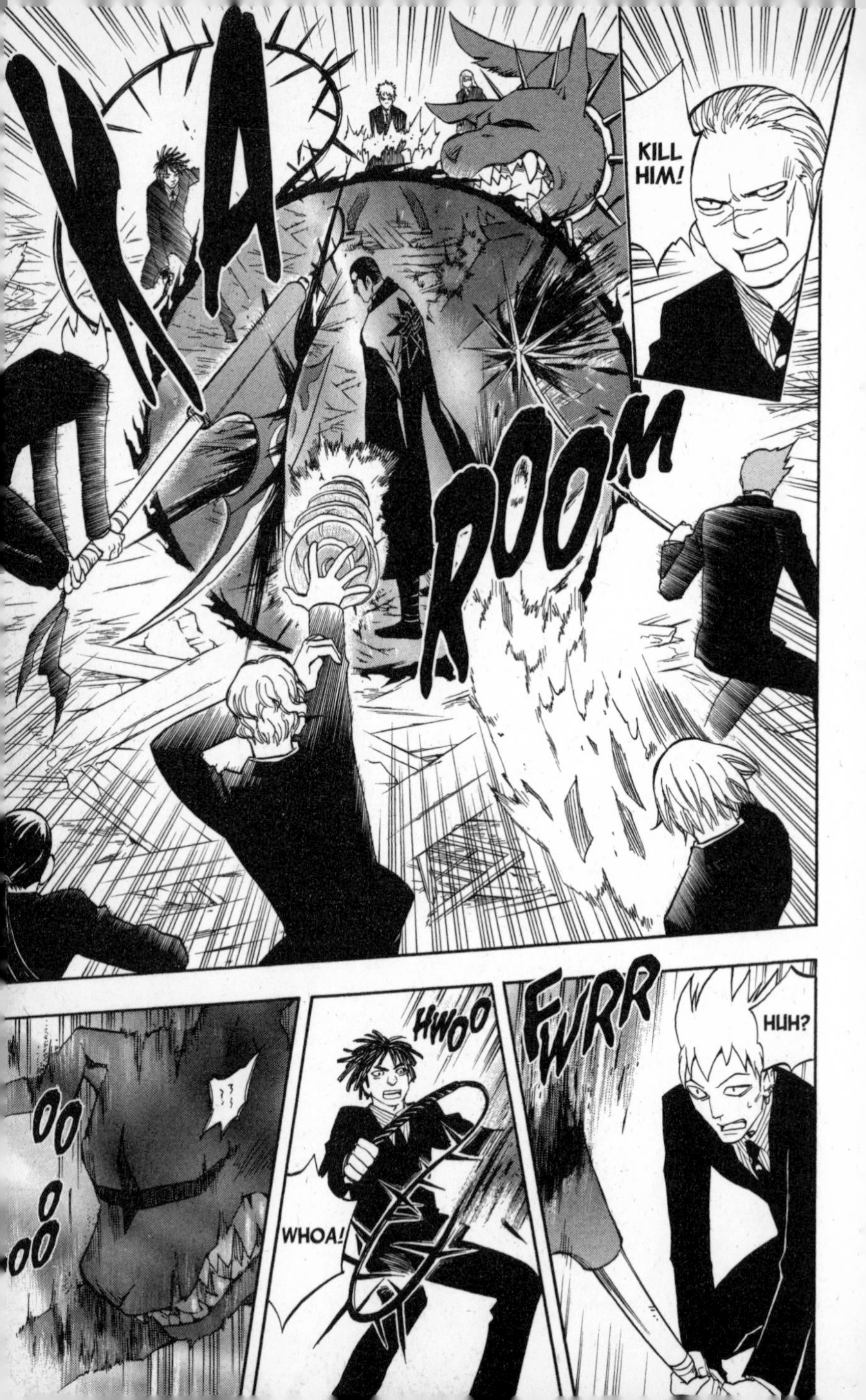
KILL HIM!
KA
ROOM
HUH?
FWRR
HWOO
WHOA!
OOOOOO
??

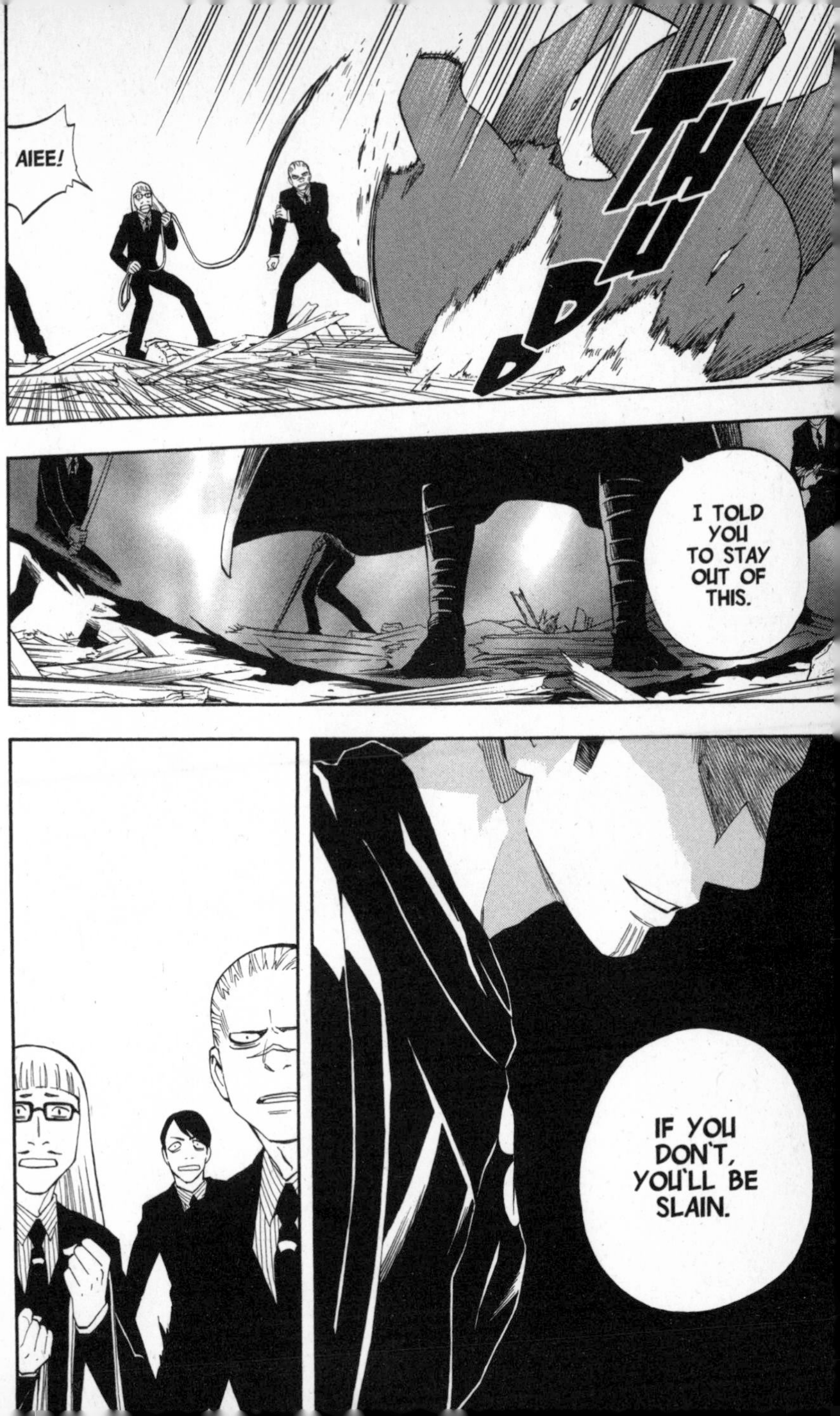
THUDD
AIEE!
I TOLD YOU TO STAY OUT OF THIS.
IF YOU DON'T, YOU'LL BE SLAIN.

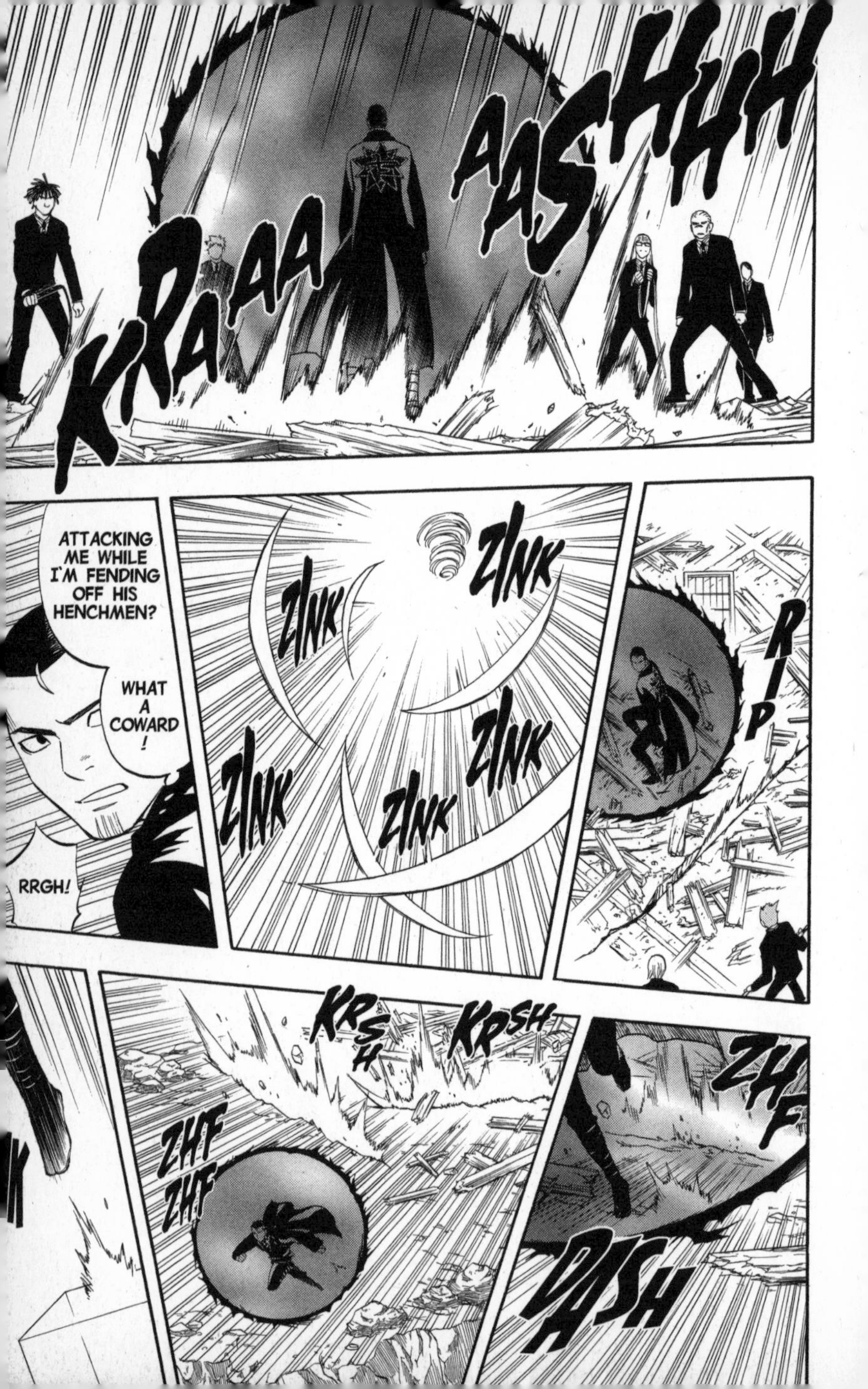
KRAAAAASHHH
RIP
ZINK
ZINK
ZINK
ZINK
ZINK
ATTACKING ME WHILE I'M FENDING OFF HIS HENCHMEN?
WHAT A COWARD!
RRGH!
ZHF
DASH
KRSH
KRSH
ZHF ZHF

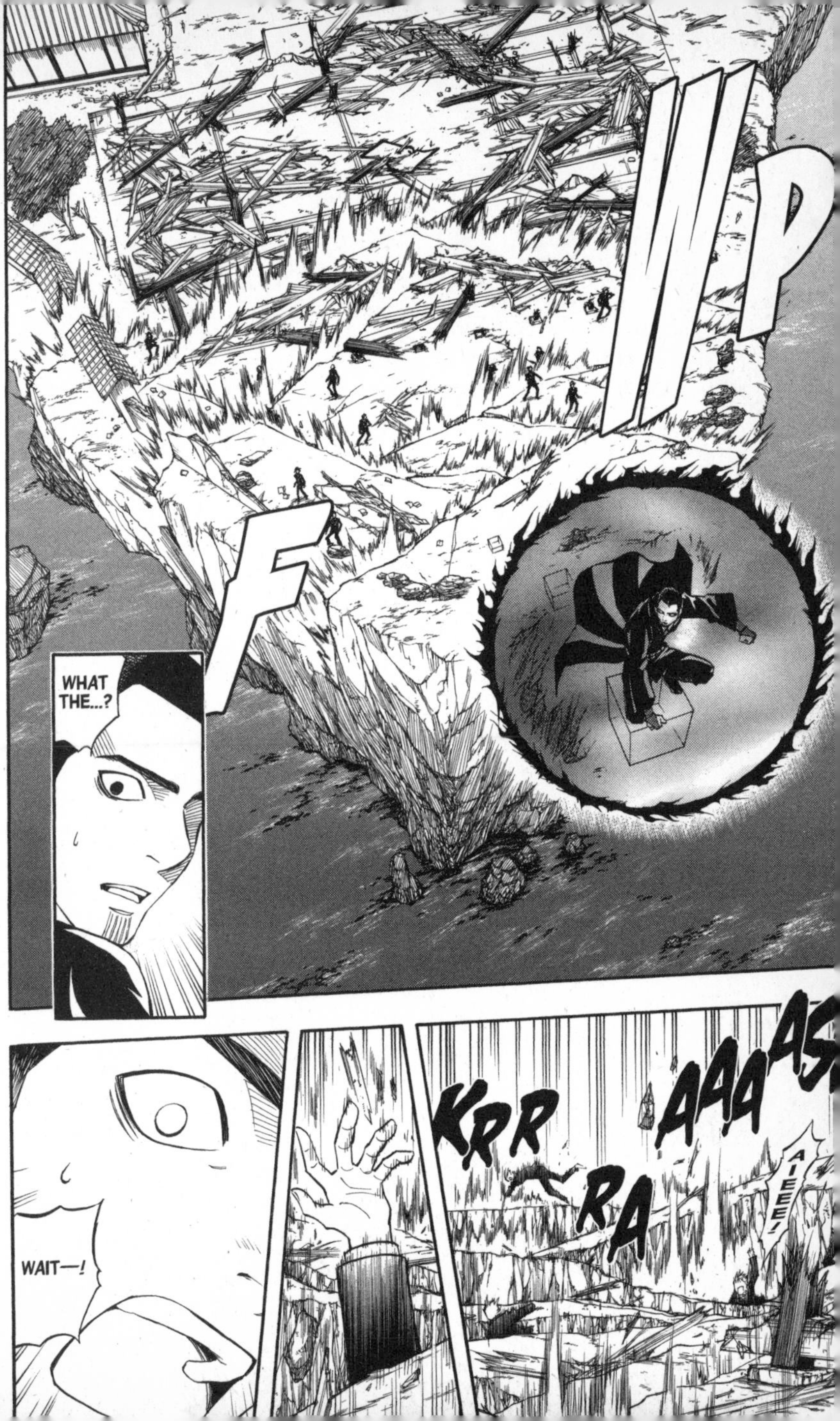
WHAT THE...?
KRR
RA
AAAAS
AIEEE!
WAIT—!

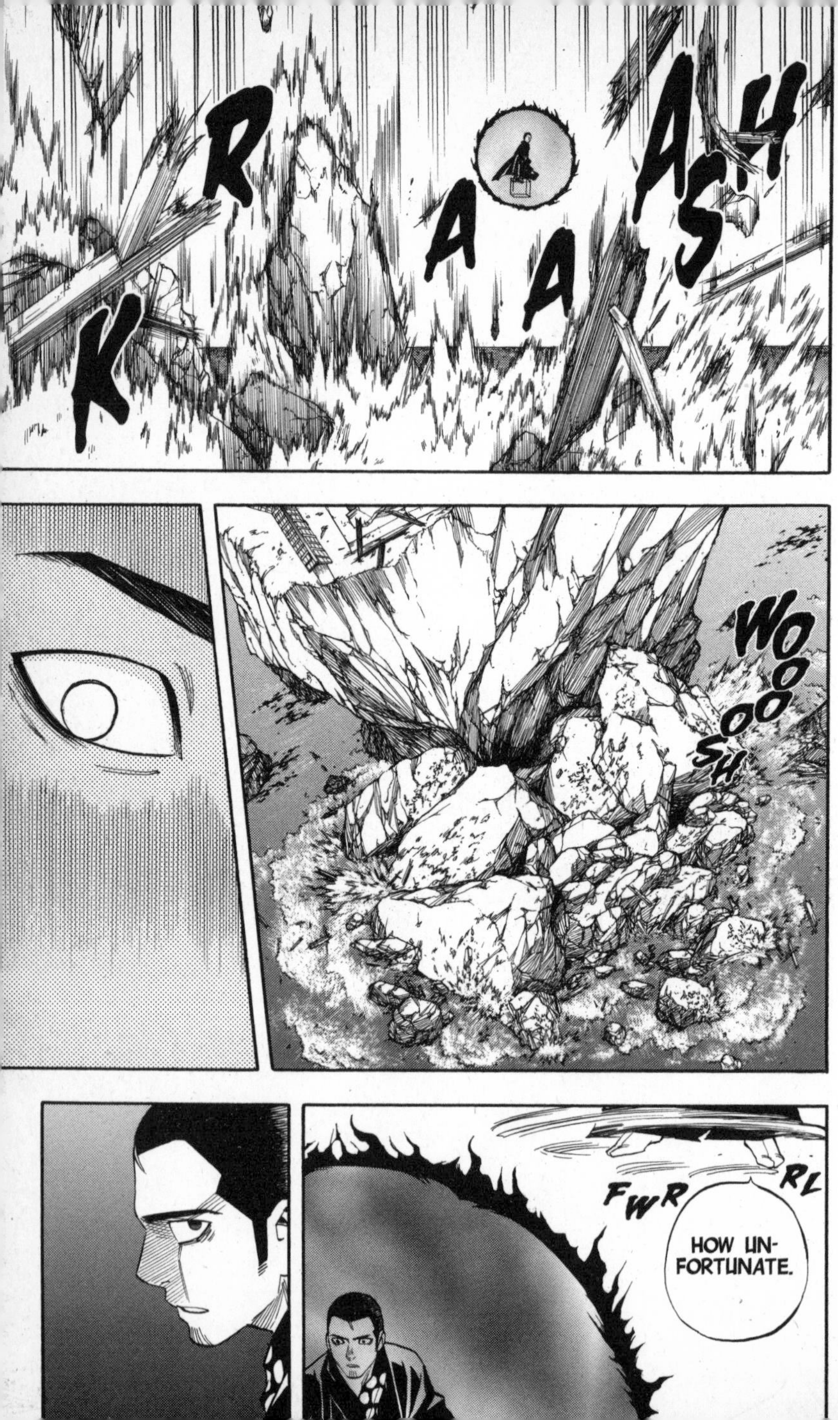
KRAAASH
WOOOOSH
FWRRL
HOW UN-FORTUNATE.

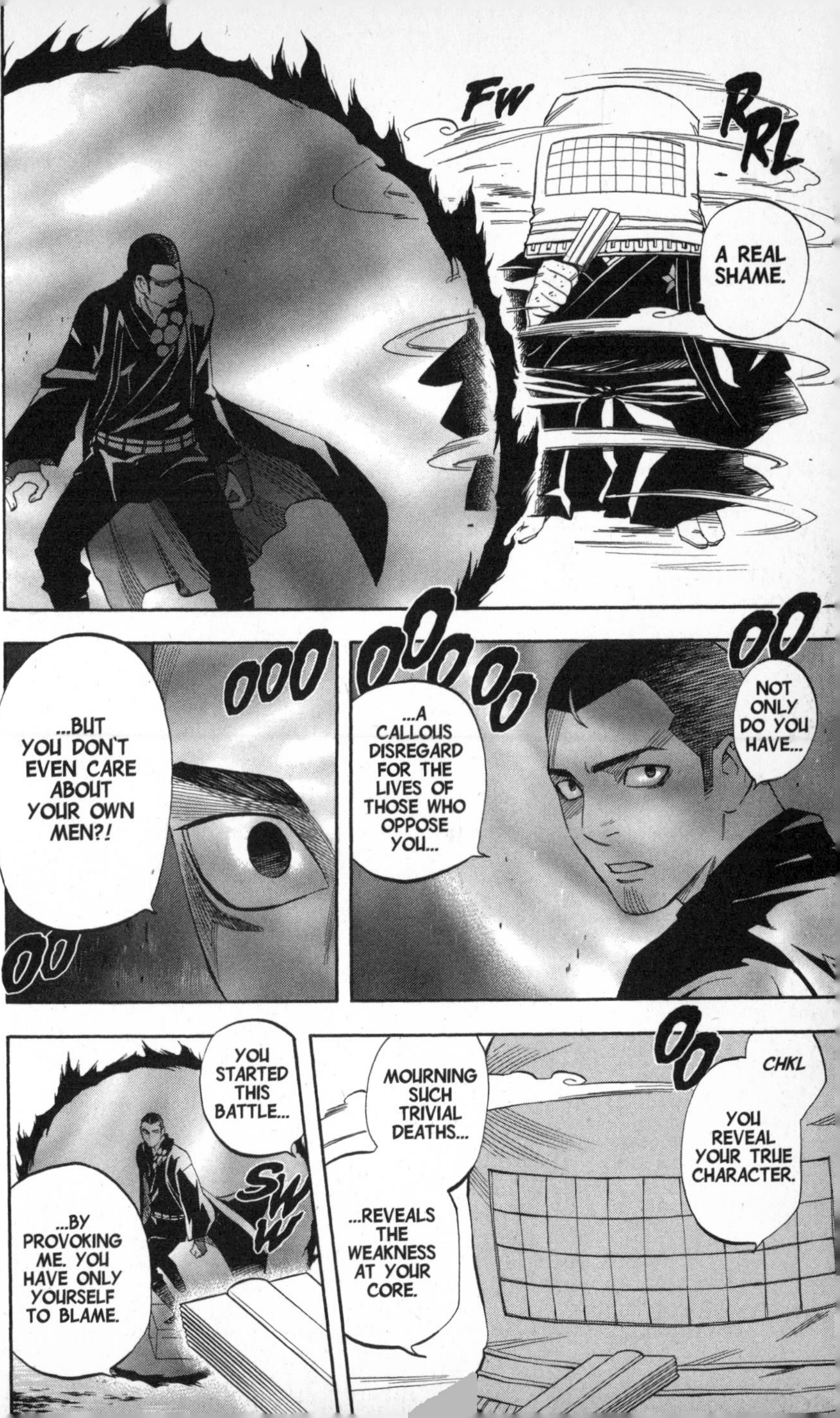
FW
RRL
A REAL SHAME.
OO
NOT ONLY DO YOU HAVE...
OOOOO
...A CALLOUS DISREGARD FOR THE LIVES OF THOSE WHO OPPOSE YOU...
OOO
...BUT YOU DON'T EVEN CARE ABOUT YOUR OWN MEN?!
OO
OO
CHKL
YOU REVEAL YOUR TRUE CHARACTER.
MOURNING SUCH TRIVIAL DEATHS...
...REVEALS THE WEAKNESS AT YOUR CORE.
YOU STARTED THIS BATTLE...
SWW
...BY PROVOKING ME. YOU HAVE ONLY YOURSELF TO BLAME.

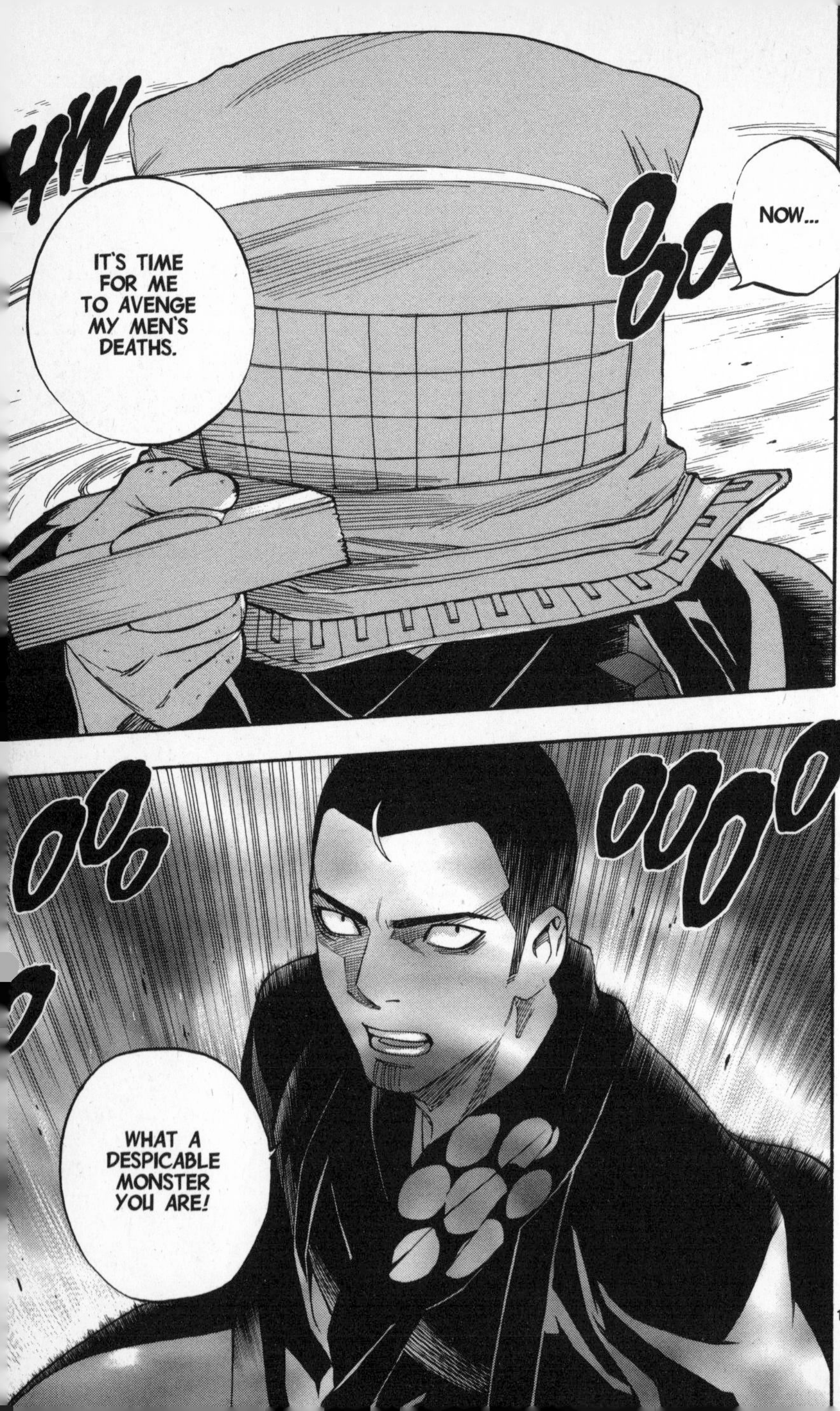
NOW...
IT'S TIME FOR ME TO AVENGE MY MEN'S DEATHS.
WHAT A DESPICABLE MONSTER YOU ARE!

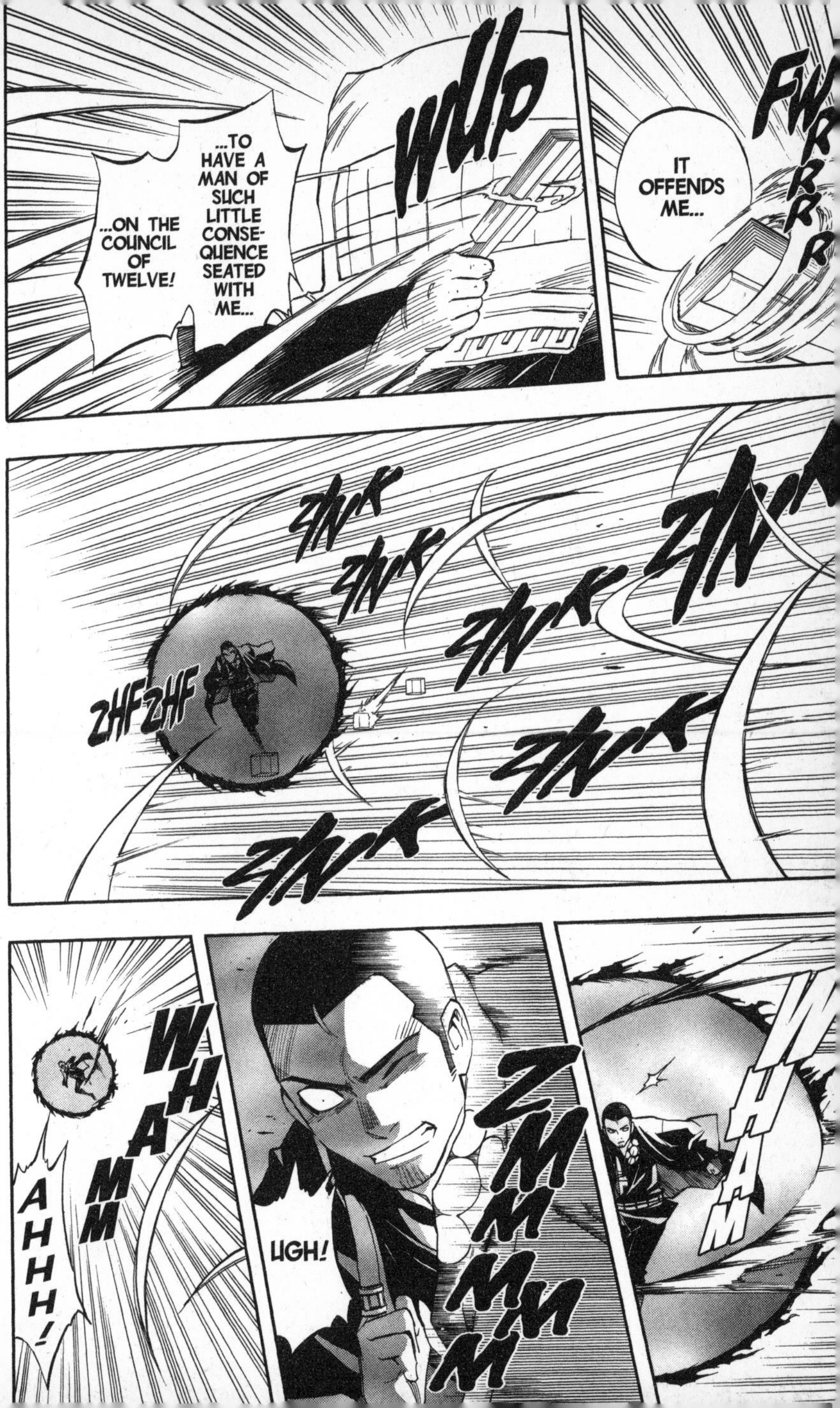
FWRRRR
IT OFFENDS ME...
WUP
...TO HAVE A MAN OF SUCH LITTLE CONSEQUENCE SEATED WITH ME...
...ON THE COUNCIL OF TWELVE!
ZANK
ZANK
ZANK
ZANK
ZANK
ZANK
ZANK
ZHFZHF
WHAM
ZMMMMMMM
UGH!
WHAMM
AHHH!

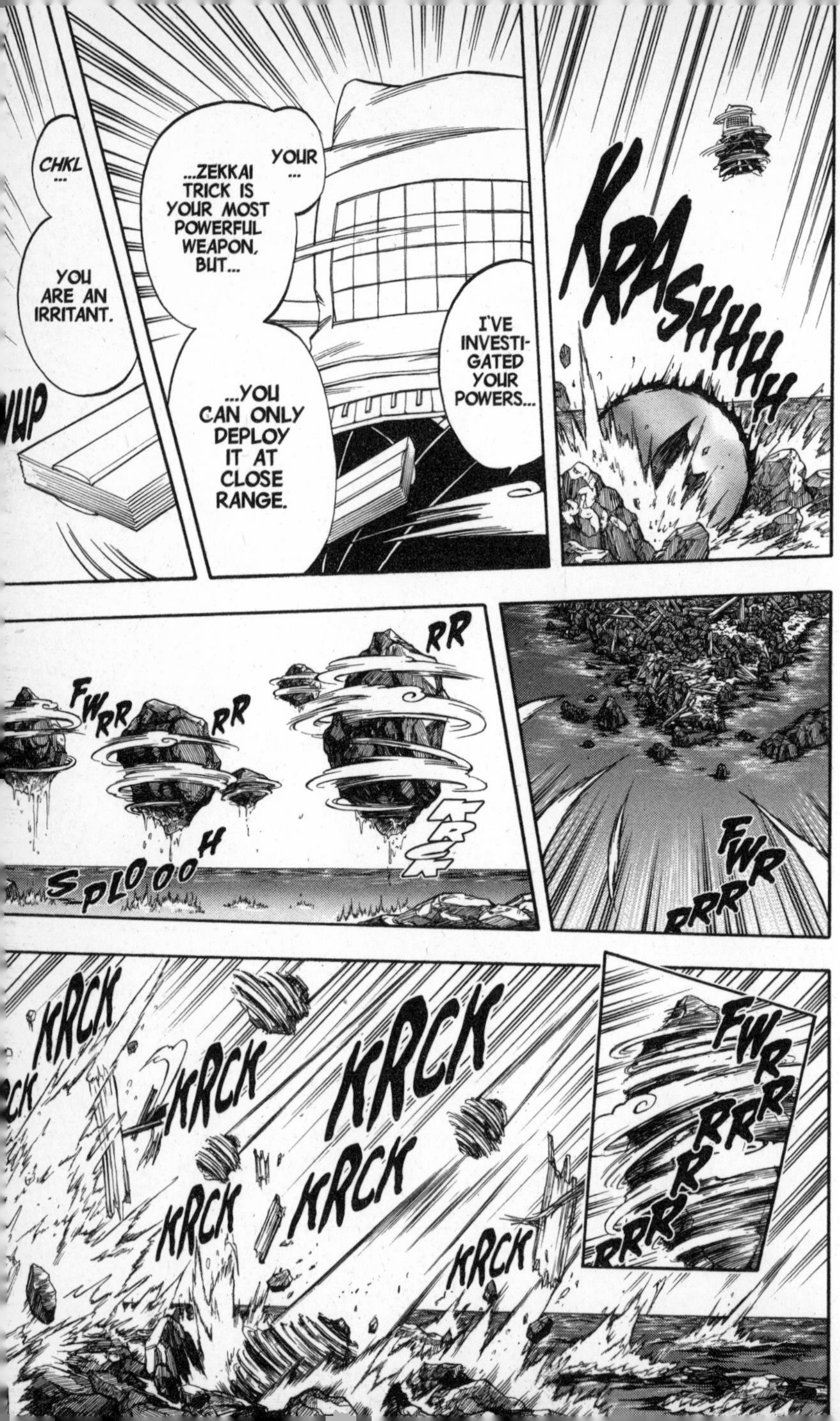
KRASHHHHH
I'VE INVESTIGATED YOUR POWERS...
YOUR ...
...ZEKKAI TRICK IS YOUR MOST POWERFUL WEAPON, BUT...
...YOU CAN ONLY DEPLOY IT AT CLOSE RANGE.
CHKL ...
YOU ARE AN IRRITANT.
WUP
FWRRRRR
RR
FWRR
RR
KRCK
SPLOOOOH
FWRRRRRRR
KRCK
KRCK
KRCK
KRCK
KRCK
KRCK

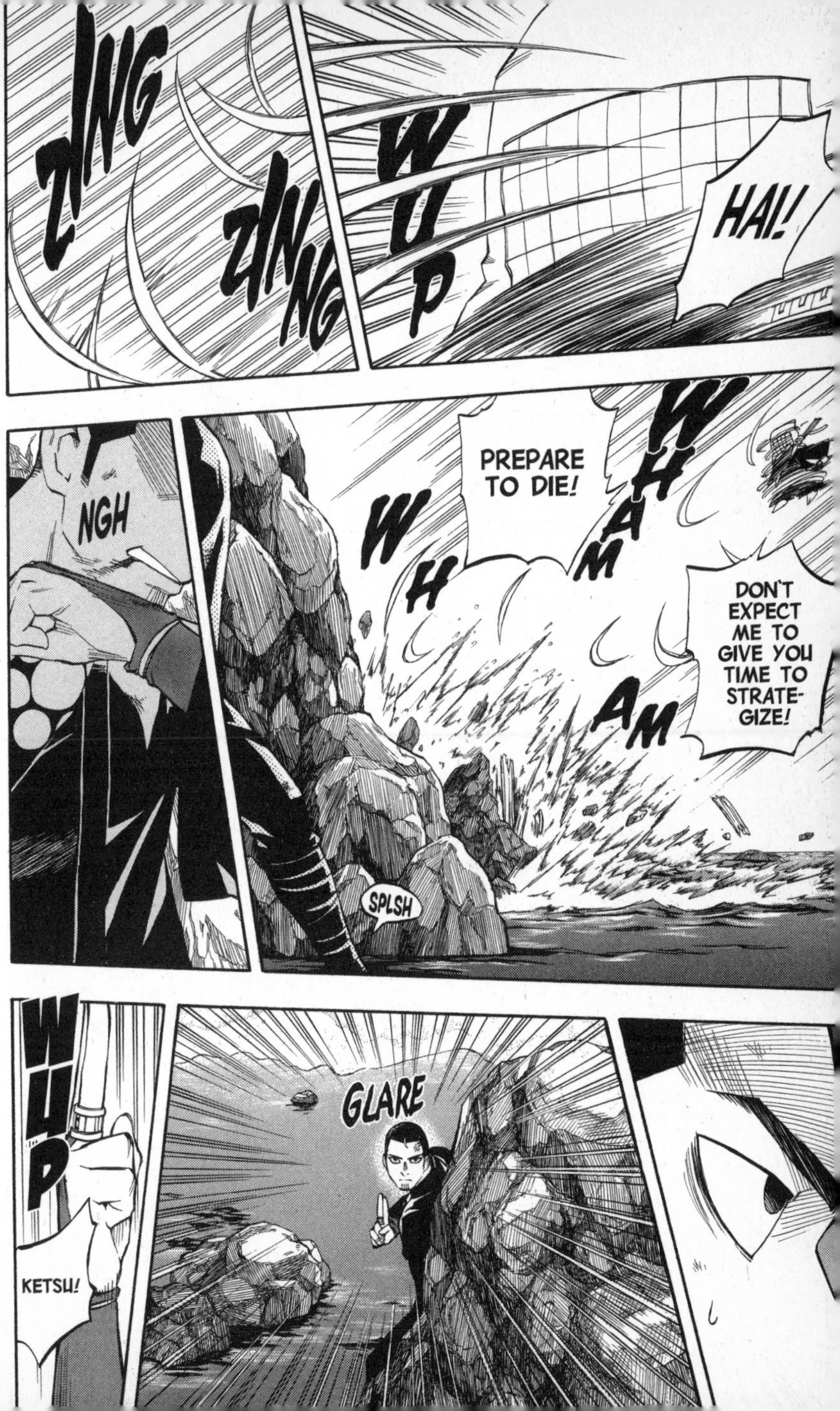
HAI!
WUP
ZING
ZING
WHAM
DON'T EXPECT ME TO GIVE YOU TIME TO STRATE-GIZE!
PREPARE TO DIE!
WHAM
SPLSH
NGH
GLARE
WUP
KETSU!

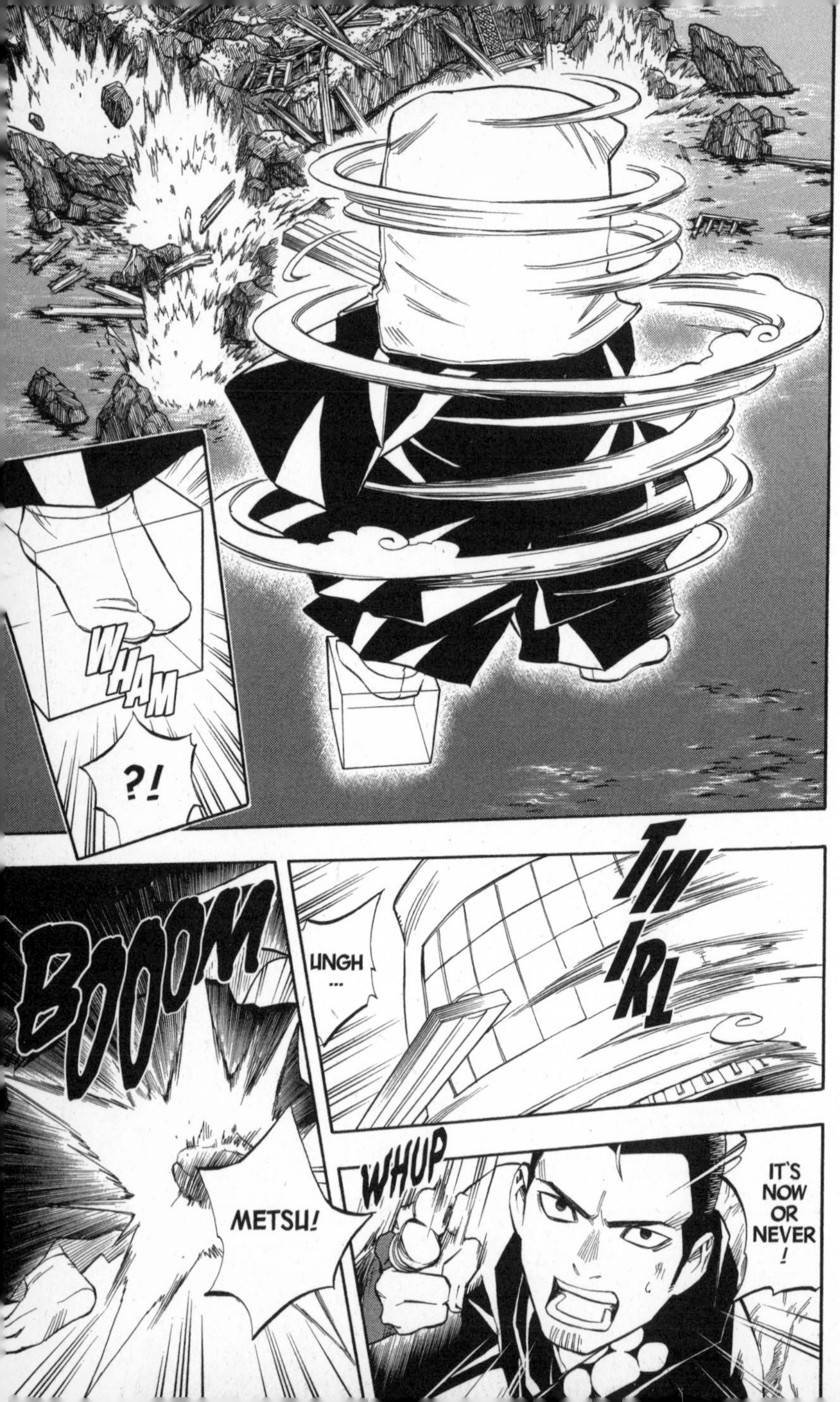
WHAM
?!
TWIRL
UNGH...
IT'S NOW OR NEVER!
WHUP
BOOOM
METSU!

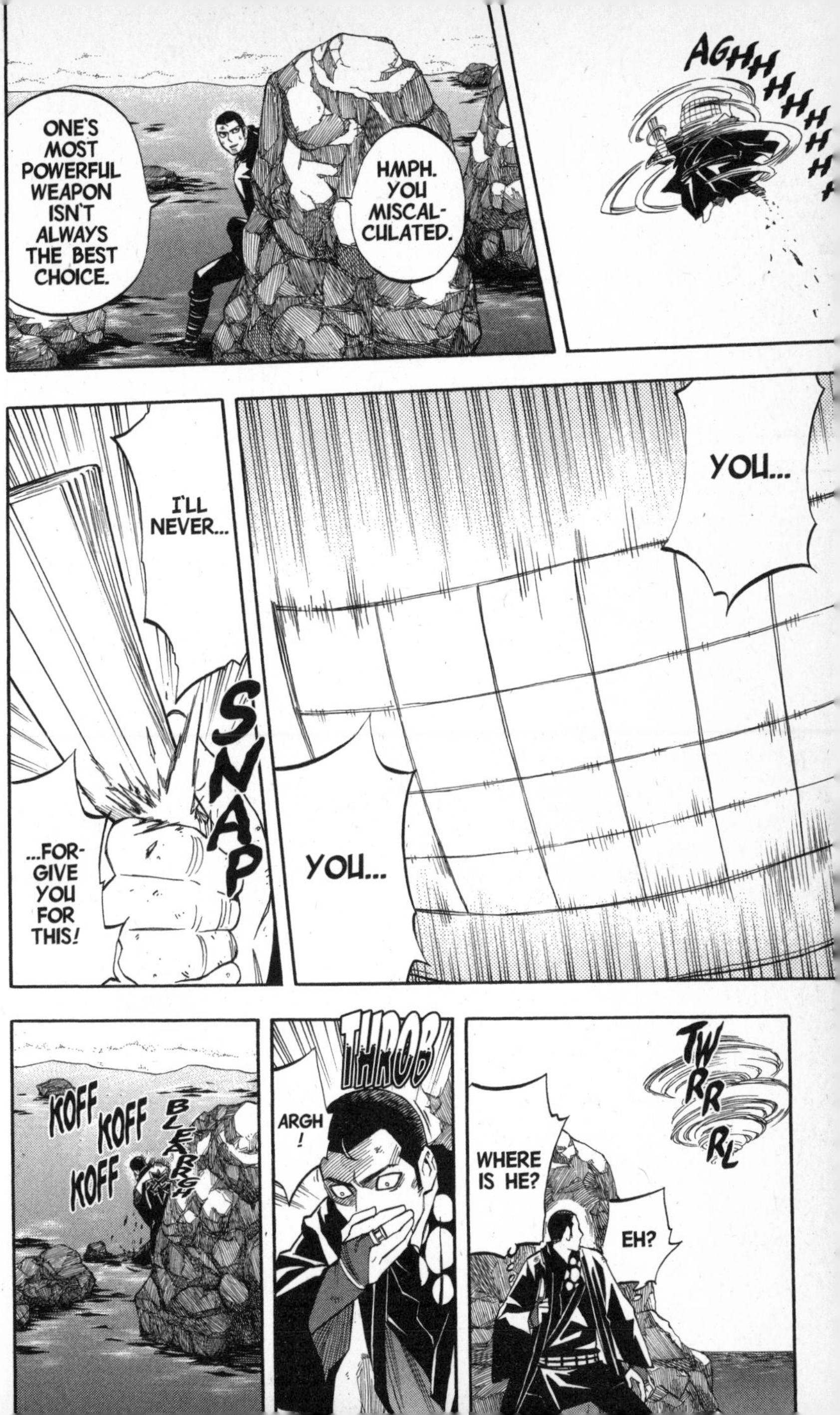
AGHHHHHHHH
HMPH. YOU MISCAL-CULATED.
ONE'S MOST POWERFUL WEAPON ISN'T ALWAYS THE BEST CHOICE.
YOU...
YOU...
I'LL NEVER...
SNAP
...FOR-GIVE YOU FOR THIS!
TWRRRL
WHERE IS HE?
EH?
THROB
ARGH!
KOFF KOFF KOFF
BLEARRGH

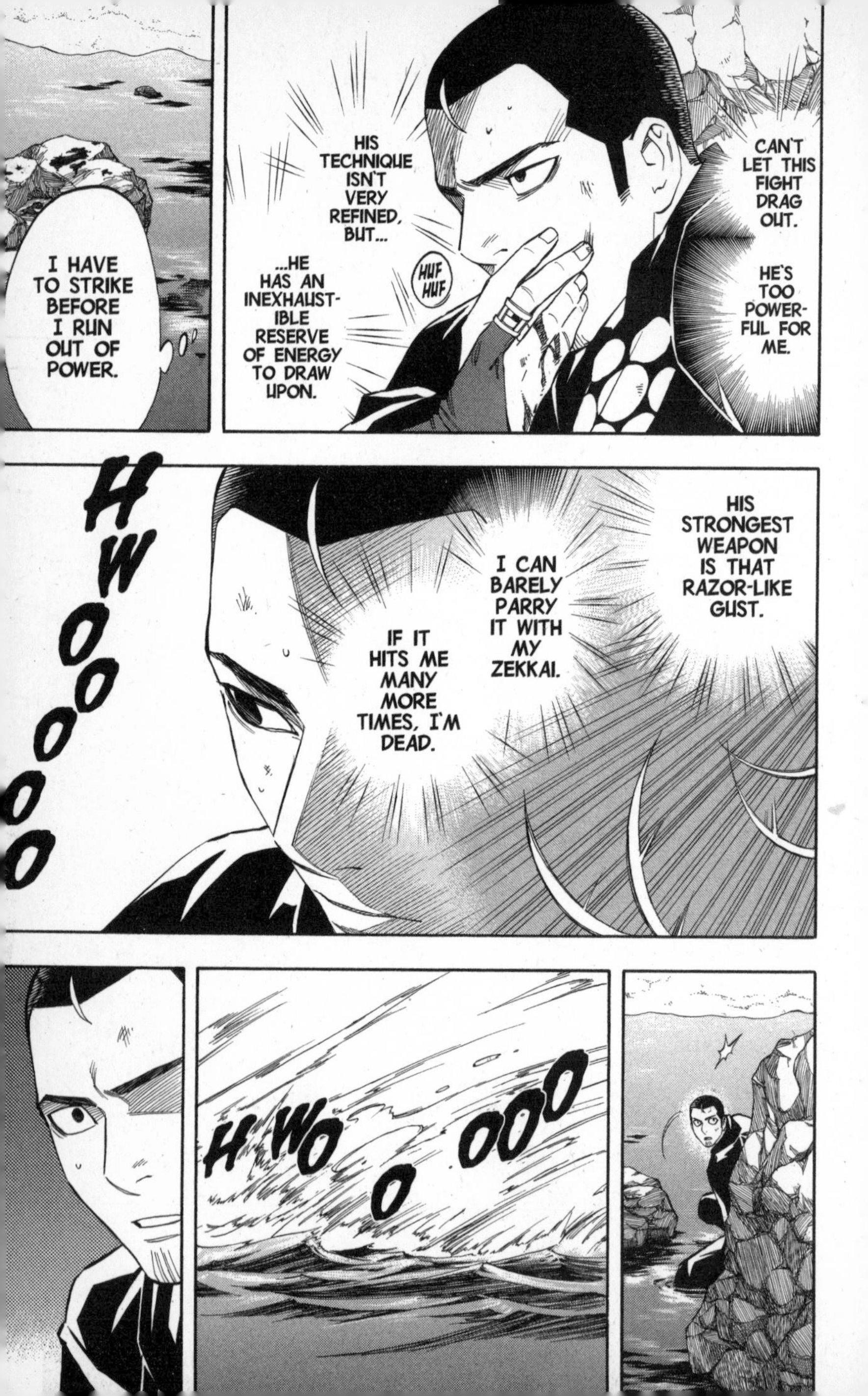
CAN'T LET THIS FIGHT DRAG OUT.
HE'S TOO POWER-FUL FOR ME.
HIS TECHNIQUE ISN'T VERY REFINED, BUT...
HUF HUF
...HE HAS AN INEXHAUST-IBLE RESERVE OF ENERGY TO DRAW UPON.
I HAVE TO STRIKE BEFORE I RUN OUT OF POWER.
HIS STRONGEST WEAPON IS THAT RAZOR-LIKE GUST.
I CAN BARELY PARRY IT WITH MY ZEKKAI.
IF IT HITS ME MANY MORE TIMES, I'M DEAD.
HWOOOOOO
HWOOOOO

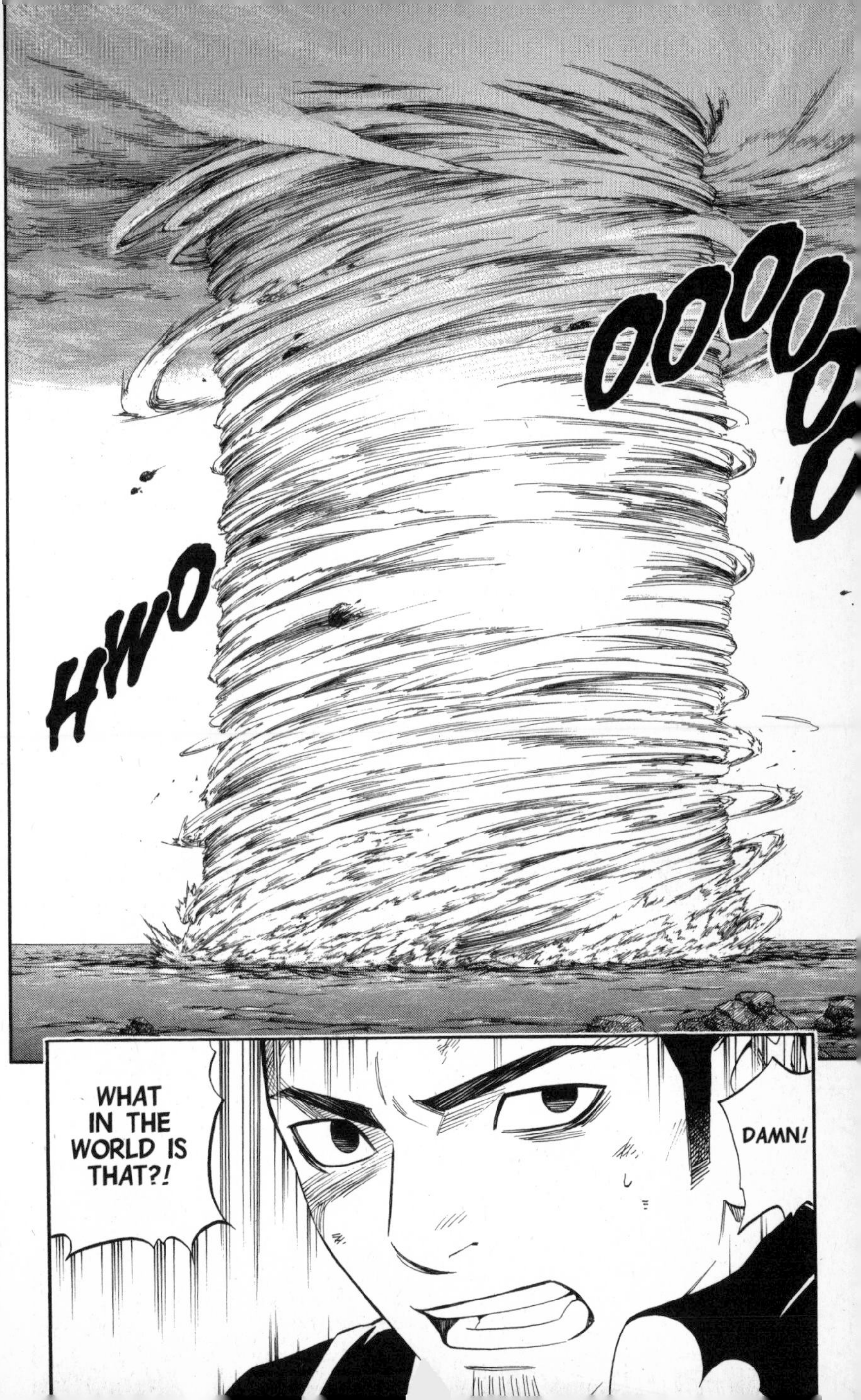
HWO
OOOOOO
DAMN!
WHAT IN THE WORLD IS THAT?!

Chapter 190: Giant Tornado

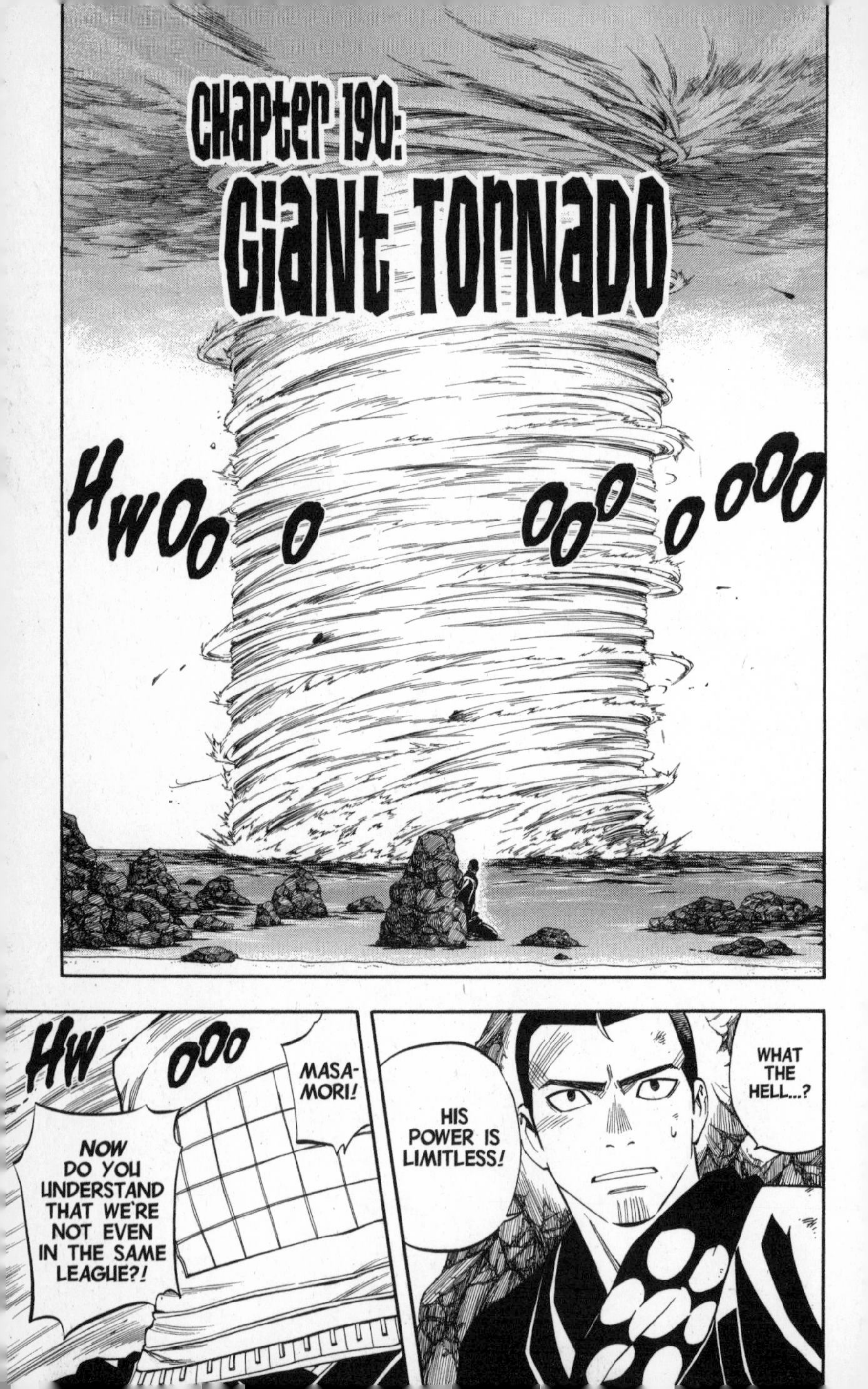
HWOOO OOOO OOOO
WHAT THE HELL...?
HIS POWER IS LIMITLESS!
MASA-MORI!
NOW DO YOU UNDERSTAND THAT WE'RE NOT EVEN IN THE SAME LEAGUE?!
HWOOO

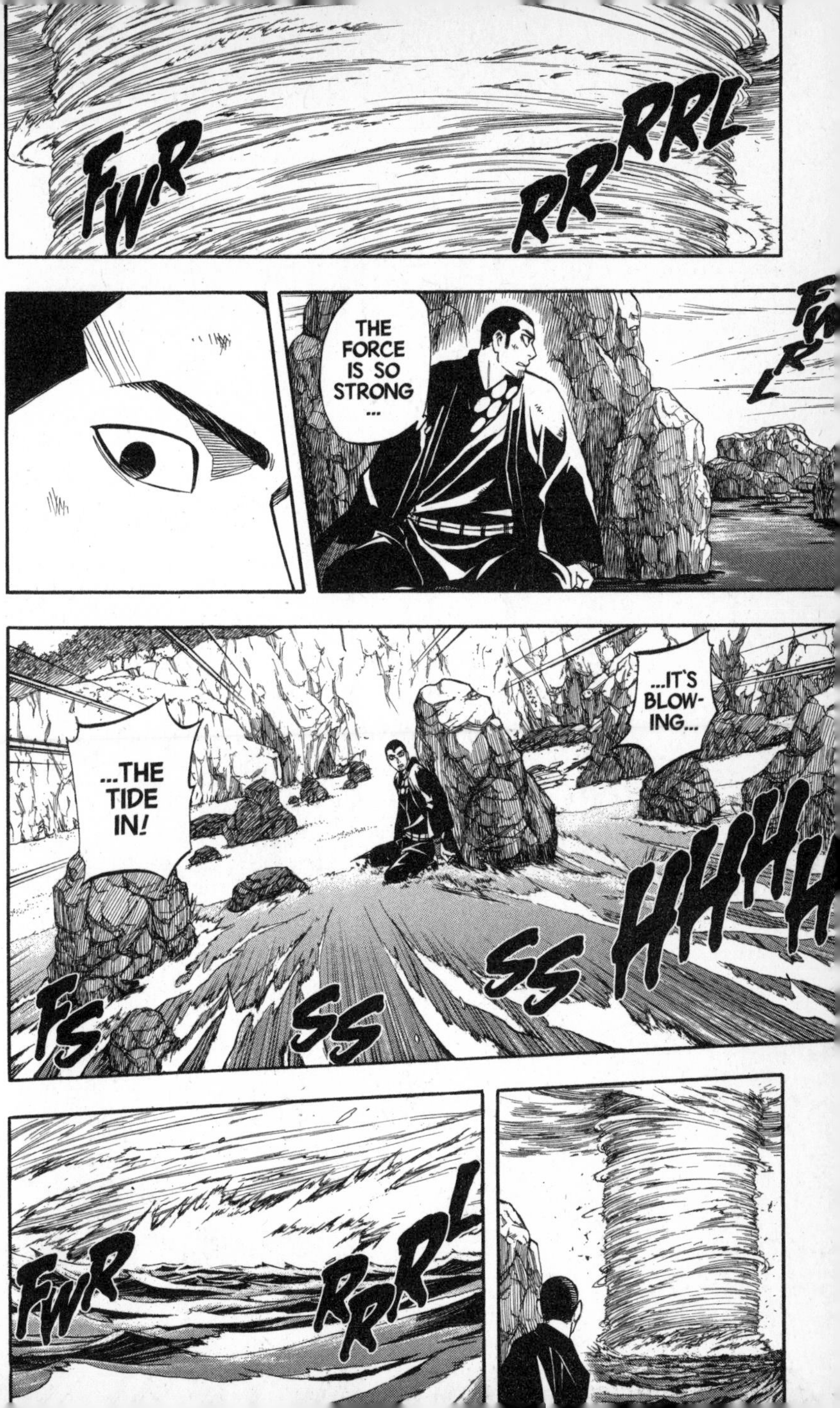
FWR
RRRRRL
FWRRL
THE FORCE IS SO STRONG...
...IT'S BLOWING...
...THE TIDE IN!
FSSSSSHHHHH
FWR
RRRL

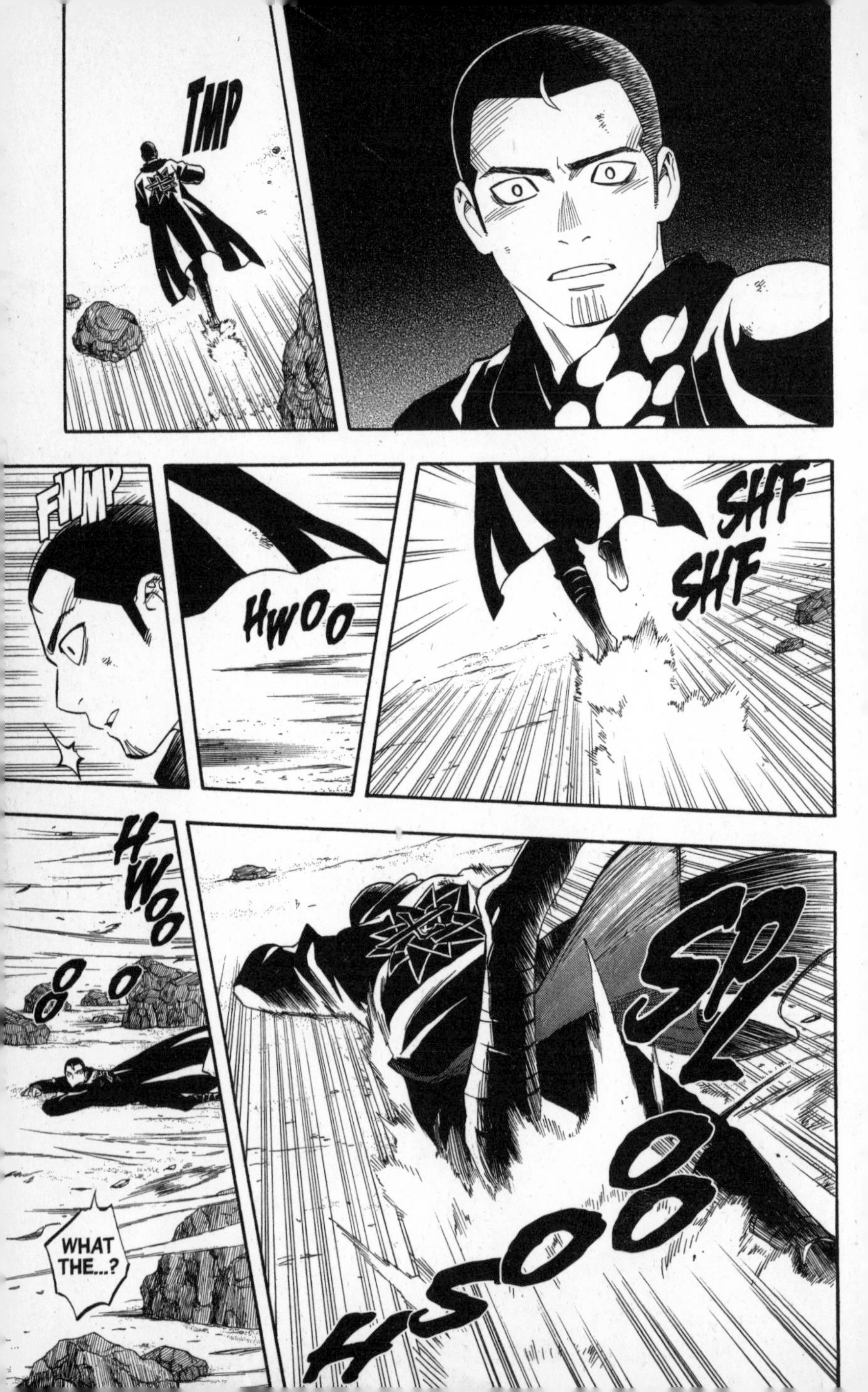
TMP
SHF
SHF
HWOO
FWMP
SP
HSOOO
HWOOOOO
WHAT THE...?

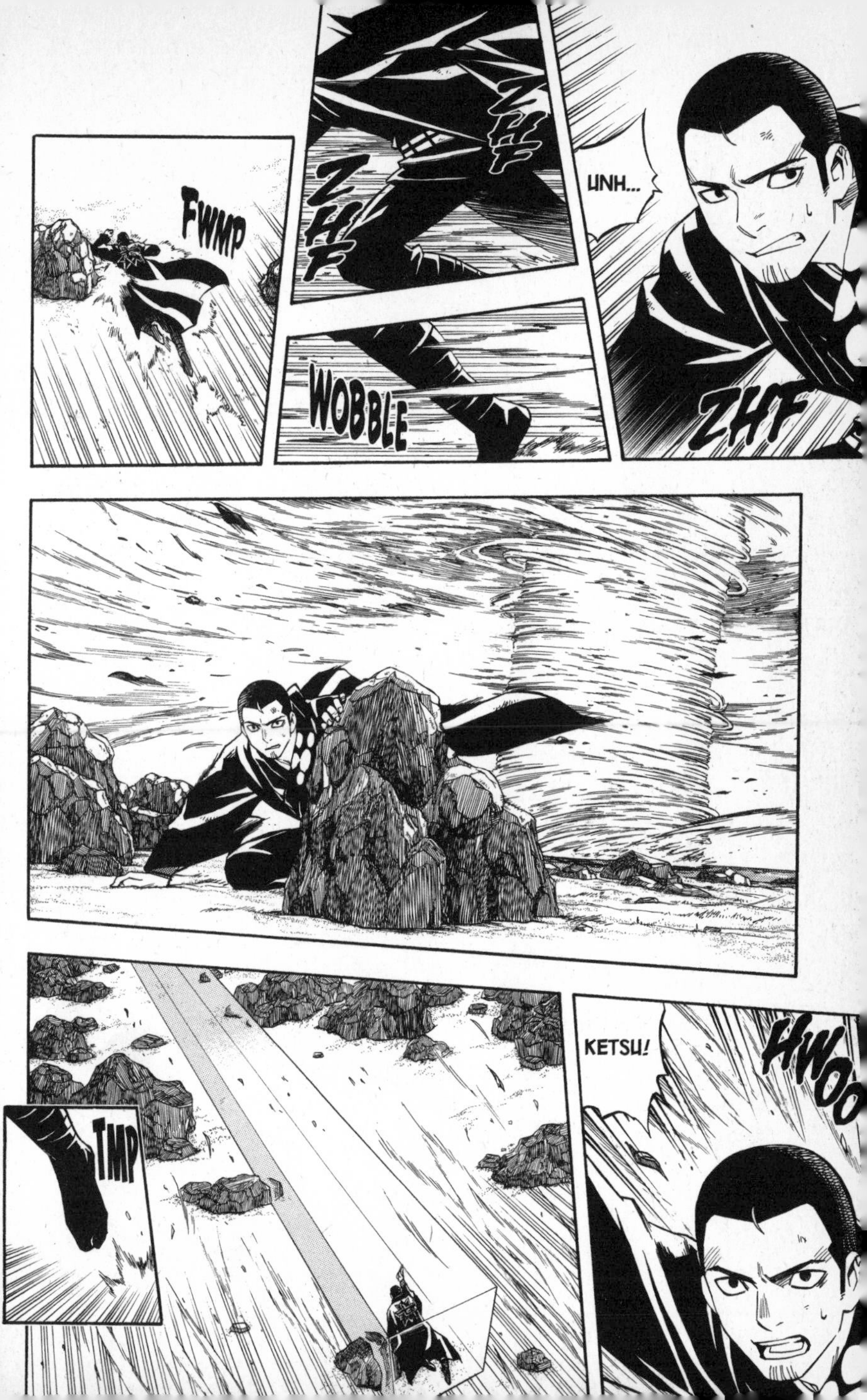

UNH...
ZHF
ZHF
ZHF
WOBBLE
FWMP
KETSU!
HWOO
TMP

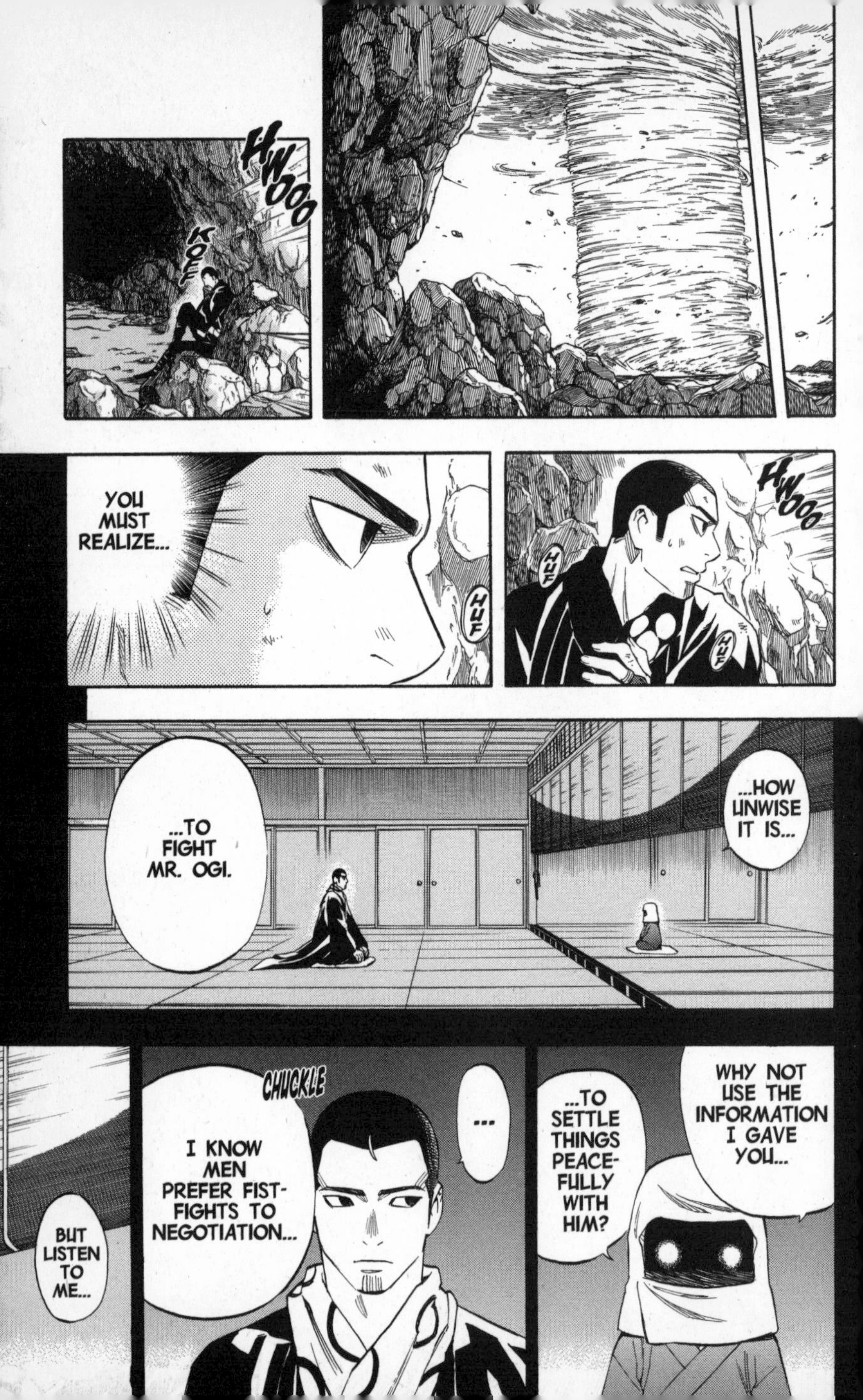
HWOOO
KOFF
HWOOO
HUF
HUF
HUF
YOU MUST REALIZE...
...HOW UNWISE IT IS...
...TO FIGHT MR. OGI.
WHY NOT USE THE INFORMATION I GAVE YOU...
...TO SETTLE THINGS PEACE-FULLY WITH HIM?
...
CHUCKLE
I KNOW MEN PREFER FIST-FIGHTS TO NEGOTIATION...
BUT LISTEN TO ME...

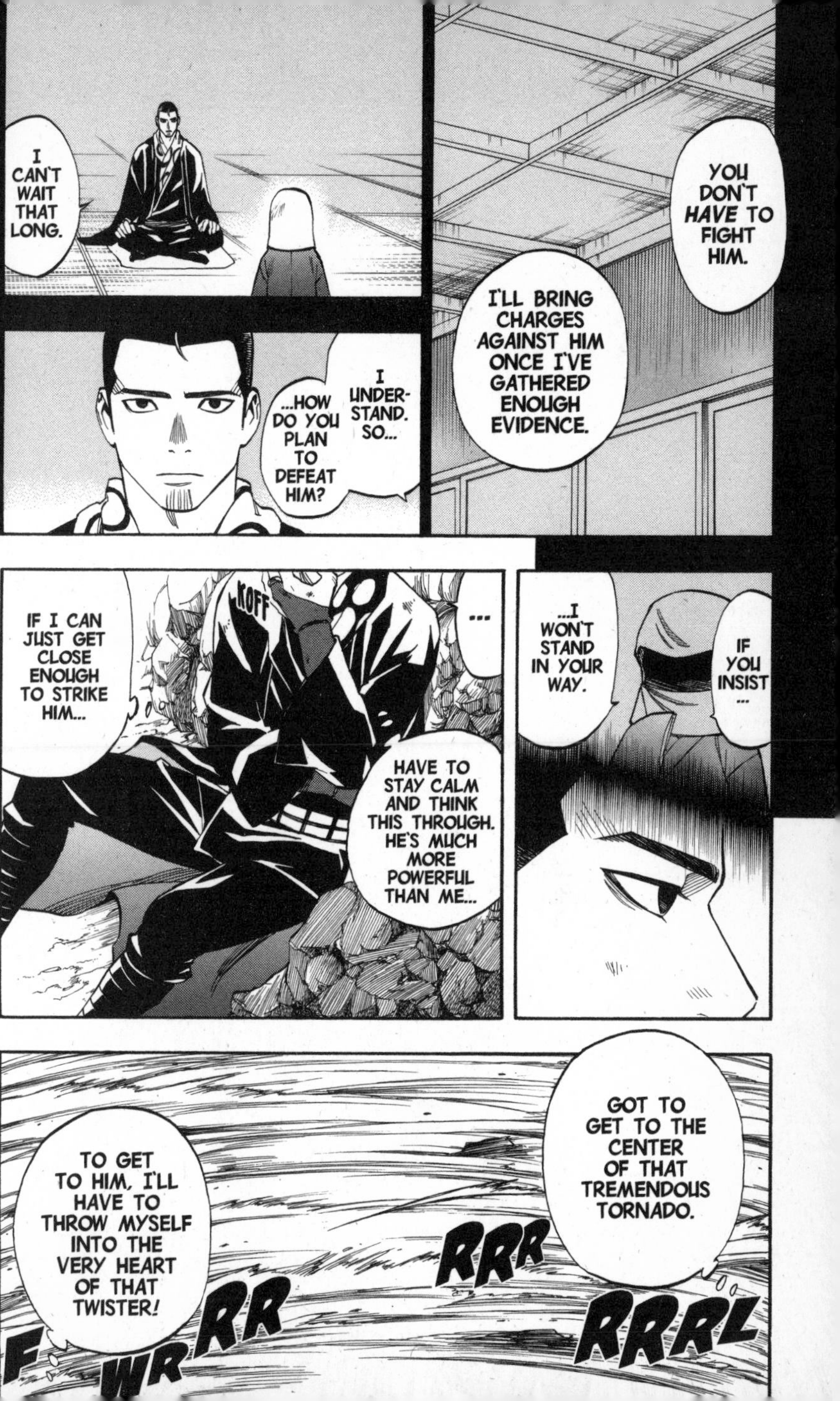
YOU DON'T *HAVE* TO FIGHT HIM.
I'LL BRING CHARGES AGAINST HIM ONCE I'VE GATHERED ENOUGH EVIDENCE.
I CAN'T WAIT THAT LONG.
I UNDERSTAND. SO...
...HOW DO YOU PLAN TO DEFEAT HIM?
IF YOU INSIST...
...I WON'T STAND IN YOUR WAY.
...
KOFF
IF I CAN JUST GET CLOSE ENOUGH TO STRIKE HIM...
HAVE TO STAY CALM AND THINK THIS THROUGH. HE'S MUCH MORE POWERFUL THAN ME...
GOT TO GET TO THE CENTER OF THAT TREMENDOUS TORNADO.
RRR
RRRL
TO GET TO HIM, I'LL HAVE TO THROW MYSELF INTO THE VERY HEART OF THAT TWISTER!
F WRRR

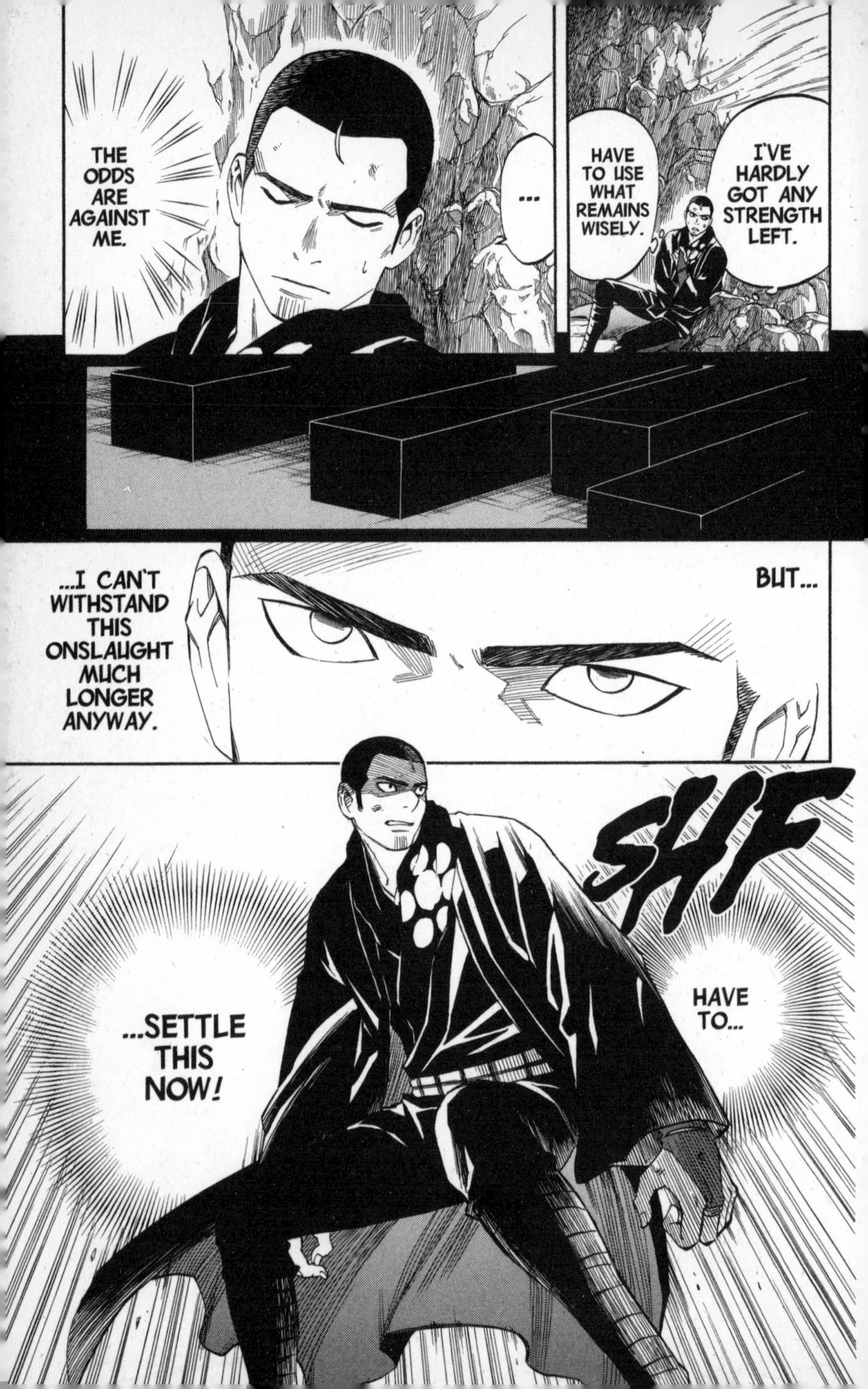
I'VE HARDLY GOT ANY STRENGTH LEFT.
HAVE TO USE WHAT REMAINS WISELY.
...
THE ODDS ARE AGAINST ME.
BUT...
...I CAN'T WITHSTAND THIS ONSLAUGHT MUCH LONGER ANYWAY.
SHF
HAVE TO...
...SETTLE THIS NOW!

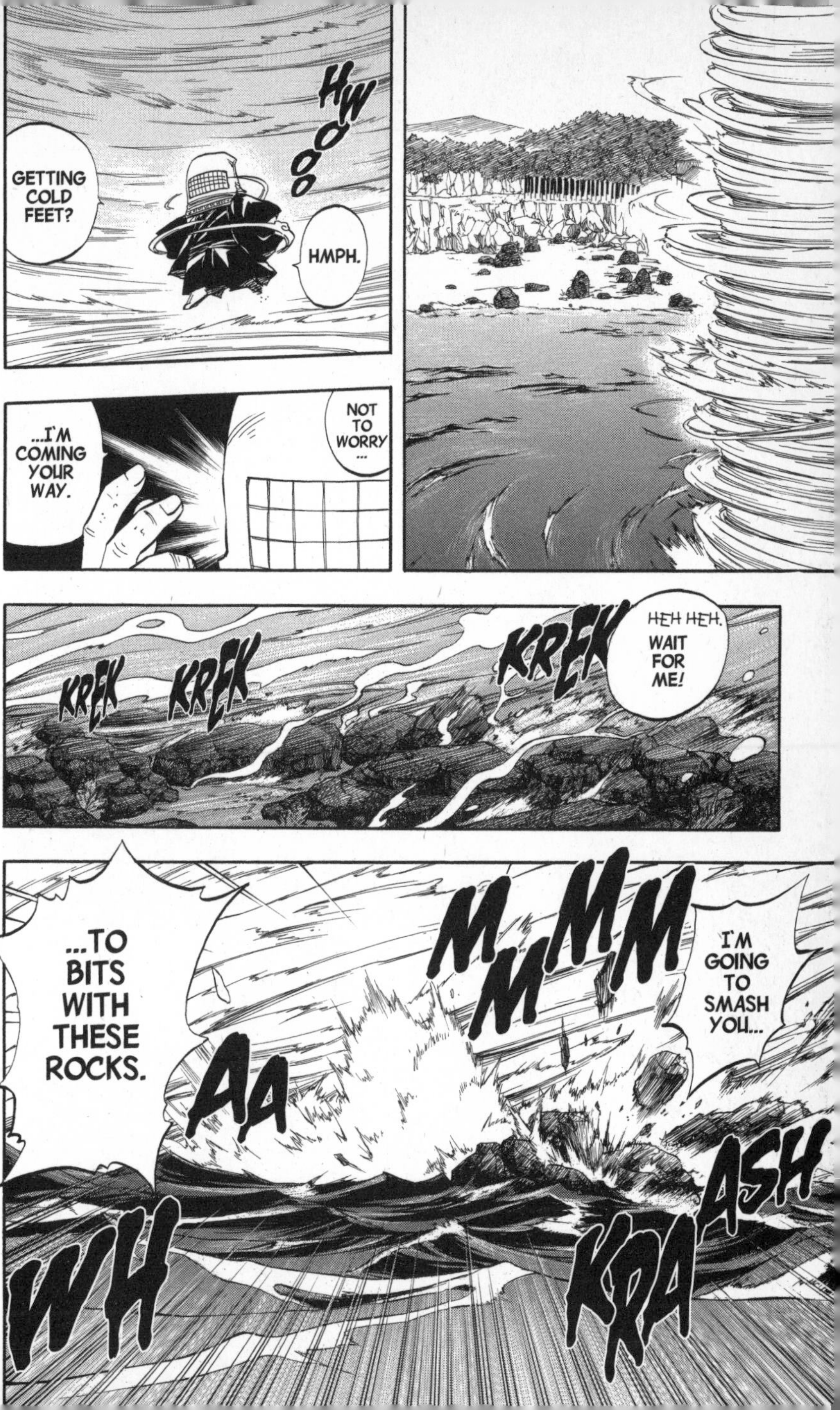
HWOOOO
GETTING COLD FEET?
HMPH.
NOT TO WORRY...
...I'M COMING YOUR WAY.
HEH HEH. WAIT FOR ME!
KREK
KREK
KREK
I'M GOING TO SMASH YOU...
MMMM
...TO BITS WITH THESE ROCKS.
AA
KRAASH
WH

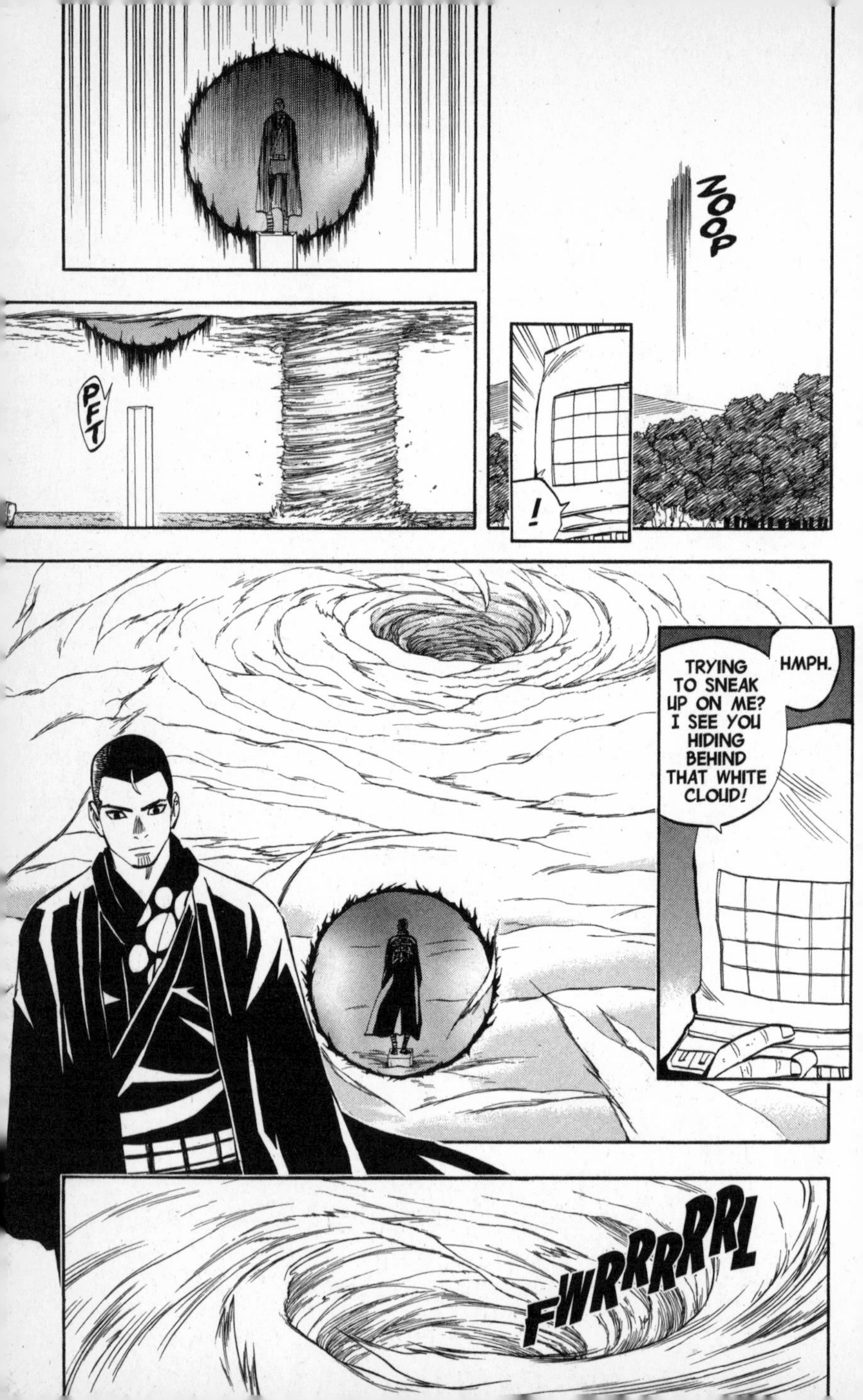
ZOOP
!
PFT
HMPH.
TRYING TO SNEAK UP ON ME? I SEE YOU HIDING BEHIND THAT WHITE CLOUD!
FWRRRRRL

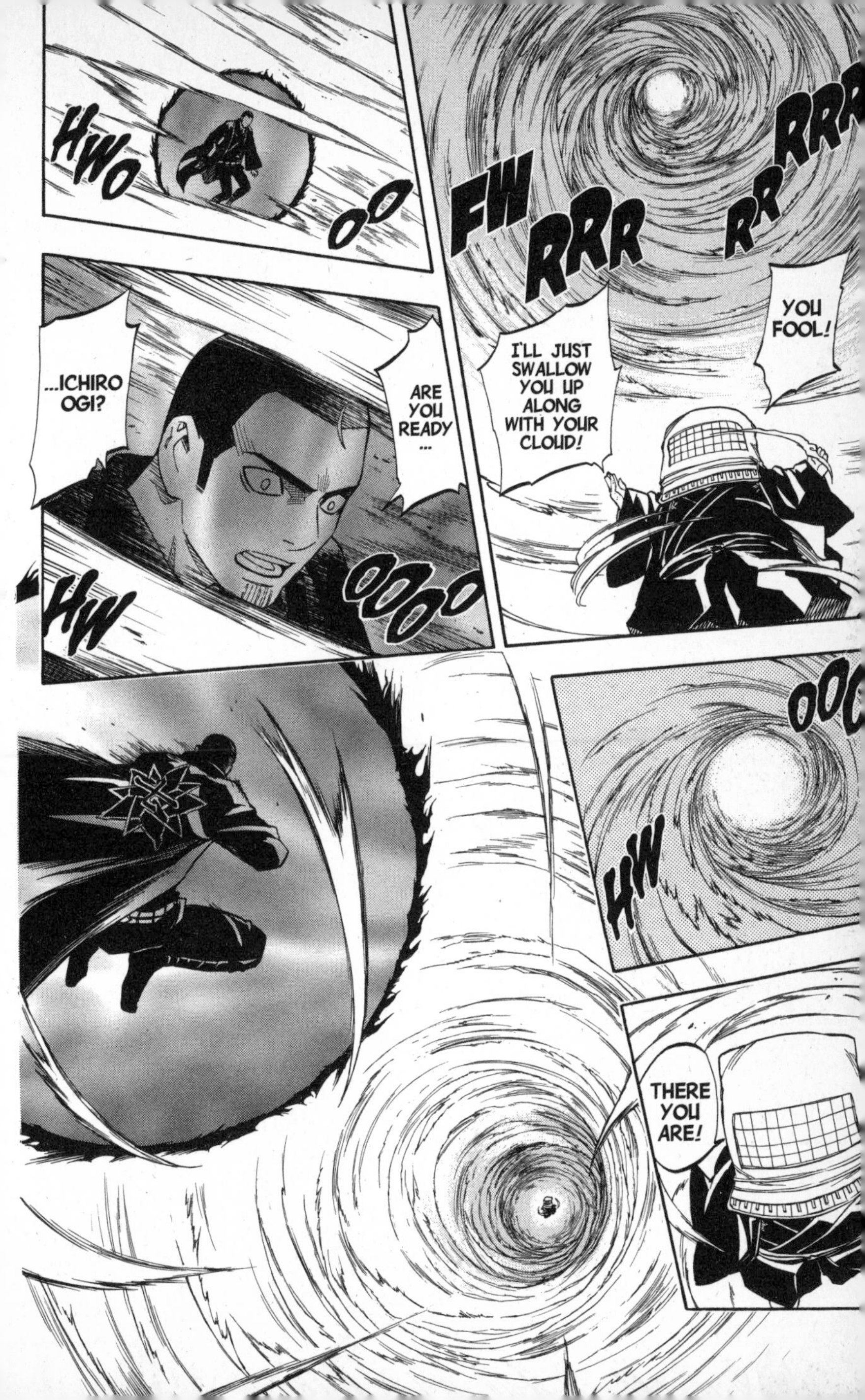
FWRRR
RRRRRR
YOU FOOL!
I'LL JUST SWALLOW YOU UP ALONG WITH YOUR CLOUD!
HWOOO
ARE YOU READY...
...ICHIRO OGI?
HWOOOOO
HWOOO
THERE YOU ARE!

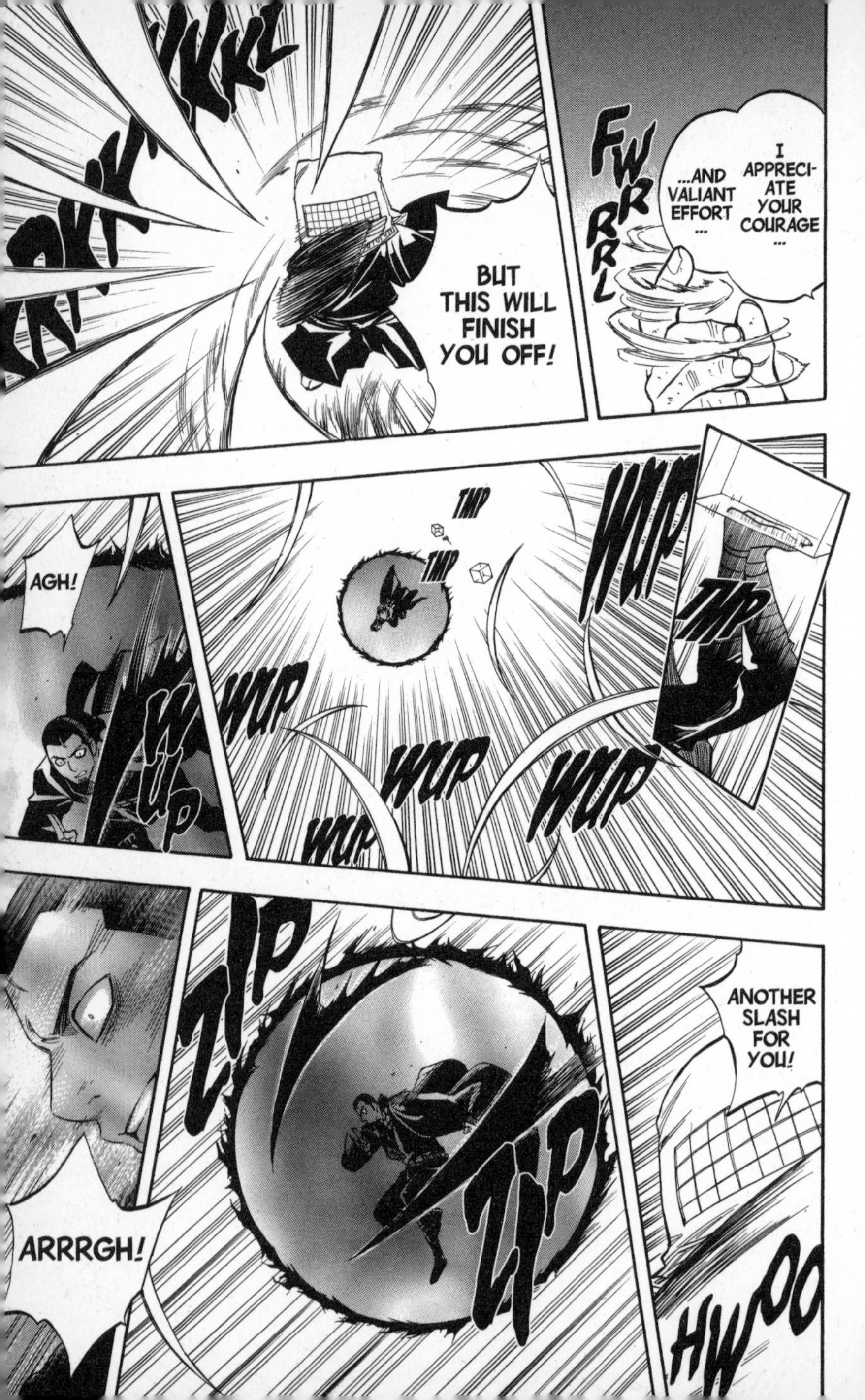
I APPRECI-ATE YOUR COURAGE...
...AND VALIANT EFFORT...
FWRRRL
BUT THIS WILL FINISH YOU OFF!
WUP
TMP
TMP
TMP
WUP
WUP
WUP
WUP
AGH!
WUP
ANOTHER SLASH FOR YOU!
HWOO
ZIP
ZIP
ARRRGH!

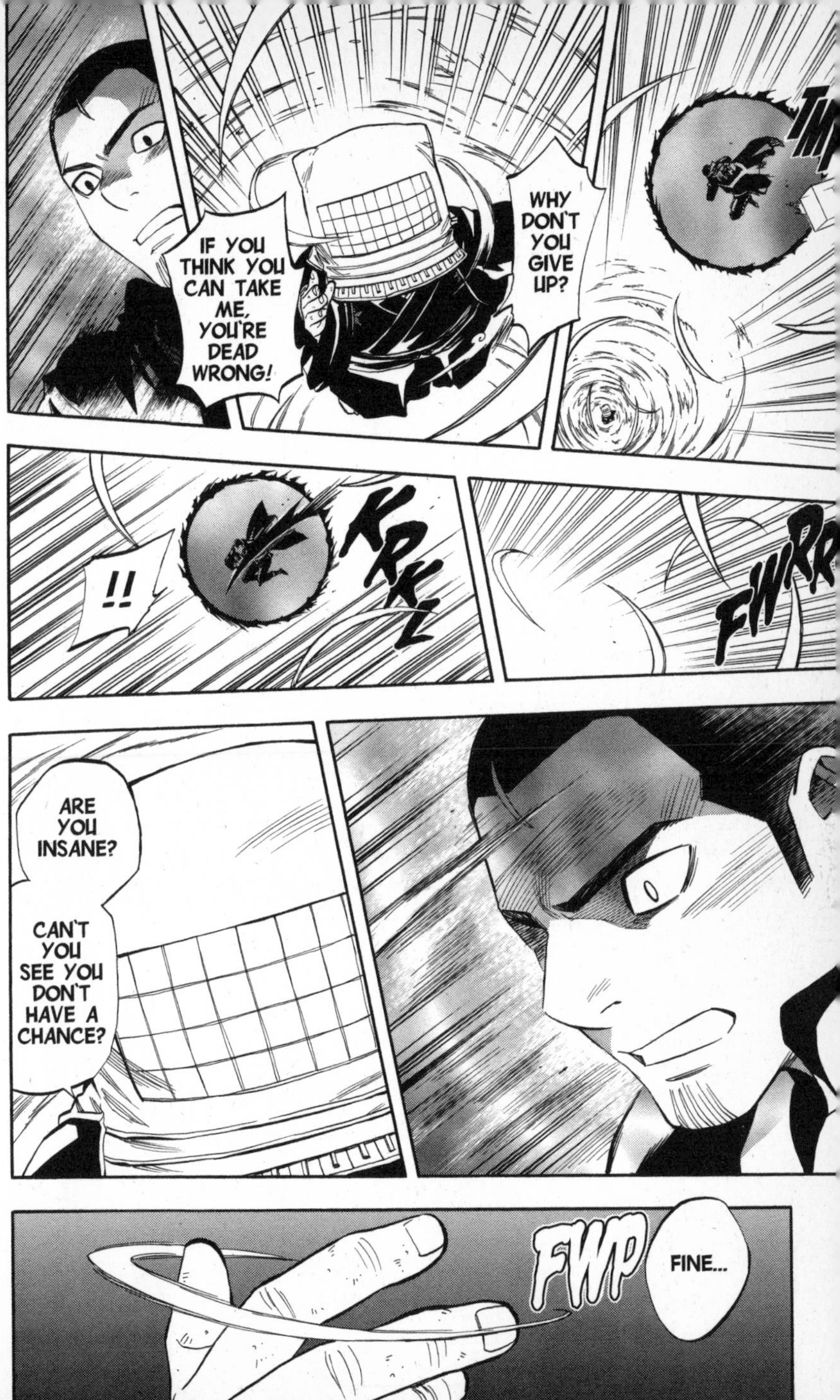
WHY DON'T YOU GIVE UP?
IF YOU THINK YOU CAN TAKE ME, YOU'RE DEAD WRONG!
KRKL
!!
ARE YOU INSANE?
CAN'T YOU SEE YOU DON'T HAVE A CHANCE?
FWP
FINE...

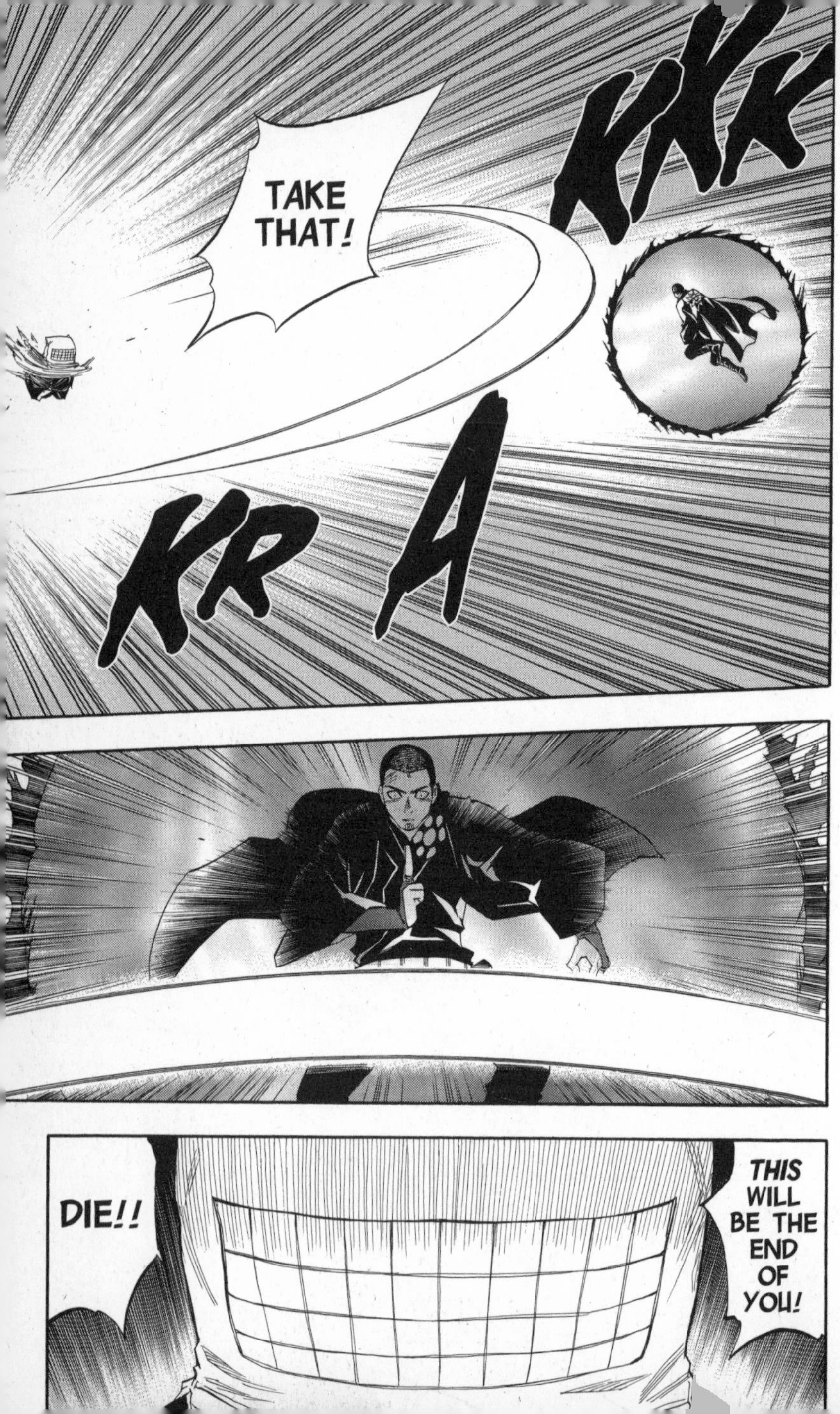
TAKE THAT!
THIS WILL BE THE END OF YOU!
DIE!!

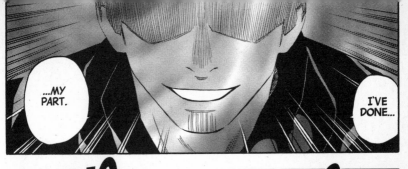

...MY PART.

I'VE DONE...

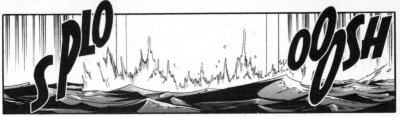

SPLO

OOSH

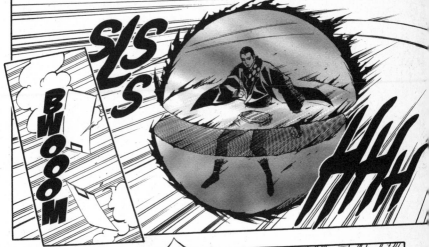

SISS

BWOOM

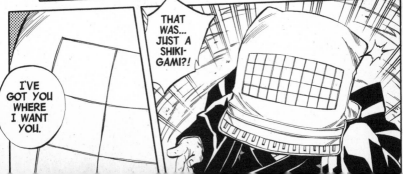

THAT WAS... JUST A SHIKI-GAMI?!

I'VE GOT YOU WHERE I WANT YOU.

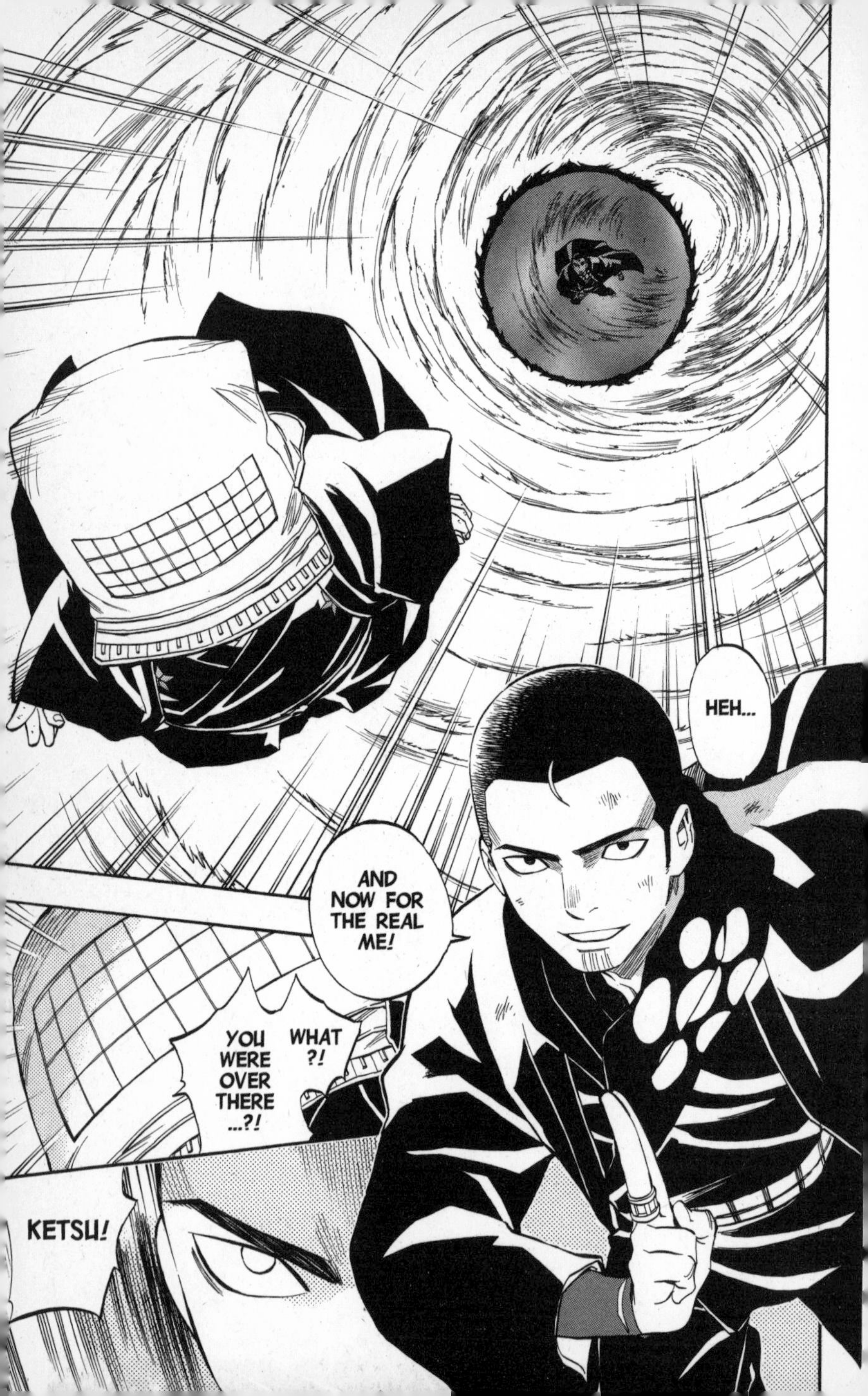
HEH...
AND NOW FOR THE REAL ME!
WHAT ?!
YOU WERE OVER THERE ...?!
KETSU!

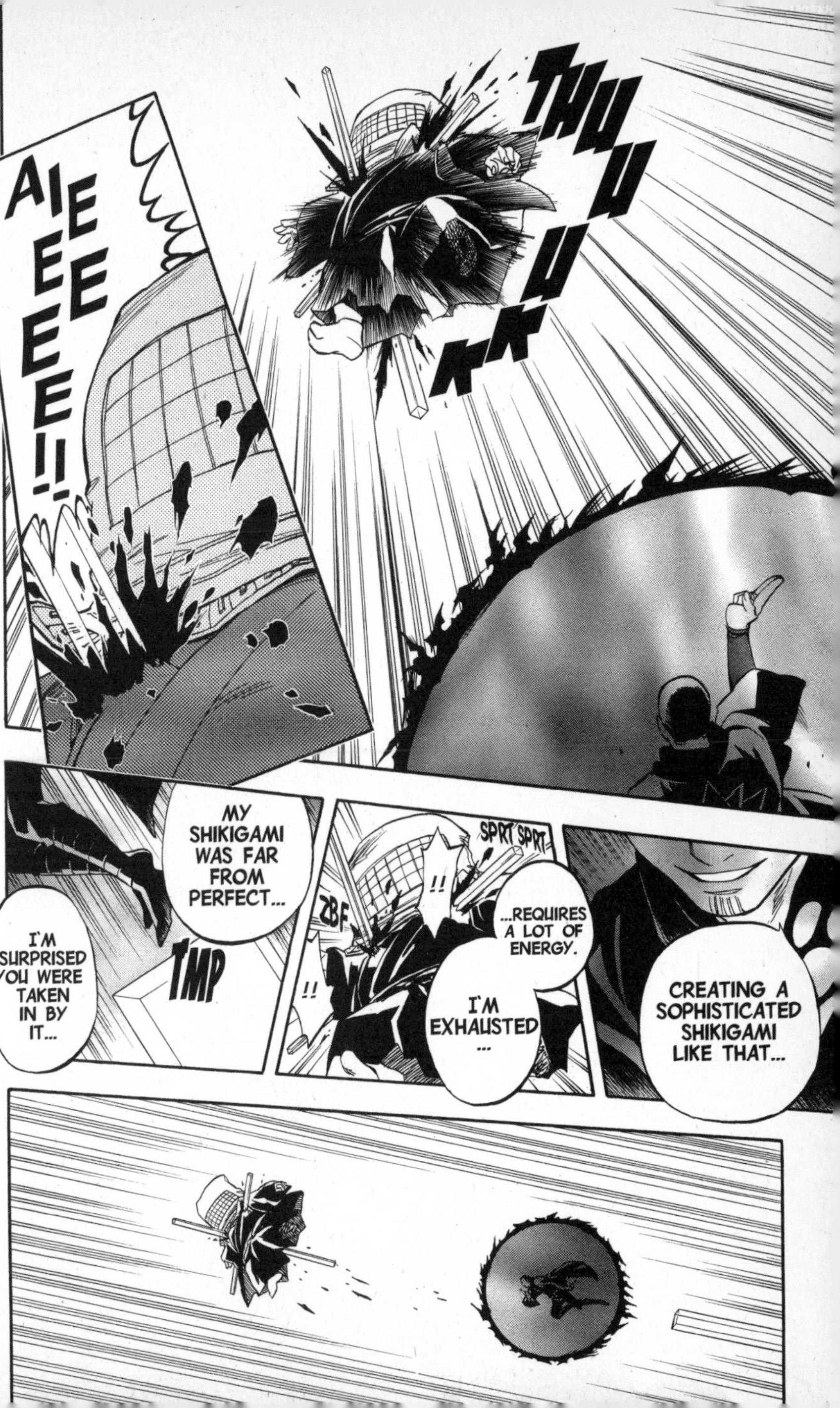
THUUUKK
AIEEEEE!!
CREATING A SOPHISTICATED SHIKIGAMI LIKE THAT...
SPRT SPRT
...REQUIRES A LOT OF ENERGY.
!!
ZBF
!!
I'M EXHAUSTED...
MY SHIKIGAMI WAS FAR FROM PERFECT...
TMP
I'M SURPRISED YOU WERE TAKEN IN BY IT...

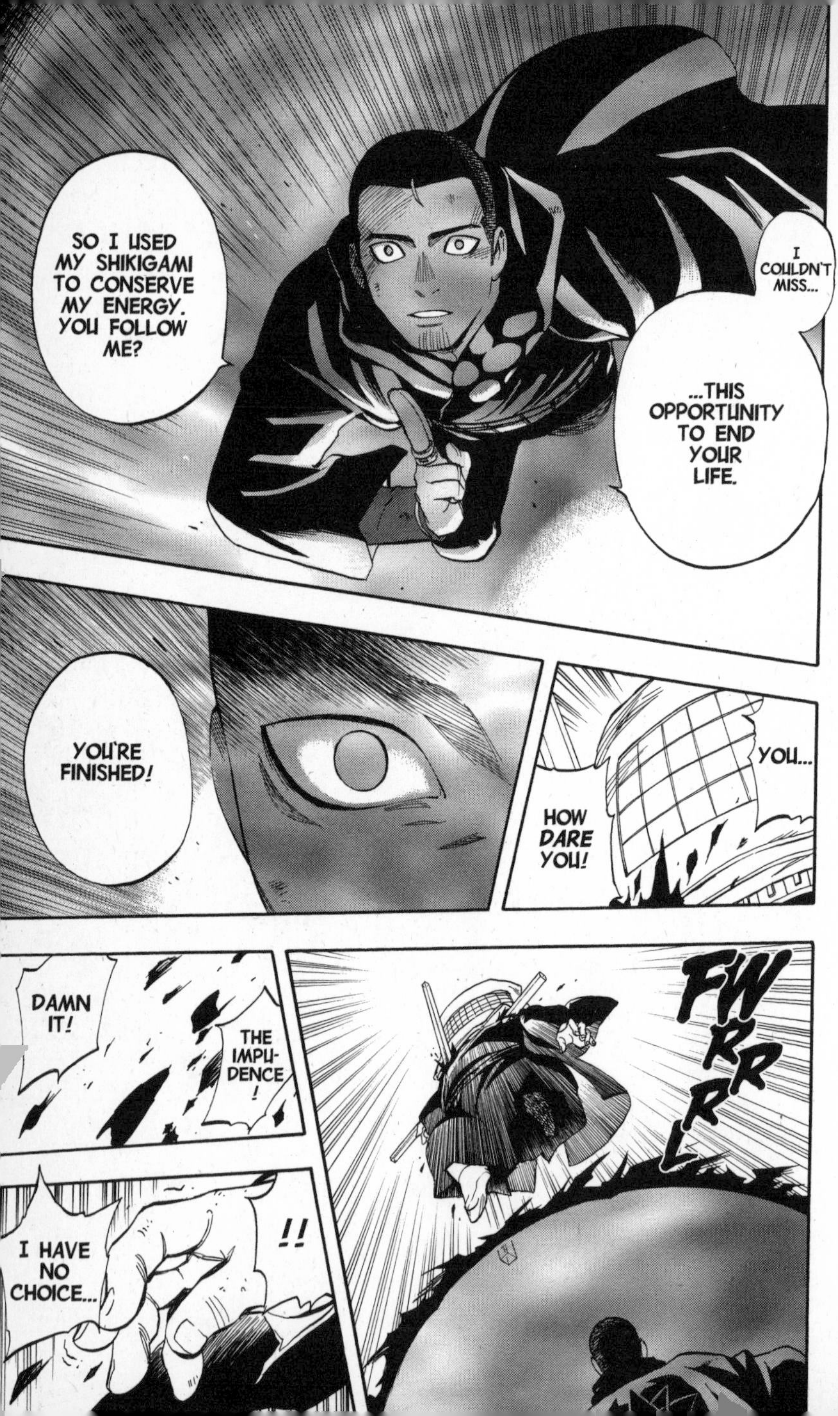
I COULDN'T MISS...
...THIS OPPORTUNITY TO END YOUR LIFE.
SO I USED MY SHIKIGAMI TO CONSERVE MY ENERGY. YOU FOLLOW ME?
YOU...
HOW DARE YOU!
YOU'RE FINISHED!
FWRRRL
THE IMPU-DENCE!
DAMN IT!
!!
I HAVE NO CHOICE...

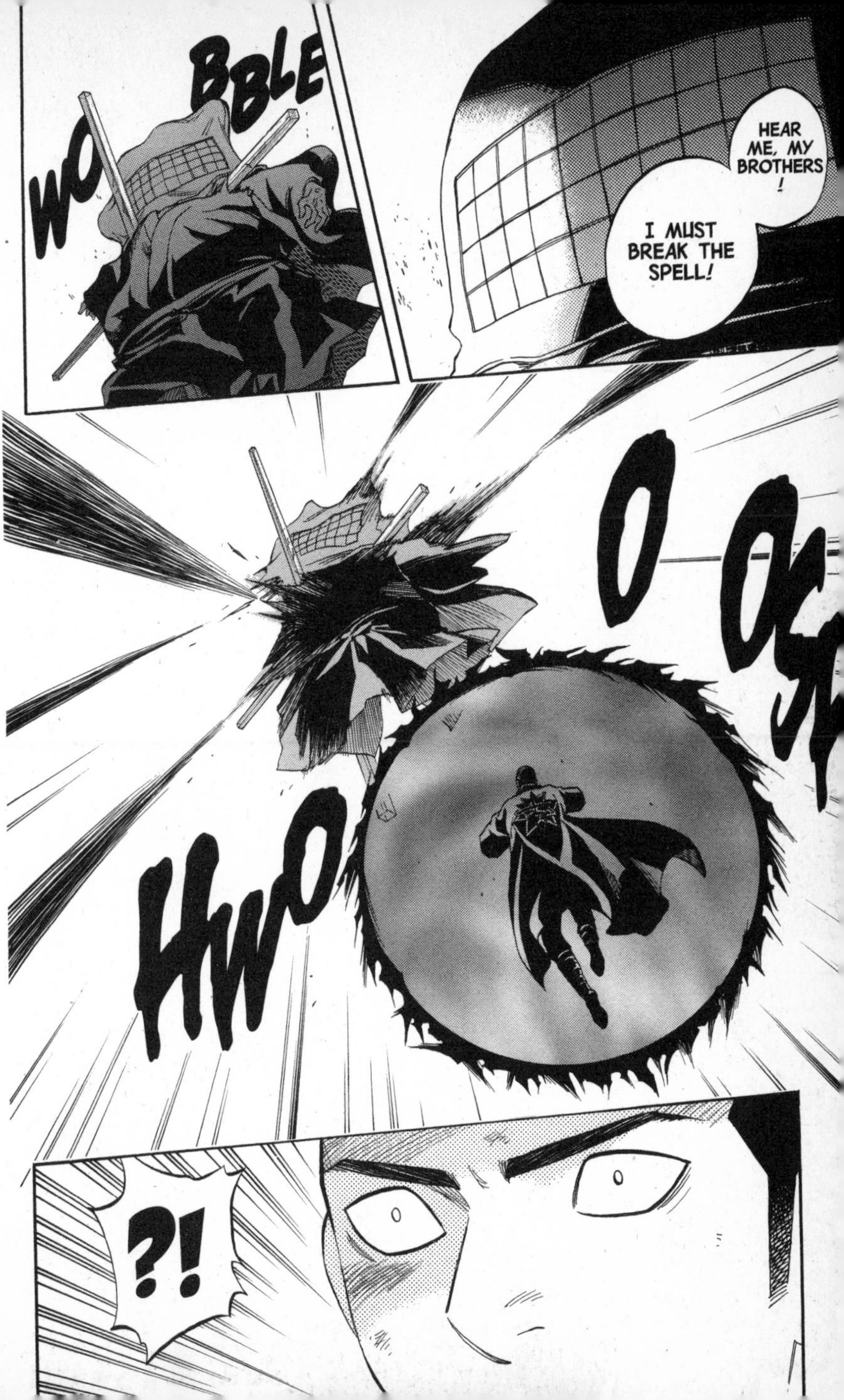
HEAR ME, MY BROTHERS!
I MUST BREAK THE SPELL!
WOBBLE
HWO
?!

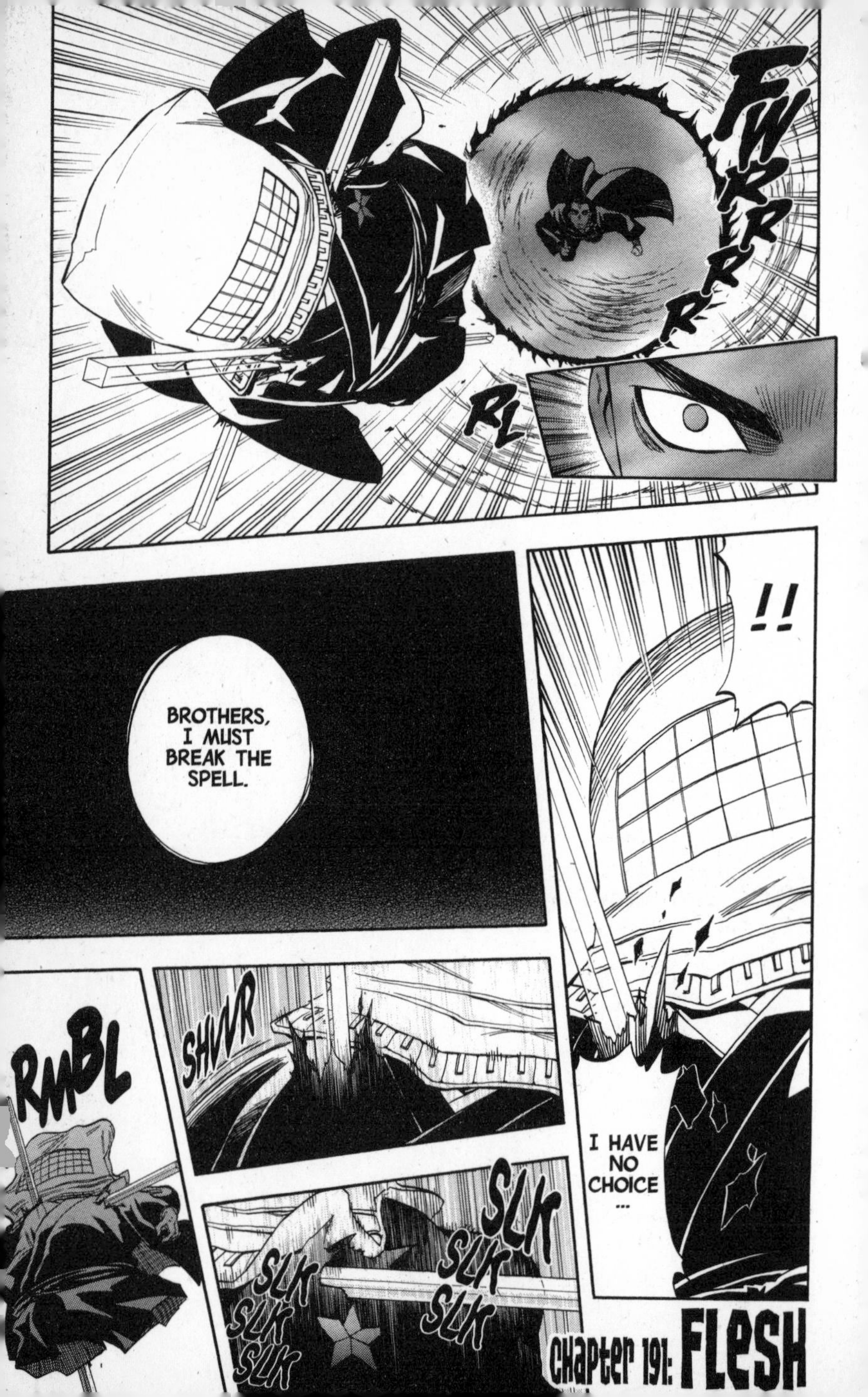
FWRRRRRL
!!
I HAVE NO CHOICE ...
BROTHERS, I MUST BREAK THE SPELL.
SHVVR
SLK SLK SLK
SLK SLK SLK
RMBL

Chapter 191: Flesh

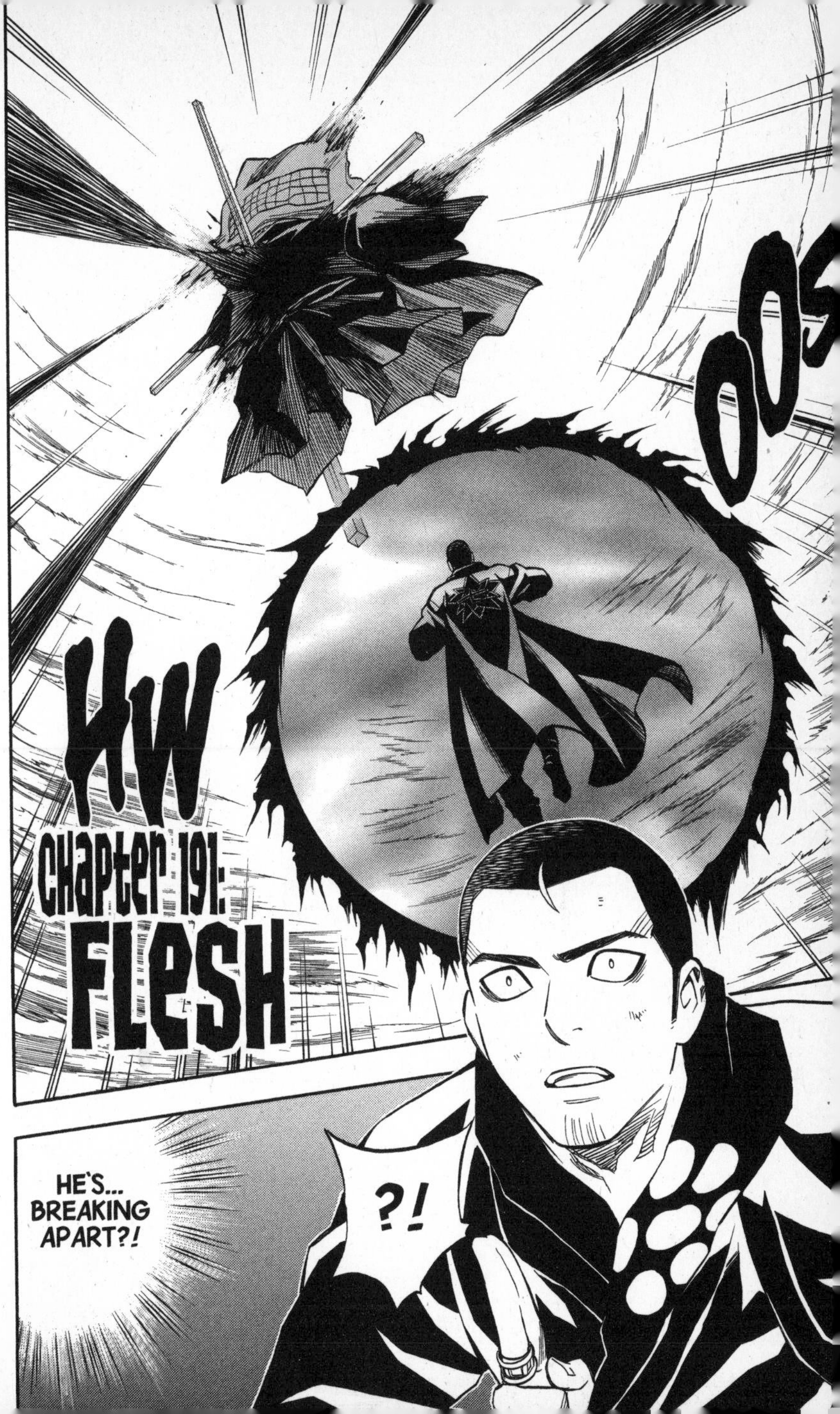
HW
CHAPTER 191: FLESH
?!
HE'S... BREAKING APART?!

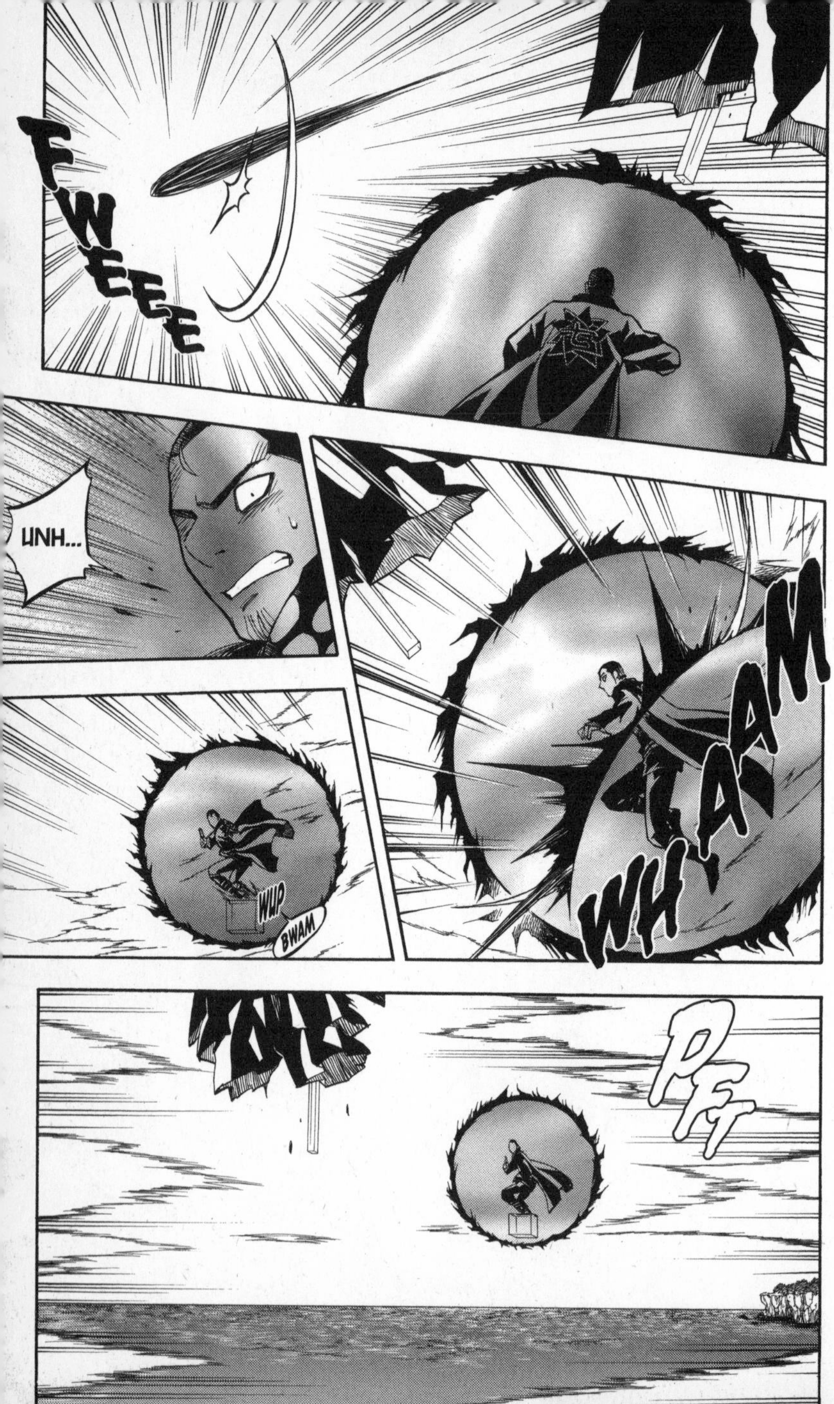
FWEEEE
WHAAAM
UNH...
WUP
BWAM
PFT

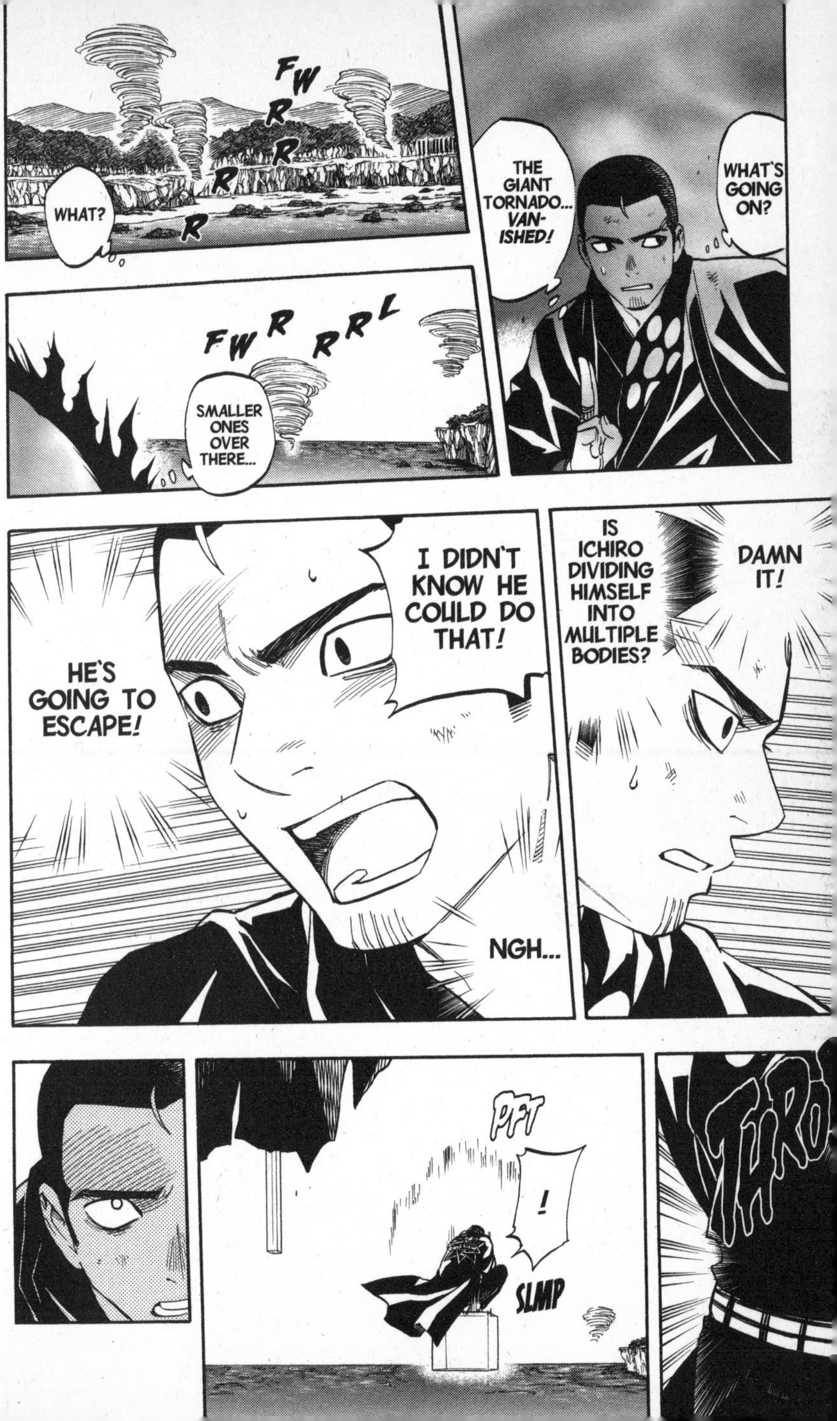
WHAT'S GOING ON?
THE GIANT TORNADO... VAN-ISHED!
FWRRRRR
WHAT?
FWRRRRL
SMALLER ONES OVER THERE...
DAMN IT!
IS ICHIRO DIVIDING HIMSELF INTO MULTIPLE BODIES?
I DIDN'T KNOW HE COULD DO THAT!
HE'S GOING TO ESCAPE!
NGH...
PFT
!
SLMP

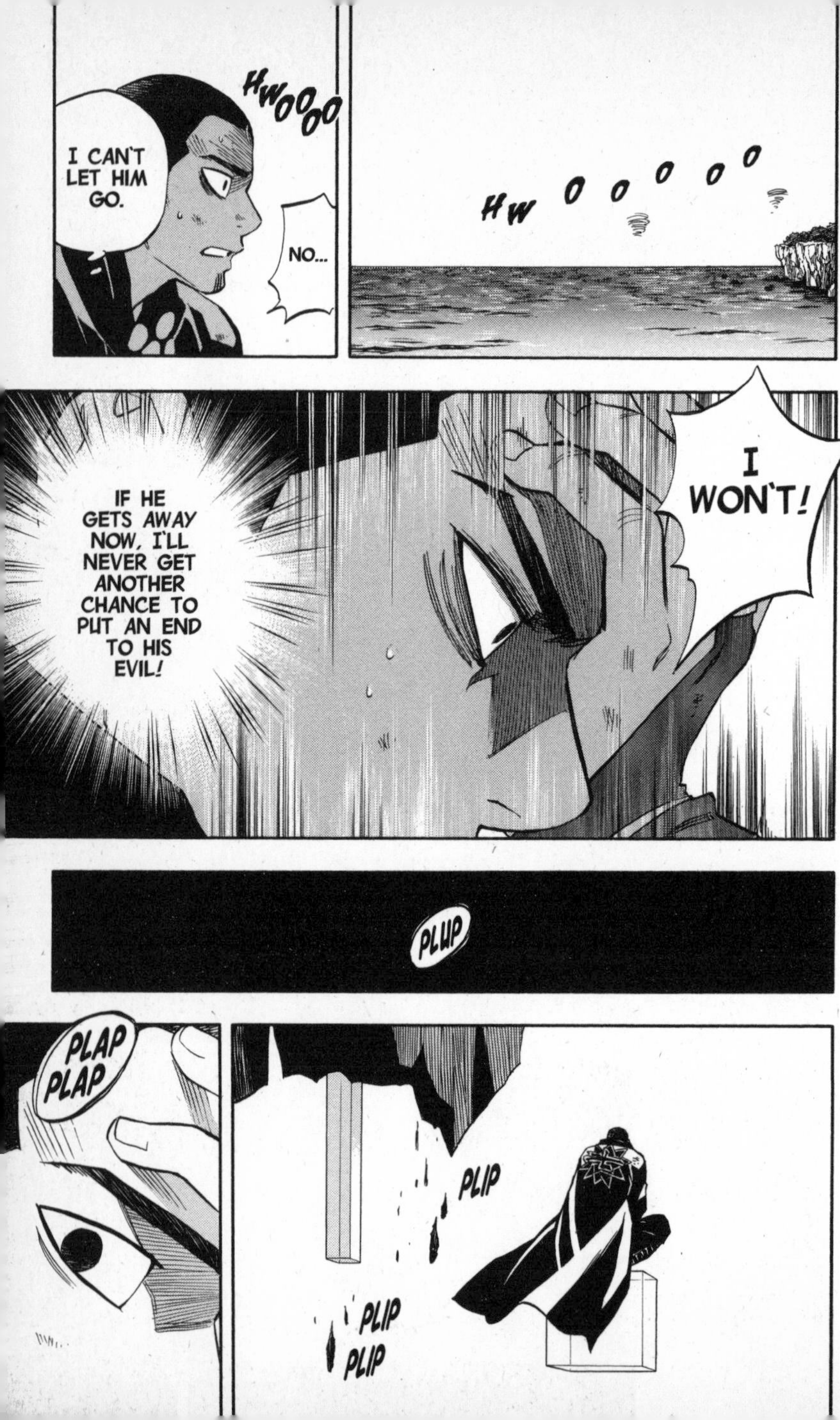
HW O O O O O
HWOOOO
NO...
I CAN'T LET HIM GO.
I WON'T!
IF HE GETS AWAY NOW, I'LL NEVER GET ANOTHER CHANCE TO PUT AN END TO HIS EVIL!
PLUP
PLIP
PLIP
PLIP
PLAP PLAP

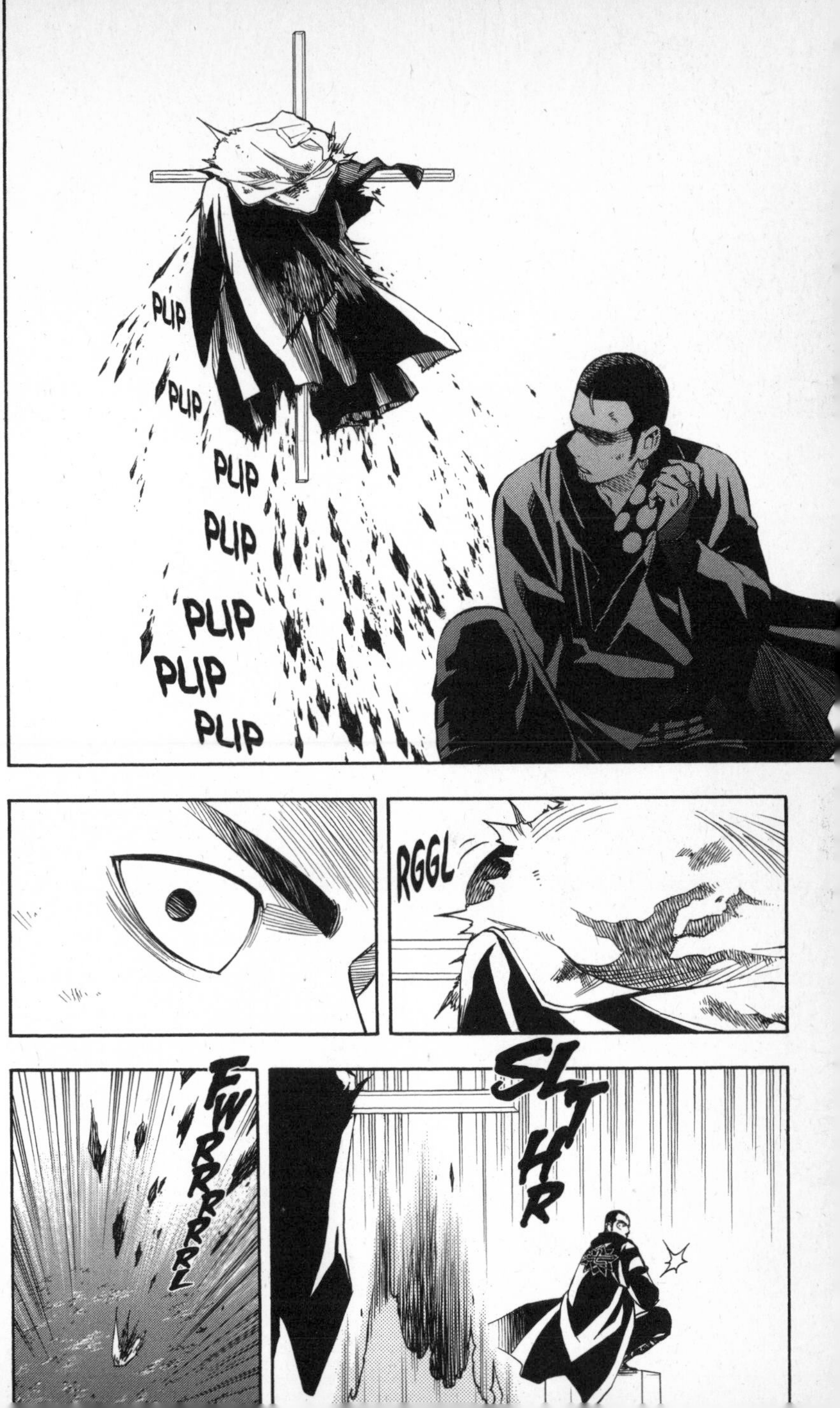
PLIP
PLIP
PLIP
PLIP
PLIP
PLIP
PLIP
RGGL
SLTHR
FWRRRRRL

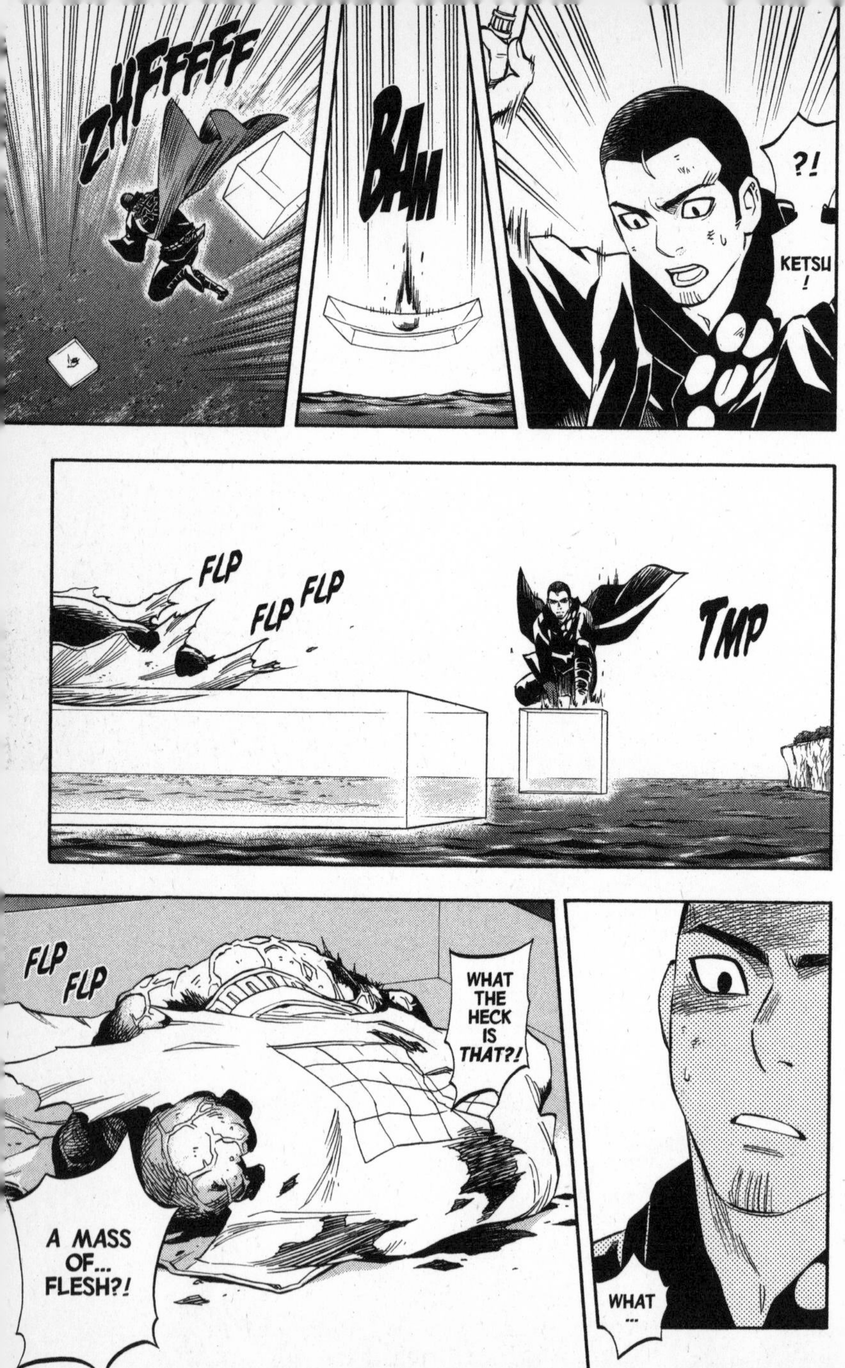
?!
KETSU!
BAM
ZHFFFFF
TMP
FLP
FLP FLP
WHAT...
WHAT THE HECK IS THAT?!
FLP FLP
A MASS OF... FLESH?!

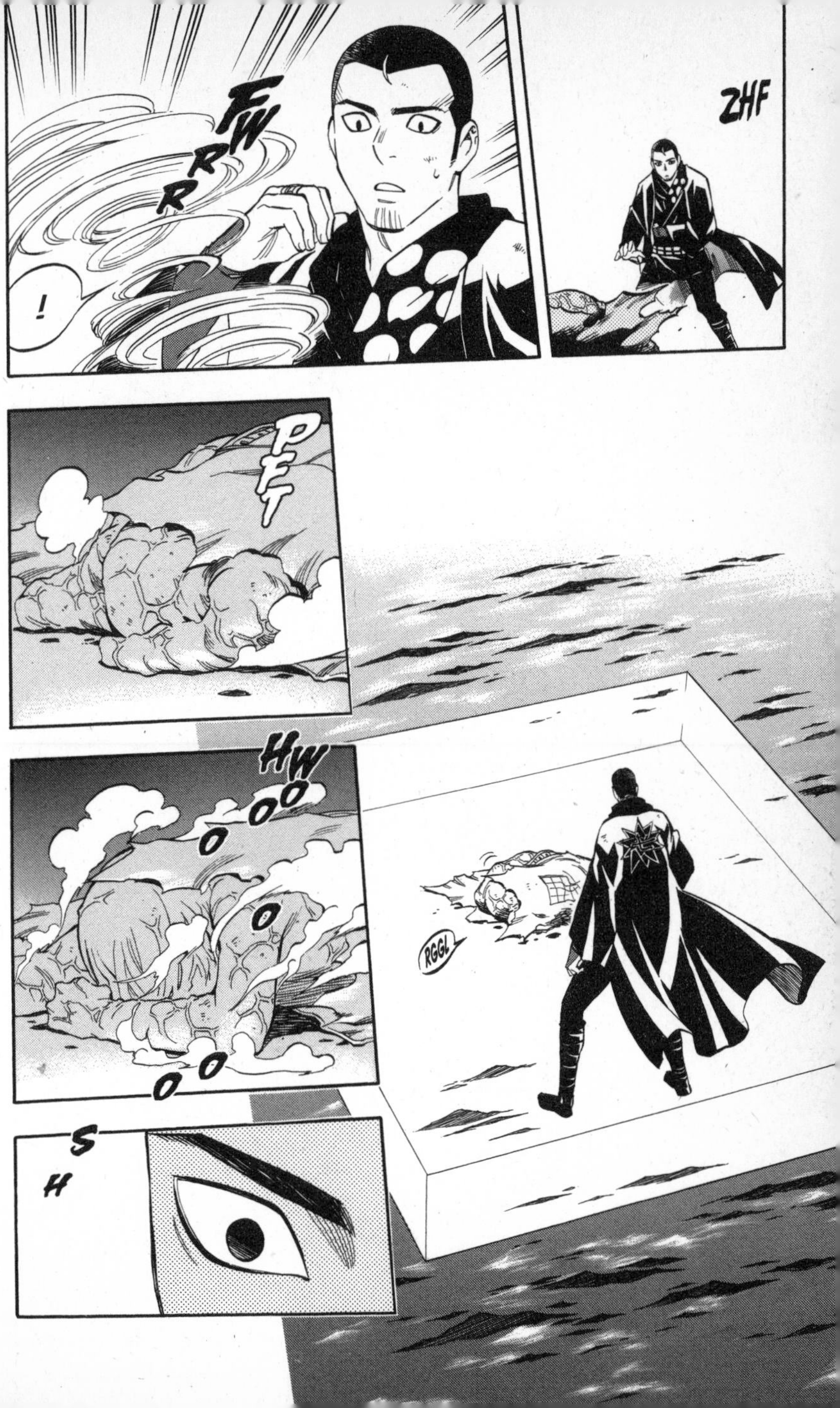
ZHF
FWRRR
!
RGGL
PFT
HWOOOOOO
SH

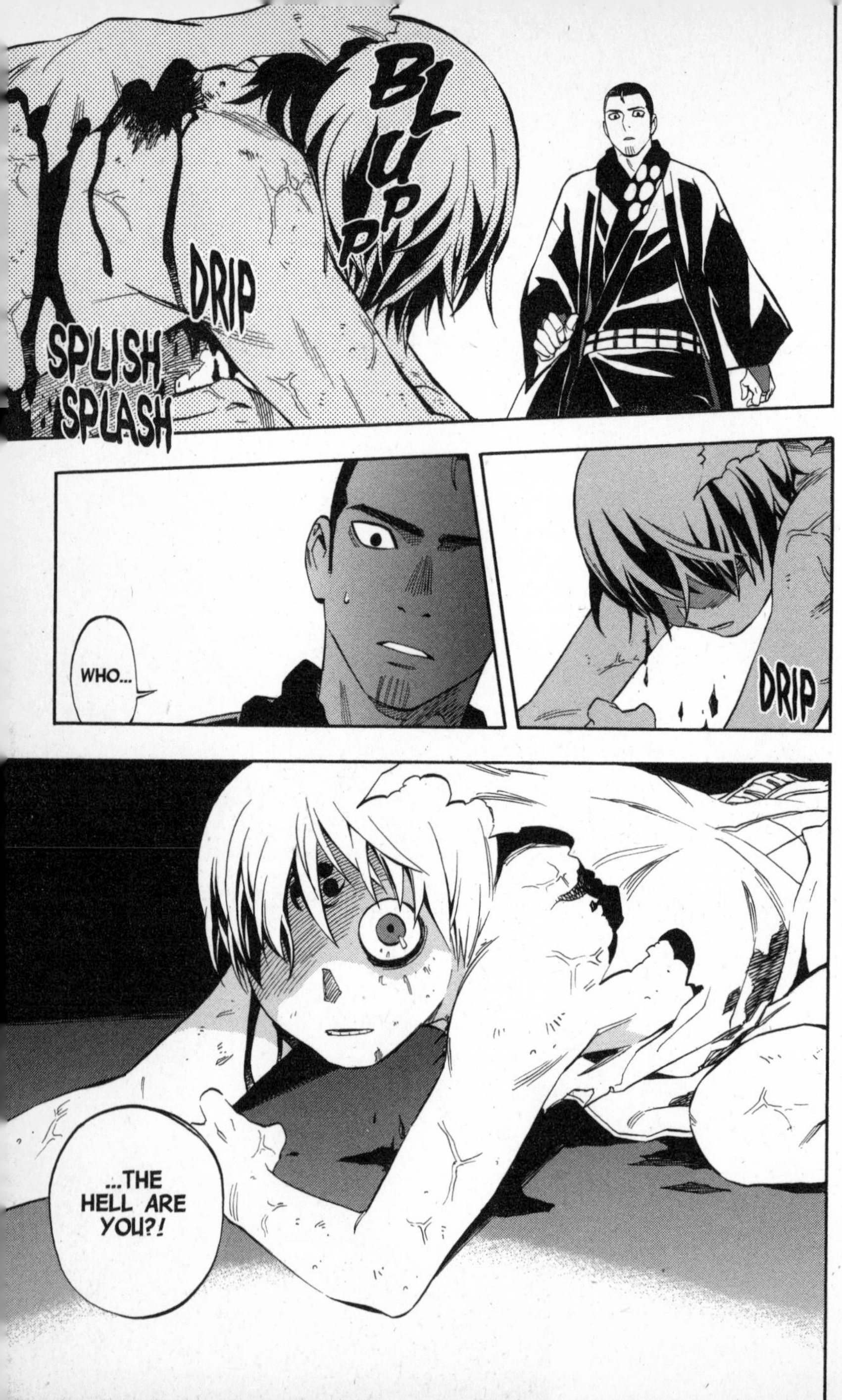
BLUPP
DRIP
SPLISH SPLASH
DRIP
WHO...
...THE HELL ARE YOU?!

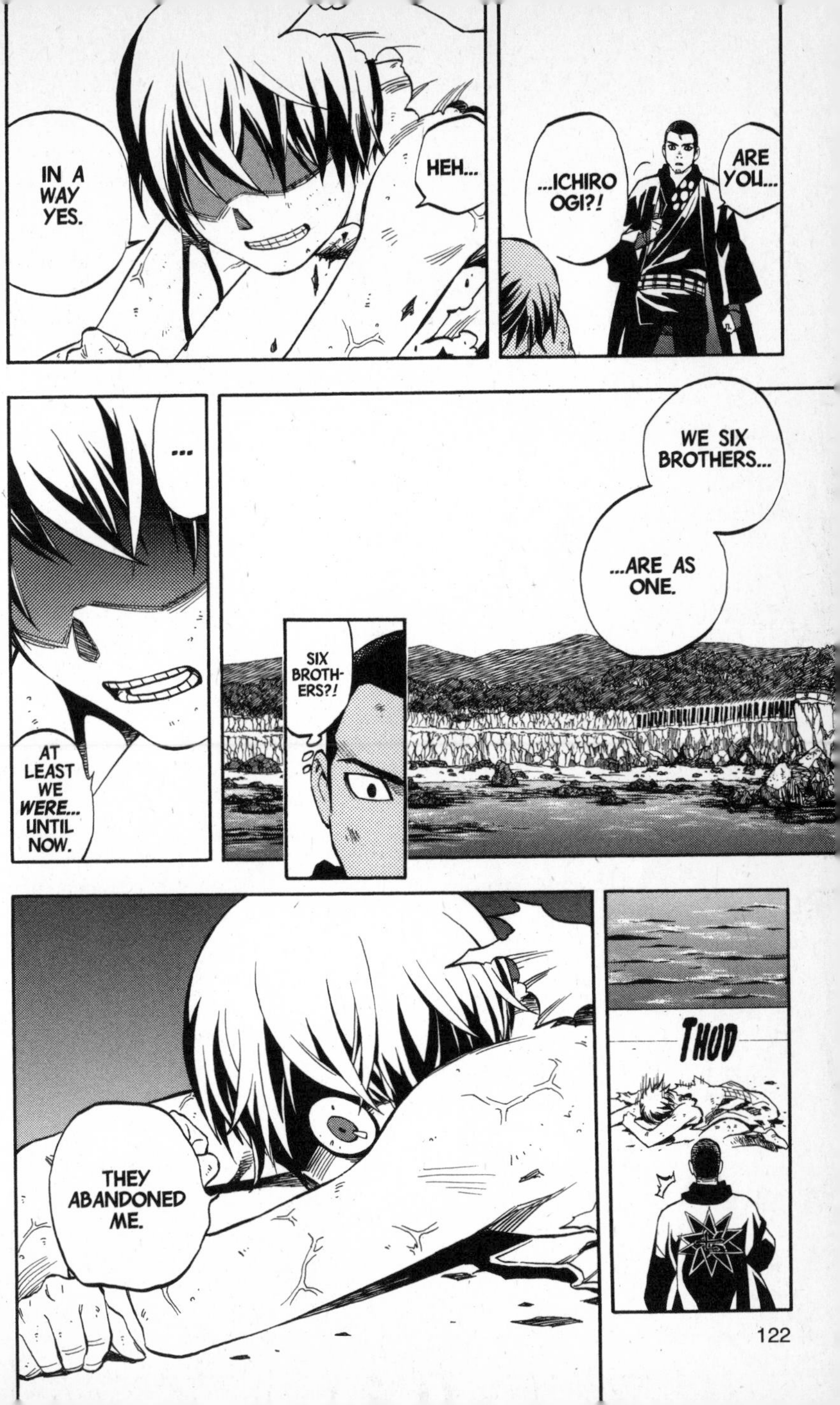
ARE YOU...
...ICHIRO OGI?!
HEH...
IN A WAY YES.
WE SIX BROTHERS...
...ARE AS ONE.
SIX BROTHERS?!
...
AT LEAST WE WERE... UNTIL NOW.
THUD
THEY ABANDONED ME.

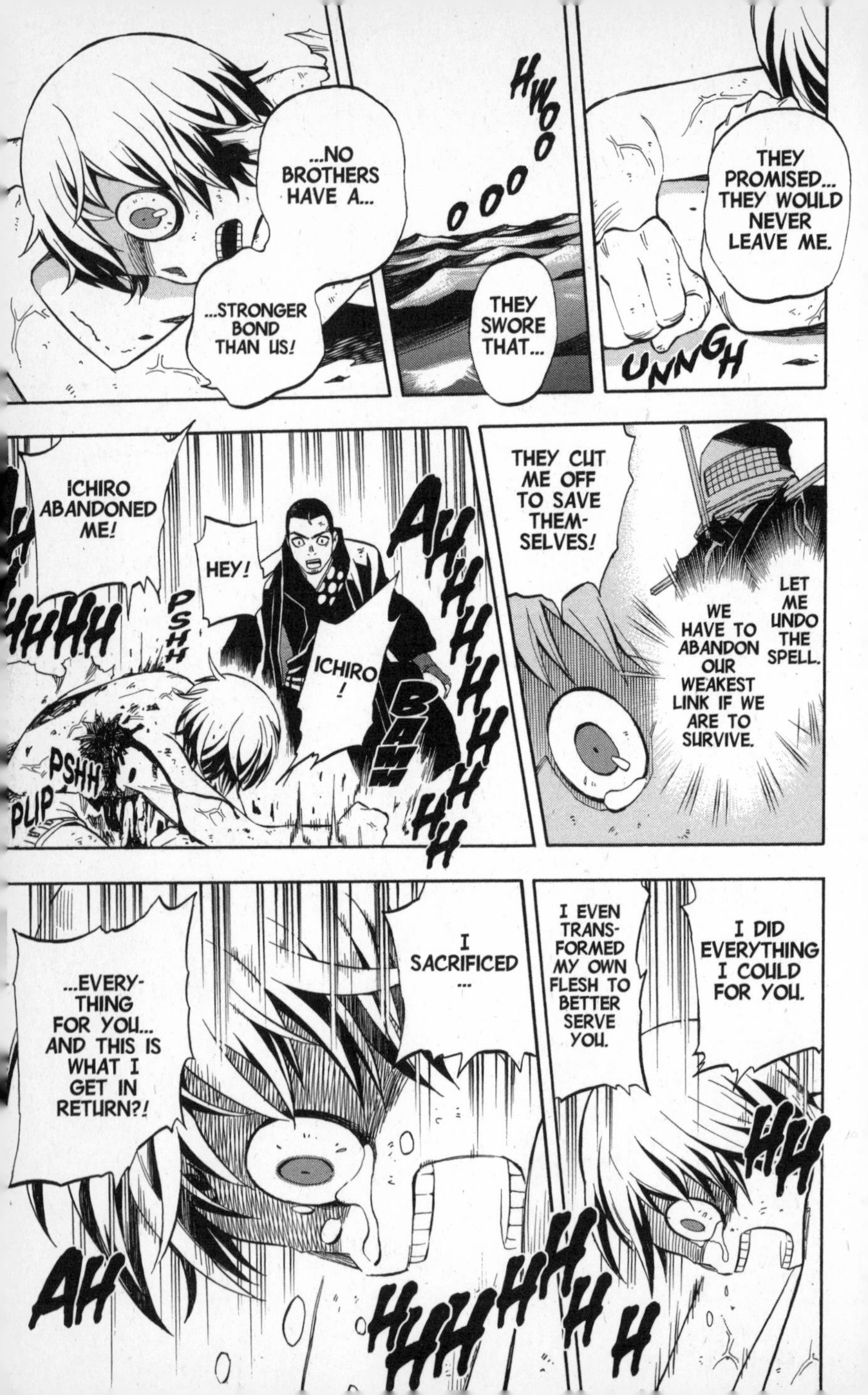
THEY PROMISED... THEY WOULD NEVER LEAVE ME.
UNNGH
HWOOOOO
THEY SWORE THAT...
...NO BROTHERS HAVE A...
...STRONGER BOND THAN US!
THEY CUT ME OFF TO SAVE THEM-SELVES!
LET ME UNDO THE SPELL.
WE HAVE TO ABANDON OUR WEAKEST LINK IF WE ARE TO SURVIVE.
AHHHHHHHHHHHH
HEY!
ICHIRO!
BAMM
ICHIRO ABANDONED ME!
PSHH
PSHH
PLIP
I DID EVERYTHING I COULD FOR YOU.
I EVEN TRANS-FORMED MY OWN FLESH TO BETTER SERVE YOU.
I SACRIFICED...
...EVERY-THING FOR YOU... AND THIS IS WHAT I GET IN RETURN?!
AHHHHHHHHHH

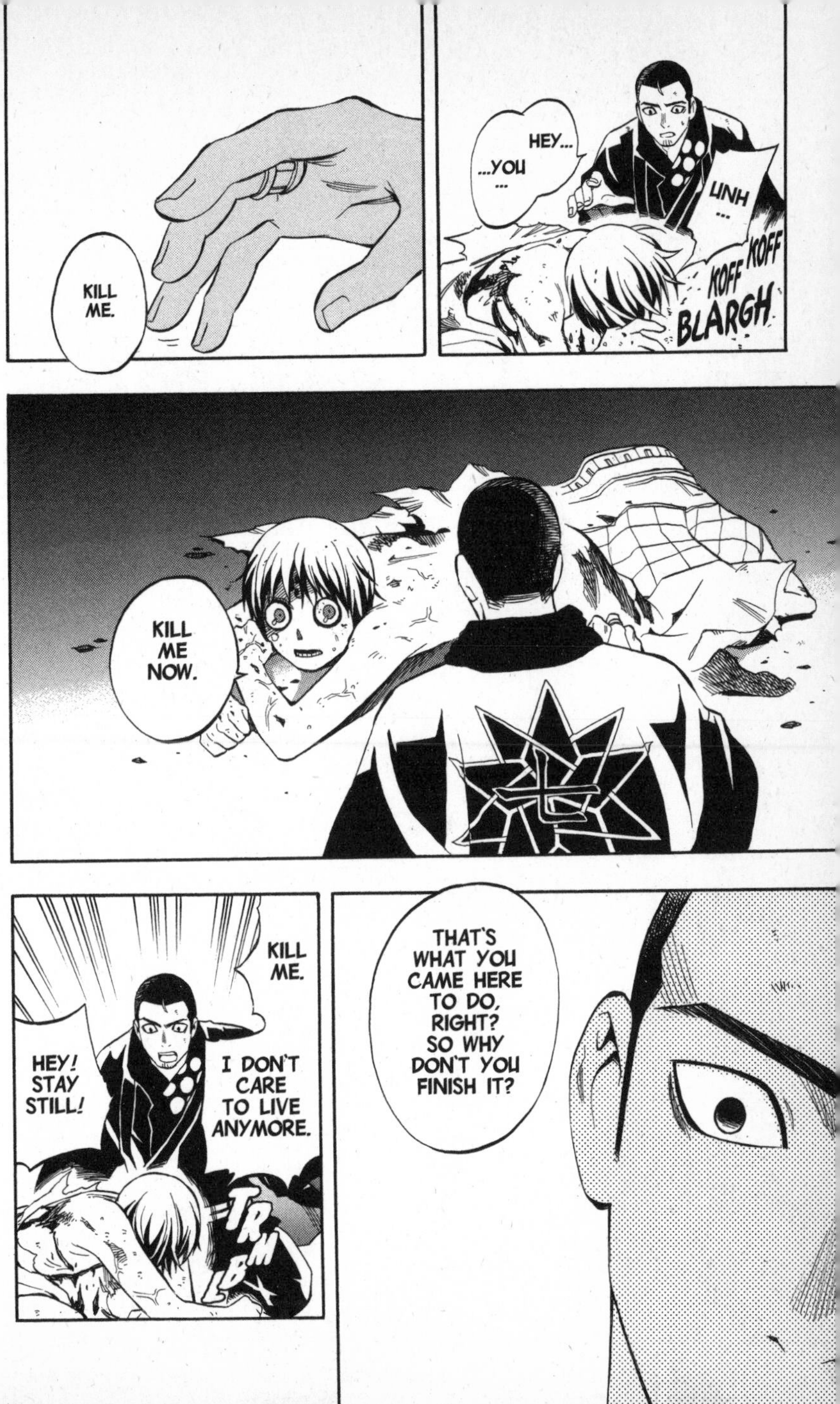
HEY...
...YOU ...
UNH ...
KOFF KOFF
BLARGH
KILL ME.
KILL ME NOW.
THAT'S WHAT YOU CAME HERE TO DO, RIGHT? SO WHY DON'T YOU FINISH IT?
KILL ME.
I DON'T CARE TO LIVE ANYMORE.
HEY! STAY STILL!
TRMBL

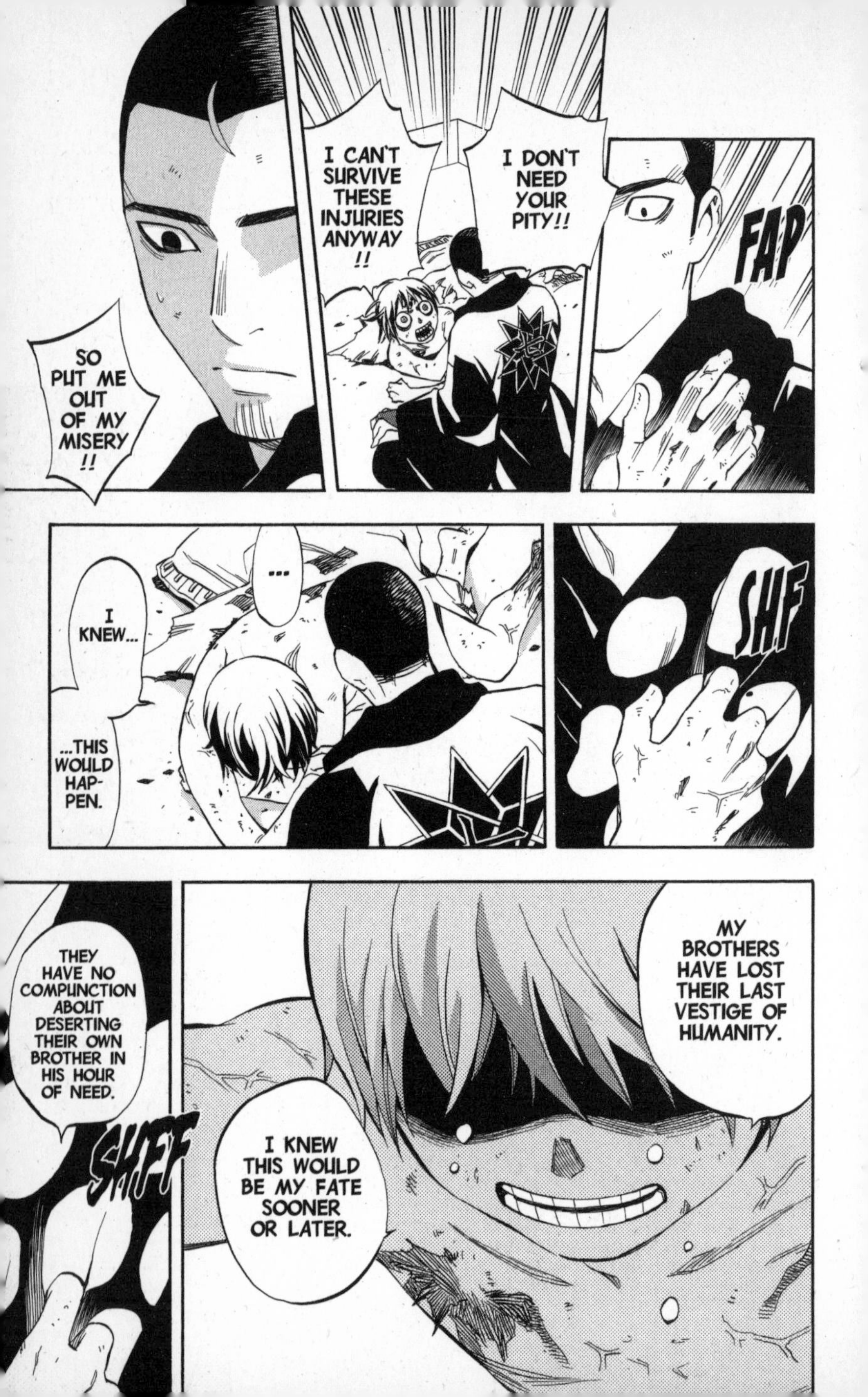
FAP
I DON'T NEED YOUR PITY!!
I CAN'T SURVIVE THESE INJURIES ANYWAY!!
SO PUT ME OUT OF MY MISERY!!
SHF
...
I KNEW...
...THIS WOULD HAP-PEN.
MY BROTHERS HAVE LOST THEIR LAST VESTIGE OF HUMANITY.
I KNEW THIS WOULD BE MY FATE SOONER OR LATER.
THEY HAVE NO COMPUNCTION ABOUT DESERTING THEIR OWN BROTHER IN HIS HOUR OF NEED.
SHFF

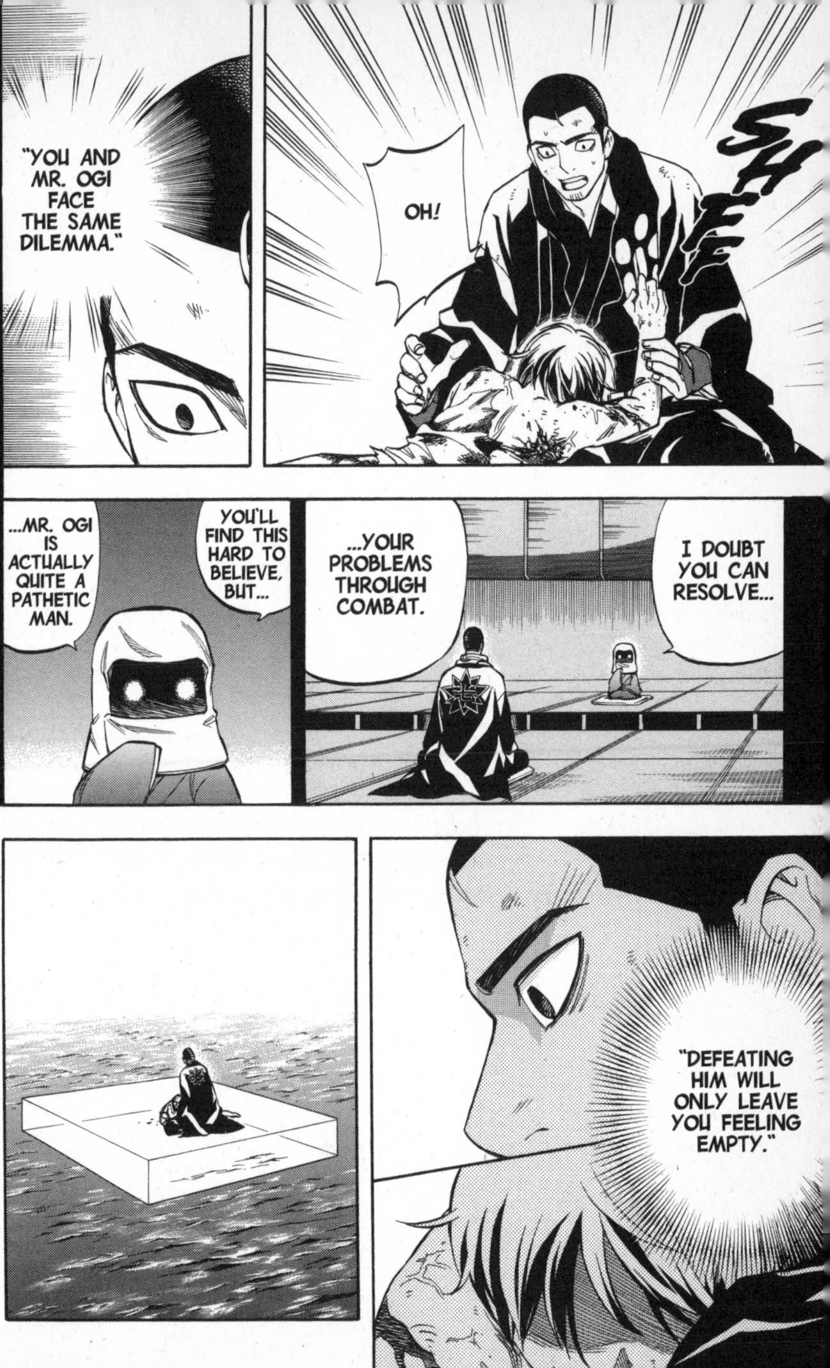
OH!
"YOU AND MR. OGI FACE THE SAME DILEMMA."
I DOUBT YOU CAN RESOLVE...
...YOUR PROBLEMS THROUGH COMBAT.
YOU'LL FIND THIS HARD TO BELIEVE, BUT...
...MR. OGI IS ACTUALLY QUITE A PATHETIC MAN.
"DEFEATING HIM WILL ONLY LEAVE YOU FEELING EMPTY."

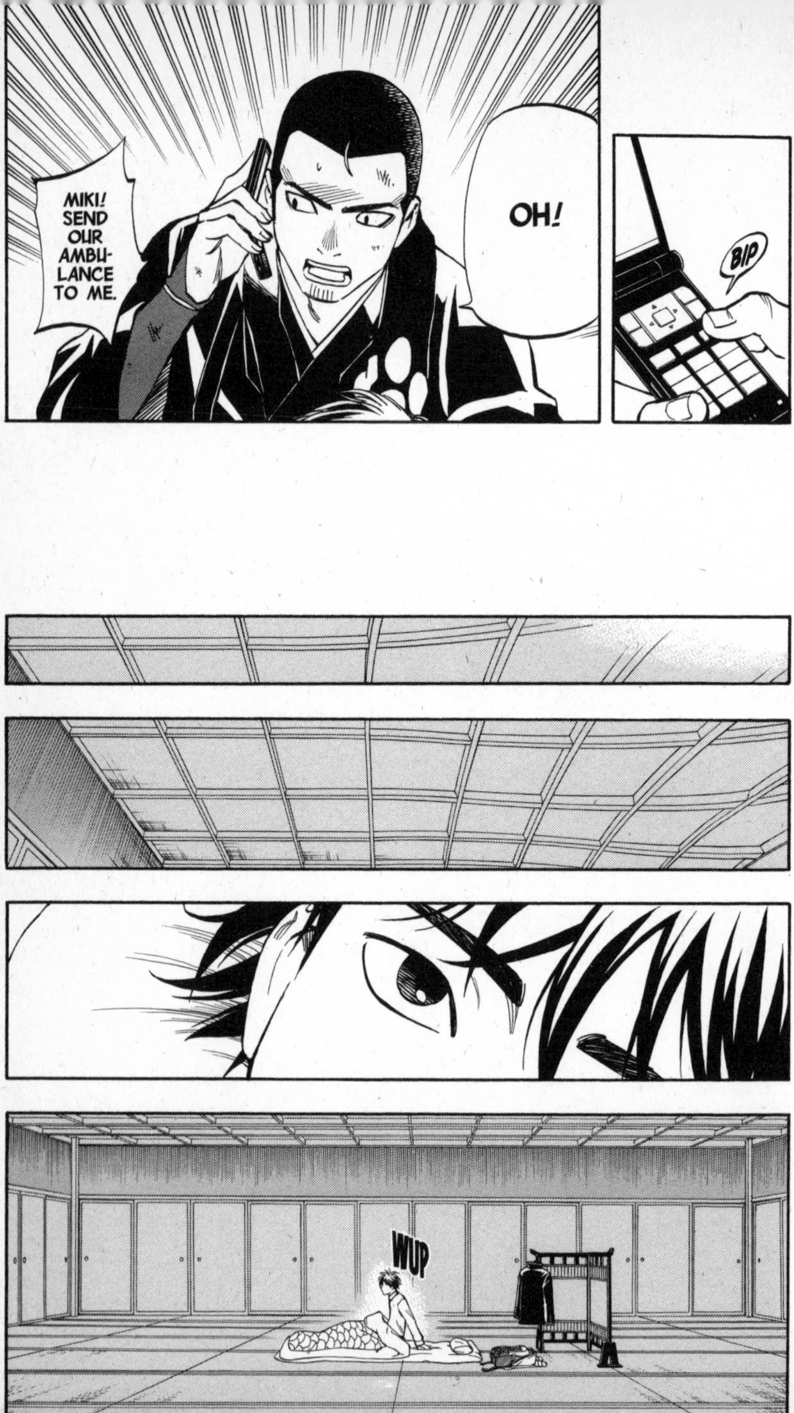
BIP
OH!
MIKI! SEND OUR AMBU-LANCE TO ME.
WUP

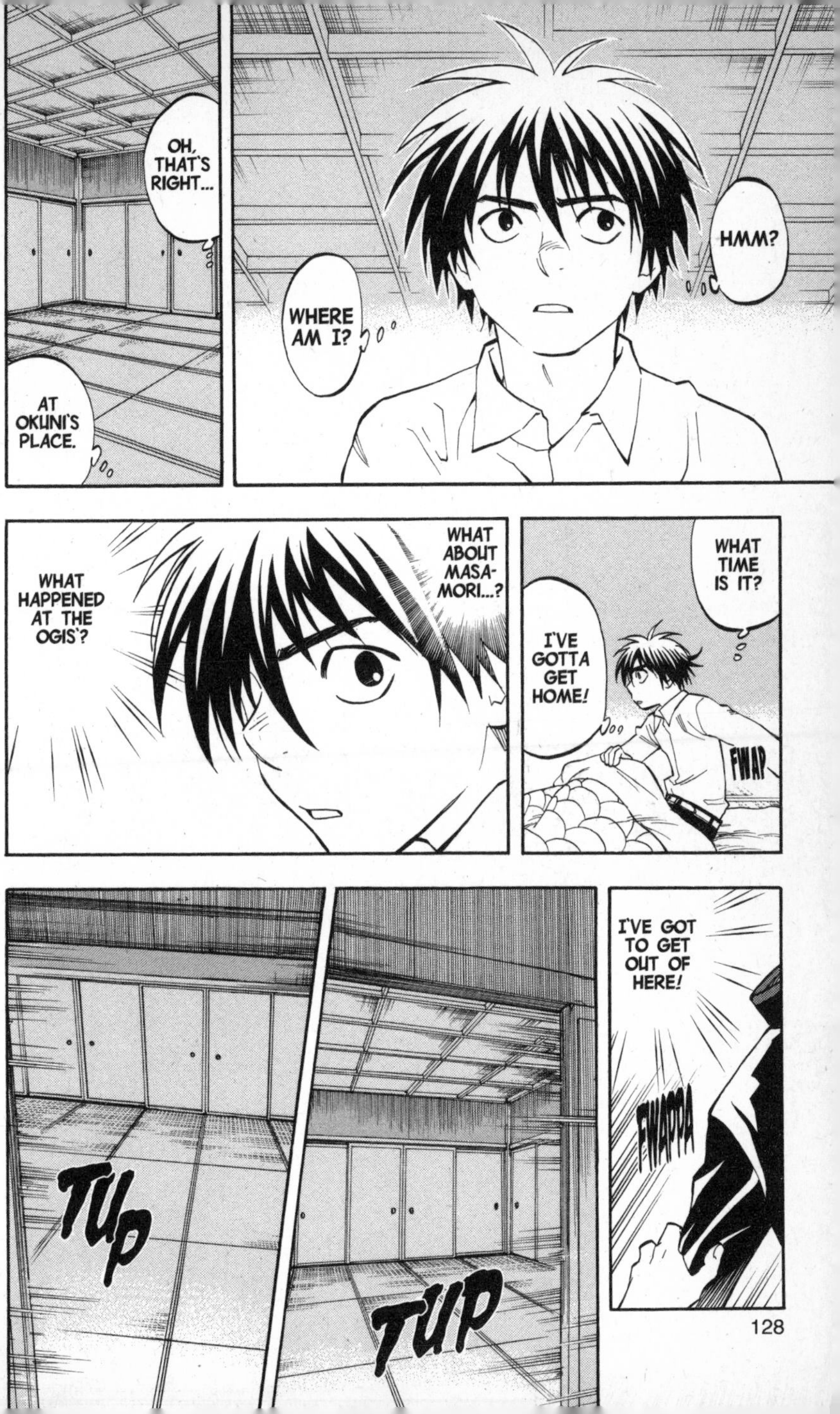
HMM?
WHERE AM I?
OH, THAT'S RIGHT...
AT OKUNI'S PLACE.
WHAT TIME IS IT?
I'VE GOTTA GET HOME!
FWAP
WHAT ABOUT MASA-MORI...?
WHAT HAPPENED AT THE OGIS'?
I'VE GOT TO GET OUT OF HERE!
FWAPPA
TUP
TUP

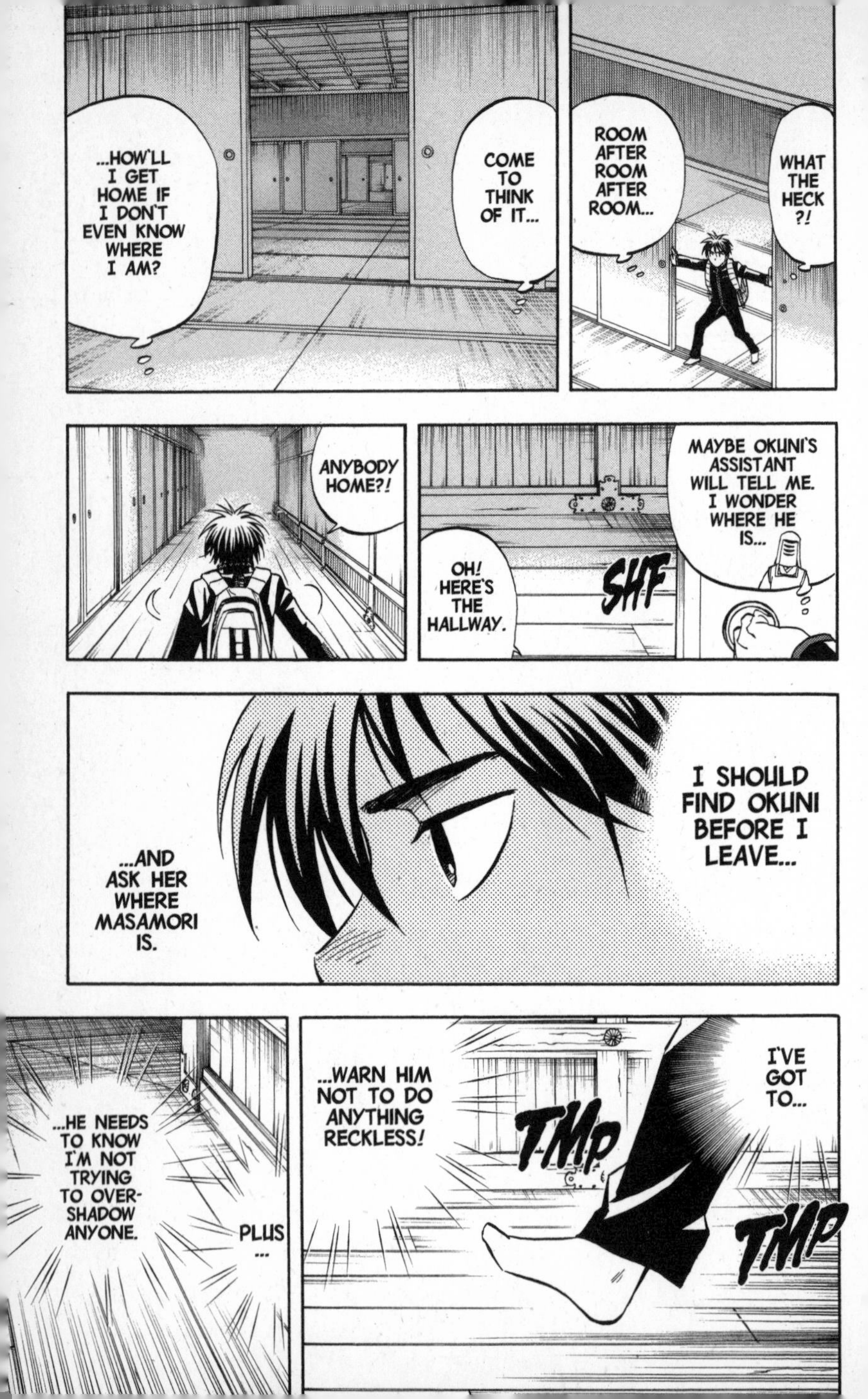
WHAT THE HECK ?!
ROOM AFTER ROOM AFTER ROOM...
COME TO THINK OF IT...
...HOW'LL I GET HOME IF I DON'T EVEN KNOW WHERE I AM?
MAYBE OKUNI'S ASSISTANT WILL TELL ME. I WONDER WHERE HE IS...
SHF
OH! HERE'S THE HALLWAY.
ANYBODY HOME?!
I SHOULD FIND OKUNI BEFORE I LEAVE...
...AND ASK HER WHERE MASAMORI IS.
I'VE GOT TO...
TMP
TMP
...WARN HIM NOT TO DO ANYTHING RECKLESS!
PLUS...
...HE NEEDS TO KNOW I'M NOT TRYING TO OVERSHADOW ANYONE.

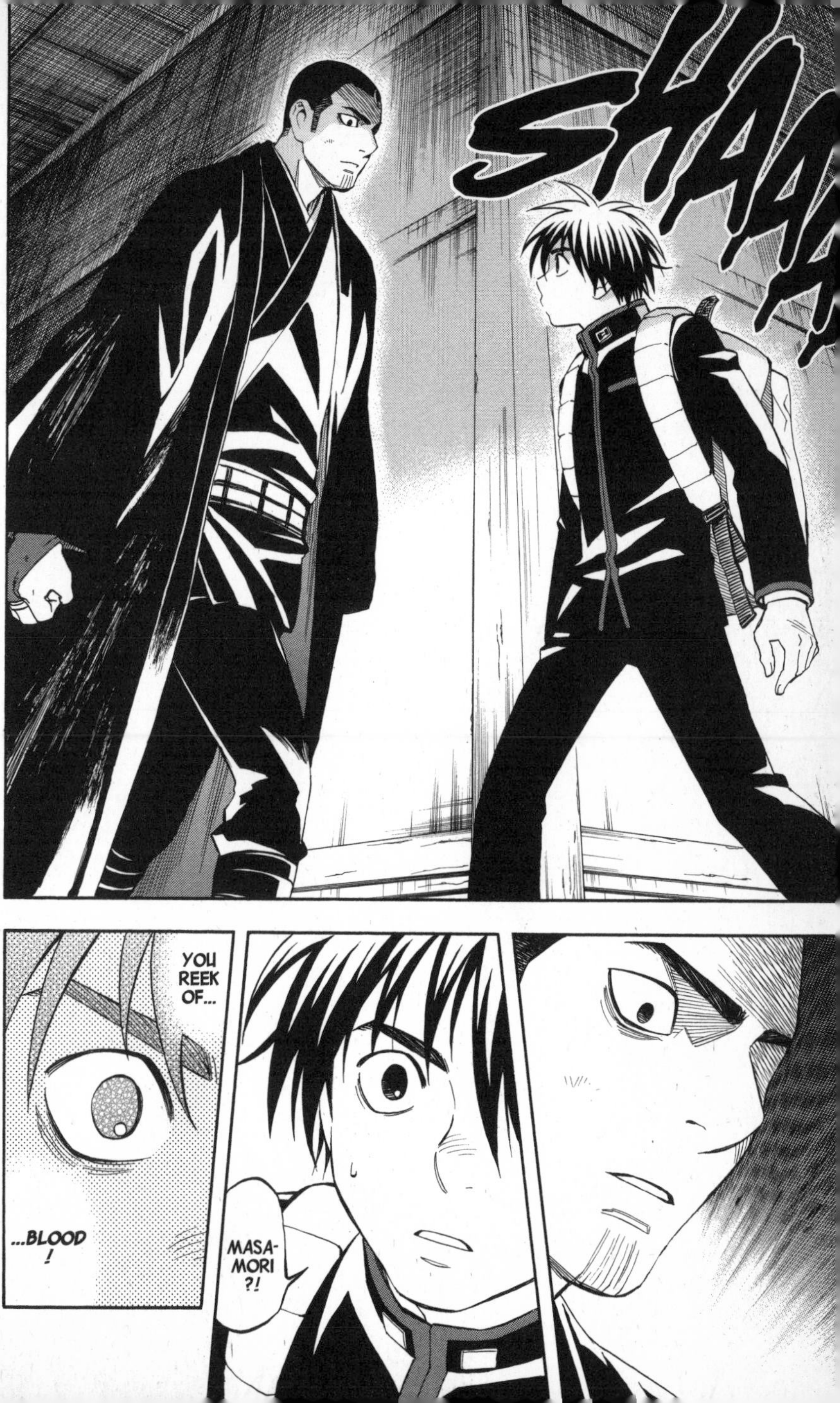
SHAAA
MASA-
MORI
?!
YOU
REEK
OF...
...BLOOD
!

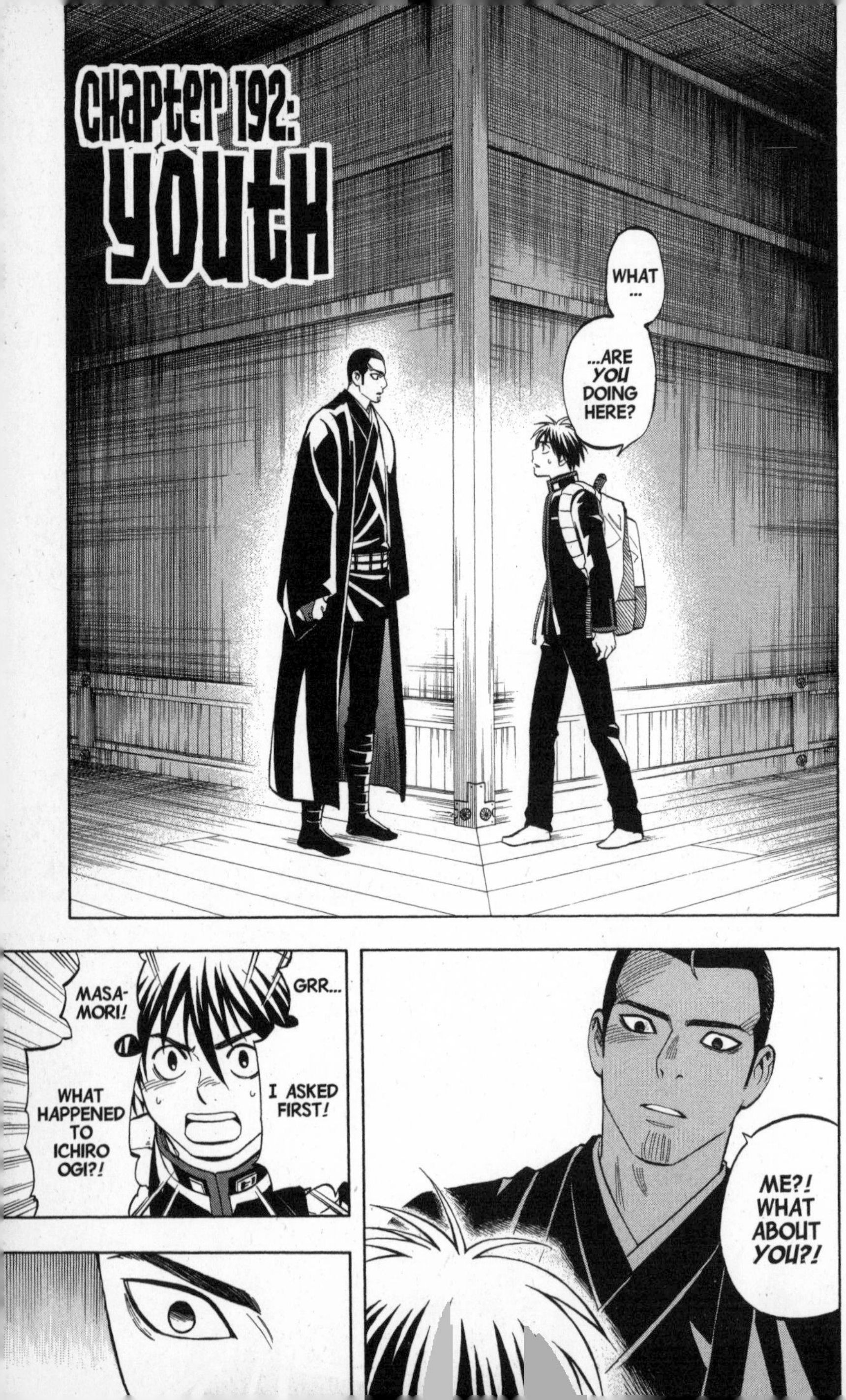
CHAPTER 192:
YOUTH
WHAT ...
...ARE YOU DOING HERE?
ME?! WHAT ABOUT YOU?!
GRR...
MASA-MORI!
I ASKED FIRST!
WHAT HAPPENED TO ICHIRO OGI?!

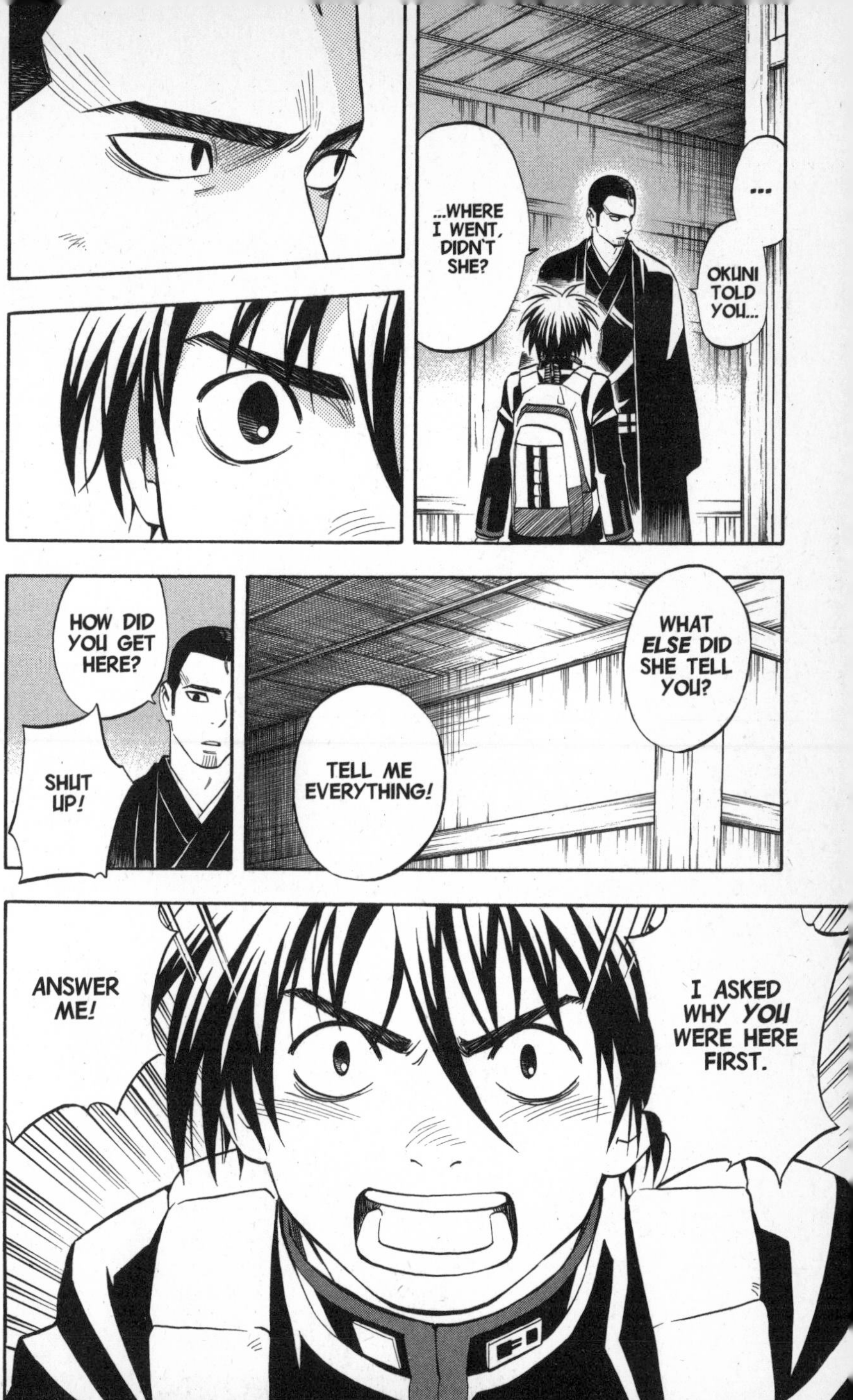
...
OKUNI TOLD YOU...
...WHERE I WENT, DIDN'T SHE?
WHAT *ELSE* DID SHE TELL YOU?
TELL ME EVERYTHING!
HOW DID YOU GET HERE?
SHUT UP!
I ASKED WHY *YOU* WERE HERE FIRST.
ANSWER ME!

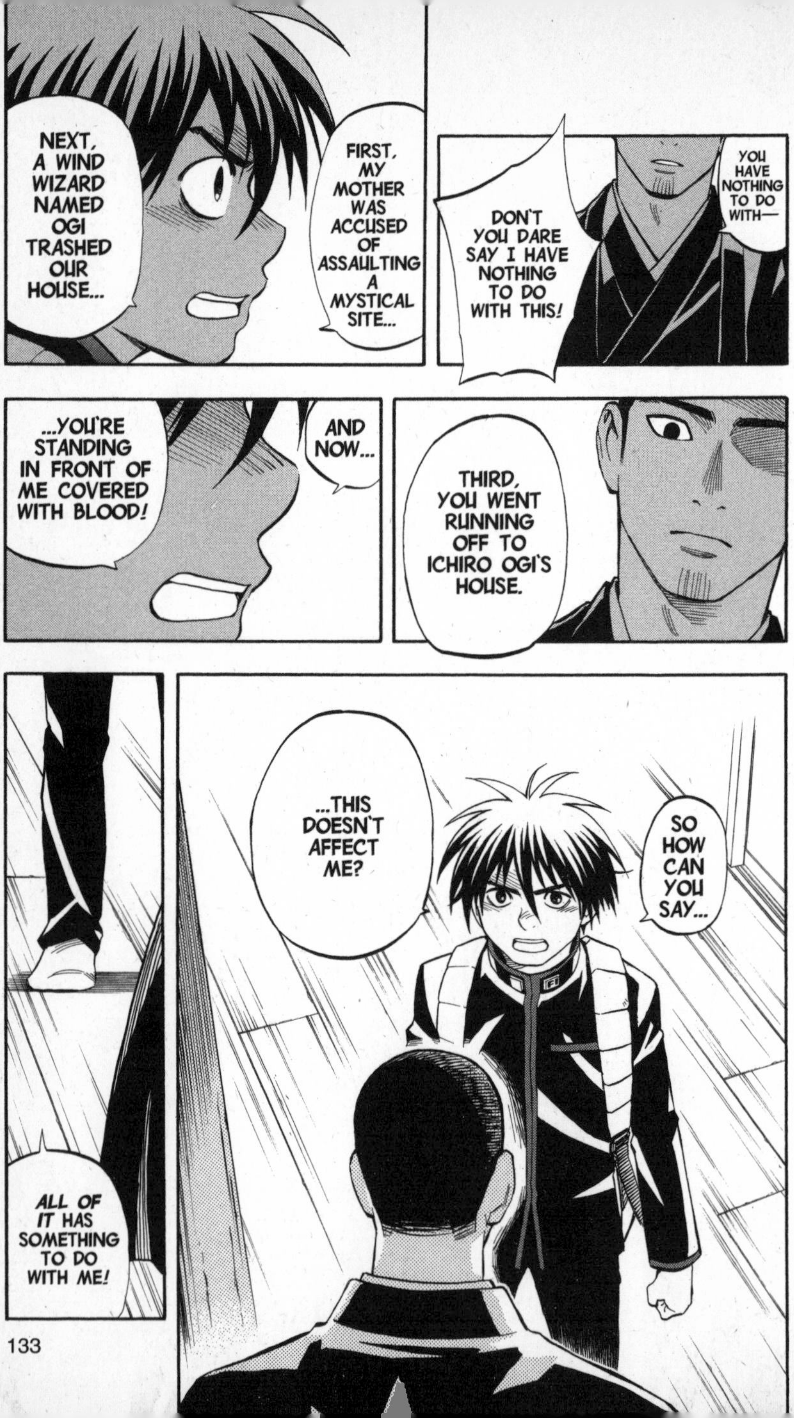
YOU HAVE NOTHING TO DO WITH—
DON'T YOU DARE SAY I HAVE NOTHING TO DO WITH THIS!
FIRST, MY MOTHER WAS ACCUSED OF ASSAULTING A MYSTICAL SITE...
NEXT, A WIND WIZARD NAMED OGI TRASHED OUR HOUSE...
THIRD, YOU WENT RUNNING OFF TO ICHIRO OGI'S HOUSE.
AND NOW...
...YOU'RE STANDING IN FRONT OF ME COVERED WITH BLOOD!
SO HOW CAN YOU SAY...
...THIS DOESN'T AFFECT ME?
ALL OF IT HAS SOMETHING TO DO WITH ME!

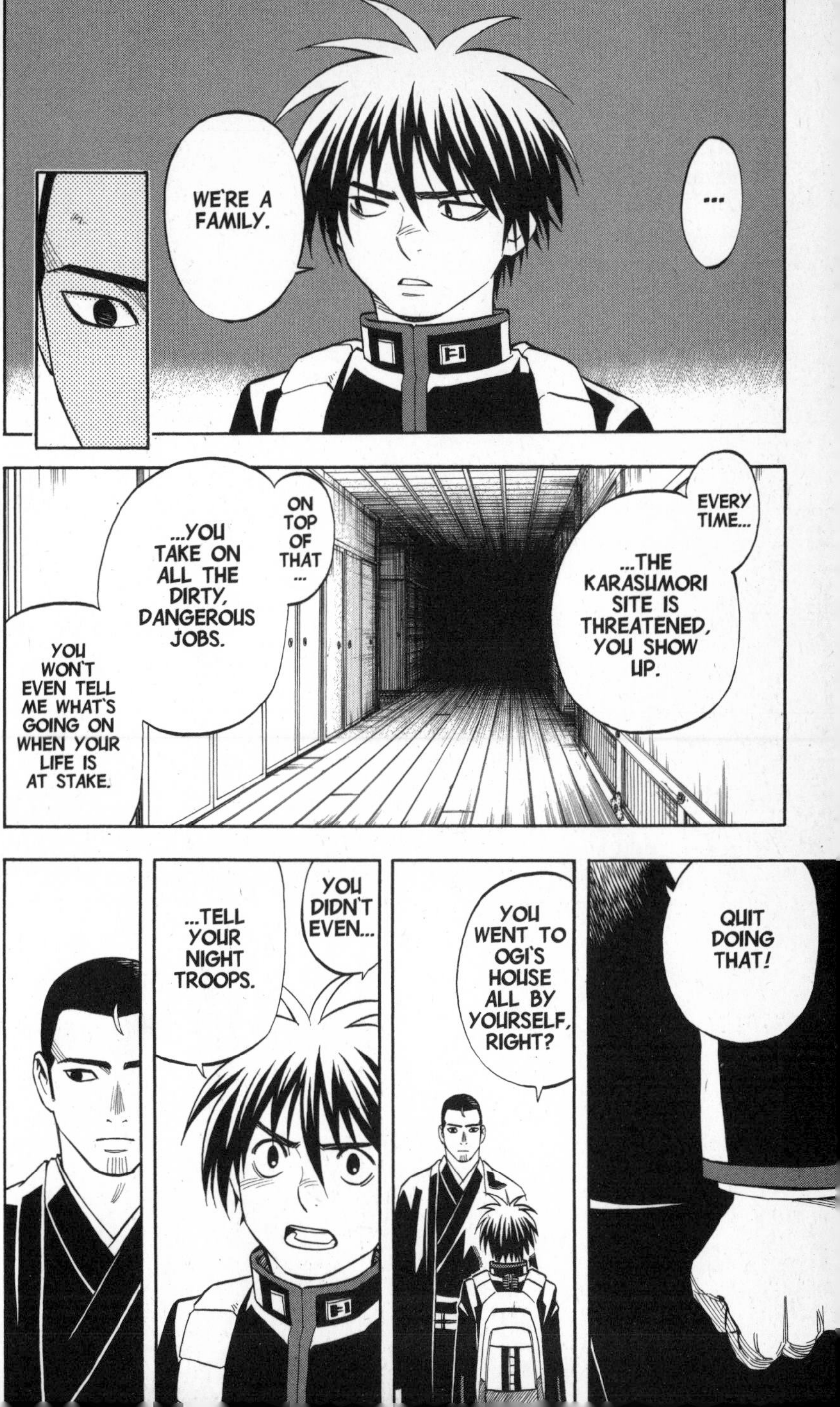
...
WE'RE A FAMILY.
EVERY TIME...
...THE KARASUMORI SITE IS THREATENED, YOU SHOW UP.
ON TOP OF THAT...
...YOU TAKE ON ALL THE DIRTY, DANGEROUS JOBS.
YOU WON'T EVEN TELL ME WHAT'S GOING ON WHEN YOUR LIFE IS AT STAKE.
QUIT DOING THAT!
YOU WENT TO OGI'S HOUSE ALL BY YOURSELF, RIGHT?
YOU DIDN'T EVEN...
...TELL YOUR NIGHT TROOPS.

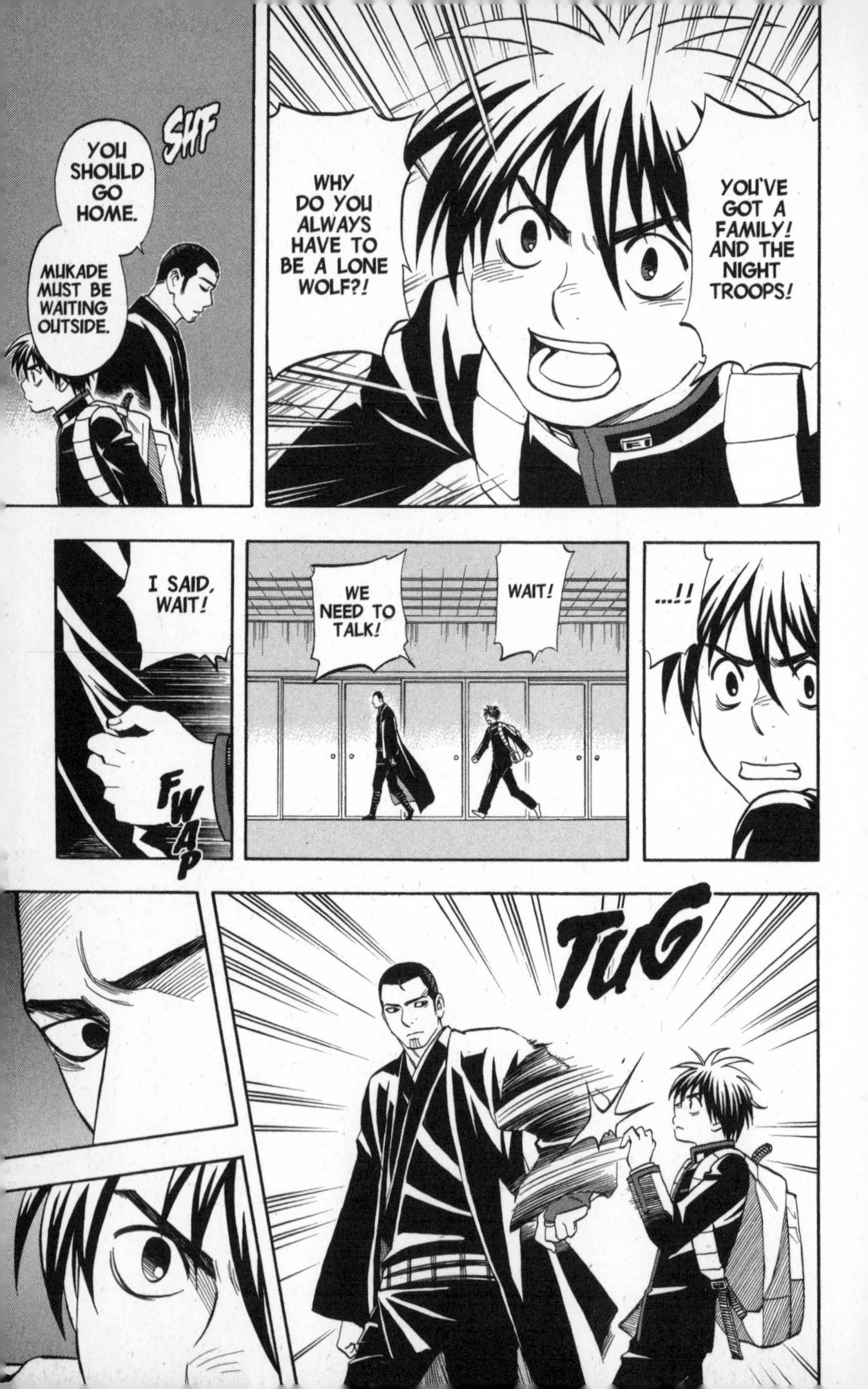
YOU'VE GOT A FAMILY! AND THE NIGHT TROOPS!
WHY DO YOU ALWAYS HAVE TO BE A LONE WOLF?!
SHF
YOU SHOULD GO HOME.
MUKADE MUST BE WAITING OUTSIDE.
...!!
WAIT!
WE NEED TO TALK!
I SAID, WAIT!
FWAP
TUG

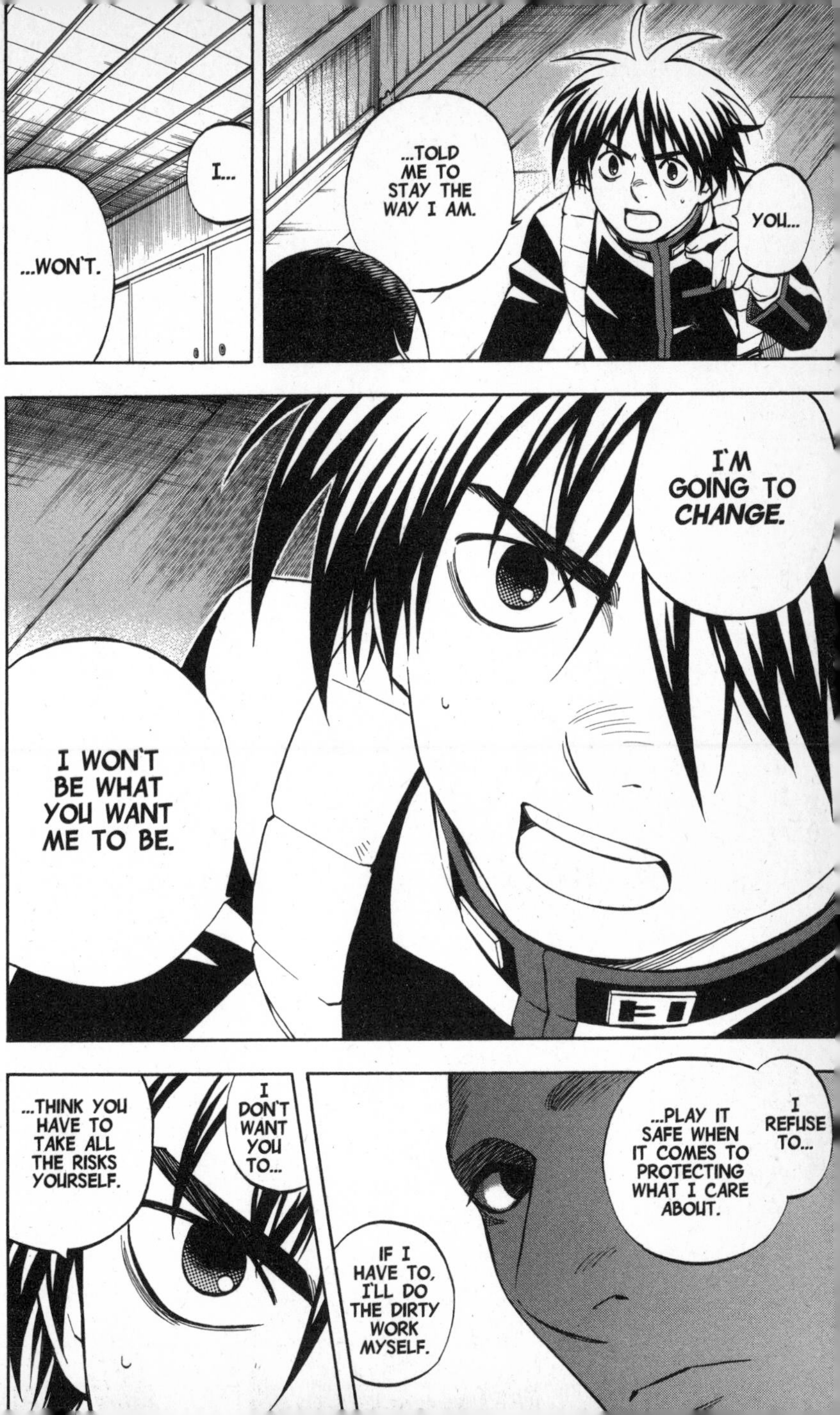
YOU...
...TOLD ME TO STAY THE WAY I AM.
I...
...WON'T.
I'M GOING TO *CHANGE.*
I WON'T BE WHAT YOU WANT ME TO BE.
I REFUSE TO...
...PLAY IT SAFE WHEN IT COMES TO PROTECTING WHAT I CARE ABOUT.
IF I HAVE TO, I'LL DO THE DIRTY WORK MYSELF.
I DON'T WANT YOU TO...
...THINK YOU HAVE TO TAKE ALL THE RISKS YOURSELF.

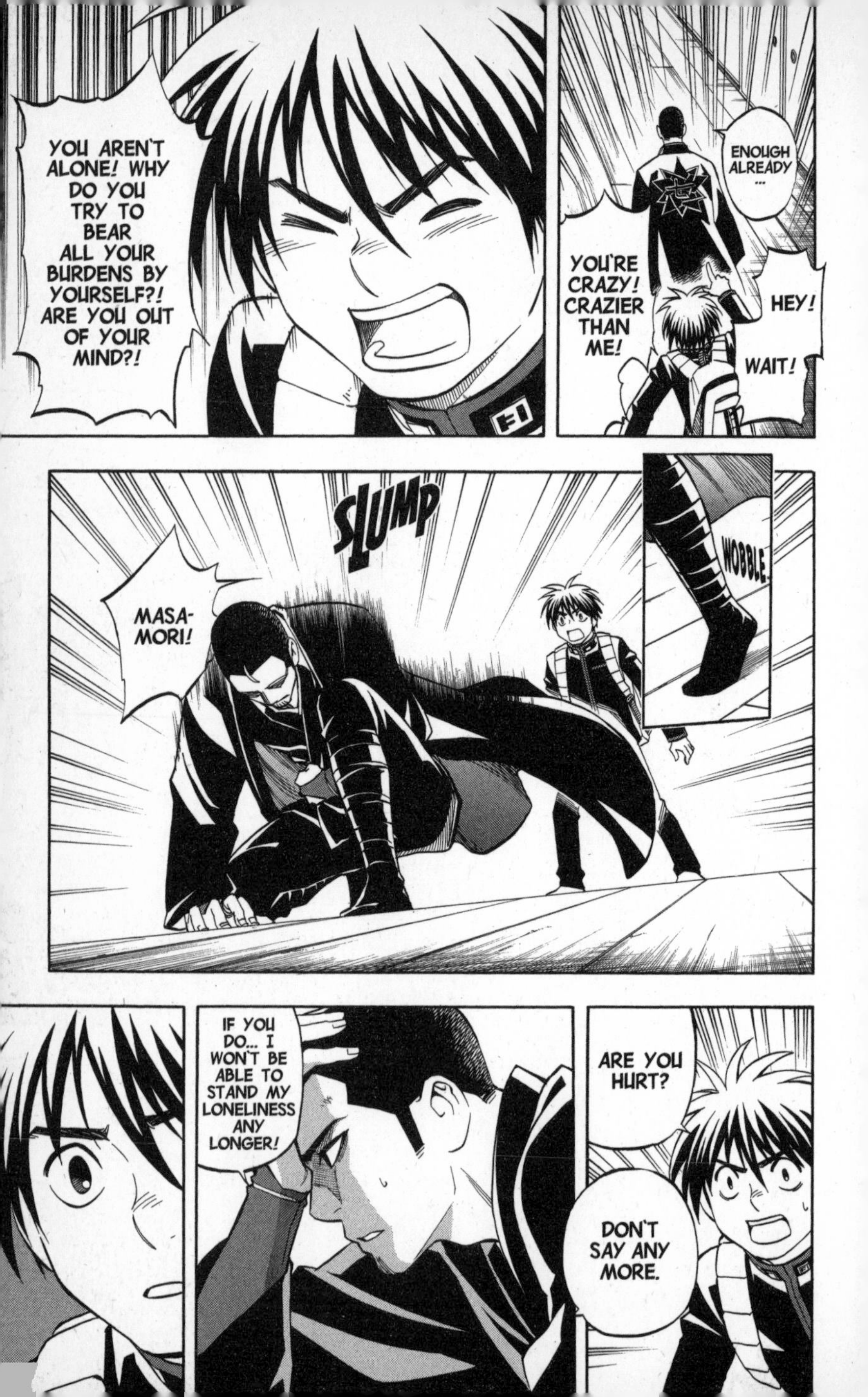
ENOUGH ALREADY ...
YOU'RE CRAZY! CRAZIER THAN ME!
HEY!
WAIT!
YOU AREN'T ALONE! WHY DO YOU TRY TO BEAR ALL YOUR BURDENS BY YOURSELF?! ARE YOU OUT OF YOUR MIND?!
WOBBLE
SLUMP
MASA-MORI!
ARE YOU HURT?
DON'T SAY ANY MORE.
IF YOU DO... I WON'T BE ABLE TO STAND MY LONELINESS ANY LONGER!

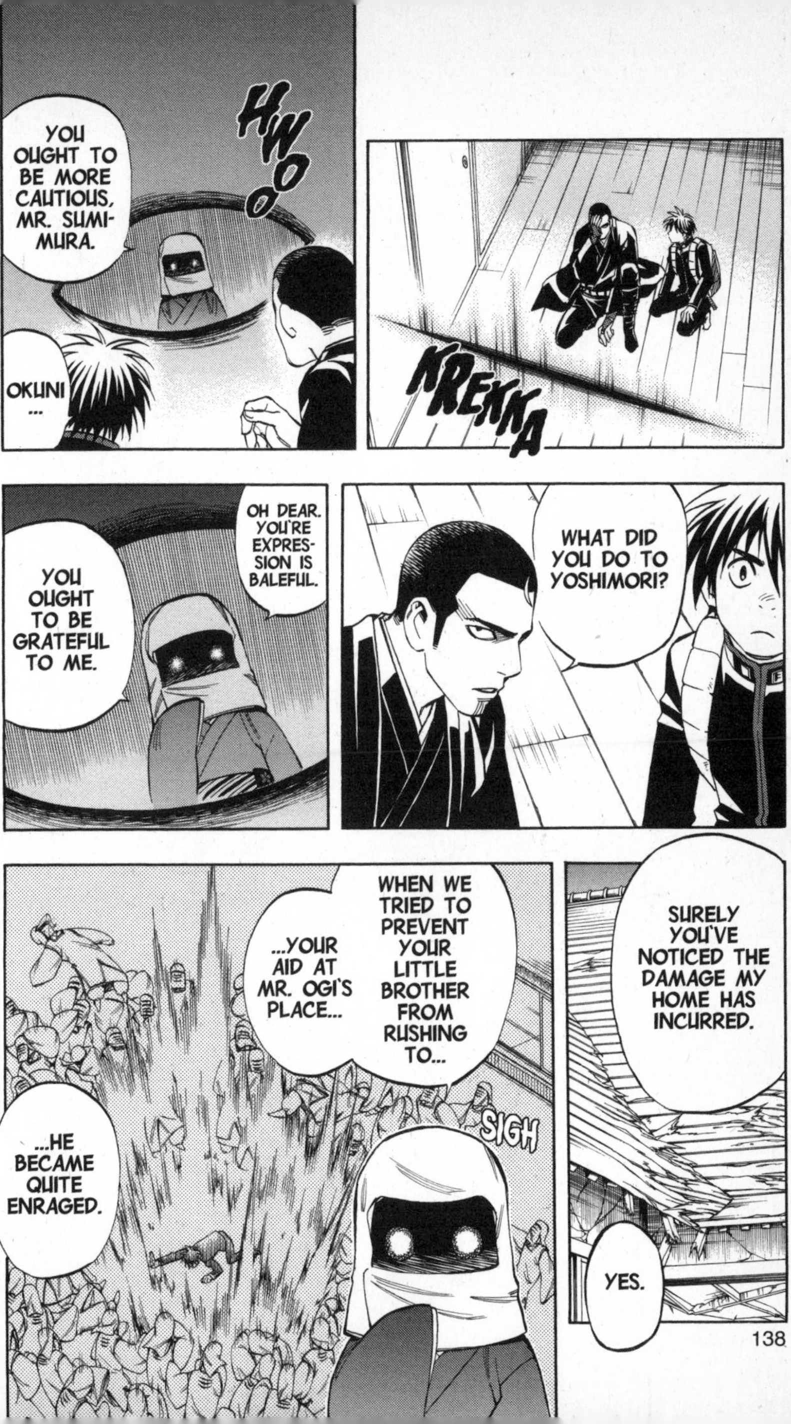
KREKKA
HWOOO
YOU OUGHT TO BE MORE CAUTIOUS, MR. SUMI-MURA.
OKUNI ...
WHAT DID YOU DO TO YOSHIMORI?
OH DEAR. YOU'RE EXPRES-SION IS BALEFUL.
YOU OUGHT TO BE GRATEFUL TO ME.
SURELY YOU'VE NOTICED THE DAMAGE MY HOME HAS INCURRED.
YES.
WHEN WE TRIED TO PREVENT YOUR LITTLE BROTHER FROM RUSHING TO...
...YOUR AID AT MR. OGI'S PLACE...
SIGH
...HE BECAME QUITE ENRAGED.

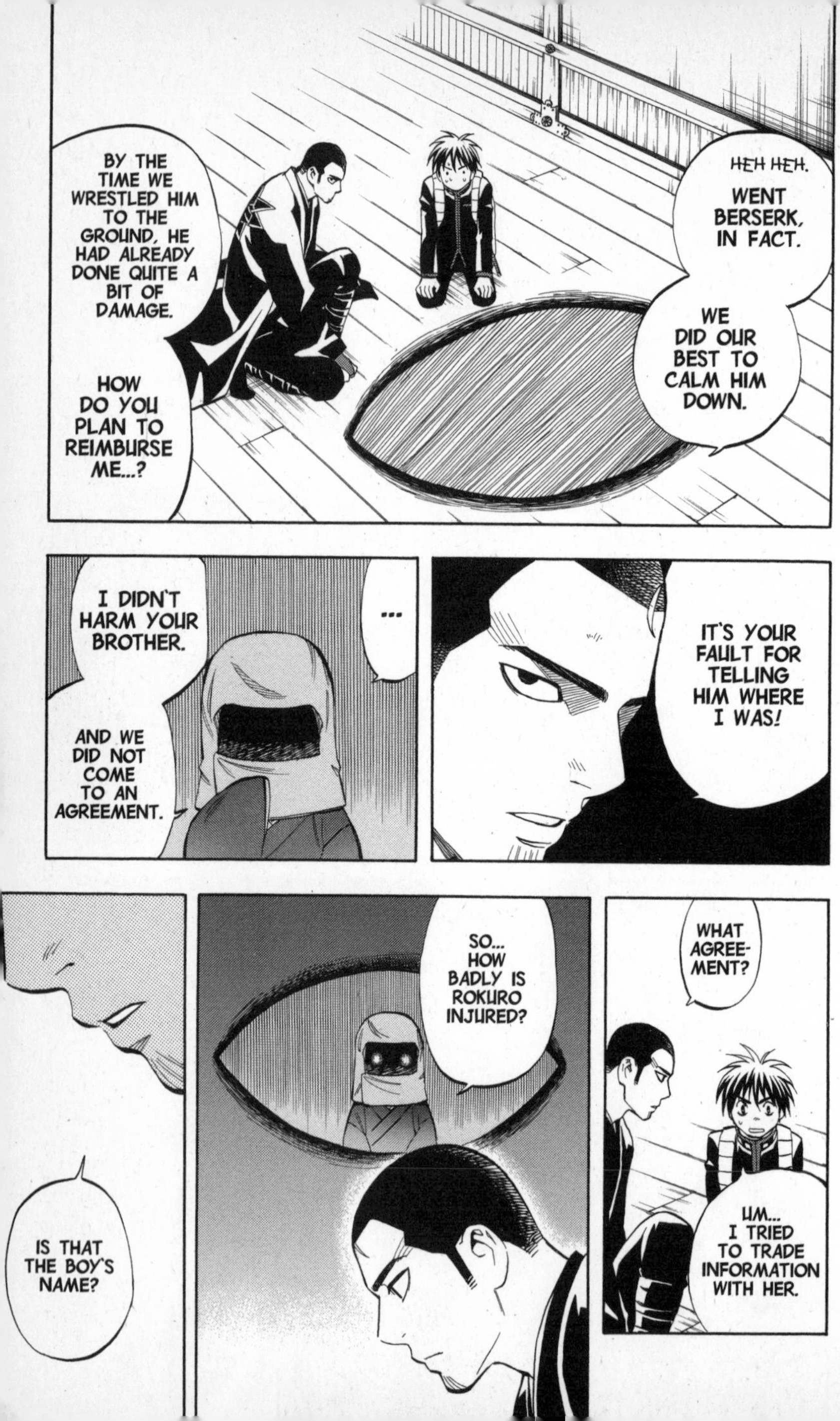
HEH HEH.
WENT BERSERK, IN FACT.
WE DID OUR BEST TO CALM HIM DOWN.
BY THE TIME WE WRESTLED HIM TO THE GROUND, HE HAD ALREADY DONE QUITE A BIT OF DAMAGE.
HOW DO YOU PLAN TO REIMBURSE ME...?
IT'S YOUR FAULT FOR TELLING HIM WHERE I WAS!
...
I DIDN'T HARM YOUR BROTHER.
AND WE DID NOT COME TO AN AGREEMENT.
WHAT AGREEMENT?
UM... I TRIED TO TRADE INFORMATION WITH HER.
SO... HOW BADLY IS ROKURO INJURED?
IS THAT THE BOY'S NAME?

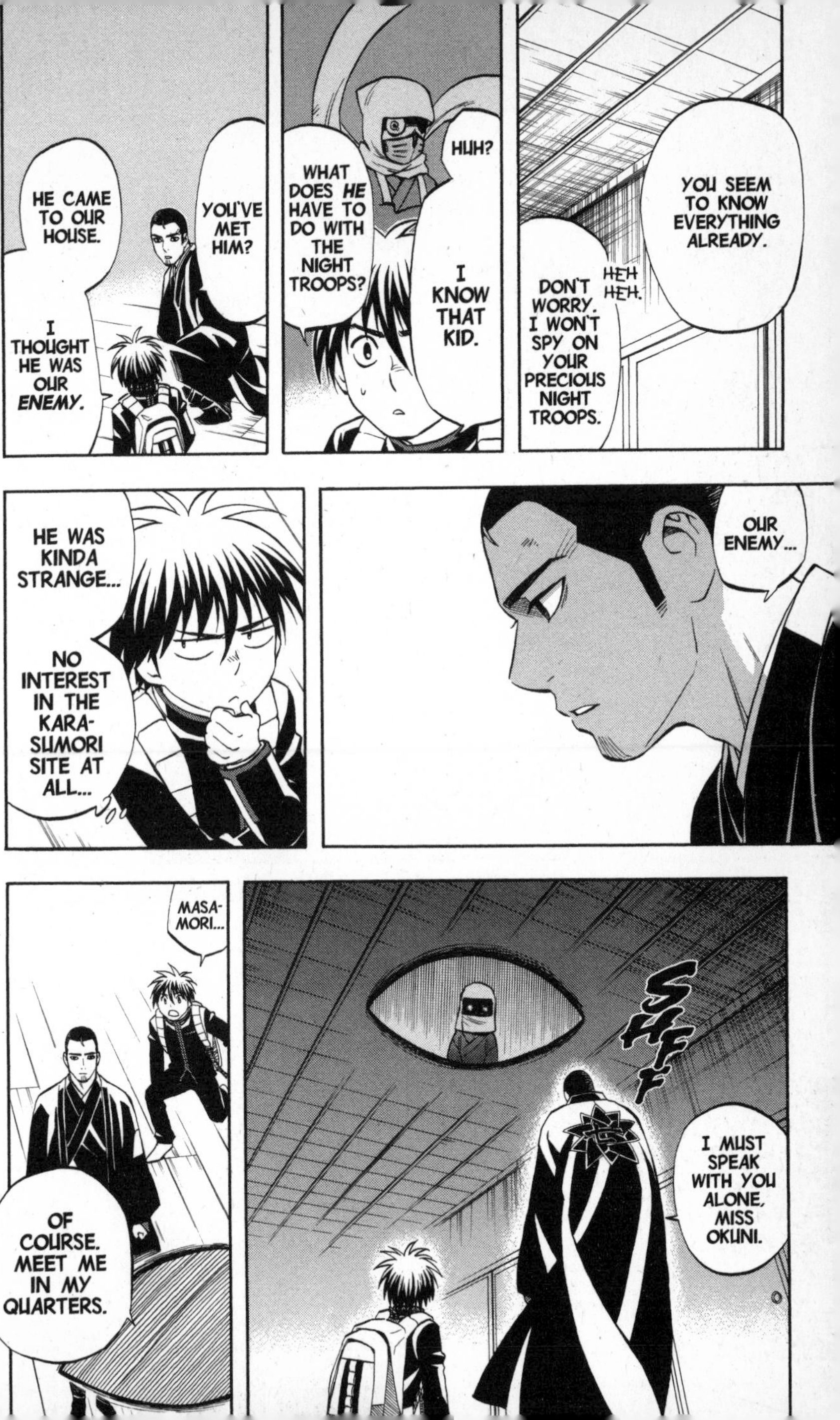
YOU SEEM TO KNOW EVERYTHING ALREADY.
HEH HEH.
DON'T WORRY. I WON'T SPY ON YOUR PRECIOUS NIGHT TROOPS.
HUH?
I KNOW THAT KID.
WHAT DOES *HE* HAVE TO DO WITH THE NIGHT TROOPS?
YOU'VE MET HIM?
HE CAME TO OUR HOUSE.
I THOUGHT HE WAS OUR *ENEMY*.
OUR ENEMY...
HE WAS KINDA STRANGE...
NO INTEREST IN THE KARA-SUMORI SITE AT ALL...
SHFF
I MUST SPEAK WITH YOU ALONE, MISS OKUNI.
MASA-MORI...
OF COURSE. MEET ME IN MY QUARTERS.

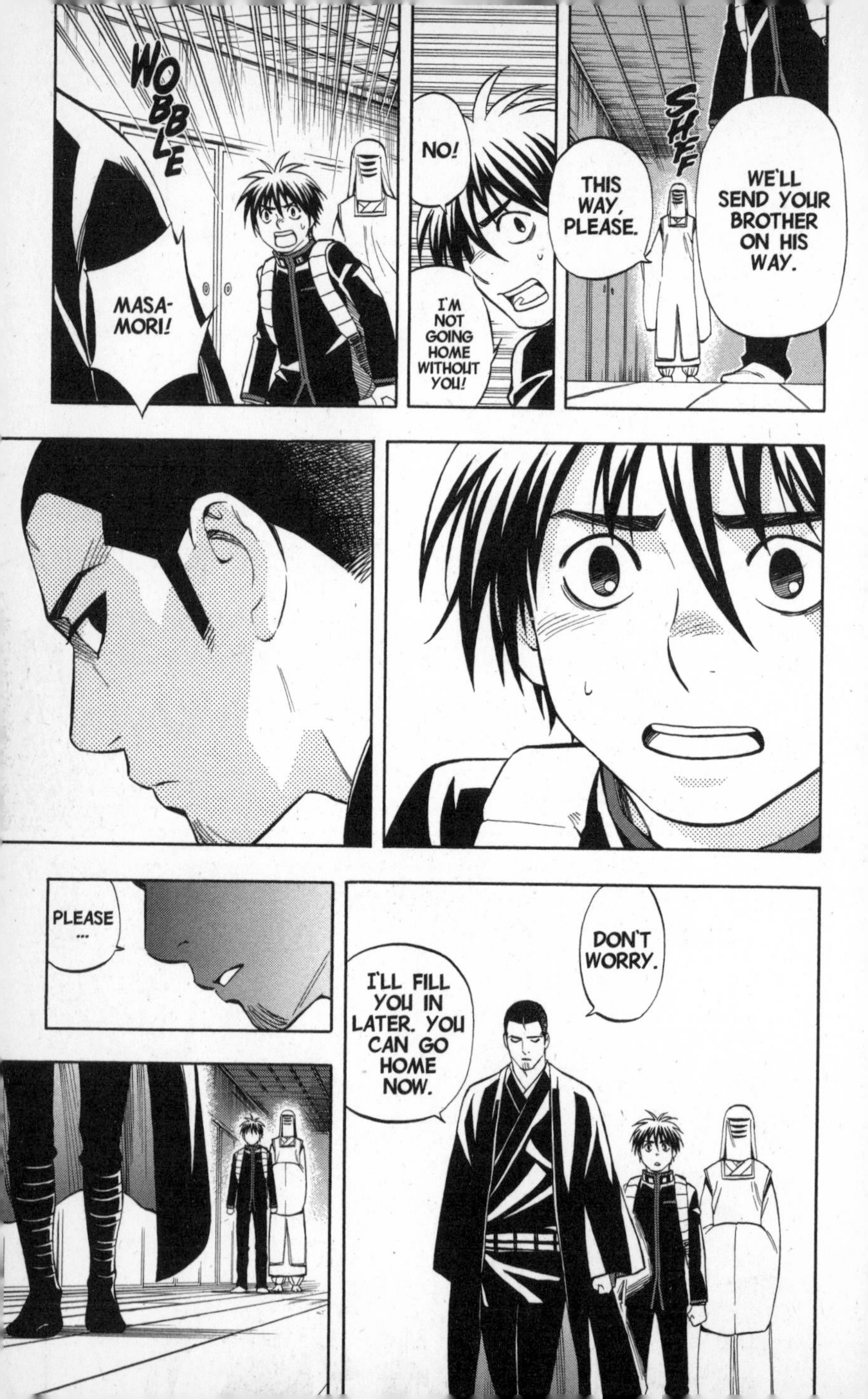
SHFF
WE'LL SEND YOUR BROTHER ON HIS WAY.
THIS WAY, PLEASE.
NO!
I'M NOT GOING HOME WITHOUT YOU!
WOBBLE
MASA-MORI!
DON'T WORRY.
I'LL FILL YOU IN LATER. YOU CAN GO HOME NOW.
PLEASE ...

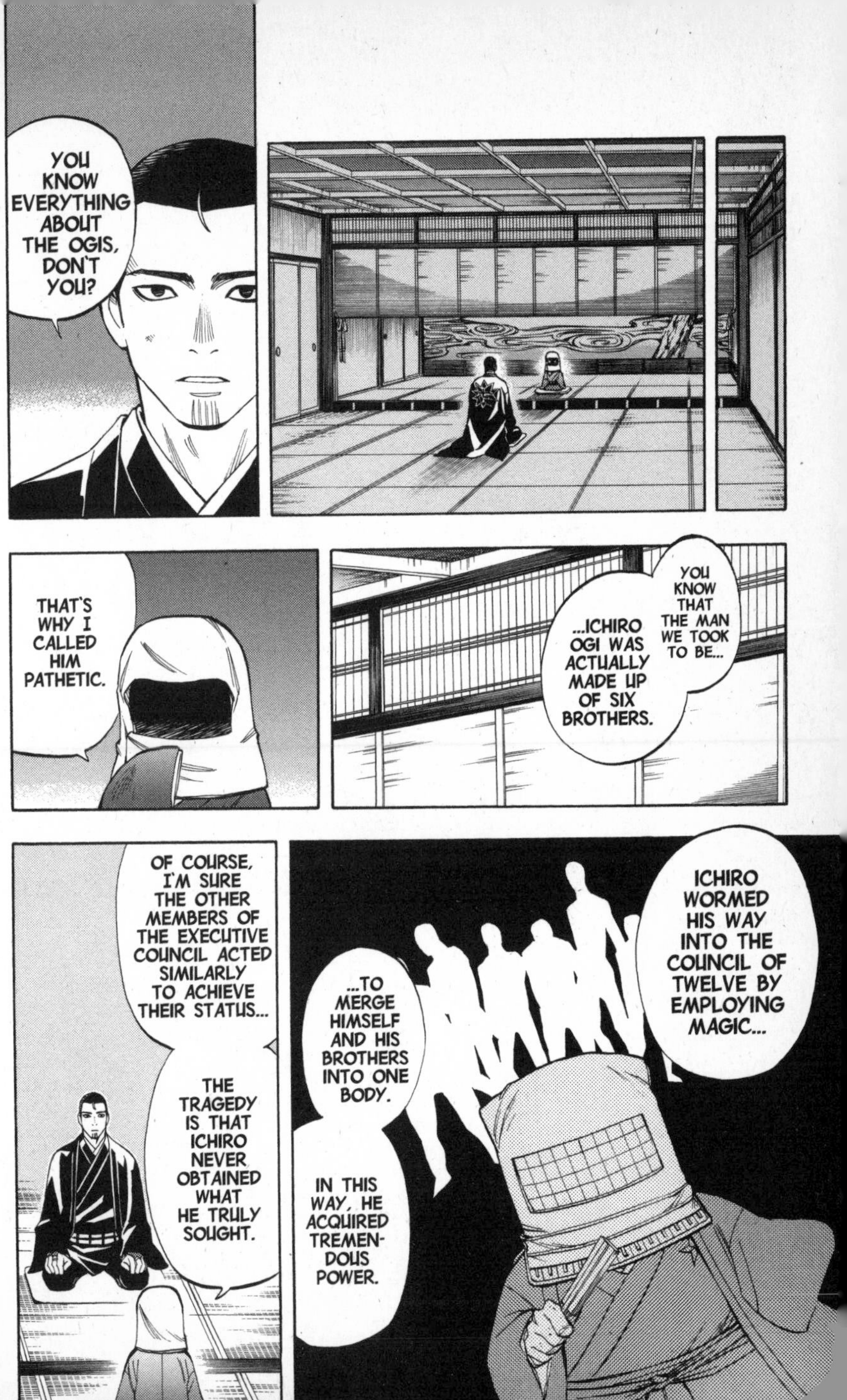
YOU KNOW EVERYTHING ABOUT THE OGIS, DON'T YOU?
YOU KNOW THAT THE MAN WE TOOK TO BE...
...ICHIRO OGI WAS ACTUALLY MADE UP OF SIX BROTHERS.
THAT'S WHY I CALLED HIM PATHETIC.
ICHIRO WORMED HIS WAY INTO THE COUNCIL OF TWELVE BY EMPLOYING MAGIC...
...TO MERGE HIMSELF AND HIS BROTHERS INTO ONE BODY.
IN THIS WAY, HE ACQUIRED TREMENDOUS POWER.
OF COURSE, I'M SURE THE OTHER MEMBERS OF THE EXECUTIVE COUNCIL ACTED SIMILARLY TO ACHIEVE THEIR STATUS...
THE TRAGEDY IS THAT ICHIRO NEVER OBTAINED WHAT HE TRULY SOUGHT.

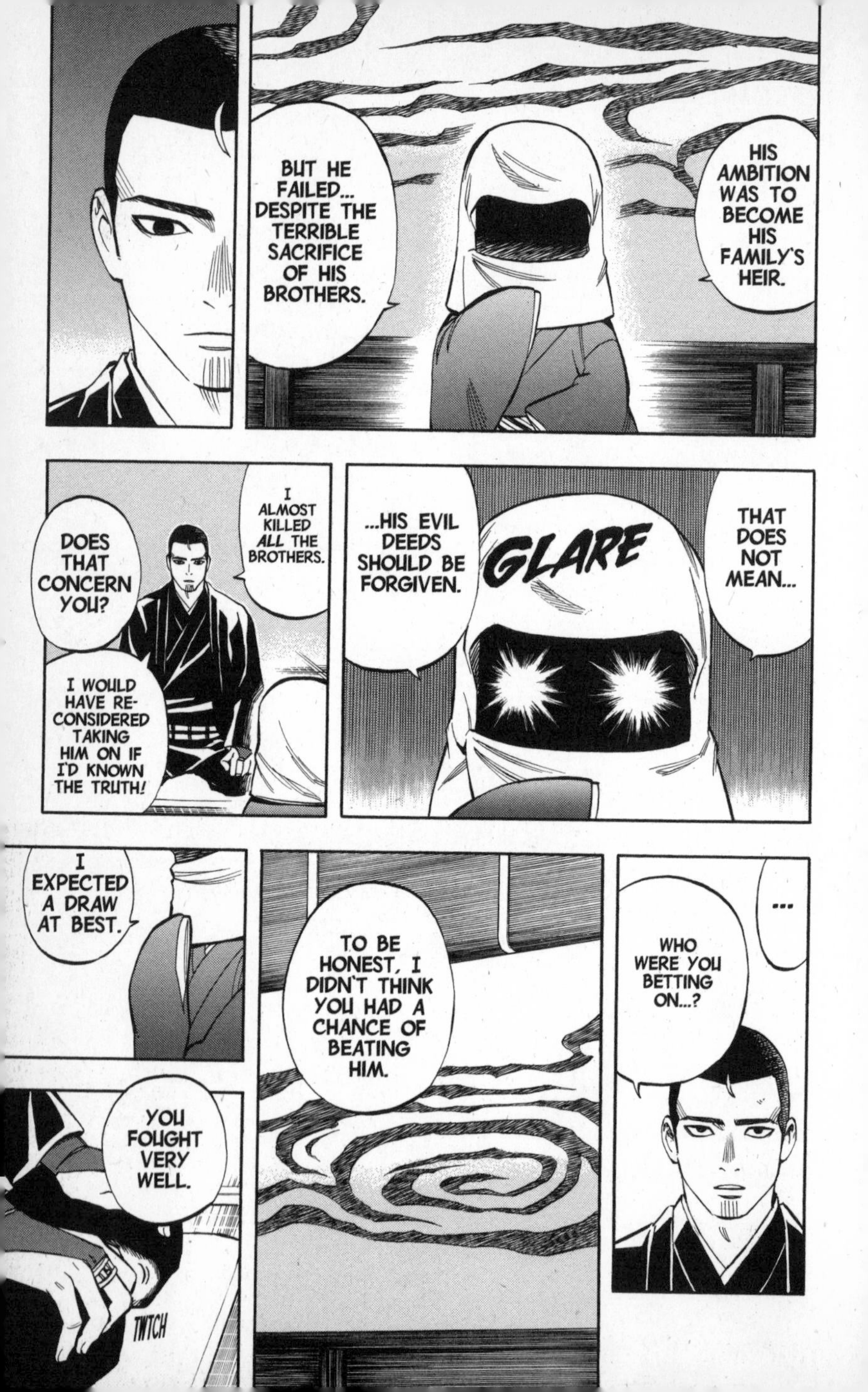
HIS AMBITION WAS TO BECOME HIS FAMILY'S HEIR.
BUT HE FAILED... DESPITE THE TERRIBLE SACRIFICE OF HIS BROTHERS.
THAT DOES NOT MEAN...
GLARE
...HIS EVIL DEEDS SHOULD BE FORGIVEN.
I ALMOST KILLED ALL THE BROTHERS.
DOES THAT CONCERN YOU?
I WOULD HAVE RE-CONSIDERED TAKING HIM ON IF I'D KNOWN THE TRUTH!
...
WHO WERE YOU BETTING ON...?
TO BE HONEST, I DIDN'T THINK YOU HAD A CHANCE OF BEATING HIM.
I EXPECTED A DRAW AT BEST.
YOU FOUGHT VERY WELL.
TWTCH

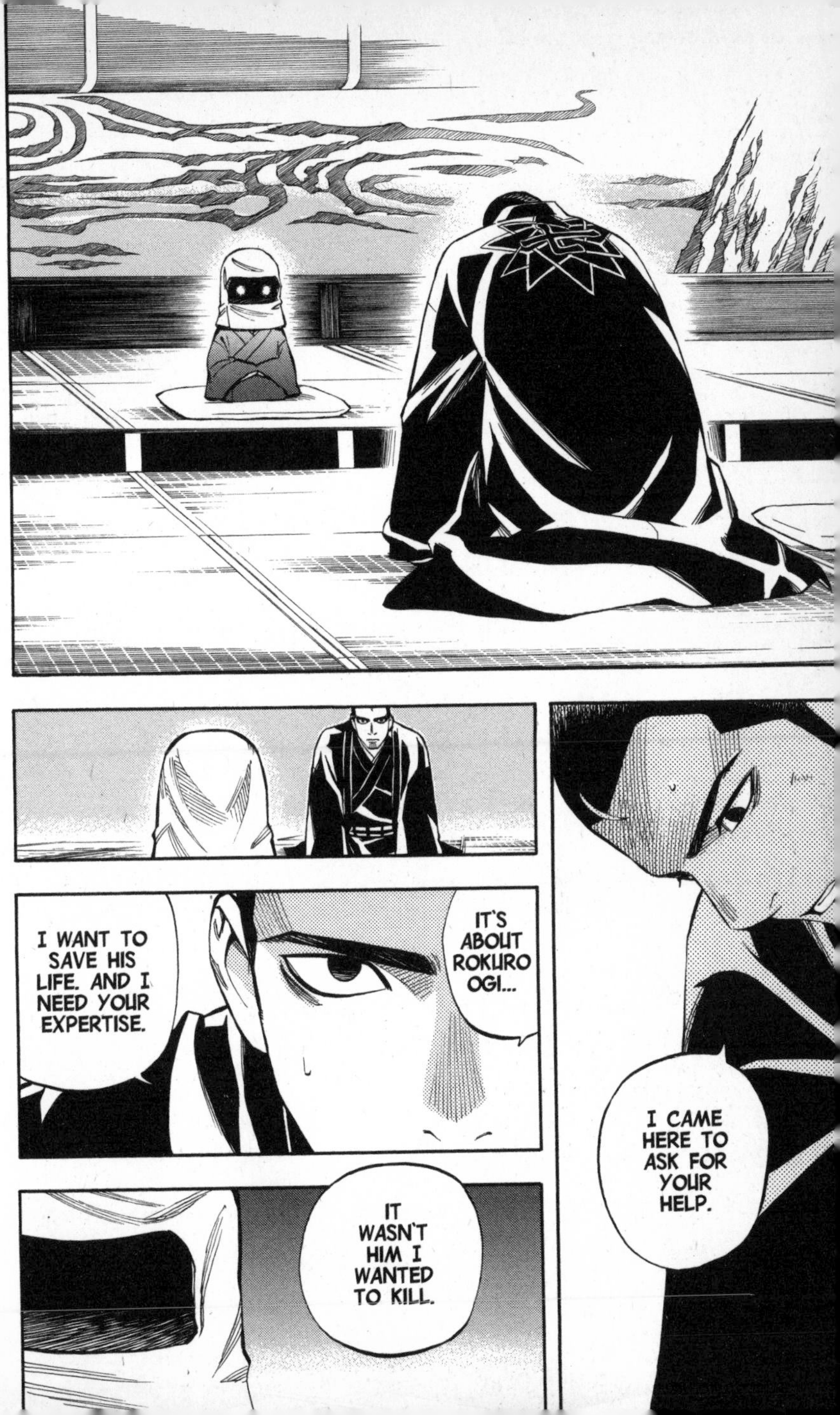
I CAME HERE TO ASK FOR YOUR HELP.
IT'S ABOUT ROKURO OGI...
I WANT TO SAVE HIS LIFE. AND I NEED YOUR EXPERTISE.
IT WASN'T HIM I WANTED TO KILL.

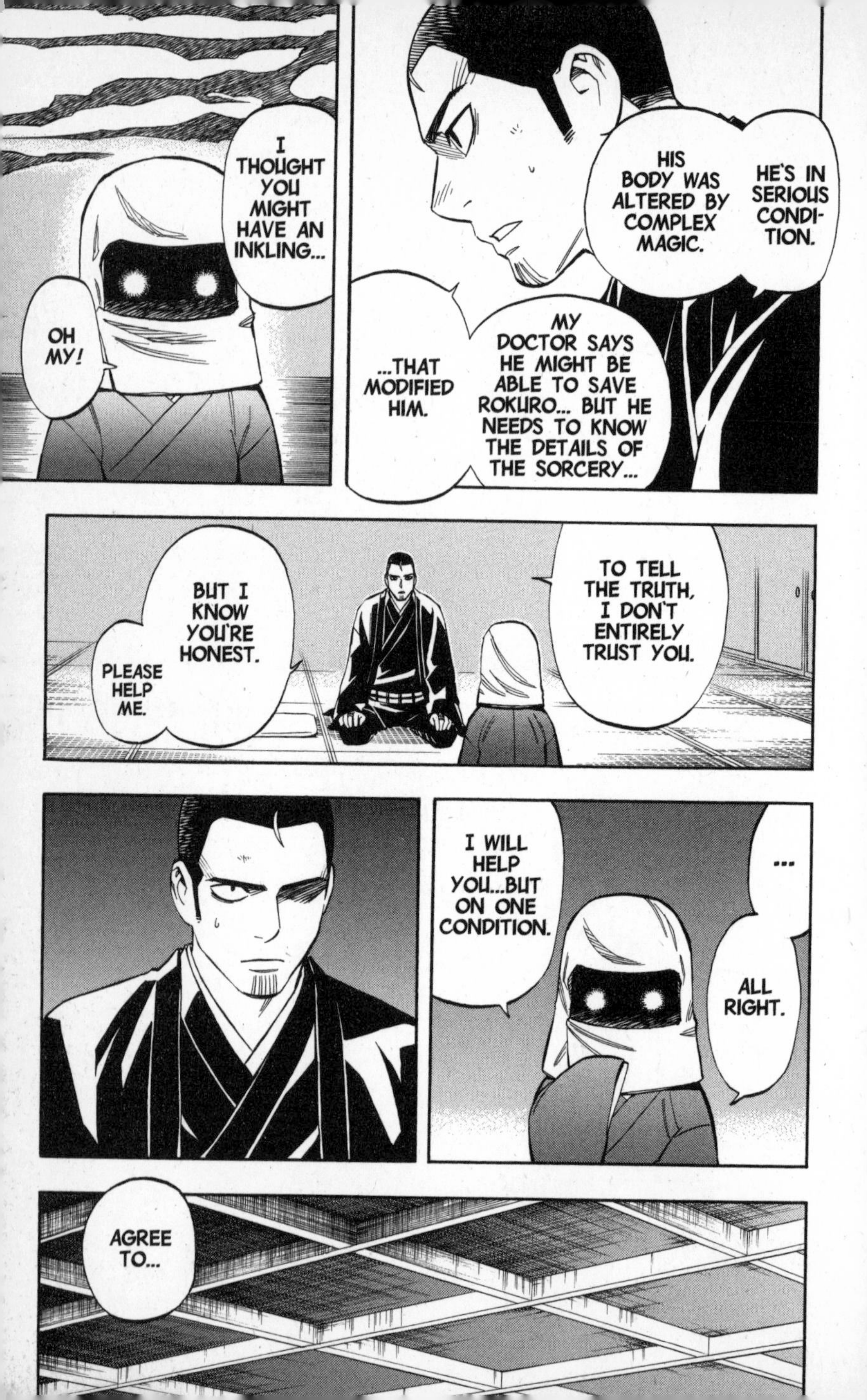
HE'S IN SERIOUS CONDITION.
HIS BODY WAS ALTERED BY COMPLEX MAGIC.
MY DOCTOR SAYS HE MIGHT BE ABLE TO SAVE ROKURO... BUT HE NEEDS TO KNOW THE DETAILS OF THE SORCERY...
...THAT MODIFIED HIM.
I THOUGHT YOU MIGHT HAVE AN INKLING...
OH MY!
TO TELL THE TRUTH, I DON'T ENTIRELY TRUST YOU.
BUT I KNOW YOU'RE HONEST.
PLEASE HELP ME.
...
ALL RIGHT.
I WILL HELP YOU...BUT ON ONE CONDITION.
AGREE TO...

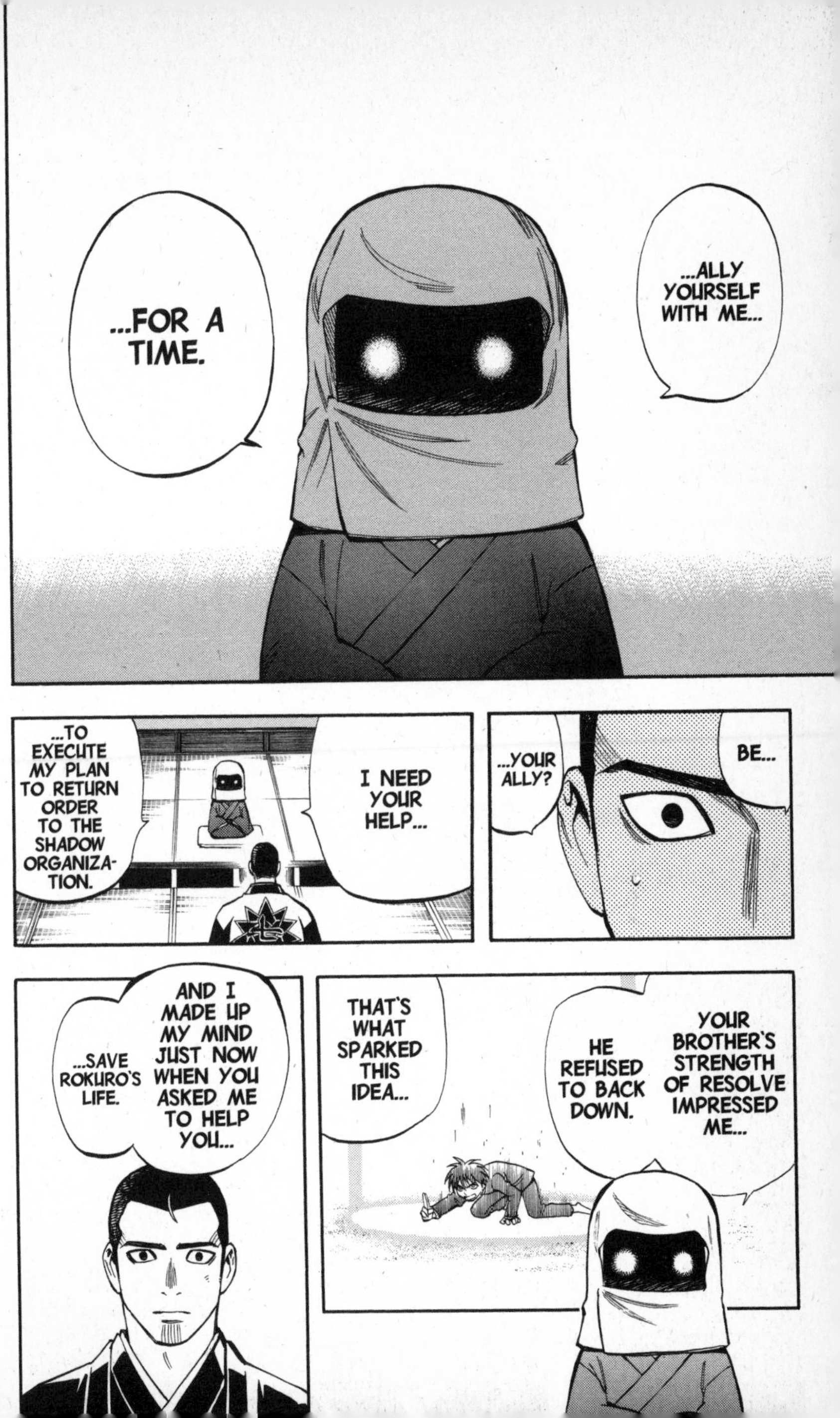
...ALLY YOURSELF WITH ME...
...FOR A TIME.
BE...
...YOUR ALLY?
I NEED YOUR HELP...
...TO EXECUTE MY PLAN TO RETURN ORDER TO THE SHADOW ORGANIZATION.
YOUR BROTHER'S STRENGTH OF RESOLVE IMPRESSED ME...
HE REFUSED TO BACK DOWN.
THAT'S WHAT SPARKED THIS IDEA...
AND I MADE UP MY MIND JUST NOW WHEN YOU ASKED ME TO HELP YOU...
...SAVE ROKURO'S LIFE.

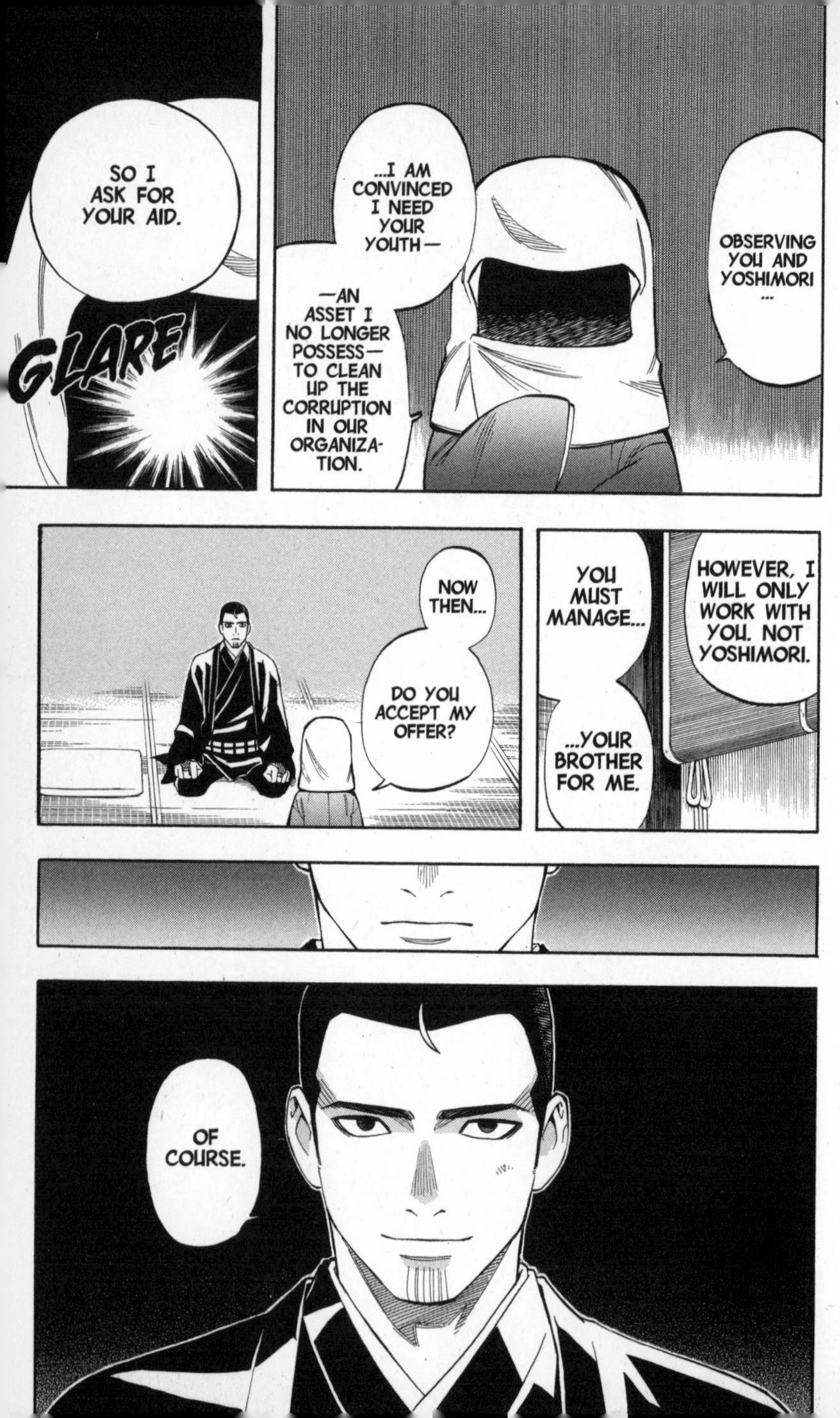
OBSERVING YOU AND YOSHIMORI ...
...I AM CONVINCED I NEED YOUR YOUTH—
—AN ASSET I NO LONGER POSSESS— TO CLEAN UP THE CORRUPTION IN OUR ORGANIZATION.
SO I ASK FOR YOUR AID.
GLARE
HOWEVER, I WILL ONLY WORK WITH YOU. NOT YOSHIMORI.
YOU MUST MANAGE...
...YOUR BROTHER FOR ME.
NOW THEN...
DO YOU ACCEPT MY OFFER?
OF COURSE.

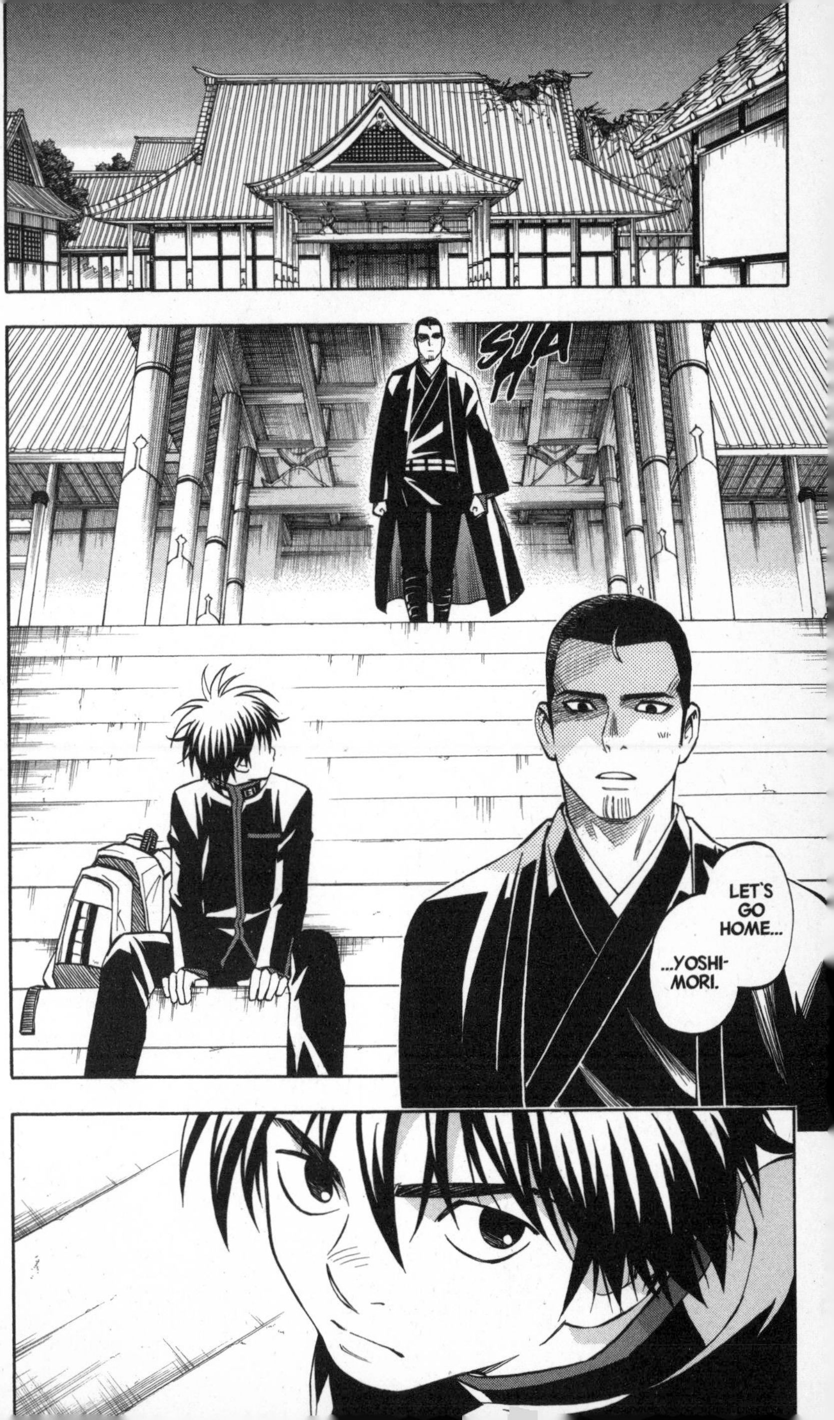
SHA
LET'S GO HOME...
...YOSHI-MORI.

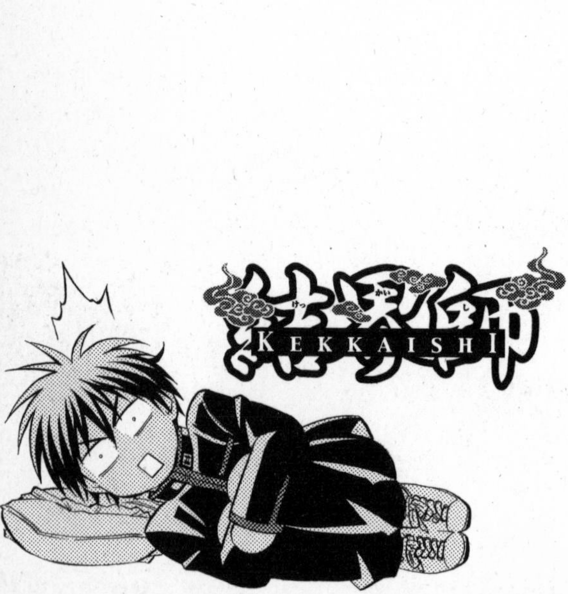
結界師
KEKKAISHI

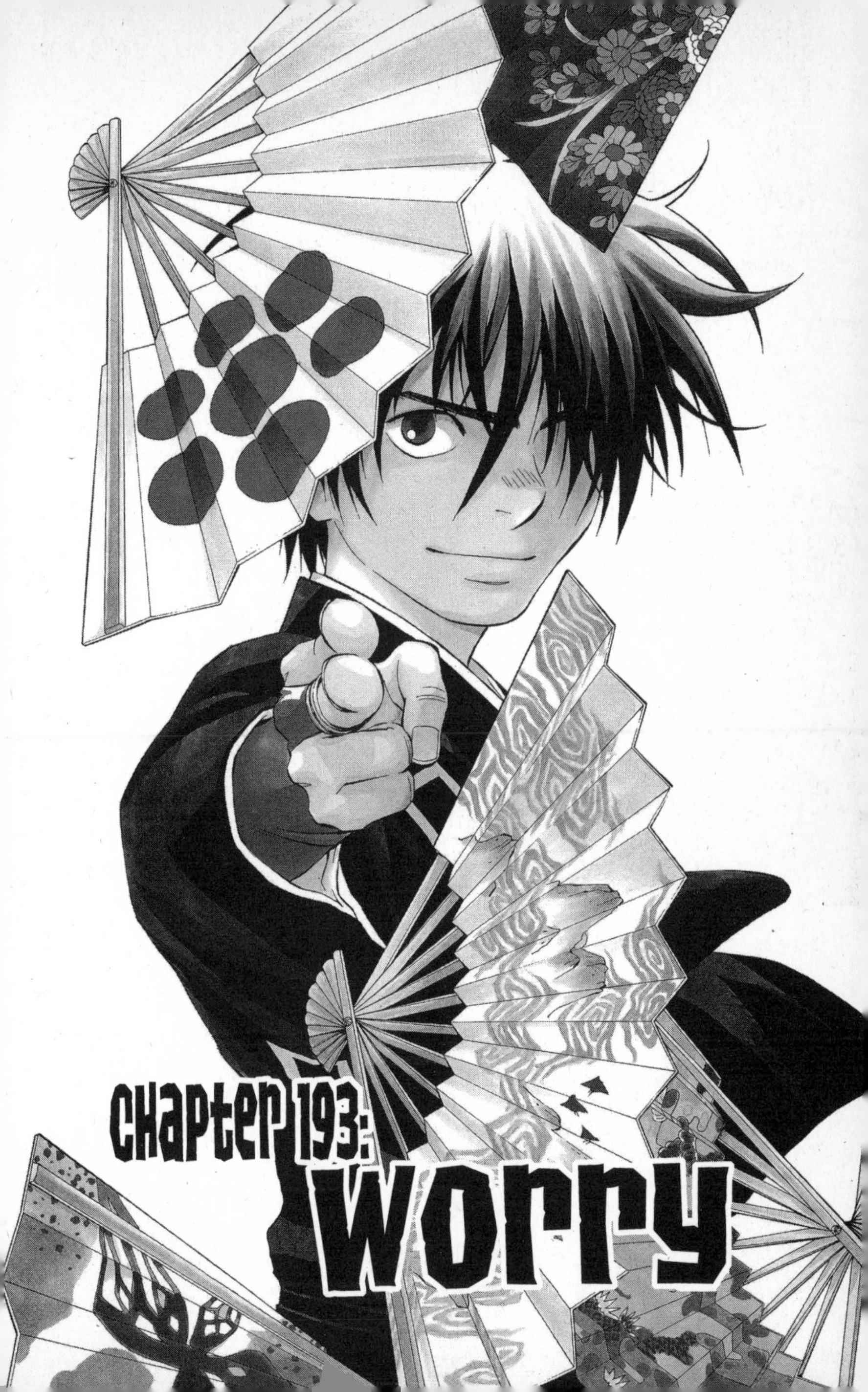
CHAPTER 193:
WORRY

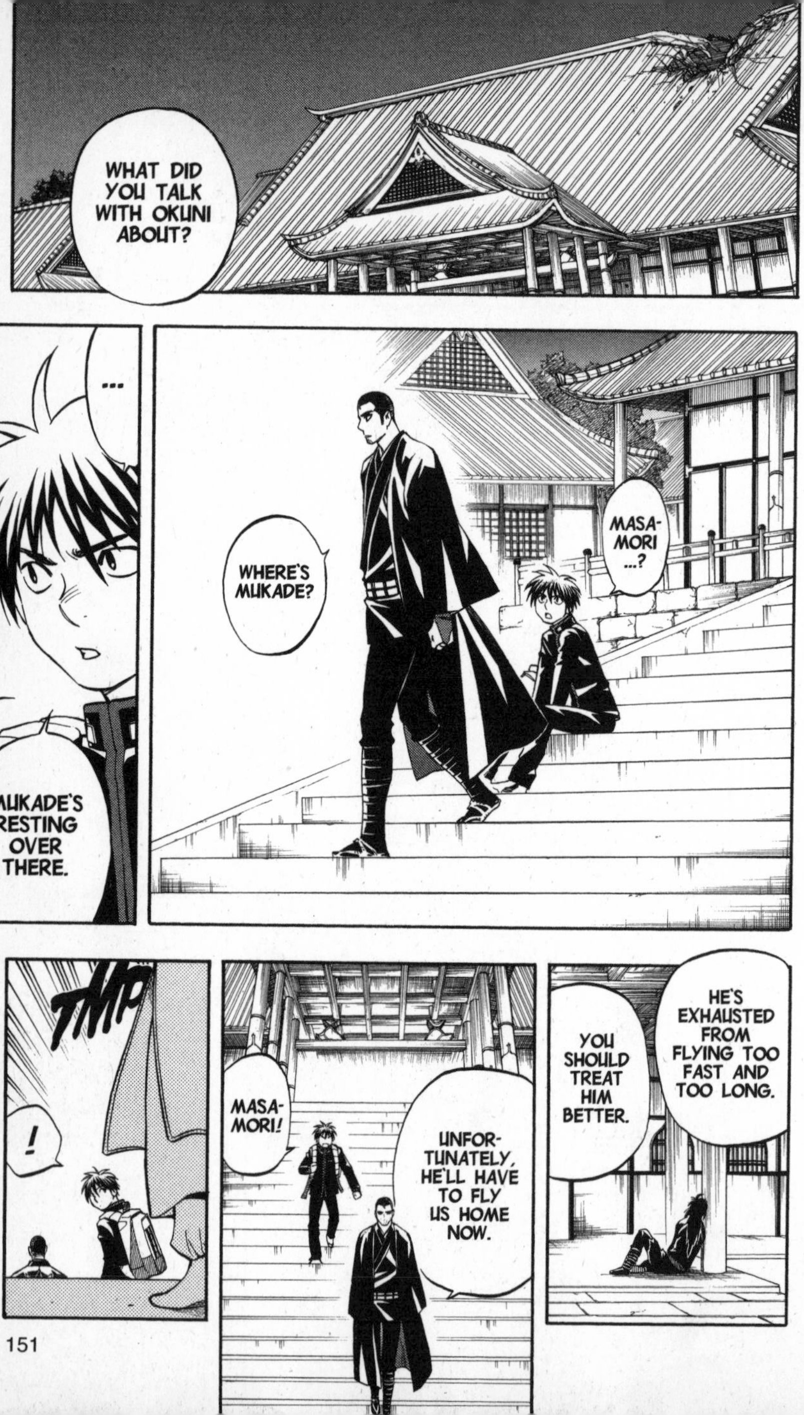
WHAT DID YOU TALK WITH OKUNI ABOUT?
MASA-MORI ...?
WHERE'S MUKADE?
...
MUKADE'S RESTING OVER THERE.
HE'S EXHAUSTED FROM FLYING TOO FAST AND TOO LONG.
YOU SHOULD TREAT HIM BETTER.
UNFOR-TUNATELY, HE'LL HAVE TO FLY US HOME NOW.
MASA-MORI!
TMP
!

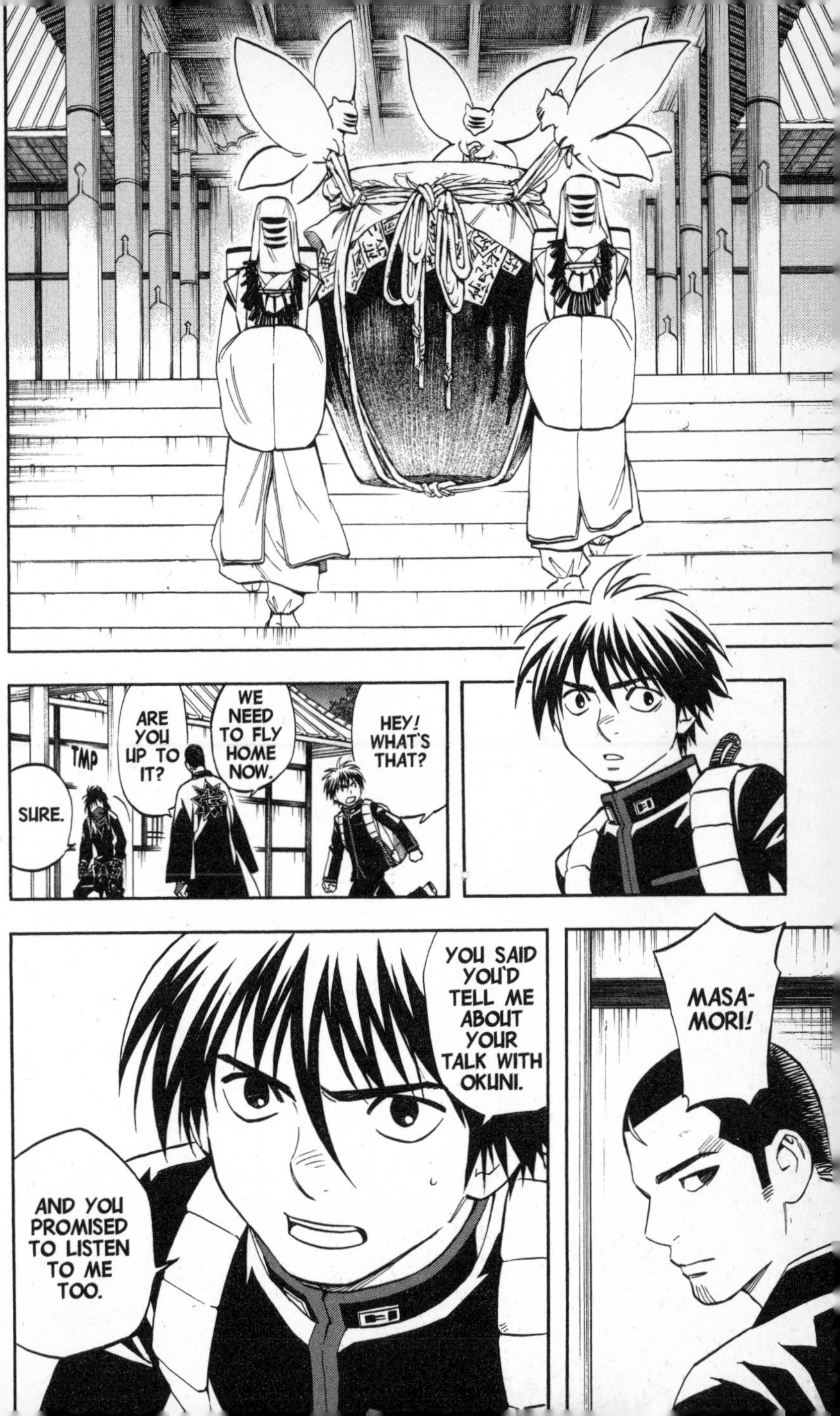
HEY! WHAT'S THAT?
WE NEED TO FLY HOME NOW.
ARE YOU UP TO IT?
TMP
SURE.
MASA-MORI!
YOU SAID YOU'D TELL ME ABOUT YOUR TALK WITH OKUNI.
AND YOU PROMISED TO LISTEN TO ME TOO.

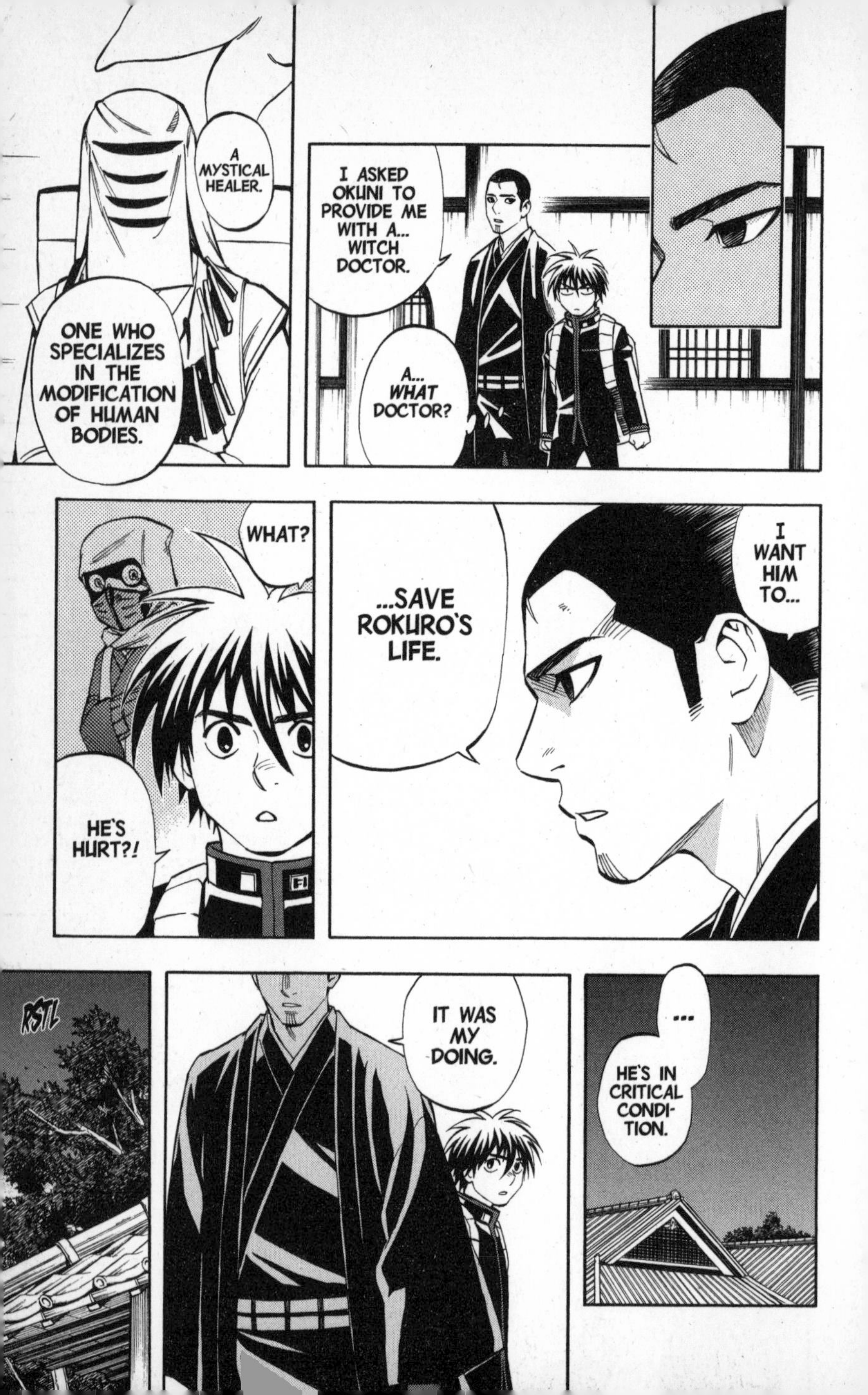
I ASKED OKUNI TO PROVIDE ME WITH A... WITCH DOCTOR.
A... WHAT DOCTOR?
A MYSTICAL HEALER.
ONE WHO SPECIALIZES IN THE MODIFICATION OF HUMAN BODIES.
I WANT HIM TO...
...SAVE ROKURO'S LIFE.
WHAT?
HE'S HURT?!
...
HE'S IN CRITICAL CONDI-TION.
IT WAS MY DOING.
RSTL

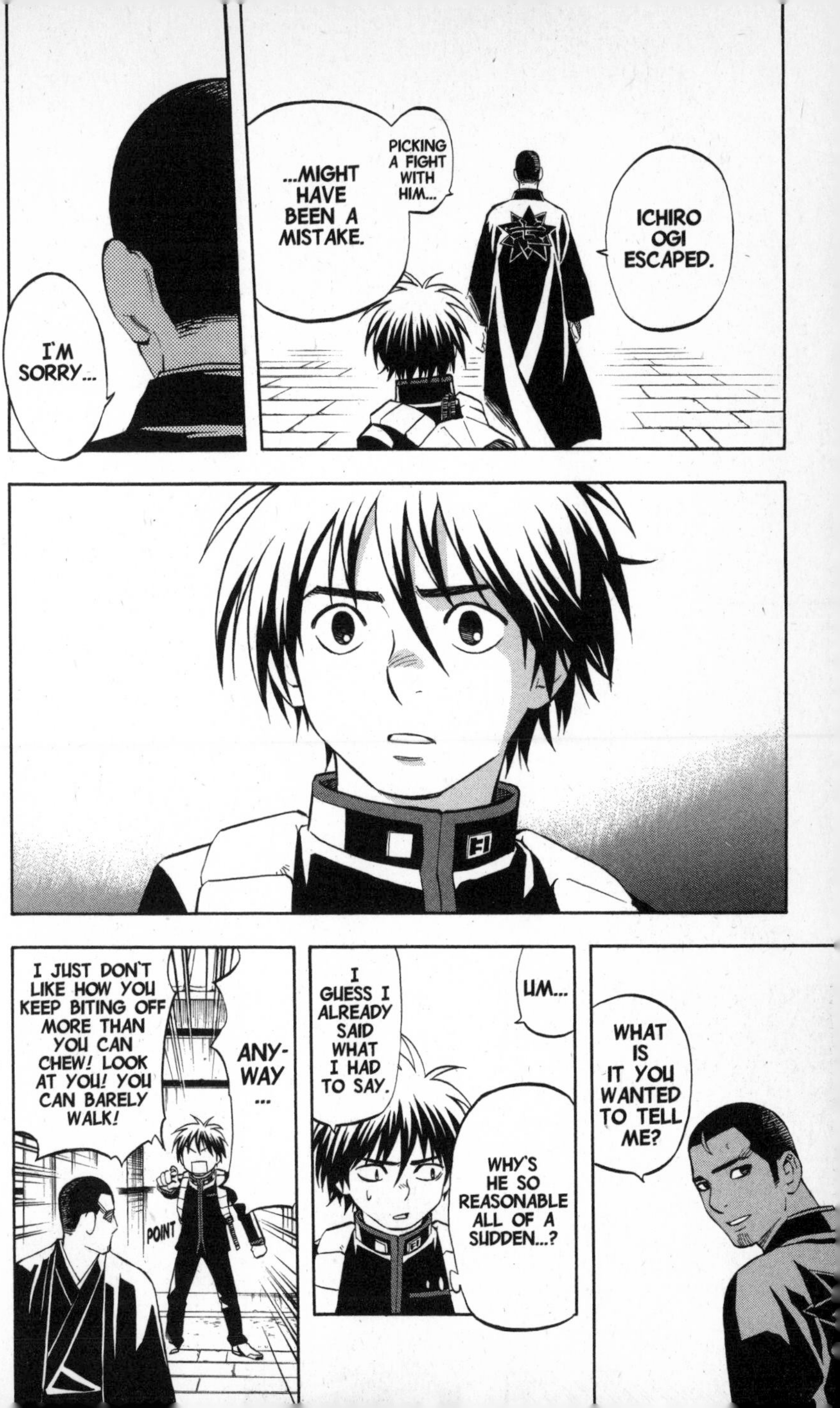
ICHIRO OGI ESCAPED.
PICKING A FIGHT WITH HIM...
...MIGHT HAVE BEEN A MISTAKE.
I'M SORRY...
WHAT IS IT YOU WANTED TO TELL ME?
UM...
I GUESS I ALREADY SAID WHAT I HAD TO SAY.
WHY'S HE SO REASONABLE ALL OF A SUDDEN...?
ANY-WAY...
I JUST DON'T LIKE HOW YOU KEEP BITING OFF MORE THAN YOU CAN CHEW! LOOK AT YOU! YOU CAN BARELY WALK!
POINT

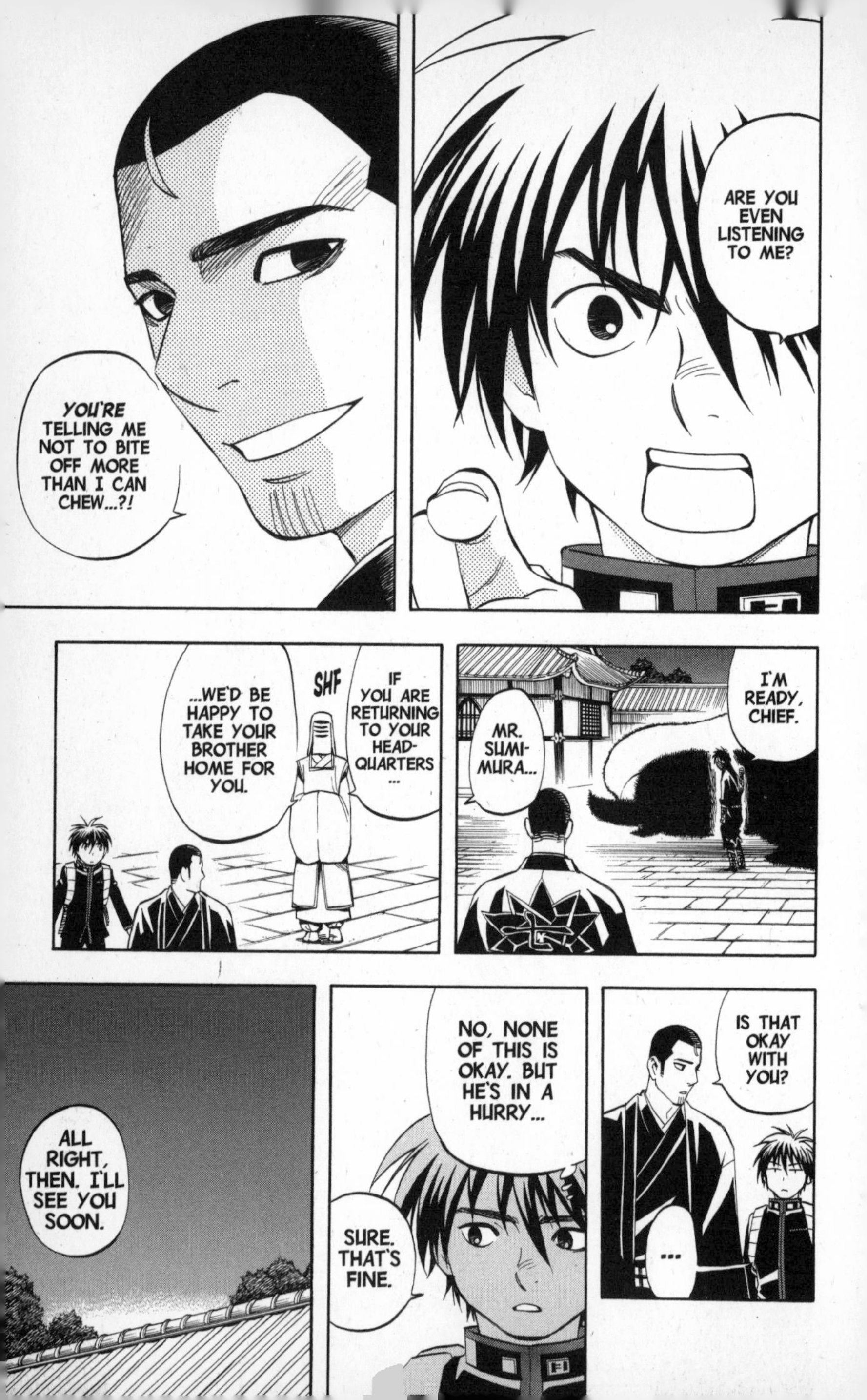
ARE YOU EVEN LISTENING TO ME?
YOU'RE TELLING ME NOT TO BITE OFF MORE THAN I CAN CHEW...?!
I'M READY, CHIEF.
MR. SUMI-MURA...
IF YOU ARE RETURNING TO YOUR HEAD-QUARTERS...
SHF
...WE'D BE HAPPY TO TAKE YOUR BROTHER HOME FOR YOU.
IS THAT OKAY WITH YOU?
...
NO, NONE OF THIS IS OKAY. BUT HE'S IN A HURRY...
SURE. THAT'S FINE.
ALL RIGHT, THEN. I'LL SEE YOU SOON.

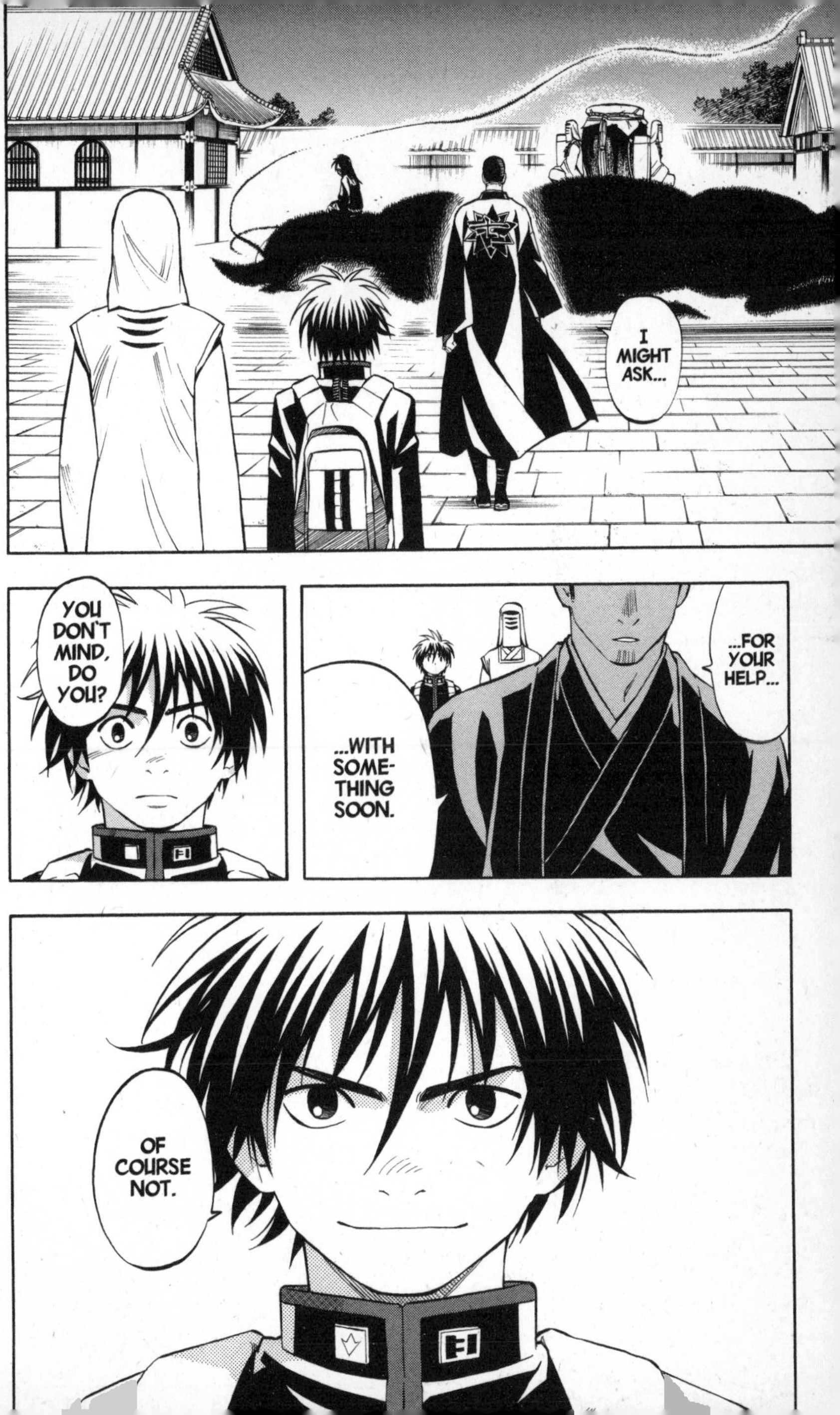
I MIGHT ASK...
...FOR YOUR HELP...
...WITH SOME-THING SOON.
YOU DON'T MIND, DO YOU?
OF COURSE NOT.

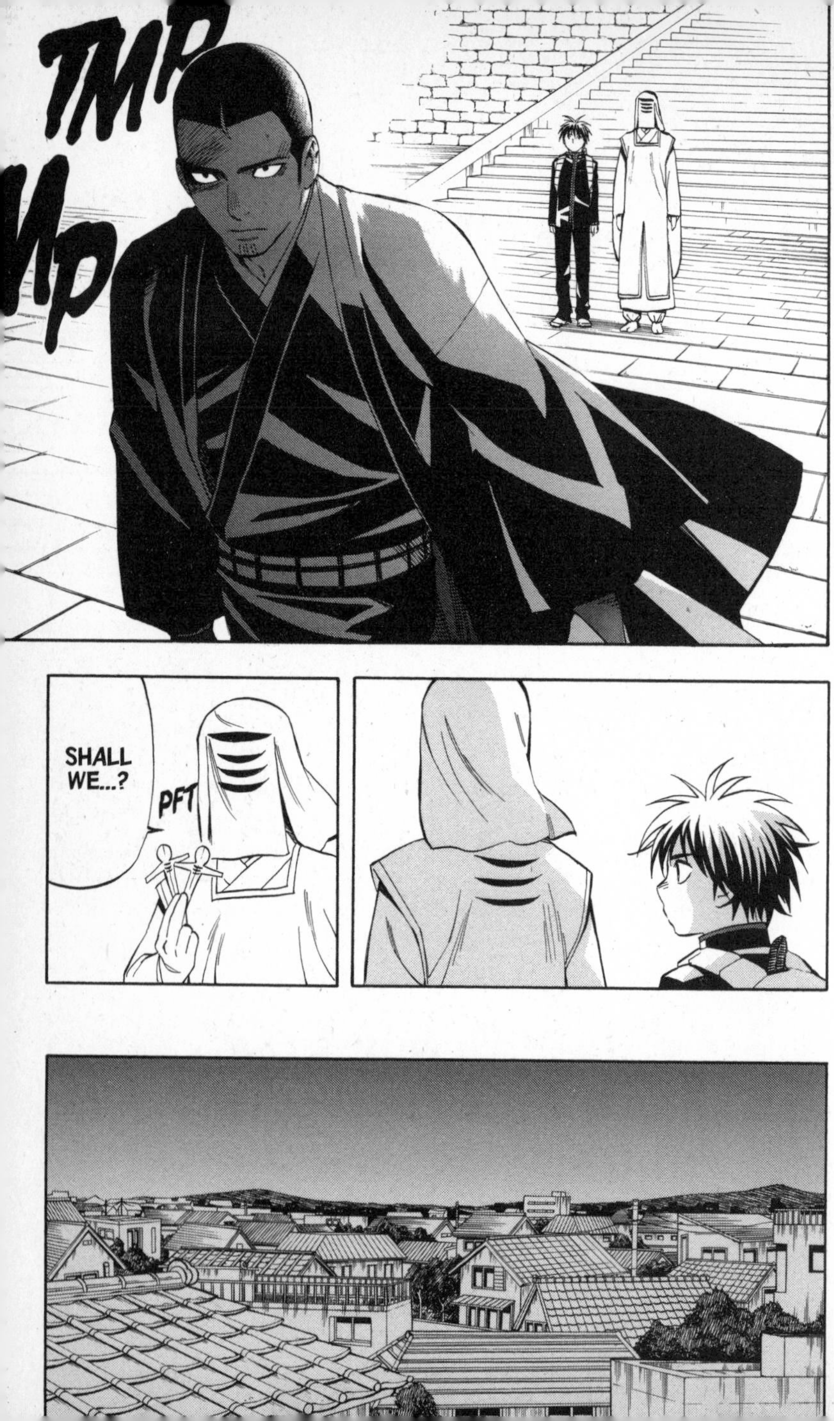
TMP TMP
SHALL WE...?
PFT

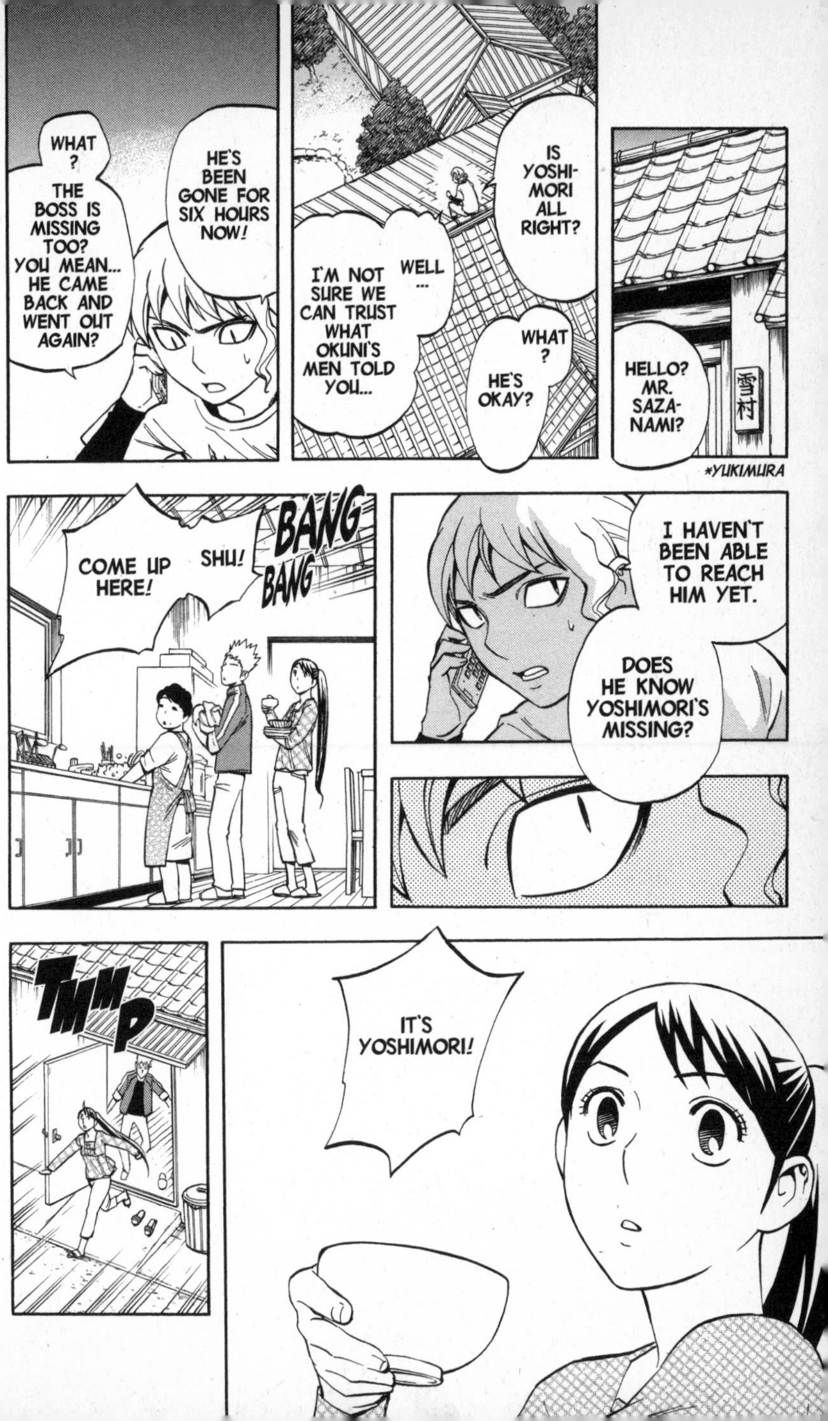
HELLO? MR. SAZA-NAMI?
雪村
*YUKIMURA
IS YOSHI-MORI ALL RIGHT?
WHAT? HE'S OKAY?
WELL...
I'M NOT SURE WE CAN TRUST WHAT OKUNI'S MEN TOLD YOU...
HE'S BEEN GONE FOR SIX HOURS NOW!
WHAT? THE BOSS IS MISSING TOO? YOU MEAN... HE CAME BACK AND WENT OUT AGAIN?
I HAVEN'T BEEN ABLE TO REACH HIM YET.
DOES HE KNOW YOSHIMORI'S MISSING?
BANG BANG
SHU!
COME UP HERE!
IT'S YOSHIMORI!
TMP

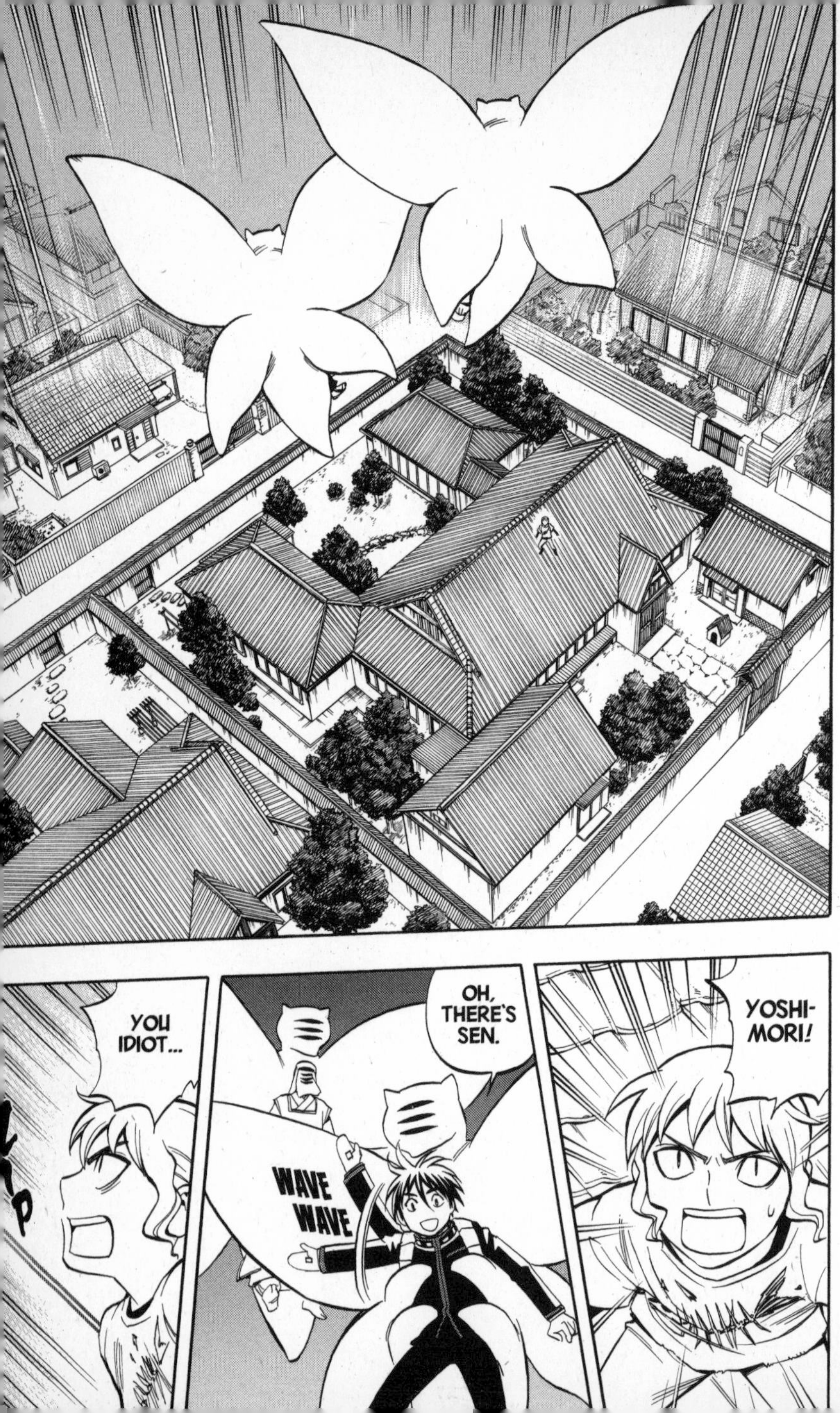
YOSHI-MORI!
OH, THERE'S SEN.
WAVE WAVE
YOU IDIOT...

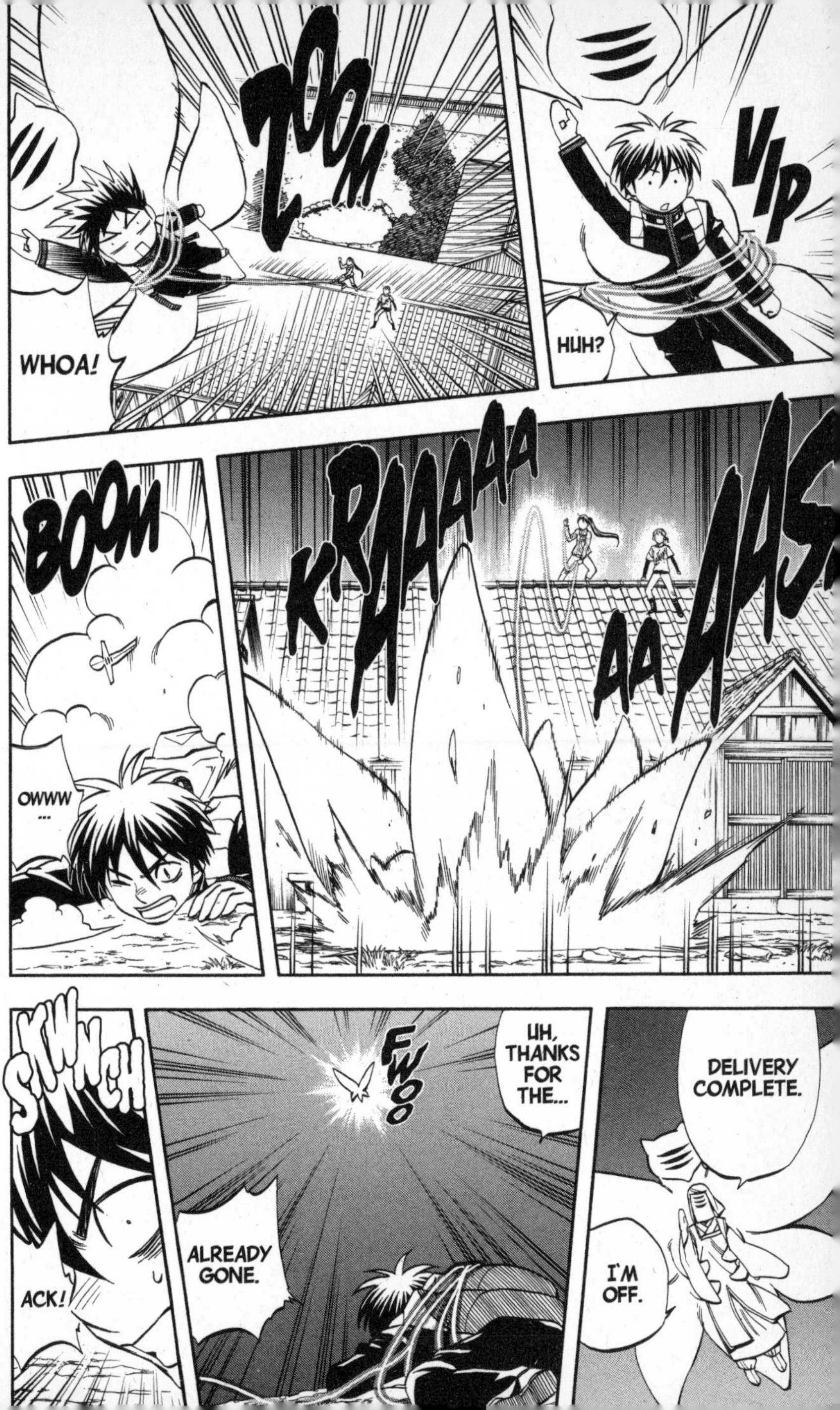
VIP
HUH?
ZOOM
WHOA!
KRAAAAAAAAAASH
BOOM
OWWW...
DELIVERY COMPLETE.
I'M OFF.
UH, THANKS FOR THE...
FWOO
ALREADY GONE.
SKWNCH
ACK!

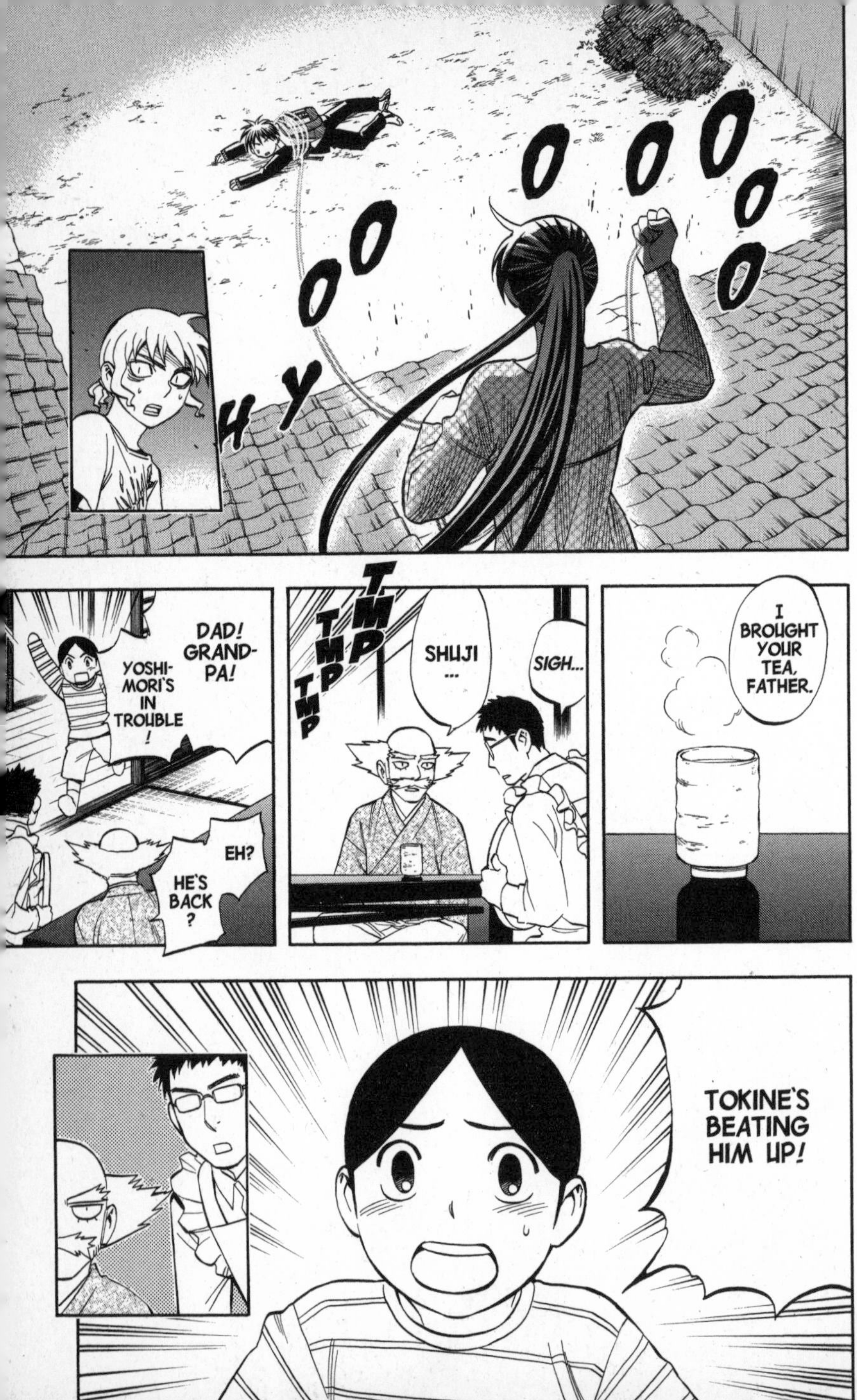
HYOOOOOOOO
I BROUGHT YOUR TEA, FATHER.
SIGH...
SHUJI ...
TMP TMP TMP TMP
DAD! GRANDPA!
YOSHIMORI'S IN TROUBLE!
EH?
HE'S BACK?
TOKINE'S BEATING HIM UP!

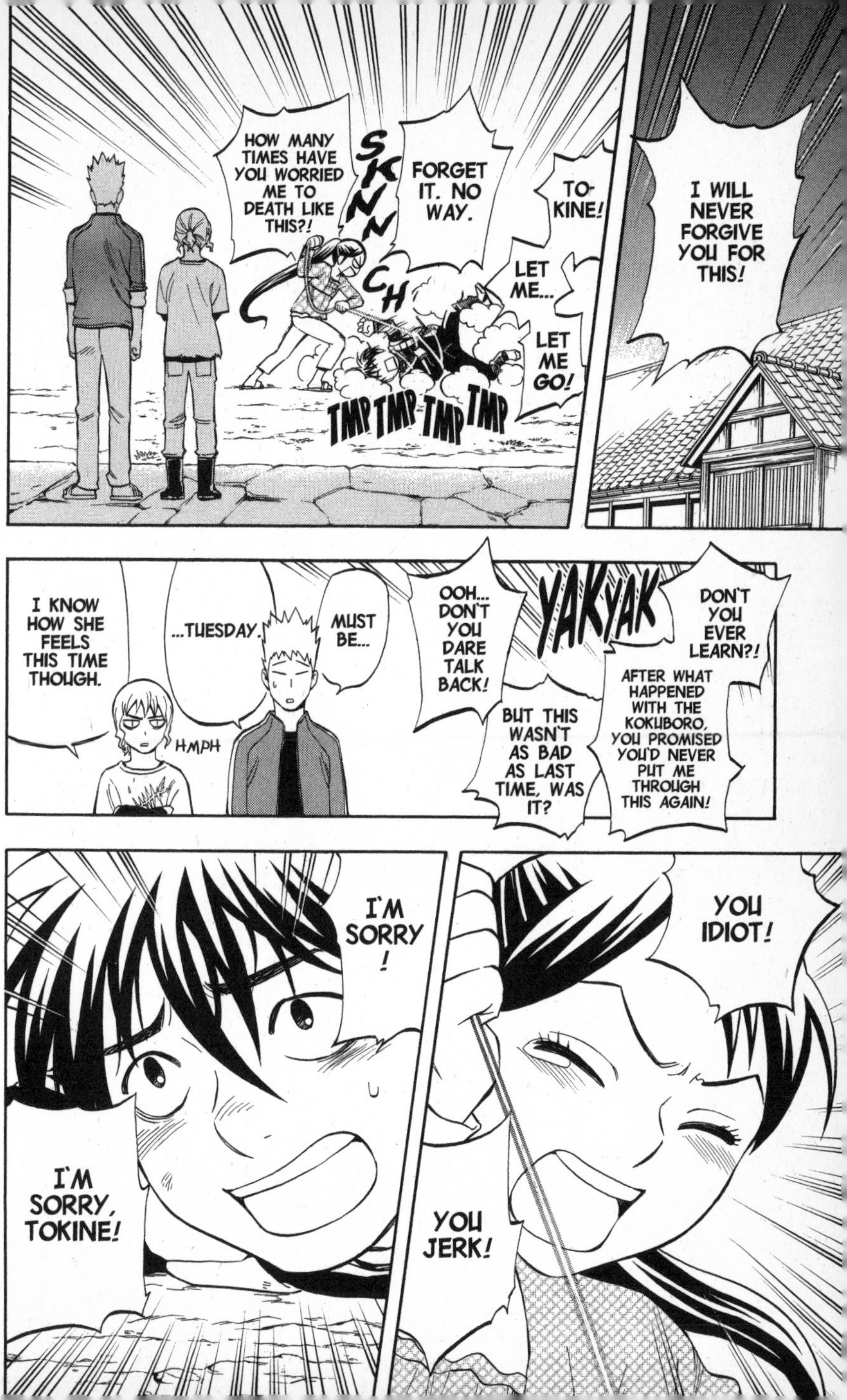
I WILL NEVER FORGIVE YOU FOR THIS!
TO-KINE!
FORGET IT. NO WAY.
SKNNCH
HOW MANY TIMES HAVE YOU WORRIED ME TO DEATH LIKE THIS?!
LET ME...
LET ME GO!
TMP TMP TMP TMP
DON'T YOU EVER LEARN?!
AFTER WHAT HAPPENED WITH THE KOKUBORO, YOU PROMISED YOU'D NEVER PUT ME THROUGH THIS AGAIN!
YAKYAK
OOH... DON'T YOU DARE TALK BACK!
BUT THIS WASN'T AS BAD AS LAST TIME, WAS IT?
MUST BE...
...TUESDAY.
I KNOW HOW SHE FEELS THIS TIME THOUGH.
HMPH
YOU IDIOT!
YOU JERK!
I'M SORRY!
I'M SORRY, TOKINE!

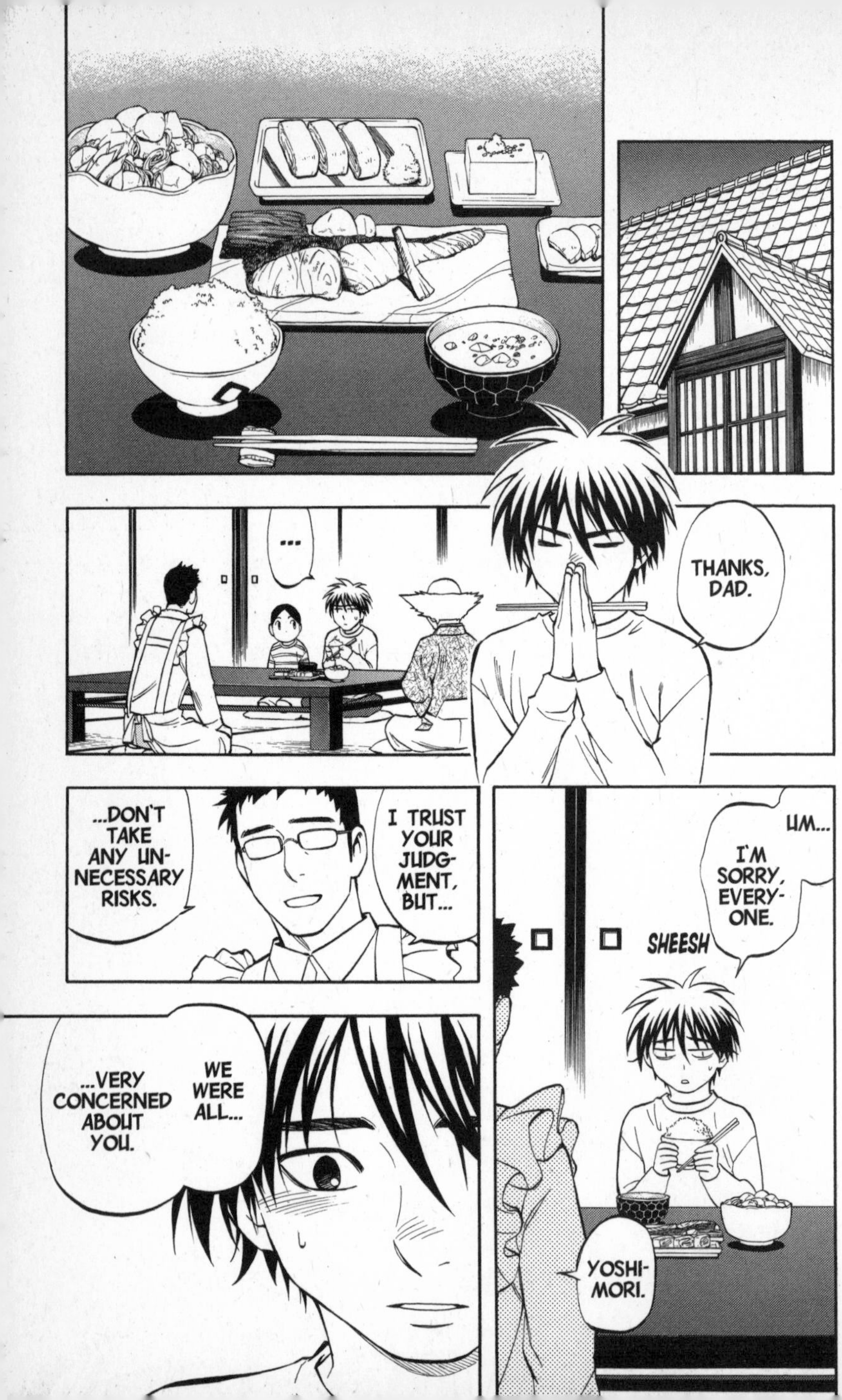
THANKS, DAD.
...
UM...
I'M SORRY, EVERY-ONE.
SHEESH
YOSHI-MORI.
I TRUST YOUR JUDG-MENT, BUT...
...DON'T TAKE ANY UN-NECESSARY RISKS.
WE WERE ALL...
...VERY CONCERNED ABOUT YOU.

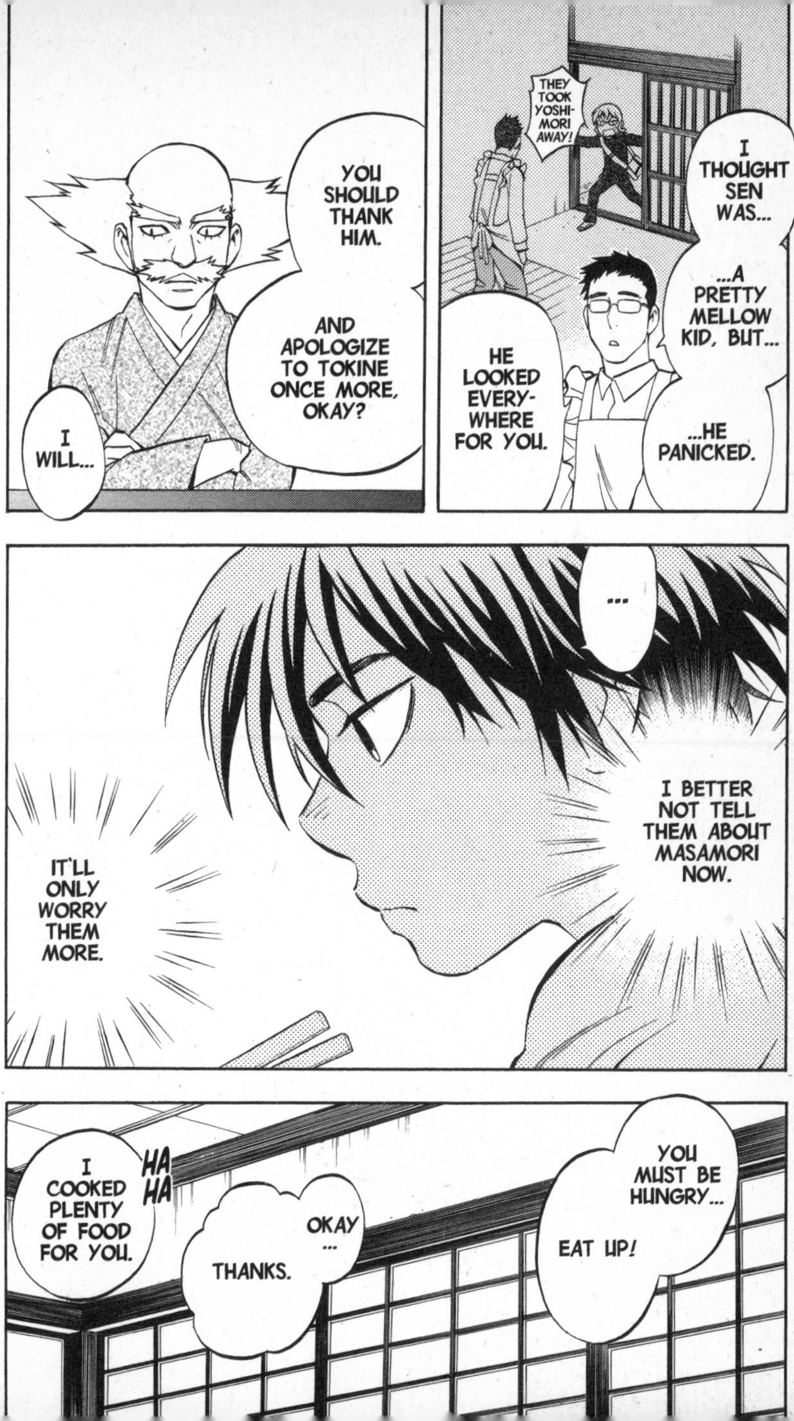

I THOUGHT SEN WAS...
...A PRETTY MELLOW KID, BUT...
THEY TOOK YOSHI-MORI AWAY!
...HE PANICKED.
HE LOOKED EVERY-WHERE FOR YOU.
YOU SHOULD THANK HIM.
AND APOLOGIZE TO TOKINE ONCE MORE, OKAY?
I WILL...
...
I BETTER NOT TELL THEM ABOUT MASAMORI NOW.
IT'LL ONLY WORRY THEM MORE.
YOU MUST BE HUNGRY...
EAT UP!
OKAY...
THANKS.
HA HA
I COOKED PLENTY OF FOOD FOR YOU.

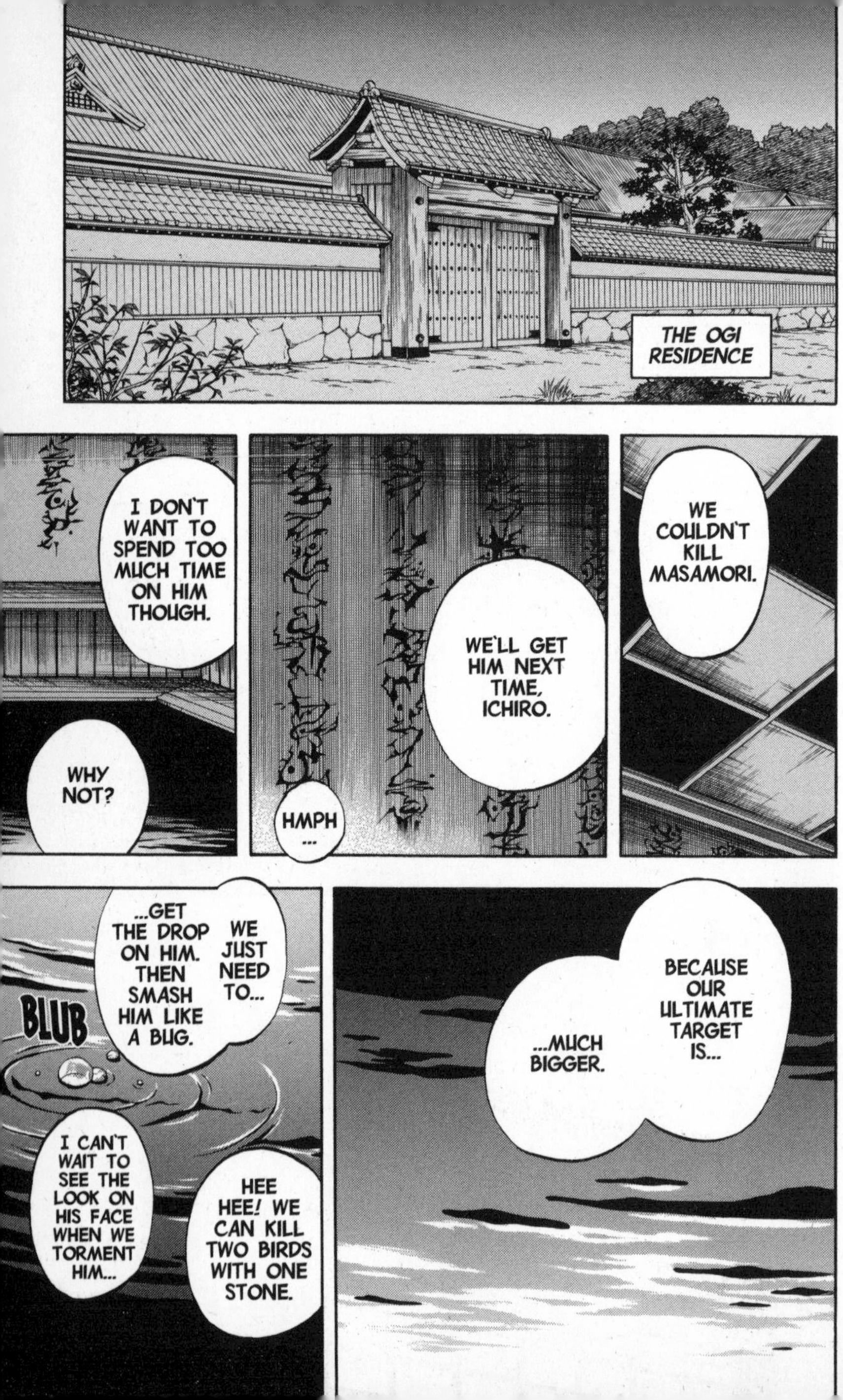
THE OGI RESIDENCE
WE COULDN'T KILL MASAMORI.
WE'LL GET HIM NEXT TIME, ICHIRO.
HMPH...
I DON'T WANT TO SPEND TOO MUCH TIME ON HIM THOUGH.
WHY NOT?
BECAUSE OUR ULTIMATE TARGET IS...
...MUCH BIGGER.
WE JUST NEED TO...
...GET THE DROP ON HIM. THEN SMASH HIM LIKE A BUG.
BLUB
HEE HEE! WE CAN KILL TWO BIRDS WITH ONE STONE.
I CAN'T WAIT TO SEE THE LOOK ON HIS FACE WHEN WE TORMENT HIM...

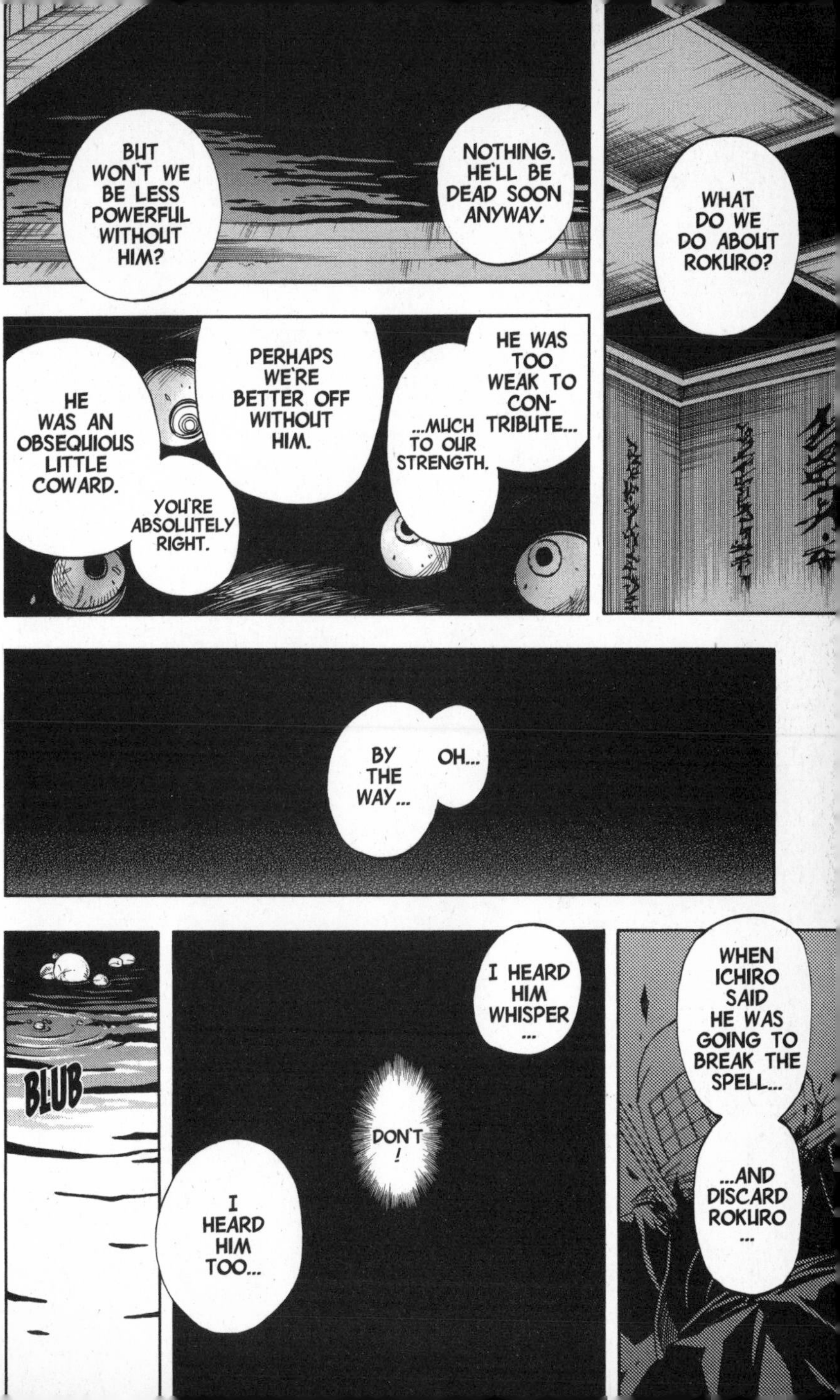
WHAT DO WE DO ABOUT ROKURO?
NOTHING. HE'LL BE DEAD SOON ANYWAY.
BUT WON'T WE BE LESS POWERFUL WITHOUT HIM?
HE WAS TOO WEAK TO CON-TRIBUTE...
...MUCH TO OUR STRENGTH.
PERHAPS WE'RE BETTER OFF WITHOUT HIM.
HE WAS AN OBSEQUIOUS LITTLE COWARD.
YOU'RE ABSOLUTELY RIGHT.
OH...
BY THE WAY...
WHEN ICHIRO SAID HE WAS GOING TO BREAK THE SPELL...
...AND DISCARD ROKURO ...
I HEARD HIM WHISPER ...
DON'T!
I HEARD HIM TOO...
BLUB

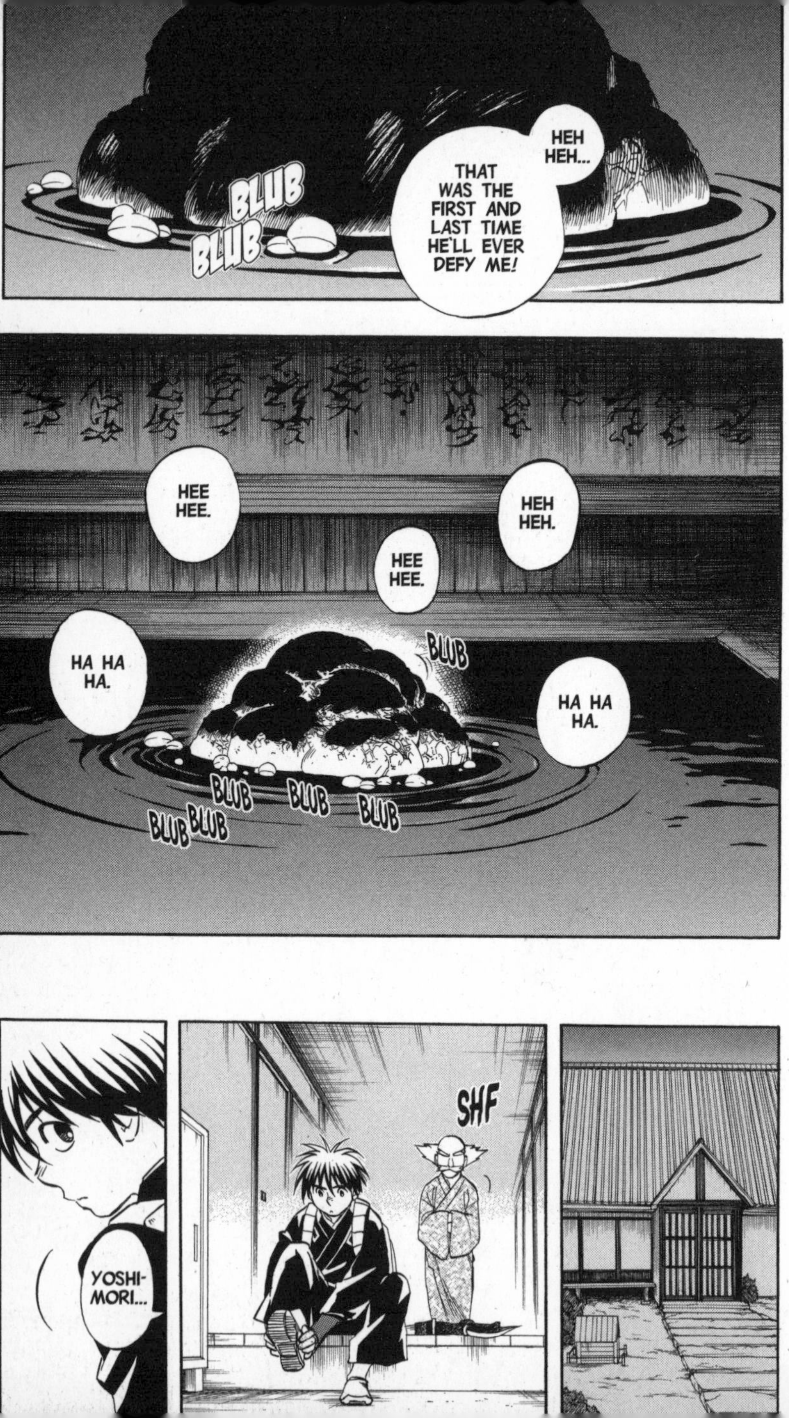
HEH HEH...
THAT WAS THE FIRST AND LAST TIME HE'LL EVER DEFY ME!
BLUB
BLUB
HEH HEH.
HEE HEE.
HEE HEE.
BLUB
HA HA HA.
HA HA HA.
BLUB
BLUB
BLUB
BLUB
BLUB
SHF
YOSHIMORI...

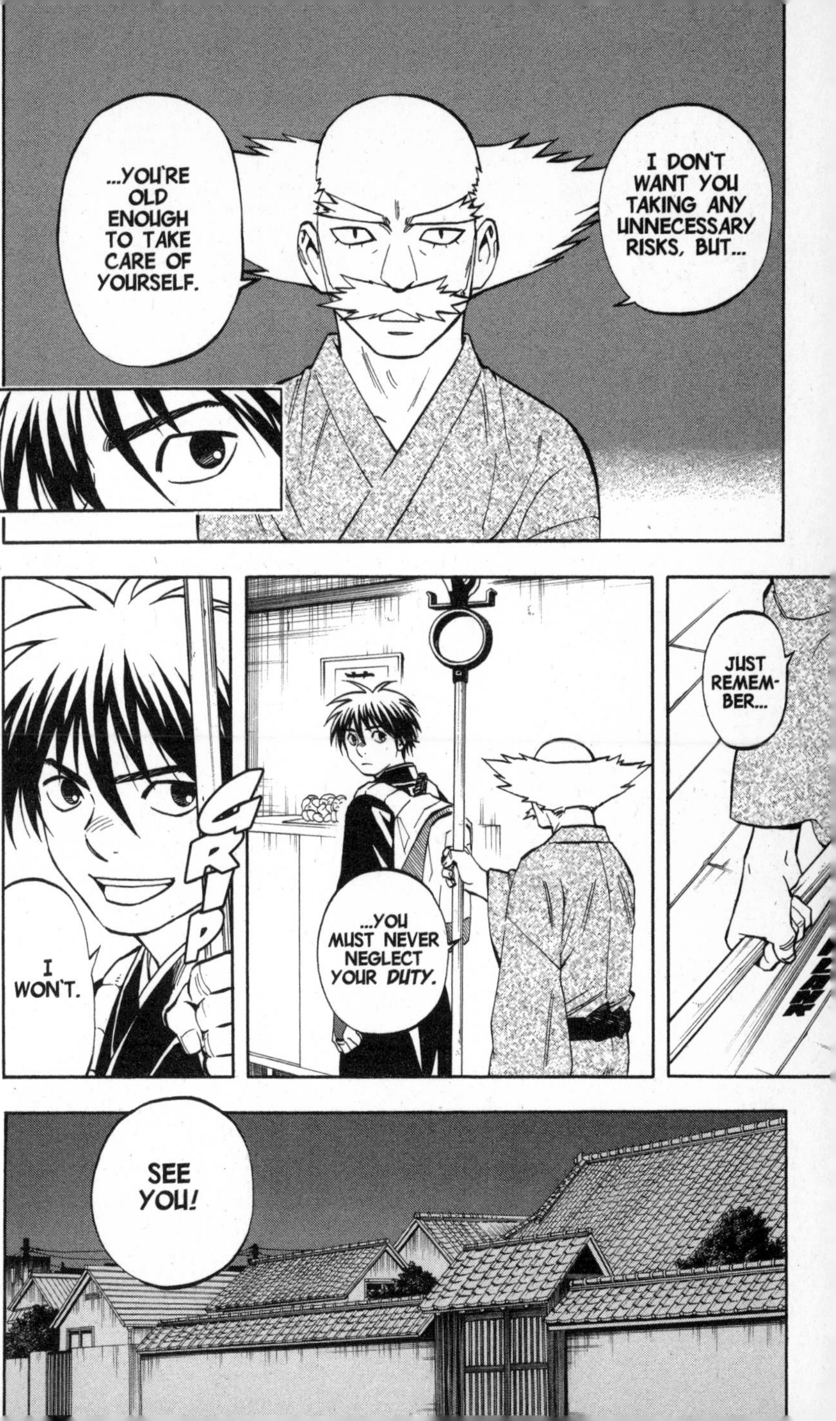
I DON'T WANT YOU TAKING ANY UNNECESSARY RISKS, BUT...
...YOU'RE OLD ENOUGH TO TAKE CARE OF YOURSELF.
JUST REMEM-BER...
...YOU MUST NEVER NEGLECT YOUR DUTY.
GRIP
I WON'T.
SEE YOU!

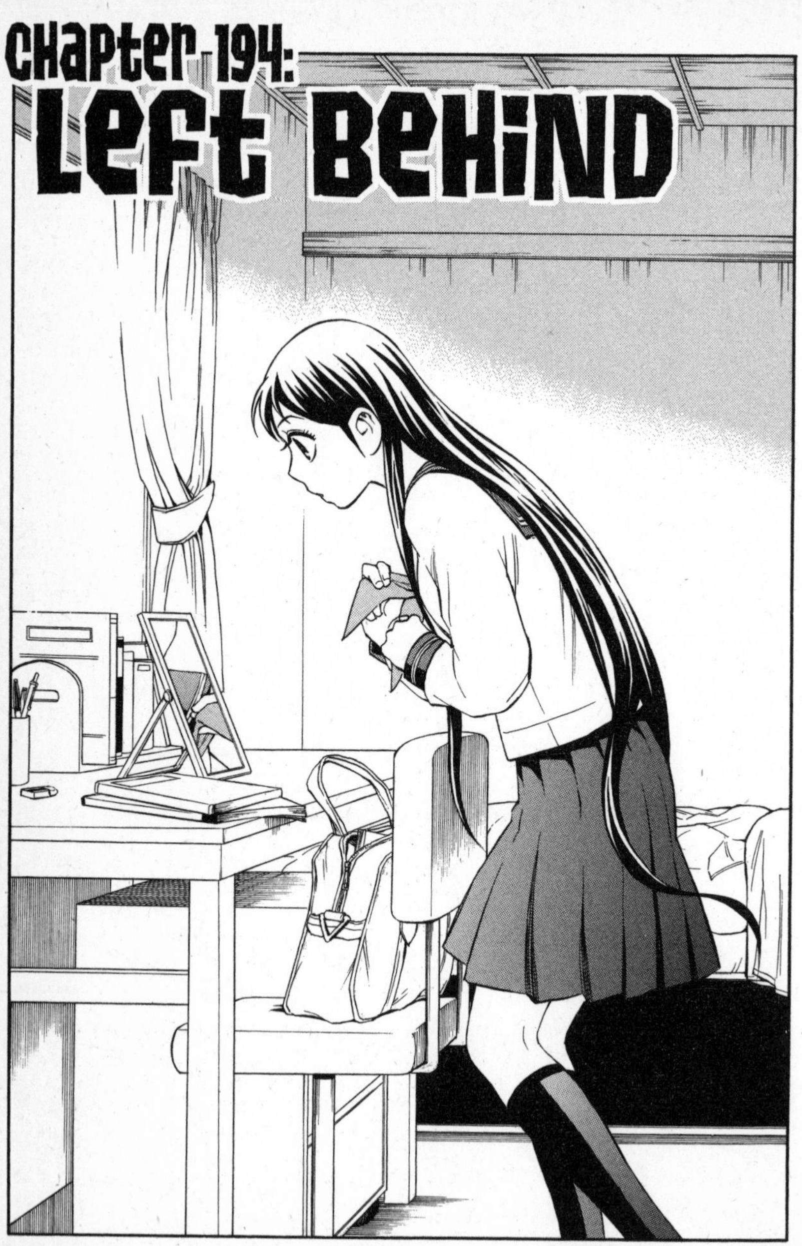
Chapter 194:
Left Behind

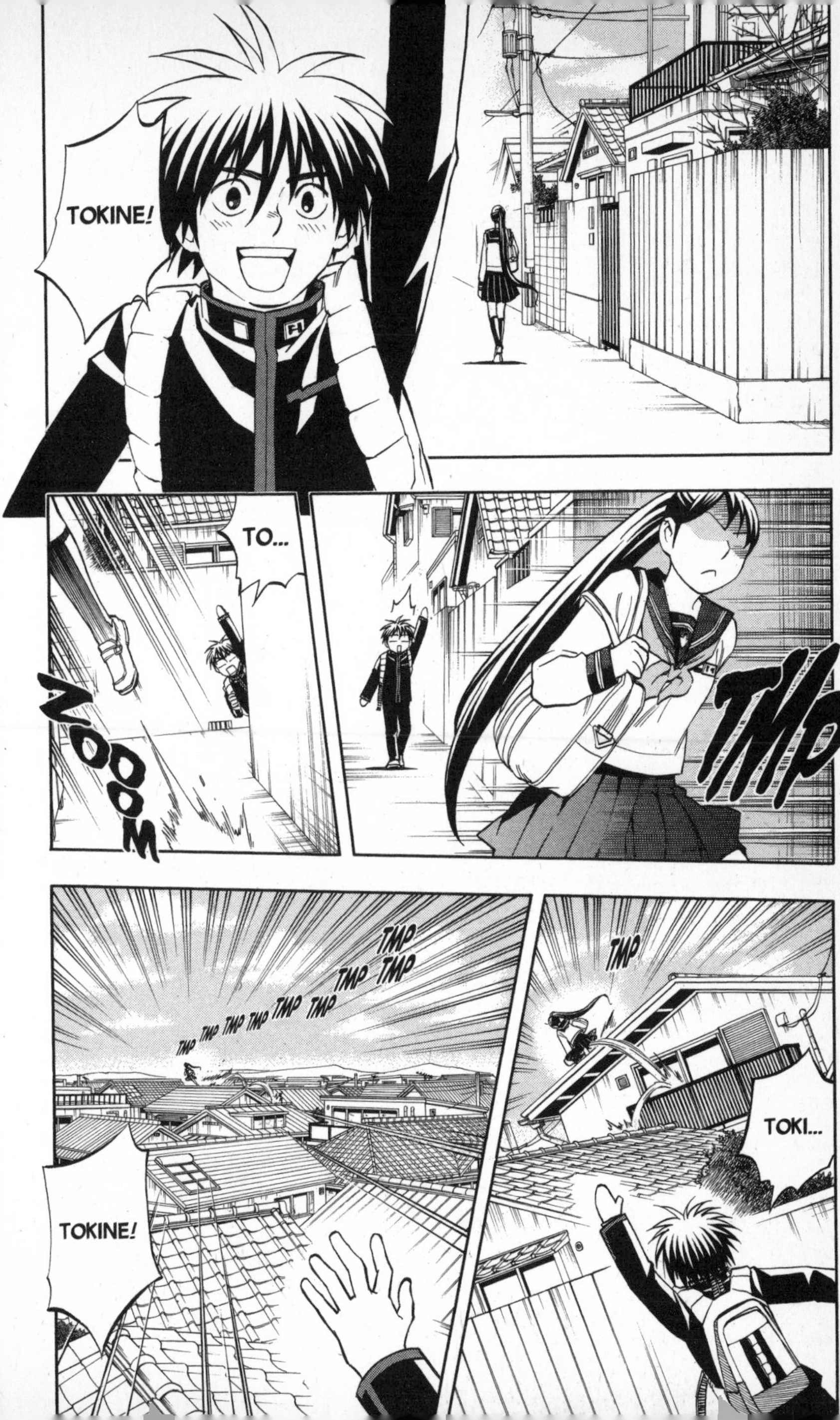
TOKINE!
TMP
TO...
ZOOOM
TMP
TOKI...
TMP TMP TMP TMP TMP TMP TMP TMP TMP
TOKINE!

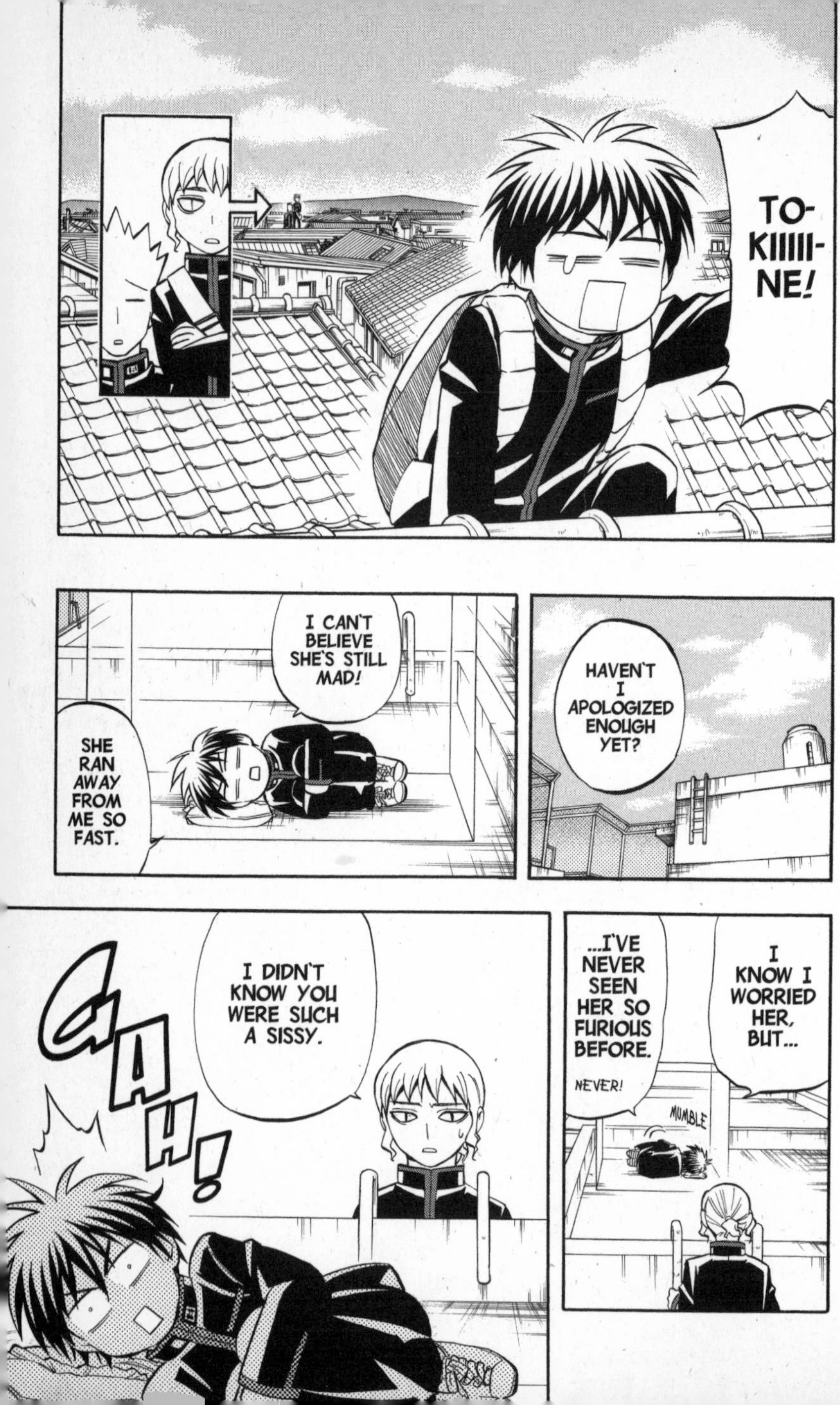
TO-KIIIII-NE!
HAVEN'T I APOLOGIZED ENOUGH YET?
I CAN'T BELIEVE SHE'S STILL MAD!
SHE RAN AWAY FROM ME SO FAST.
I KNOW I WORRIED HER, BUT...
...I'VE NEVER SEEN HER SO FURIOUS BEFORE.
NEVER!
MUMBLE
I DIDN'T KNOW YOU WERE SUCH A SISSY.
GAH!

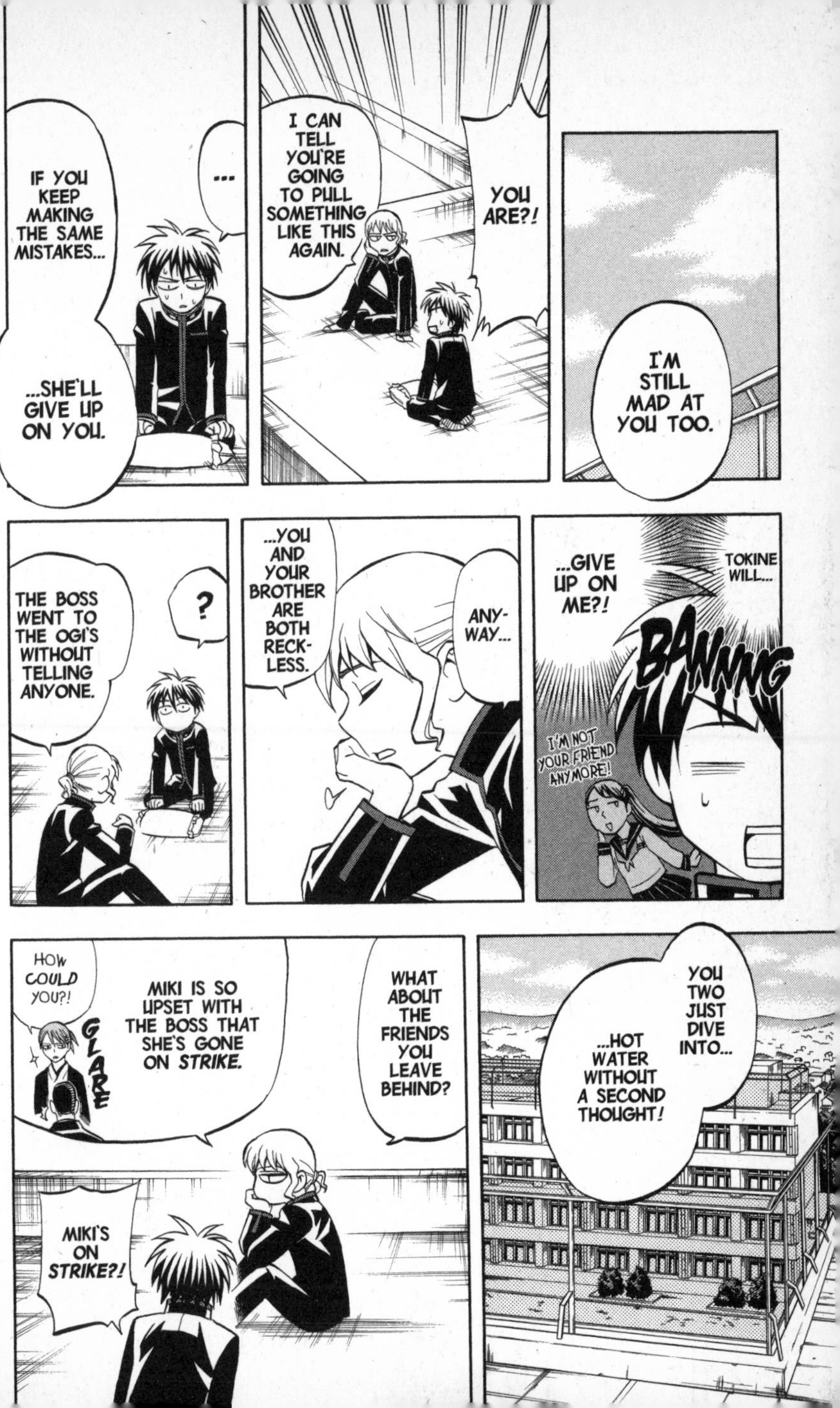
I'M STILL MAD AT YOU TOO.
YOU ARE?!
I CAN TELL YOU'RE GOING TO PULL SOMETHING LIKE THIS AGAIN.
...
IF YOU KEEP MAKING THE SAME MISTAKES...
...SHE'LL GIVE UP ON YOU.
TOKINE WILL...
...GIVE UP ON ME?!
BANNNG
I'M NOT YOUR FRIEND ANYMORE!
ANY-WAY...
...YOU AND YOUR BROTHER ARE BOTH RECK-LESS.
?
THE BOSS WENT TO THE OGI'S WITHOUT TELLING ANYONE.
YOU TWO JUST DIVE INTO...
...HOT WATER WITHOUT A SECOND THOUGHT!
WHAT ABOUT THE FRIENDS YOU LEAVE BEHIND?
MIKI IS SO UPSET WITH THE BOSS THAT SHE'S GONE ON *STRIKE.*
HOW COULD YOU?!
GLARE
MIKI'S ON *STRIKE?!*

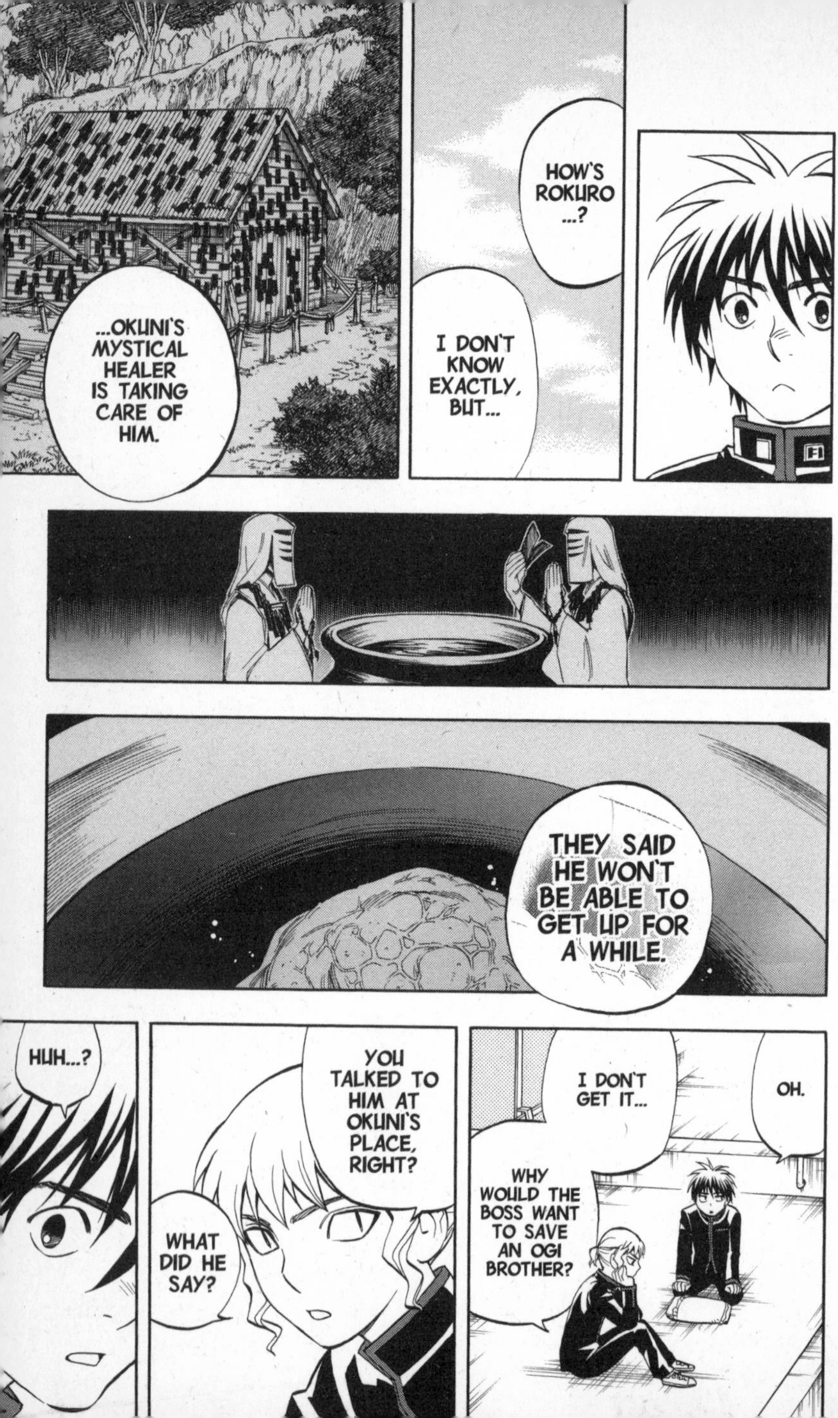
HOW'S ROKURO ...?
I DON'T KNOW EXACTLY, BUT...
...OKUNI'S MYSTICAL HEALER IS TAKING CARE OF HIM.
THEY SAID HE WON'T BE ABLE TO GET UP FOR A WHILE.
OH.
I DON'T GET IT...
WHY WOULD THE BOSS WANT TO SAVE AN OGI BROTHER?
YOU TALKED TO HIM AT OKUNI'S PLACE, RIGHT?
WHAT DID HE SAY?
HUH...?

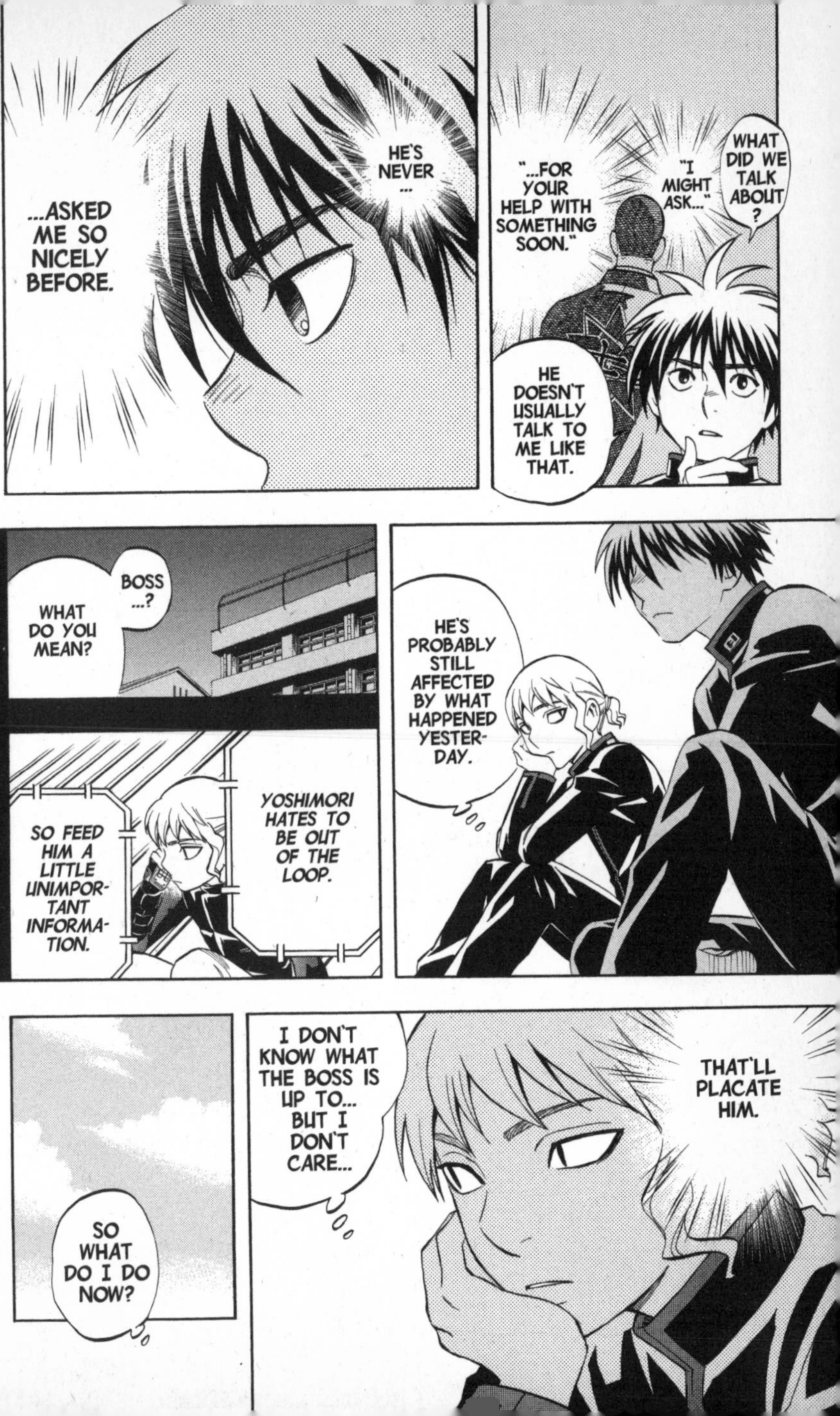
WHAT DID WE TALK ABOUT?
"I MIGHT ASK..."
"...FOR YOUR HELP WITH SOMETHING SOON."
HE DOESN'T USUALLY TALK TO ME LIKE THAT.
HE'S NEVER ...
...ASKED ME SO NICELY BEFORE.
HE'S PROBABLY STILL AFFECTED BY WHAT HAPPENED YESTER-DAY.
BOSS ...?
WHAT DO YOU MEAN?
YOSHIMORI HATES TO BE OUT OF THE LOOP.
SO FEED HIM A LITTLE UNIMPOR-TANT INFORMA-TION.
THAT'LL PLACATE HIM.
I DON'T KNOW WHAT THE BOSS IS UP TO... BUT I DON'T CARE...
SO WHAT DO I DO NOW?

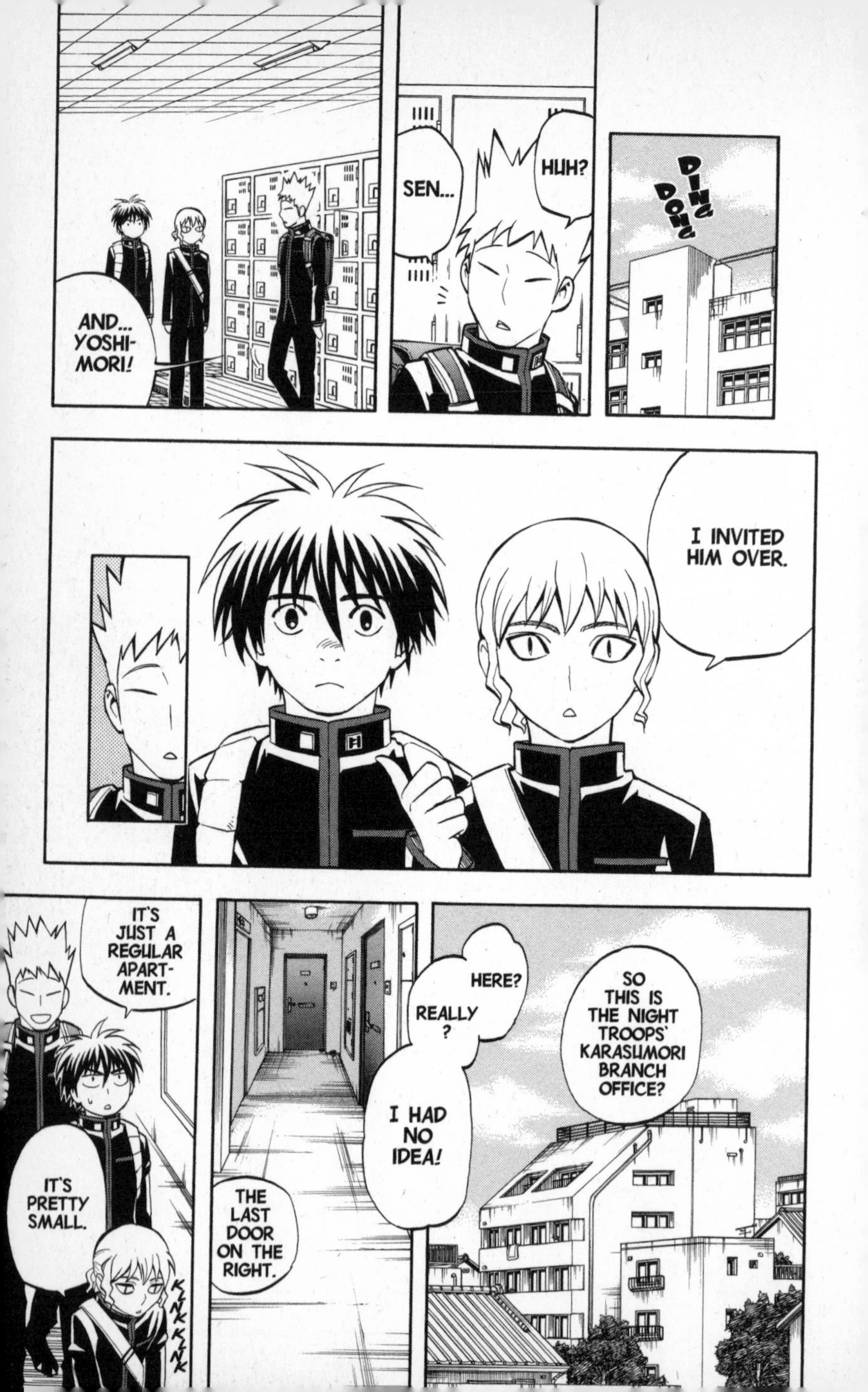
DING DONG
SEN...
HUH?
AND... YOSHIMORI!
I INVITED HIM OVER.
SO THIS IS THE NIGHT TROOPS' KARASUMORI BRANCH OFFICE?
HERE?
REALLY?
I HAD NO IDEA!
THE LAST DOOR ON THE RIGHT.
IT'S JUST A REGULAR APARTMENT.
IT'S PRETTY SMALL.
KLINK KLINK

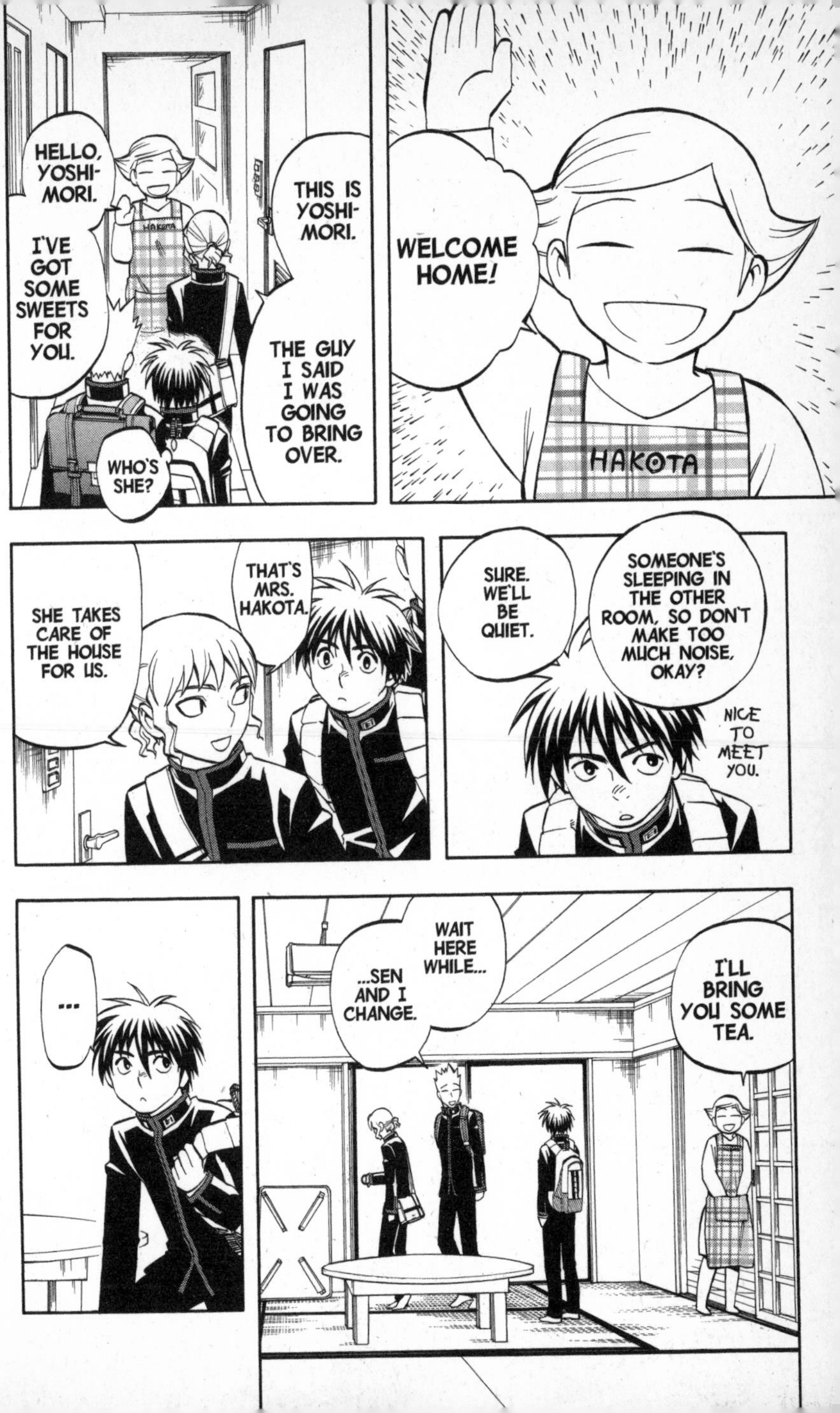
WELCOME HOME!
THIS IS YOSHI-MORI.
THE GUY I SAID I WAS GOING TO BRING OVER.
HELLO, YOSHI-MORI.
I'VE GOT SOME SWEETS FOR YOU.
HAKOTA
WHO'S SHE?
SOMEONE'S SLEEPING IN THE OTHER ROOM, SO DON'T MAKE TOO MUCH NOISE, OKAY?
SURE. WE'LL BE QUIET.
NICE TO MEET YOU.
THAT'S MRS. HAKOTA.
SHE TAKES CARE OF THE HOUSE FOR US.
I'LL BRING YOU SOME TEA.
WAIT HERE WHILE...
...SEN AND I CHANGE.
...

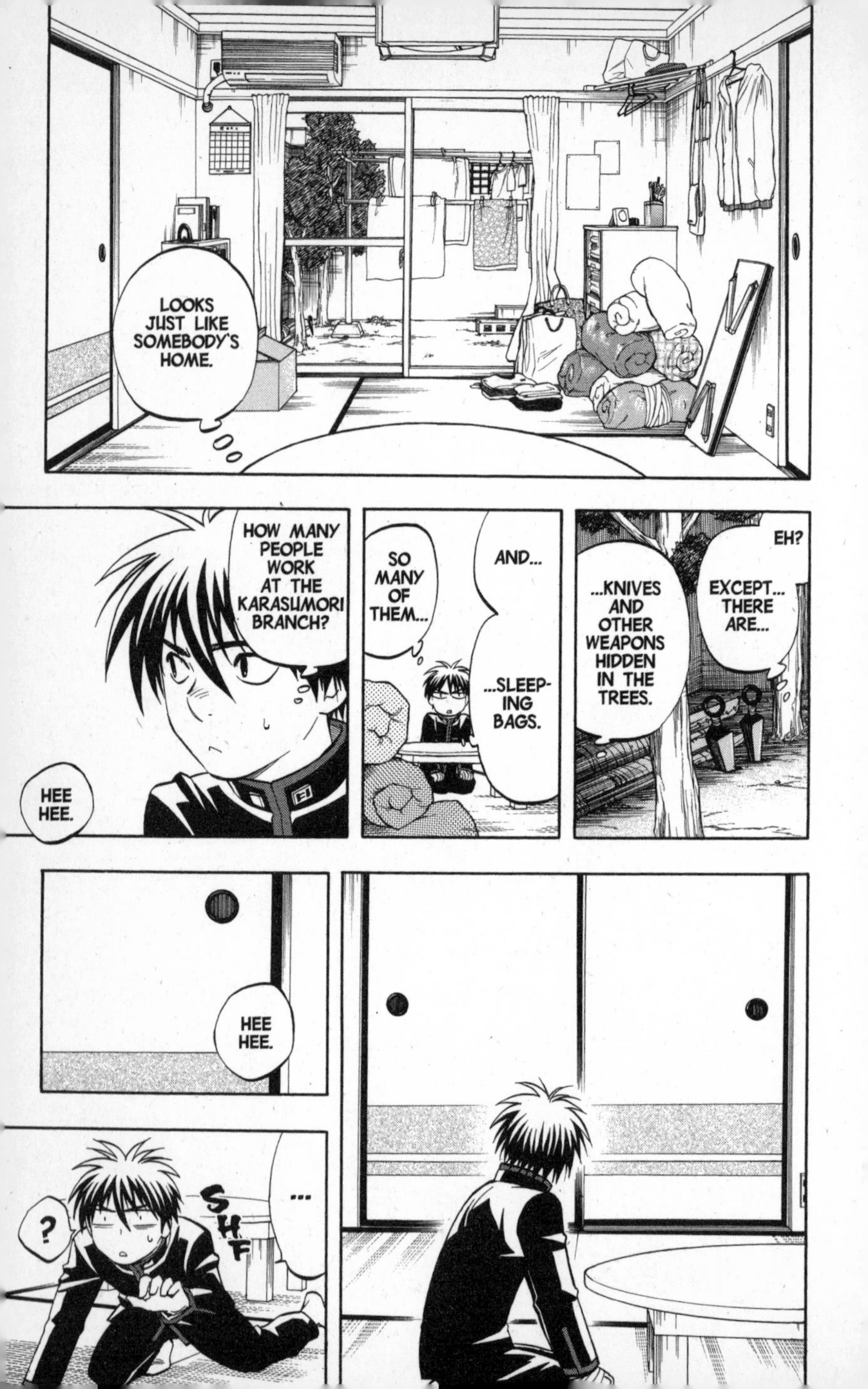

LOOKS JUST LIKE SOMEBODY'S HOME.
EH?
EXCEPT... THERE ARE...
...KNIVES AND OTHER WEAPONS HIDDEN IN THE TREES.
AND...
...SLEEP-ING BAGS.
SO MANY OF THEM...
HOW MANY PEOPLE WORK AT THE KARASUMORI BRANCH?
HEE HEE.
HEE HEE.
...
SHF
?

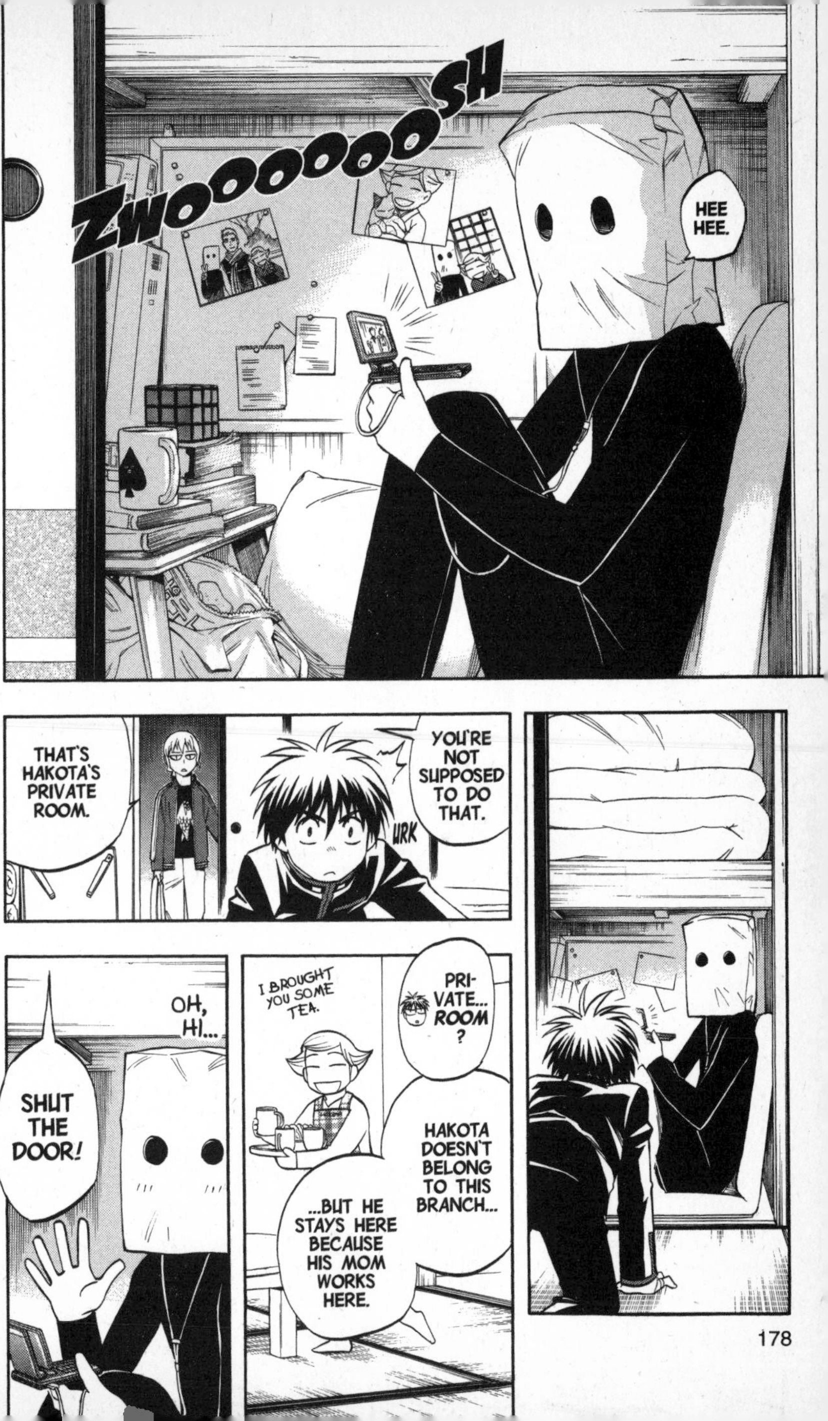
ZWOOOOOOOSH
HEE HEE.
YOU'RE NOT SUPPOSED TO DO THAT.
URK
THAT'S HAKOTA'S PRIVATE ROOM.
PRI-VATE... ROOM?
I BROUGHT YOU SOME TEA.
HAKOTA DOESN'T BELONG TO THIS BRANCH...
...BUT HE STAYS HERE BECAUSE HIS MOM WORKS HERE.
OH, HI...
SHUT THE DOOR!

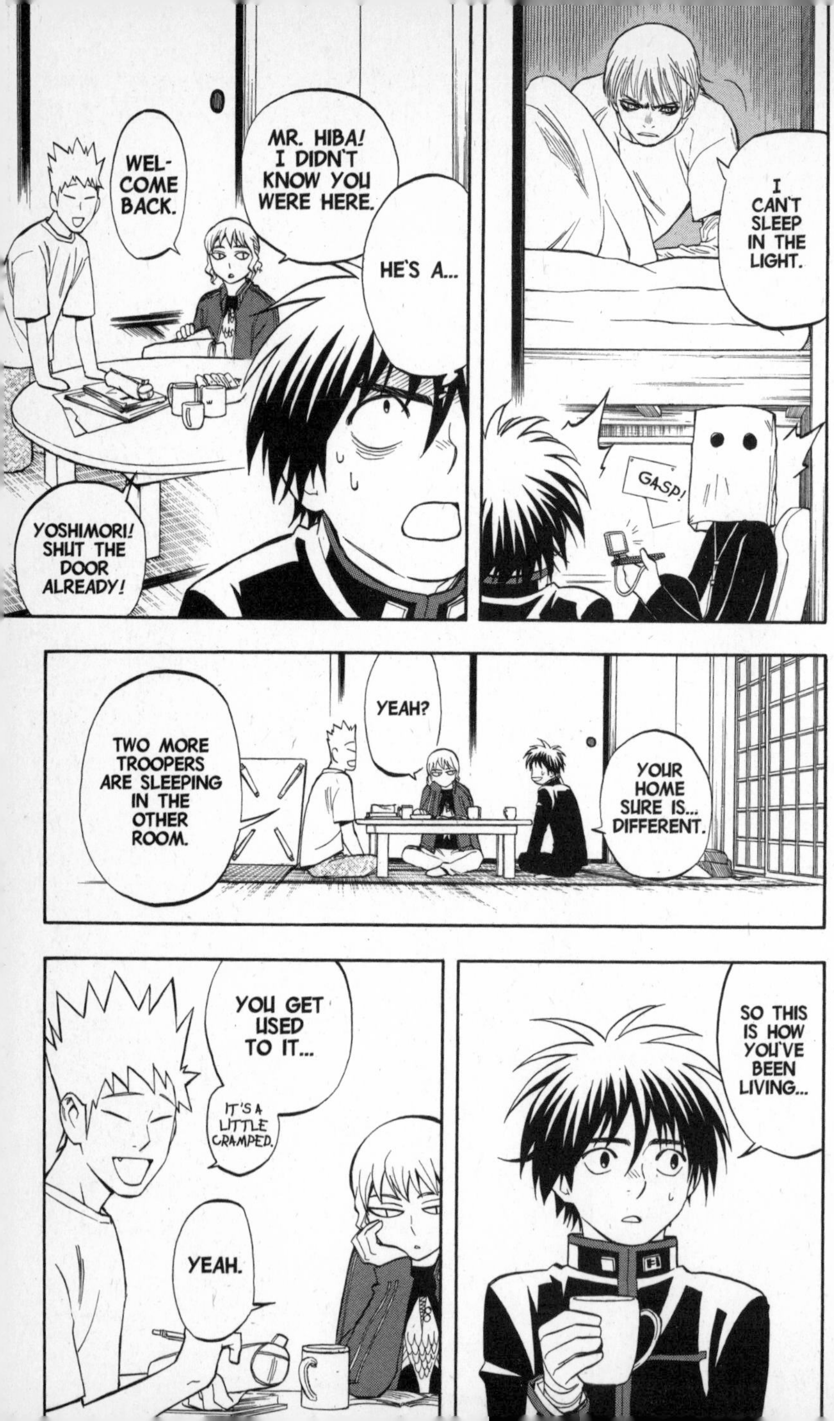
I CAN'T SLEEP IN THE LIGHT.
GASP!
MR. HIBA! I DIDN'T KNOW YOU WERE HERE.
HE'S A...
WEL-COME BACK.
YOSHIMORI! SHUT THE DOOR ALREADY!
YOUR HOME SURE IS... DIFFERENT.
YEAH?
TWO MORE TROOPERS ARE SLEEPING IN THE OTHER ROOM.
SO THIS IS HOW YOU'VE BEEN LIVING...
YOU GET USED TO IT...
IT'S A LITTLE CRAMPED.
YEAH.

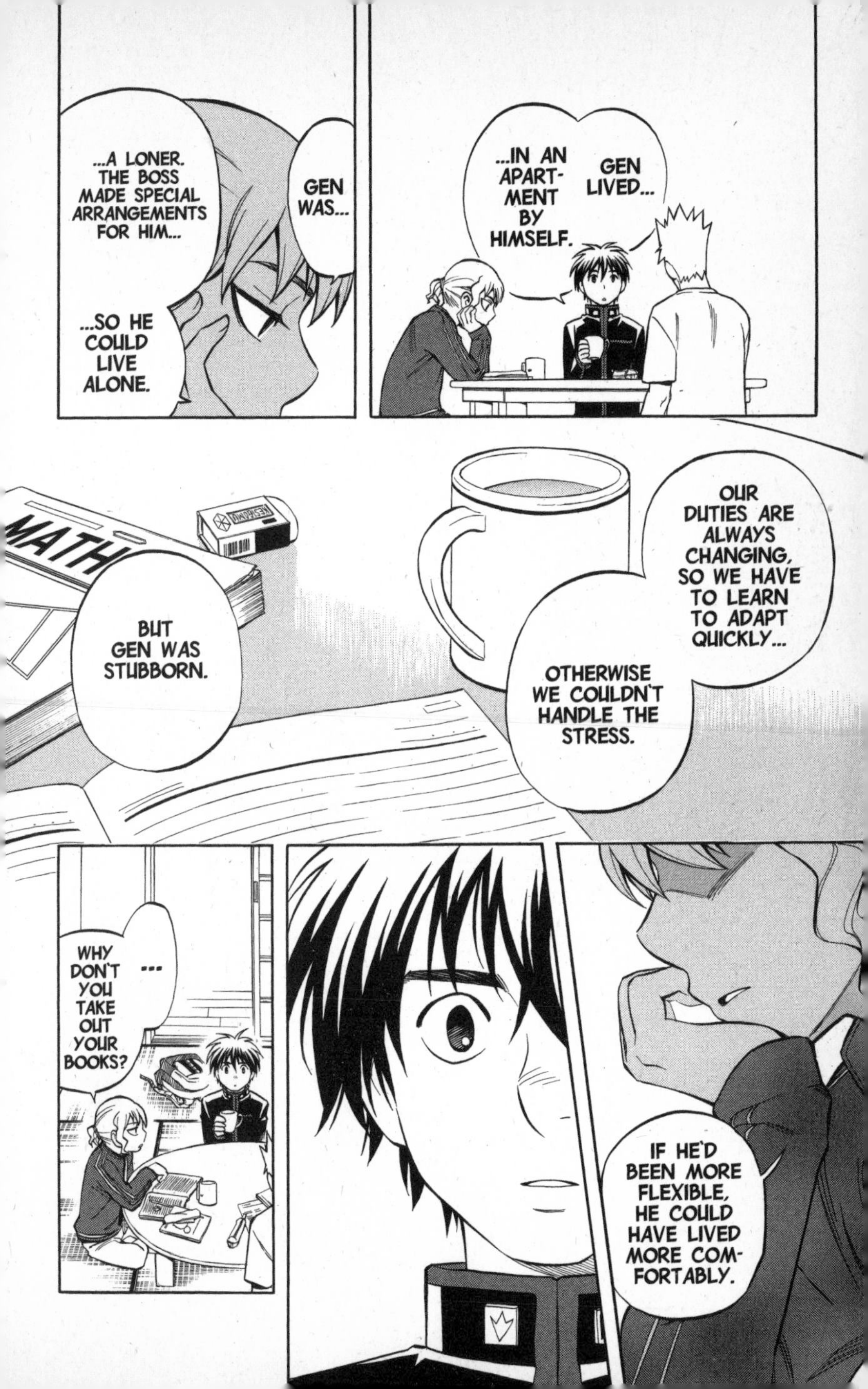
GEN LIVED...
...IN AN APARTMENT BY HIMSELF.
GEN WAS...
...A LONER. THE BOSS MADE SPECIAL ARRANGEMENTS FOR HIM...
...SO HE COULD LIVE ALONE.
OUR DUTIES ARE ALWAYS CHANGING, SO WE HAVE TO LEARN TO ADAPT QUICKLY...
OTHERWISE WE COULDN'T HANDLE THE STRESS.
MATH
BUT GEN WAS STUBBORN.
IF HE'D BEEN MORE FLEXIBLE, HE COULD HAVE LIVED MORE COMFORTABLY.
...
WHY DON'T YOU TAKE OUT YOUR BOOKS?

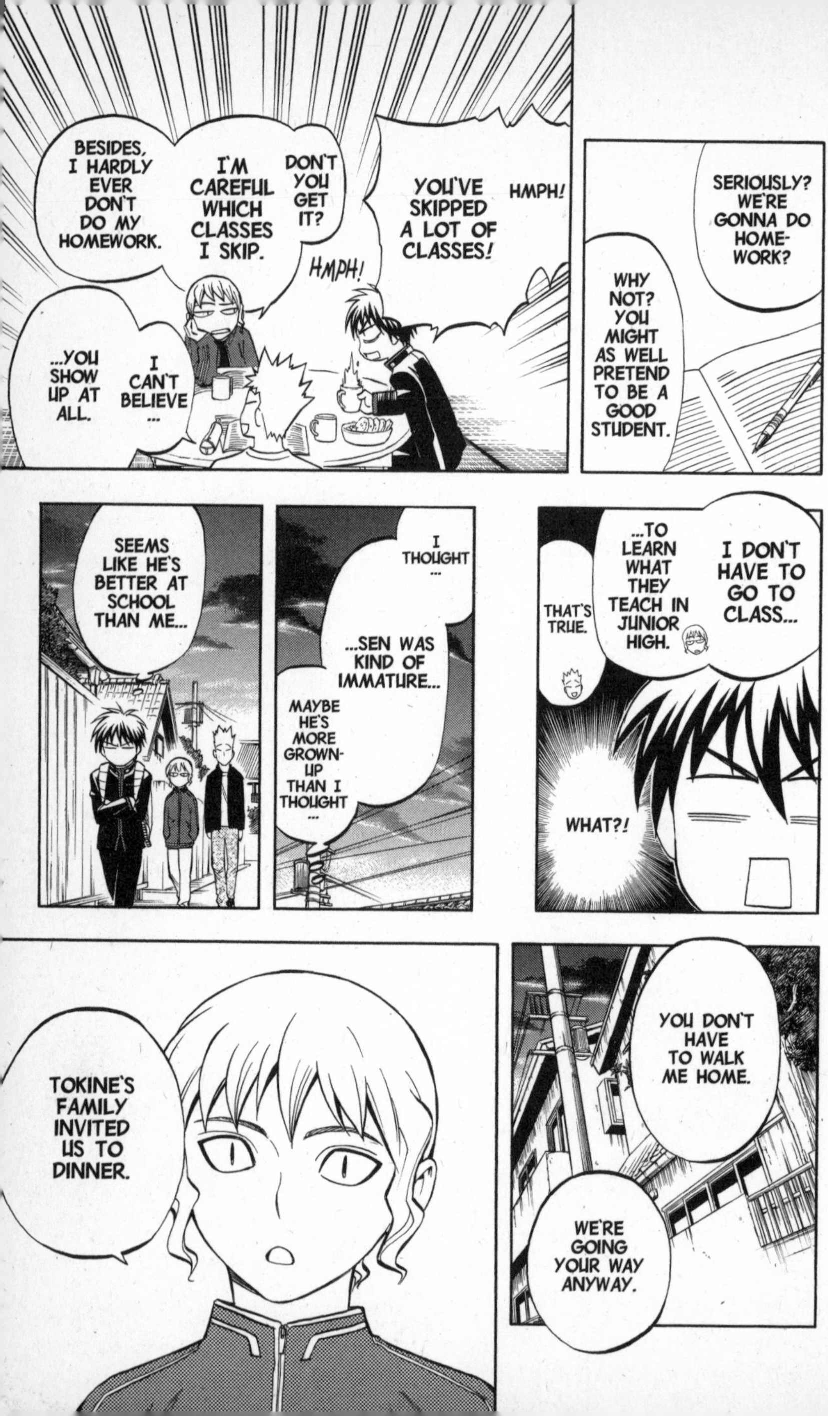
SERIOUSLY? WE'RE GONNA DO HOME-WORK?
WHY NOT? YOU MIGHT AS WELL PRETEND TO BE A GOOD STUDENT.
HMPH!
YOU'VE SKIPPED A LOT OF CLASSES!
HMPH!
DON'T YOU GET IT?
I'M CAREFUL WHICH CLASSES I SKIP.
BESIDES, I HARDLY EVER DON'T DO MY HOMEWORK.
I CAN'T BELIEVE...
...YOU SHOW UP AT ALL.
I DON'T HAVE TO GO TO CLASS...
...TO LEARN WHAT THEY TEACH IN JUNIOR HIGH.
THAT'S TRUE.
WHAT?!
I THOUGHT...
...SEN WAS KIND OF IMMATURE...
MAYBE HE'S MORE GROWN-UP THAN I THOUGHT...
SEEMS LIKE HE'S BETTER AT SCHOOL THAN ME...
YOU DON'T HAVE TO WALK ME HOME.
WE'RE GOING YOUR WAY ANYWAY.
TOKINE'S FAMILY INVITED US TO DINNER.

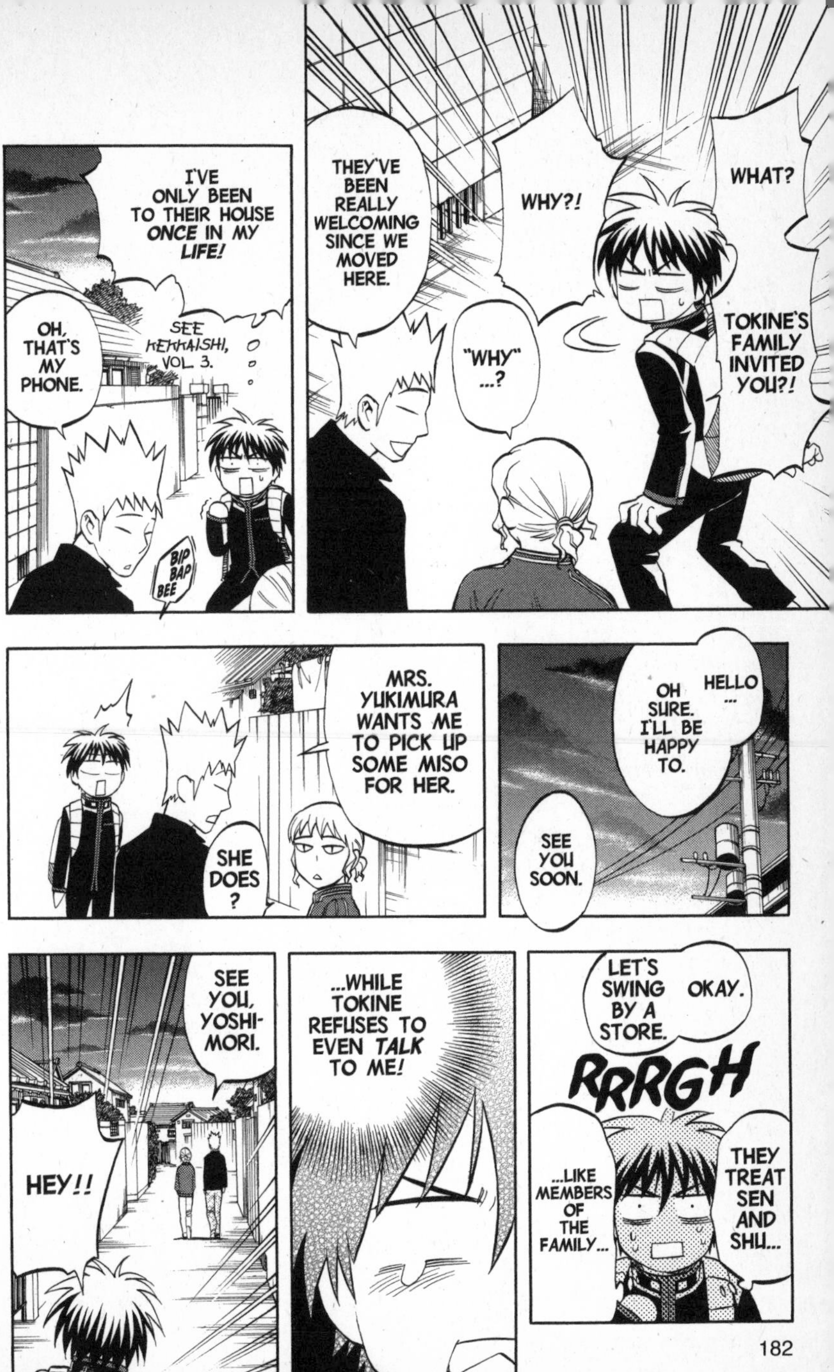
WHAT?
TOKINE'S FAMILY INVITED YOU?!
WHY?!
THEY'VE BEEN REALLY WELCOMING SINCE WE MOVED HERE.
"WHY" ...?
I'VE ONLY BEEN TO THEIR HOUSE *ONCE* IN MY *LIFE!*
SEE KEKKAISHI, VOL. 3.
OH, THAT'S MY PHONE.
BIP BAP BEE
HELLO...
OH SURE. I'LL BE HAPPY TO.
SEE YOU SOON.
MRS. YUKIMURA WANTS ME TO PICK UP SOME MISO FOR HER.
SHE DOES?
OKAY.
LET'S SWING BY A STORE.
RRRGH
THEY TREAT SEN AND SHU...
...LIKE MEMBERS OF THE FAMILY...
...WHILE TOKINE REFUSES TO EVEN *TALK* TO ME!
SEE YOU, YOSHIMORI.
HEY!!

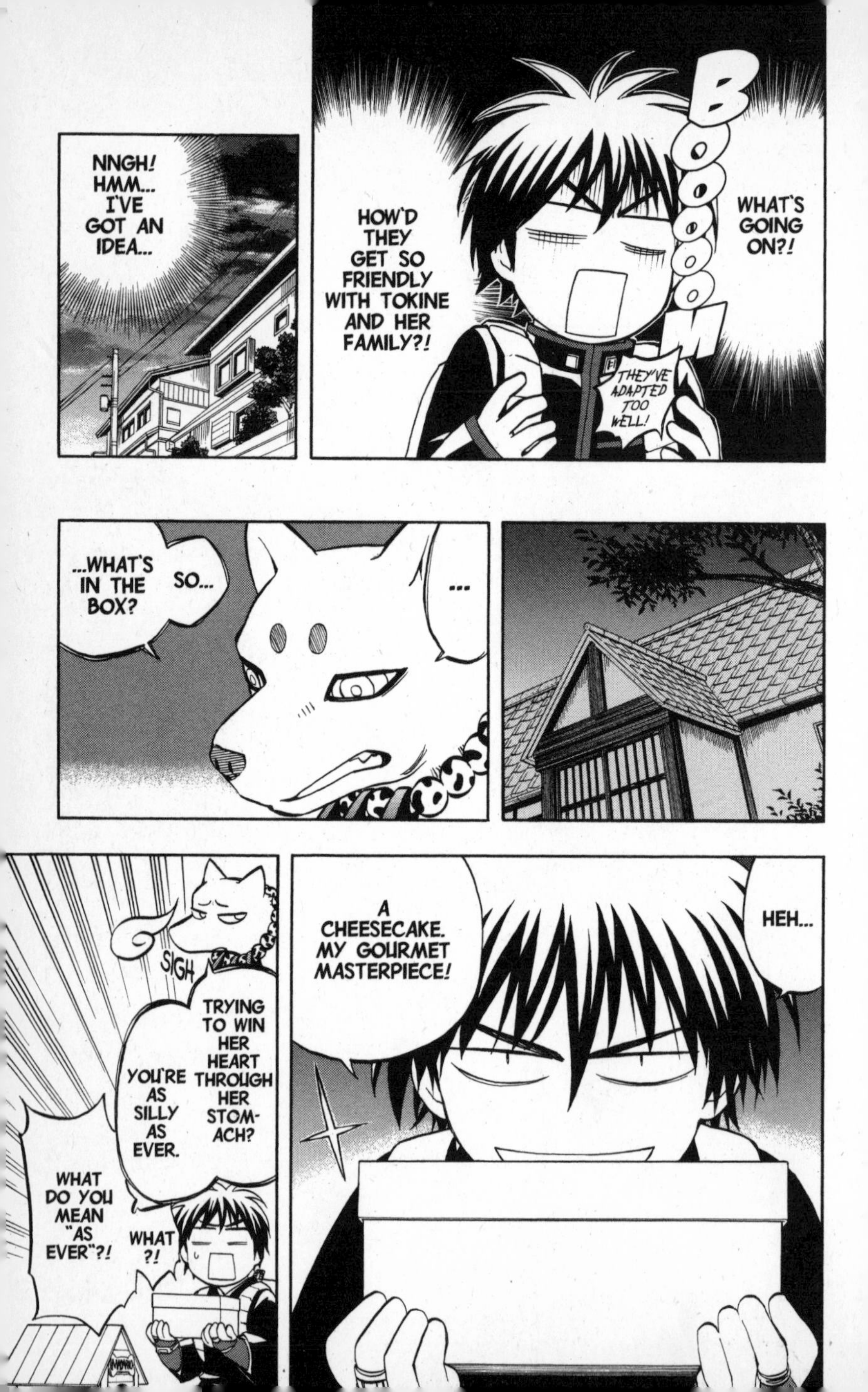
WHAT'S GOING ON?!
BOOOOOOM
HOW'D THEY GET SO FRIENDLY WITH TOKINE AND HER FAMILY?!
THEY'VE ADAPTED TOO WELL!
NNGH! HMM... I'VE GOT AN IDEA...
...
SO...
...WHAT'S IN THE BOX?
HEH...
A CHEESECAKE. MY GOURMET MASTERPIECE!
SIGH
TRYING TO WIN HER HEART THROUGH HER STOMACH?
YOU'RE AS SILLY AS EVER.
WHAT?!
WHAT DO YOU MEAN "AS EVER"?!

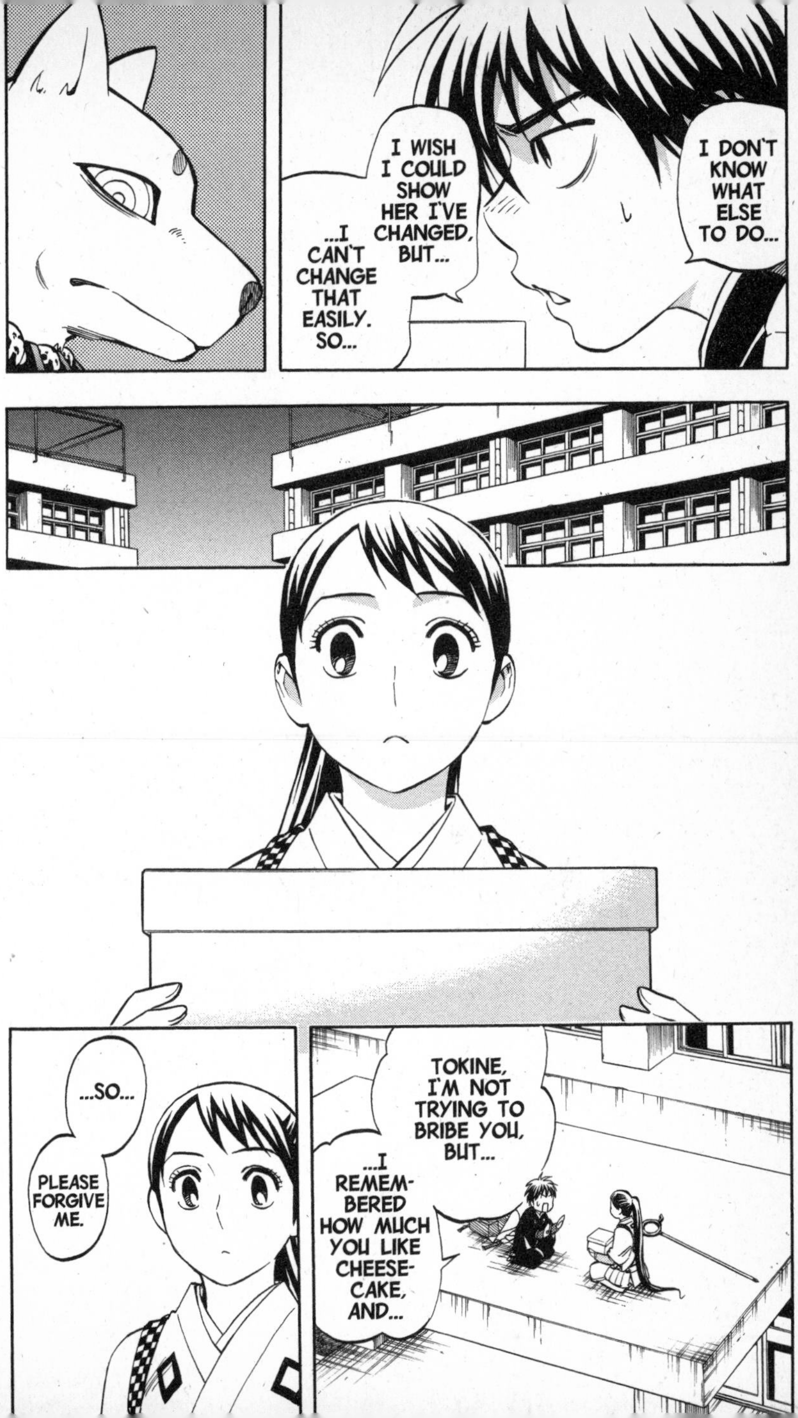
I DON'T KNOW WHAT ELSE TO DO...
I WISH I COULD SHOW HER I'VE CHANGED, BUT...
...I CAN'T CHANGE THAT EASILY. SO...
TOKINE, I'M NOT TRYING TO BRIBE YOU, BUT...
...I REMEMBERED HOW MUCH YOU LIKE CHEESECAKE, AND...
...SO...
PLEASE FORGIVE ME.

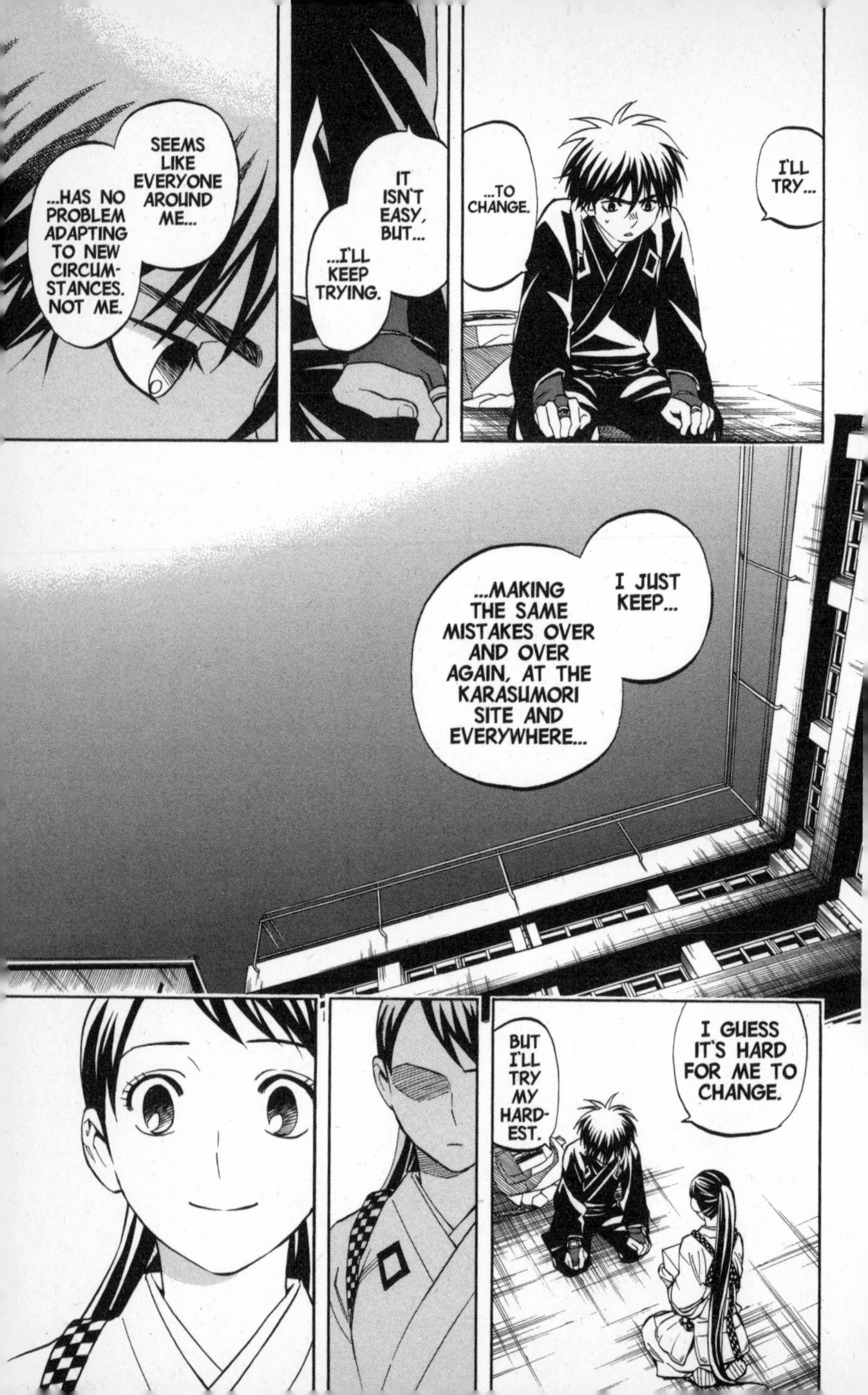
I'LL TRY...
...TO CHANGE.
IT ISN'T EASY, BUT...
...I'LL KEEP TRYING.
SEEMS LIKE EVERYONE AROUND ME...
...HAS NO PROBLEM ADAPTING TO NEW CIRCUM-STANCES. NOT ME.
I JUST KEEP...
...MAKING THE SAME MISTAKES OVER AND OVER AGAIN, AT THE KARASUMORI SITE AND EVERYWHERE...
I GUESS IT'S HARD FOR ME TO CHANGE.
BUT I'LL TRY MY HARD-EST.

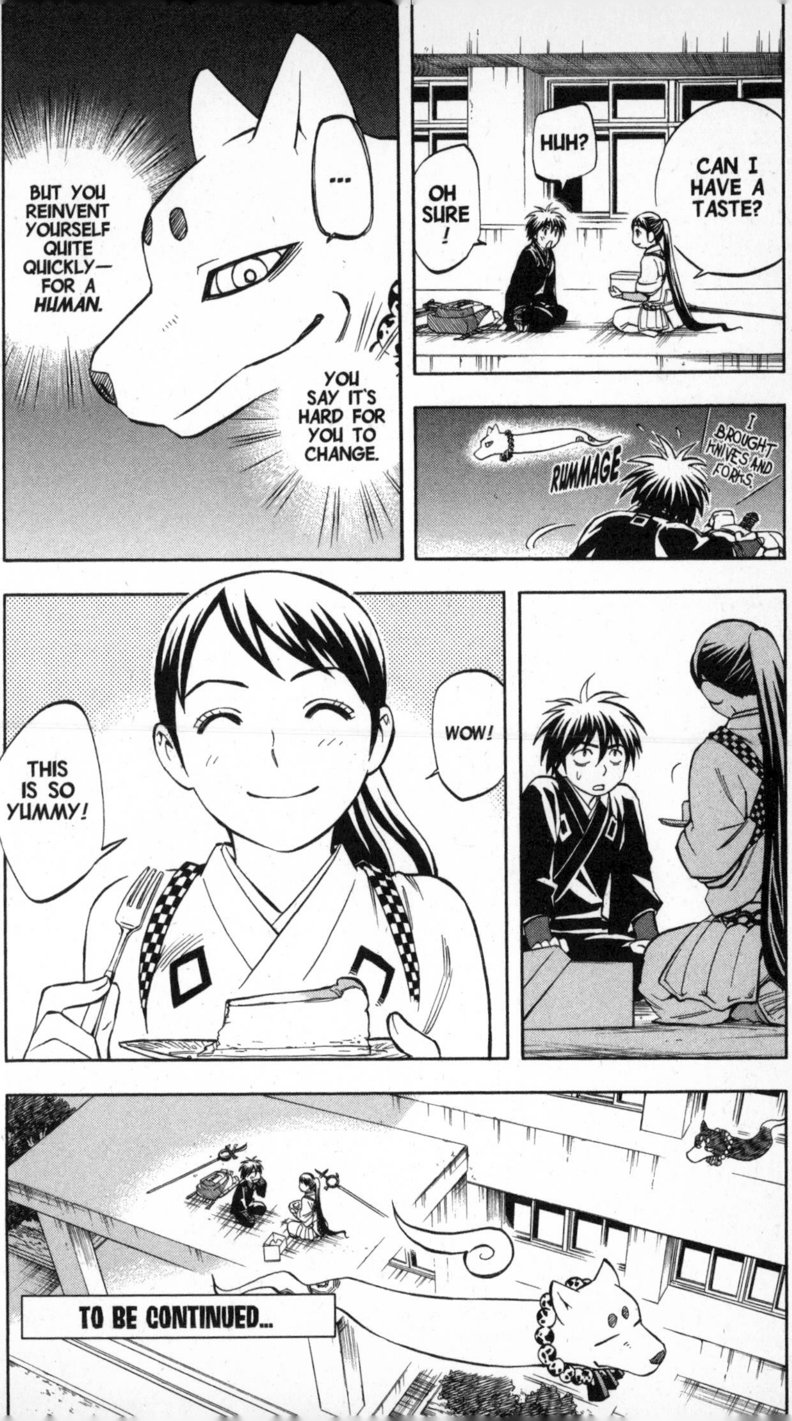
CAN I HAVE A TASTE?
HUH?
OH SURE!
I BROUGHT KNIVES AND FORKS.
RUMMAGE
...
BUT YOU REINVENT YOURSELF QUITE QUICKLY—FOR A *HUMAN.*
YOU SAY IT'S HARD FOR YOU TO CHANGE.
WOW!
THIS IS SO YUMMY!
TO BE CONTINUED...

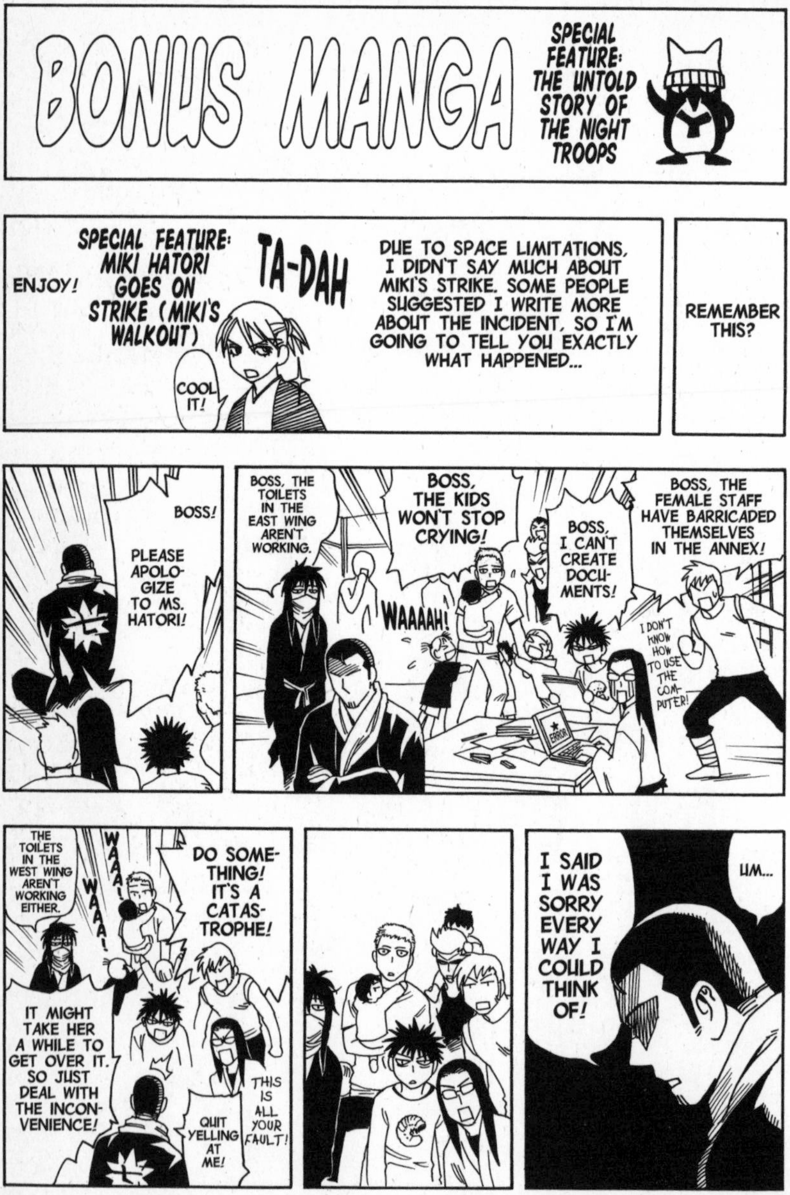
BONUS MANGA
SPECIAL FEATURE: THE UNTOLD STORY OF THE NIGHT TROOPS
REMEMBER THIS?
DUE TO SPACE LIMITATIONS, I DIDN'T SAY MUCH ABOUT MIKI'S STRIKE. SOME PEOPLE SUGGESTED I WRITE MORE ABOUT THE INCIDENT, SO I'M GOING TO TELL YOU EXACTLY WHAT HAPPENED...
TA-DAH
SPECIAL FEATURE: MIKI HATORI GOES ON STRIKE (MIKI'S WALKOUT)
ENJOY!
COOL IT!
BOSS, THE FEMALE STAFF HAVE BARRICADED THEMSELVES IN THE ANNEX!
BOSS, I CAN'T CREATE DOCU-MENTS!
BOSS, THE KIDS WON'T STOP CRYING!
BOSS, THE TOILETS IN THE EAST WING AREN'T WORKING.
I DON'T KNOW HOW TO USE THE COM-PUTER!
WAAAAH!
ERROR
BOSS!
PLEASE APOLO-GIZE TO MS. HATORI!
UM...
I SAID I WAS SORRY EVERY WAY I COULD THINK OF!
DO SOME-THING! IT'S A CATAS-TROPHE!
WAAA!
WAAA!
THE TOILETS IN THE WEST WING AREN'T WORKING EITHER.
IT MIGHT TAKE HER A WHILE TO GET OVER IT. SO JUST DEAL WITH THE INCON-VENIENCE!
THIS IS ALL YOUR FAULT!
QUIT YELLING AT ME!

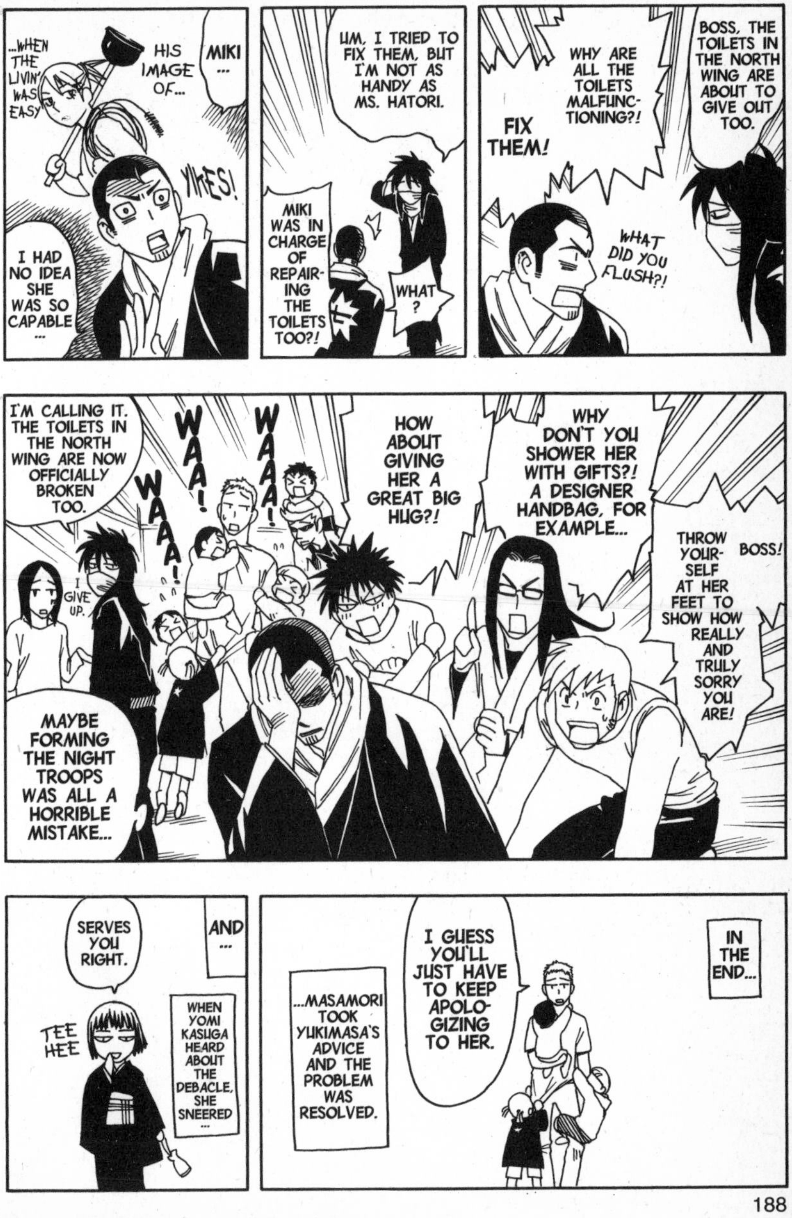

BOSS, THE TOILETS IN THE NORTH WING ARE ABOUT TO GIVE OUT TOO.
WHY ARE ALL THE TOILETS MALFUNCTIONING?!
FIX THEM!
WHAT DID YOU FLUSH?!
UM, I TRIED TO FIX THEM, BUT I'M NOT AS HANDY AS MS. HATORI.
WHAT?
MIKI WAS IN CHARGE OF REPAIRING THE TOILETS TOO?!
MIKI...
HIS IMAGE OF...
...WHEN THE LIVIN' WAS EASY
YIKES!
I HAD NO IDEA SHE WAS SO CAPABLE...
BOSS!
THROW YOURSELF AT HER FEET TO SHOW HOW REALLY AND TRULY SORRY YOU ARE!
WHY DON'T YOU SHOWER HER WITH GIFTS?! A DESIGNER HANDBAG, FOR EXAMPLE...
HOW ABOUT GIVING HER A GREAT BIG HUG?!
WAAAA!
WAAA!
WAAAA!
I'M CALLING IT. THE TOILETS IN THE NORTH WING ARE NOW OFFICIALLY BROKEN TOO.
I GIVE UP.
MAYBE FORMING THE NIGHT TROOPS WAS ALL A HORRIBLE MISTAKE...
IN THE END...
I GUESS YOU'LL JUST HAVE TO KEEP APOLOGIZING TO HER.
...MASAMORI TOOK YUKIMASA'S ADVICE AND THE PROBLEM WAS RESOLVED.
AND...
WHEN YOMI KASUGA HEARD ABOUT THE DEBACLE, SHE SNEERED...
SERVES YOU RIGHT.
TEE HEE

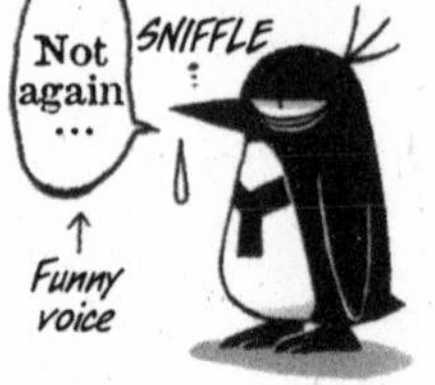

Not again... SNIFFLE!

↑ Funny voice

I had a cold while writing the last volume. And now I have another one.

MESSAGE FROM YELLOW TANABE

With the approach of spring, I started to get the sniffles and a runny nose. I thought to myself, "It must be hay fever season!" But it turns out I just have a plain old cold.

Seems like the older I get, the longer my colds last. But I never get a fever.

I wonder if my immune system is going downhill as I age...

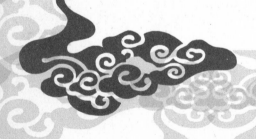

KEKKAISHI

VOLUME 20

SHONEN SUNDAY EDITION

STORY AND ART BY YELLOW TANABE

Original Japanese edition "KEKKAISHI" published by SHOGAKUKAN Inc.

Translation/Yuko Sawada
Touch-up Art & Lettering/Stephen Dutro
Cover Design & Graphic Layout/Julie Behn
Editor/Annette Roman

VP, Production/Alvin Lu
VP, Sales & Product Marketing/Gonzalo Ferreyra
VP, Creative/Linda Espinosa
Publisher/Hyoe Narita

Printed in the U.S.A.

Published by VIZ Media, LLC
P.O. Box 77010
San Francisco, CA 94107

10 9 8 7 6 5 4 3 2 1
First printing, February 2010

viz media
www.viz.com

RATED T FOR TEEN
PARENTAL ADVISORY
KEKKAISHI is rated T for Teen and is recommended for ages 13 and up. It contains fantasy violence.
ratings.viz.com

SHONEN SUNDAY
WWW.SHONENSUNDAY.COM

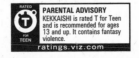

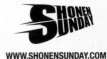

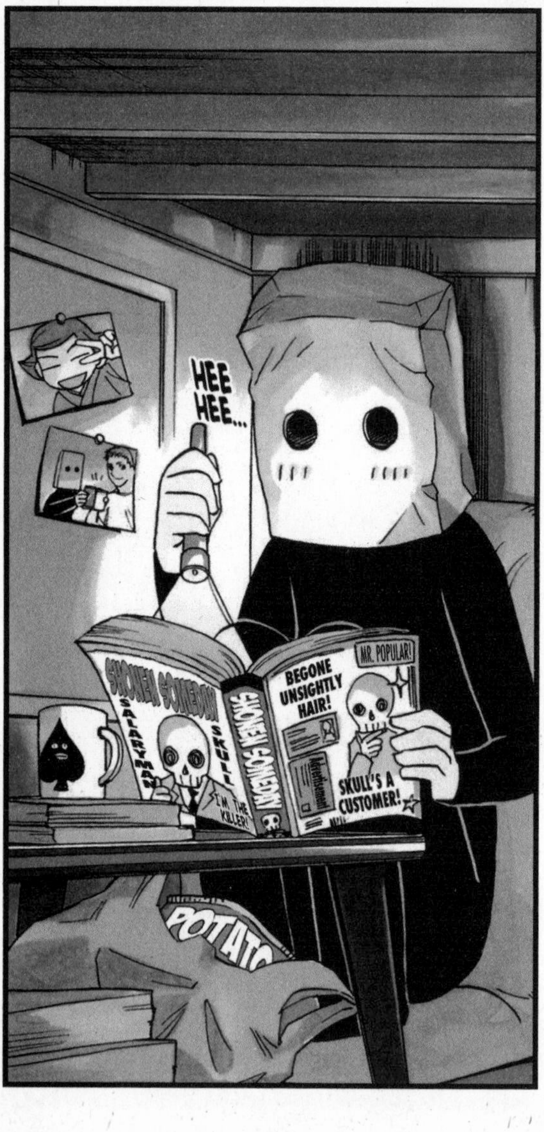
HEE HEE...
MR. POPULAR!
BEGONE UNSIGHTLY HAIR!
SKULL'S A CUSTOMER!
SHONEN SOMEDAY
SHONEN SOMEDAY
SALARYMAN SKULL
I'M THE KILLER!

LO
MA

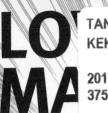
...nk!

...RVEY is
ONLINE.

Please visit: **VIZ.COM/MANGASURVEY**

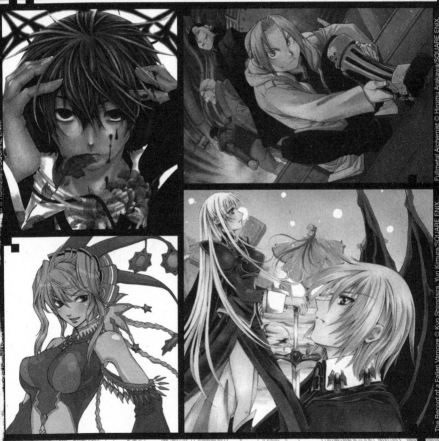

Help us make the **manga** you love **better!**